MAY   1994

Great Christian Thinkers

Great Christian Thinkers

Hans Küng

Continuum · New York

1994
The Continuum Publishing Company
370 Lexington Avenue, New York, NY 10017

Translated by John Bowden from the German *Grosse
Christliche Denker* copyright © R. Piper GmbH &
Co. KG 1994
Translation copyright © John Bowden 1994

Library of Congress Cataloging-in-Publication Data
Küng, Hans, 1928–
    [Grosse christliche Denker.   English]
    Great Christian thinkers / Hans Küng.
        p.   cm.
    Includes bibliographical references.
    Contents: Paul—Origen—Augustine—
    Thomas Aquinas—Martin
Luther—Friedrich Schleiermacher—Karl Barth.
    ISBN 0-8264-0643-2
    1. Theology—Introductions.   2. Theologians.
    I. Title.
BT77.K79 1994   94-883
230'.092'2—dc20   CIP

Printed in Great Britain

Contents

For Eberhard Jüngel and Jürgen Moltmann,
my theological companions in Tübingen,
in gratitude for many intimate ecumenical discussions,
always inspiring, sometimes passionate.

A Brief Introduction to Theology

This short book offers a somewhat unusual but, I hope, relatively simple **introduction to Christian theology**, what it is focussed on and how it is done. There are many introductions to theology; most have a thematic approach, using abstract methodological or hermeneutical principles. With some satisfaction, here I have adopted another course. Here is theology in the doing, theology in the living, theology as reflected by paradigmatic figures of the history of Christianity – great Christian thinkers who are representative of whole eras.

Can Christians, may Christians, call **Christian thinkers 'great'**? May some Christians say of others that they are 'great' theologians? We need to be careful: someone who regards others as great theologians, indeed who even regards himself as the greatest theologian, may well be the greatest – ass! That, at any rate is the view of one of the seven 'greats' that we have to discuss here: 'If, however, you feel and are inclined to think that you have made it, flattering yourself with your own little books, teaching, or writing, because you have done it beautifully and preached excellently; if you are highly pleased when someone praises you in the presence of others; if you perhaps look for praise, and would sulk or quit what you are doing if you did not get it – if you are of that stripe, dear friend, then take yourself by the ears, and if you do this in the right way you will find a beautiful pair of big, long, shaggy, ass's ears. Then do not spare any expense! Decorate them with golden bells, so that people will be able to hear you wherever you go, point their fingers at you, and say, "See, see, there goes that clever beast, who can write such exquisite things and even so remarkably well." That very moment you will be blessed and blessed beyond measure in the kingdom of heaven. Yes, in that heaven where hellfire is ready for the devil and his angels.' Thus Martin Luther, when at a late stage in his career, in 1539, he had to compose a preface to the first volume of his German writings ('Preface to the Wittenberg Edition of Luther's German Writings', in *Martin Luther's Basic Theological Writings*, ed. Timothy F. Lull, Minneapolis 1989, 67f.).

So we have been warned: those who think that they can measure the 'greatness' of a theologian by the extent of his or her work, the influence of his or her words or popular admiration are doing the work of the devil! The greatness of at least a Christian theologian is measured only by whether **the Christian message**, Holy Scripture, God's very Word, comes to light through his or her work. The theologian is to be the first servant of the Logos, the Word. Not the theologian's ideas but God's Word is to be translated for the men and women of a time. Through their indefatigable questioning and research, theologians have to understand God's cause anew and make it understandable to each new age – in season, out of season; whether it pleases the spirit of an age or not.

So in these seven brief portraits we shall always have two concerns, **description** and **criticism**, not least because of the influence exerted by these great thinkers, which has lasted down to the present day. By their work they have not only understood the world in different ways but also changed it. It will not be easy to condense into a few pages thinkers who (apart from the first) have all written small libraries and (without exception) have had a large library written about them, to describe their basic views against the background of their lives and at the same time to make a critical evaluation of them. Specialists in the history of theology (listed in the bibliographical surveys), to whom I owe so much, in particular will understand this. Not everything can be mentioned in such an undertaking. A broad perspective has to be combined with concentration on what is central for these great figures. My little book cannot and should not be a substitute for reading their works. On the contrary, the greatest reward would be if sometimes it could lead readers to immerse themselves personally in the world and work of these great figures.

This short book is a **forerunner** to the second volume of my trilogy 'The Religious Situation of Our Time', which is to be devoted to **Christianity**. In that book I shall be returning in a wider historical context to the theologians discussed here. As already in *Credo*, which preceded the present book on the Christian thinkers, I am deeply grateful to my team for their intensive collaboration, above all to Dr Karl-Josef Kuschel, Privat-dozent in the Catholic Theological Faculty and Deputy Director of the Institute for Ecumenical Research, and to my colleague Frau Marianne Saur. Once again the overall design of the book and checking of notes was in the hands of Stephan Schlensog, and the manuscript was prepared by Frau Eleonore Henn and Frau Franziska Heller-Manthey; the proofs were read by my doctoral student Matthias Schnell and Michel Hofmann. Once again I would like to thank the Robert Bosch Jubilee Foundation for its generous support of our research project 'No world peace without peace among the religions', within the overall framework of which it also proved possible to write this short book.

I warmly invite readers to enter with me into the world of these seven great Christian thinkers, which at first is very strange, not only for their own sakes, but also in order to have a better understanding of today's reality.

Tübingen, September 1993   Hans Küng

Paul
Christianity becomes a World Religion

Chronology (following Helmut Koester)

35	Conversion.
35-38	Missionary activity in Arabia (Gal.1.17f.).
38	Visits Peter in Jerusalem (Gal.1.18).
38-48	Activity in Cilicia and Syria (Gal.1.21).
48	Apostolic Council in Jerusalem (Gal.2.1ff.; Acts 15).
48-49	Episode in Antioch (Gal.2.11ff.).
49	Mission in Galatia (against Acts 16.6).
50	Mission in Philippi, Thessalonica and Beroea (Acts 16.11-17.14).
50	Autumn: via Athens to Corinth (Acts 17.15; 18.1); composition of I Thessalonians.
50	Autumn to 52 spring: mission in Corinth (Acts 18.11).
52	Summer: journey to Antioch, then through Asia Minor to Ephesus, including second visit to Galatia (Acts 18.18-23; cf. Gal.4.13).
54	Intermediate visit to Corinth (presupposed in II Cor.13.1, etc.).
54-55	Winter: Imprisonment in Ephesus; composition of correspondence with Philippi and the letter to Philemon.
55	Summer: journey through Macedonia to Corinth.
55-56	Winter: stay in Corinth; composition of Romans.
56	Journey to Jerusalem (Acts 20); preparations for handing over the collection (Acts 21.15ff.); arrest.
56-58	Imprisonment in Caesarea.
58	Felix replaced by Festus; Paul sent to Rome.
58-60	Imprisonment in Rome (Acts 28.30).
60	Martyrdom.

1. The most controversial figure for Christians and Jews

A word in advance: Paul the Jew, the first Christian author and theologian, who came from the city of Tarsus in Cilicia (now Turkey), which at that time was a significant trading city on the through route from Anatolia to Syria, is the most controversial figure for Jews and Christians – to the present day. For many Jews this rabbinic scholar has remained **the** Jewish apostate. For most Christians he is **the** apostle, to be mentioned in the same breath as Peter (they are often both patrons of the same church) – not least because according to the Roman calendar the two rivals are celebrated together every year on 29 June!

Paul is a controversial man. Did he ever give up his Jewish faith? That is the question for Jews. And did he really understand Jesus of Nazareth rightly, or did he make something else of him? That is the question for Christians.

Nietzsche already put this decisive question. In his late work *The Antichrist*, he portrayed Paul as the real founder of Christianity, who was at the same time its great falsifier. It was Nietzsche who focussed modern criticism of Paul by playing off Jesus against Paul. Nietzsche could say of Jesus: 'Basically there was only one Christian, and he **died** on the cross. The "gospel" died on the cross.'[1] By contrast Paul is abused by Nietzsche as the 'dysangelist' and 'counterfeiter out of hatred': 'the opposite type to the "bringer of joyful news", the genius in hatred, in the vision of hatred, in the inexorable logic of hatred'.[2] But even Christian theologians were superficial and foolish enough to call for a 'repudiation of Pauline Christianity' with the cry 'back to Jesus!'.

However, Paul was controversial from the beginning. His case disturbed the young Christian community more than any comparable one. For here a man had appeared who was **not a direct disciple of Jesus,** who knew Jesus at best by hearsay, and yet who claimed – on the basis of a quite personal and therefore unverifiable call – to be an apostle of Jesus Christ. Here moreover a man had appeared who had at first come into prominence as a **persecutor of Christians.** Both the sources for Paul's life at our disposal – the authentic Pauline letters and the Acts of the Apostles – agree on one point, that the name of Paul was feared in the young community: 'But Saul laid waste the church, and entering house after house, he dragged off men and women and committed them to prison' – thus the Acts of the Apostles.[3] And the authenticity of this report is endorsed by Paul's own confession: 'Circumcised on the eighth day, of the people of Israel, of the tribe of Benjamin, a Hebrew born of Hebrews; as to the law a Pharisee, as to zeal a persecutor of the church, as to righteousness under the law blameless.'[4]

This very text from Philippians gives us important **basic biographical information**. Here we have sure biographical ground under our feet. For the picture that Acts draws of Paul is strongly influenced by the intentions of its author Luke and the ideas of the communities in the post-apostolic period; it is not always confirmed by the authentic letters of Paul. So restraint is called for: we should not simply take over the accounts of Paul in Acts. However, Tarsus as his birthplace can hardly have been invented, and the original name of the Jew Paul may have been 'Saul' (after the Israelite king of that name), as Acts tells us, even if Paul himself always uses only his Roman name 'Paul' in his letters. The proverbial change of name from Saul to Paul as a result of a conversion experience is, however, less probable, as 'Paul' may well have been a Hellenistic parallel name to Saul from the beginning, chosen (as was customary at the time) because of the similar sound. It is also uncertain whether Paul, who still earned his living as a craftsman (probably a tent-maker) on his missionary journeys, had inherited Roman citizenship from his father, since as a Roman citizen he could more easily have avoided the manifold punishments that he had to endure in the course of his missionary activity, as Acts also in fact reports.[5] Finally, it is uncertain whether Paul grew up in Jerusalem and studied there under the famous rabbi Gamaliel I.

So the authentic letters of Paul have priority for his biography (cf. the chronological table); all the later sources must be checked, and sometimes corrected, by them. On the basis of his own testimony[6] we may certainly assume that Paul came from a Jewish family of the tribe of Benjamin, had been circumcised on the eighth day according to Jewish tradition, after that had had a strict Jewish upbringing, and joined the sect of the Pharisees. This included a formal training in the exegesis of the law and the Hebrew Bible, which presupposed a knowledge of Hebrew (and probably also of Aramaic). So we must imagine the young Paul as a reflective, deeply serious Pharisee of strict observance, influenced by contemporary Jewish apocalyptic, zealous for the law and the preservation of the traditions of the fathers. He was probably born at almost the same time as Jesus, but he grew up in a Hellenistic environment in which Greek was the everyday language and therefore was his mother tongue. His letters bear witness to some command of Greek and a knowledge of popular philosophical views and rhetoric, which can indicate a Greek education.

But this Pharisaic zealot for God and the law saw himself challenged by the emergence of the Jewish Christianity of the Hellenists (probably outside Jerusalem), which was free of the law.[7] Fanatic that he was, he resolved to combat it actively, 'beyond measure', as he writes in Galatians.[8] The scandal presented to every Jew by the assertion of a Messiah who had been crucified under the curse of the law evidently strengthened him further in his boundless zeal for persecution.[9] However, he now arrived at a surprising turning point.

2. A change in life at the end of an age

Paul is virtually the archetypal figure for a great **change in life**, from persecuting Christians to proclaiming Christ – however difficult this may be for us to explain in our day either historically or psychologically. At any rate, Paul himself does not attribute this radical turning point - presumably around 35 near Damascus – to human instruction, a new self-understanding or a heroic effort. Rather, he attributes it to an experience of the living Christ on which he does not elaborate, a 'revelation' (a 'vision') of the risen Crucified One. Paul himself understood this visionary experience - Acts[10] turns it into a legendary story of an appearance of Jesus – less as an individual conversion than as a **call to be an apostle**, a plenipotentiary – **to missionize the Gentiles**.[11] And if we do not doubt an authentic nucleus in the stories of the calls of Hebrew prophets like Isaiah, Jeremiah and Ezekiel, we may not *a priori* doubt an authentic nucleus in the story of the calling of Paul the Pharisee either.

At any rate, it is now the former persecutor of Christians himself who manifests a different attitude to the law and therefore must endure discrimination, persecution, imprisonment and physical punishment from the Jewish establishment and probably also from Jewish Christian agitators. Acts is full of this, and here too Paul himself confirms the authenticity of such accounts – above all when he has to defend himself: 'Three times I have been beaten with rods; once I was stoned. Three times I have been shipwrecked; a night and a day I have been adrift at sea; on frequent journeys, in danger from rivers, danger from robbers, danger from my own people, danger from Gentiles, danger in the city, danger in the wilderness, danger at sea, danger from false brethren.'[12] It is all the more astonishing that this constant **pressure of suffering** did not quench the confidence, hope and joy of the apostle which keeps breaking through.

The inner conversion of Paul from persecuting Christians to proclaiming Christ ultimately remains a mystery which we cannot decipher. However, its consequences were manifest: an **epoch-making shift** in early Christianity, indeed in the ancient world generally. For no matter what is controversial about Paul, **the significance of the apostle and his theology for world history** is indisputable.

But it is quite wrong to depict Paul as the real founder of Christianity, as Nietzsche already did. For long before Paul's personal conversion there was a faith in Christ: in other words, Jewish followers of Jesus experienced the Crucified Jesus as the Messiah (Christ) now elevated to God. So Paul is not responsible for the fundamental shift from Jesus' faith to the community's faith in Christ. What is 'responsible' for that is the Easter experience of the Jesus who was raised to life; from then on it was impossible for a certain group of Jews to believe in the God of Israel apart from the Messiah Jesus.[13]

But what is Paul responsible for? He is responsible for the fact that despite its universal monotheism, it was not Hellenistic Judaism, which was already carrying on an intensive mission among the Gentiles before Paul, but Christianity which became a universal religion of humankind. Paul succeeded in doing what neither prophets nor rabbis had been able to do: to disseminate belief in the one God of Israel all over the world. Paul, who was far and away the best-known and most influential figure of early Christianity, was quite justified in saying in his own defence that he had done more than other apostles. From the most important centres of trade, industry and administration like Antioch, Ephesus, Thessalonika and Corinth, with a whole network of colleagues and intensive correspondence, in a few years he had organized missionary work in Syria, Asia Minor, Macedonia and Greece as far as Illyria.[14]

So that is the significance of the apostle Paul for world history. The one who primarily preached everywhere to Jews, but was mostly rejected by them, opened up access to Jewish belief in God for non-Jews and thus **initiated the first paradigm shift in Christianity** – from Jewish Christianity to Hellenistic Gentile Christianity. To what extent? To the extent that at the Apostolic Council in Jerusalem in 48 he pushed through the decision, in the face of the early Christian circles in Jerusalem, that **Gentiles too can have access to the universal God of Israel**, and can do so **without** first having to accept **circumcision** and the Jewish laws of cleanness, the regulations about food and the sabbath – the 'works of the law' – that they found so alien. Paul recognizes the historical priority of the Jerusalem community and supports it effectively with a large-scale collection in the new Gentile Christian communities, but only when he has gained recognition of his mission to the Gentiles apart from the law from the people in Jerusalem.

In practice all this means that a Gentile can become a Christian without having to become a Jew first. The **consequences** of this basic decision **for the whole Western world** (and not only the Western world) are incalculable:
– Only through Paul did the Christian mission to the Gentiles (which already existed before and alongside Paul) become a resounding success, in contrast to the Jewish-Hellenistic mission.
– Only through Paul did Christianity find a new language of original freshness, direct force and passionate sensitivity.
– Only through Paul did the community of Palestinian and Hellenistic Jews become a community of Jews and Gentiles.
– Only through Paul did the small Jewish 'sect' eventually develop into a 'world religion' in which West and East became more closely bound together even than through Alexander the Great.

– So, without Paul there would have been no Catholic church, without Paul there would have been no Greek and Latin patristic theology, without Paul there would have been no Hellenistic Christian culture, and finally without Paul the change under Constantine would never have taken place. Indeed, later paradigm shifts in Christian theology associated with the names of Augustine, Luther and Barth are also unthinkable without Paul.

However, now we cannot put off an answer to our initial question any longer: did Paul really understand Jesus correctly, or did he make out of him something that Jesus did not want?

3. Uninterested in Jesus?

This question has not been plucked out of thin air. For is it not striking that Paul, who did not know Jesus personally, **hardly refers to the person and preaching of the historical Jesus** in his letters either? Is it not striking that nothing either of the parables of Jesus or the Sermon on the Mount or Jesus's miracles seems to occur in Paul's letters, nor anything at all of the content of Jesus' message? My reply is that it is indeed striking, but that must not lead us to false conclusions. Of course one could go on at great length about the differences between the 'rustic' Jesus of Nazareth, who spoke in the language of fishermen, shepherds and peasants, and Paul the city-dweller and Diaspora Jew, who draws his imagery from city life, from athletics and wrestling, from military service, the theatre and seafaring. But that does not contribute very much. We do not even know whether Paul was tall or short, handsome or ugly, nor what the 'thorn' in his flesh means and what his mystical experiences were. Here above all we must reflect on two important perspectives:

1. The centre of Pauline theology is not human beings generally or the church, or even the history of salvation, but **Jesus Christ himself, crucified and risen**. One must be either blind to what Jesus himself quite radically sought, lived out and endured, or fail to recognize under the Jewish Hellenistic presentation the elemental driving force in Paul, if one cannot see that the letters of Paul in particular keep crying out, 'Back to Jesus, God's Christ!' The crucified Jesus Christ who has been raised to life by God

stands in the centre of Paul's view of God and man. So in favour of human beings there is a christocentricity which is grounded and comes to a climax in a theocentricity. 'God through Jesus Christ' – 'through Jesus Christ to God': this is a basic formula of Pauline theology.

2. Paul is more interested in the **historical Jesus** than the theologians who followed Karl Barth and Rudolf Bultmann were inclined to accept. Certainly, Paul did not want to know about a 'Christ after the flesh'. But that did not mean that he wanted to play the historical or even crucified Jesus off against the risen, exalted Christ, as the representatives of dialectical theology in the twentieth century did. For when Paul says that he wants to know nothing of a 'Christ after the flesh', he is referring to a Jesus Christ who at that time (when he was a persecutor) was known – or better, misunderstood – in a natural human, unbelieving, i.e., 'fleshly' way. This Jesus Christ was contrary to the Jesus Christ whom he now knew (after his conversion) in a pneumatic and believing, 'spiritual' way. So Paul is not concerned to devalue the historical Jesus but with a fundamentally changed relation to him – a relation to Jesus Christ in the Spirit.

Paul was no enlightened sage like Confucius, nor an inward-looking mystic like Buddha. He was a **prophetic figure** through and through, who was stamped by an intense spirituality. He was a great thinker in his own way! He was a completely coherent theologian, but like the prophets of Israel he was not a balanced systematic theologian who has left us a closed system of faith with no contradictions in it. He did not develop an abstract theological problematic of law and gospel, faith and works, like a scholar in an ivory tower; later Lutheran theologians did that. But in the midst of his restless activity as a missionary and a 'worker priest' he reflected on the consequences of his conversion from Pharisaism to belief in Christ and on all the implications of this faith for the Jewish Christian and especially the Gentile Christian communities.

In doing so, this **pioneer thinker of early Christianity** refers relatively rarely to the Gospel tradition about Jesus. But beyond doubt he is positive towards it. At any rate, at least twenty important passages can be cited from the authentic Pauline writings – mostly occasional works, some of which (like Philippians and II Corinthians) consist of several fragments of letters put together afterwards and in any case are not preserved in their completeness – in which Paul is clearly basing himself on the Gospel tradition of Jesus.[15] We can conclude from this that over and above what has been preserved in a highly fortuitous way, Paul could tell his communities a good deal more of what he had heard about the message, conduct and fate of the earthly, historical Jesus in Jerusalem, Damascus, Antioch or elsewhere. Or should we perhaps assume that, say, in Corinth, where he lived for a good eighteen months, in his preaching and catechesis Paul constantly repeated and varied only an abstract 'kerygma' of the crucified and risen Jesus? That he told his hearers nothing about Jesus himself? Did not hand on anything of what he must have heard in his contacts with Peter and other eyewitnesses in Jerusalem, and then again later at the Apostolic Council and elsewhere? That would be to think unhistorically. But in that case where does the continuity between Jesus and Paul lie?

4. The connection between Paul and Jesus

It has already become abundantly clear that early Christianity changed decisively through Paul and his restless missionary activity. But this did not happen in contradiction to Jesus. It happened **in connection with Jesus**. For if we look closer, we recognize that in Paul, who always modestly and proudly called himself simply a fully authorized 'messenger', an 'apostle of Jesus Christ' for the Gentiles, very much more of the preaching of Jesus is preserved than individual 'words of the Lord' indicate. Indeed, the 'substance' of the preaching of Jesus has quite smoothly been transformed through the paradigm change into the preaching of Paul. We might reflect on the following seven key words.

1. **Kingdom of God.** Paul, too, lived quite intensely in the expectation of an imminent kingdom of God, which was expected by many Jews. If Jesus had looked to the future here, Paul at the same time now looks back on the kingdom of God that has already dawned through the death and resurrection of Jesus. Now already the name of Jesus Christ stands for God's kingdom.

2. **Sin.** Paul, too, begins from actual human sinfulness (but not

sexually transmitted original sin as with Augustine), particularly the sinfulness of righteous, pious people who are loyal to the law but nevertheless lost. But he develops this insight theologically, using biblical, rabbinic and Hellenistic material, and above all by contrasting Adam-Christ as the types of the old and the new.

3. **Conversion.** Paul, too, sees human beings in crisis, calls for faith and requires repentance. However, for him the message of the kingdom of God is concentrated in the word of Christ's cross, which in a scandalous way causes a crisis for Jewish or Hellenistic sages who 'boast of themselves' before God. On the one hand Paul criticizes the legalistic obedience of Jewish Christians to the law (e.g. in Galatians), and on the other hand he criticizes the arrogant wisdom speculation of the Gentile Christians (for example in I Corinthians).

4. **Revelation.** Paul, too, claims God for his activity. But he does so in the light of the death and resurrection of Jesus, where for him the activity of God, a God of the living and not of the dead, has manifestly broken through in a definitive way. After his death and resurrection, Jesus's own *de facto* christology became the explicit, express christology of the community already before Paul and then through Paul.

5. **Universalism.** Paul, too, caused offence to many of his contemporaries. He turned in a quite practical way, beyond the limits of the law, to the poor, the lost, the oppressed, the outsiders, the lawless, the law-breakers, and advocated a universalism in word and deed. But now, in Paul, Jesus' universalism in principle in respect of Israel and his *de facto* or virtual universalism in respect of the Gentile world has become – in the light of the crucified and risen Jesus – a direct universalism in respect of **the world of Israel and the Gentiles,** which virtually requires the preaching of the good news among the Gentiles.

6. **Justification.** Paul, too, presents the forgiveness of sins from sheer grace, the acquittal, vindication, justification of the sinner not on the basis of the works of the law (Jesus' parable of the Pharisee in the temple) but on the basis of an unconditional trust (faith) in the gracious and merciful God. But his message of the justification of the sinner without the works of the law (without circumcision and other ritual actions) presupposes Jesus' death on the cross, where the Messiah was executed by the guardians

of law and order in the name of the law as an accursed criminal, but then appears justified over against the law as the one who is raised by the God who gives life, so that for Paul the negative side of the law has now also been made manifest.

7. Love. Paul, too, proclaimed the **love of God and neighbour** as the actual fulfilment of the law and lived it out in the most radical way in unconditional obedience to God and in selfless existence for fellow men and women, including enemies. But precisely in the death of Jesus Paul recognized the deepest revelation of this love of God and of Jesus himself, which may now be a ground and an example for human love towards God and neighbours. So it has now become clear that both have:

5. The same cause

In Paul we certainly find high emotionalism and powerful rhetoric, which also includes irony and sarcasm; there are some highly polemical statements and harsh quarrels with his opponents. But this man of passion for the cause he represents is never a man of personal hatred and resentment. Rather he is a man of service, of love, of joy even in suffering, a real 'messenger of good news' who neither wanted to found a new religion nor in fact invented one.

No, Paul did not create a new system, a new 'substance of faith'. As a Jew – albeit in a completely new paradigmatic constellation – he built on that foundation which according to his own words has been laid once for all: Jesus Christ.[16] Christ is the origin, content and critical norm of Paul's preaching, and that distinguishes Paul from the majority of his contemporaries. So, in the light of a fundamentally different situation after the death and resurrection of Jesus, Paul did not advocate another cause, but the same cause. And this – to put it in a phrase – is the cause of Jesus, which is none other than God's cause and the human cause – but which now, sealed by death and resurrection, is summed up briefly by Paul in the formula '**the things of Jesus Christ**'.[17]

So Paul's preaching is ultimately about a **radicalized understanding of God in the light of Jesus Christ**! Since then Jews and Christians have struggled over it, each in their different ways –

and the distinguished New Testament scholar Ernst Käsemann has recently spelt this out in a response to the Jewish scholar Pinchas Lapide. In fact, if we regard the history of Israel from the wandering in the wilderness through the history of the prophets and the Qumran sect to the present, the people of Israel always faced the need to depart from false worship. Indeed the writings of the Hebrew Bible are full of this: God is not only not known properly among the heathen; he is not even known properly by the people of God themselves. And this people constantly experienced dramatic and tragic tensions and splits, constantly struggled with apostates and rebels over the true God and correct, perfect worship. Precisely this, too, was the deepest, the ultimate concern of Jesus: 'Where and when and how is the God who is hidden in heaven rightly known and appropriately worshipped on earth? The Jew Paul also asks this question, and he answers it by giving belief in God a christological orientation... Today we perhaps honour the rabbi of Nazareth on both sides, whether as teacher, as prophet or as brother. For Paul, the crucified Christ alone is the sole image of the divine will, the countenance of the God who seeks out the godless, who scandalizes the pious and moral, those faithful to the law and bound by norms at all times, and blesses the fallen and lost world as his creation. From there we can and must understand the whole of his theology.'[18]

So Paul did no more and no less than to draw out consistently and translate into Hellenistic language that line which had been drawn first in the proclamation, conduct and fate of Jesus. In so doing he attempted to make the Christian message understandable beyond Israel to the whole inhabited world of his time. And the one who as a disciple of his master, after the tremendous commitment of the whole of his life, suffered the violent death of a martyr in Rome under the emperor Nero (probably around 60), has continued to give constant new impetus all down to the centuries to Christianity, in a way second only to Jesus, through the few letters and fragments of his letters that have been preserved: impetus to rediscover and follow the true Christ in Christianity, which is by no means an obvious matter. For since his time it has become clear that the difference between the 'essence' of **Christianity** and Judaism, for the old world religions and the modern humanisms, is this **Christ Jesus himself**. Precisely as the crucified one he is distinct from the many risen, exalted, living gods and divinized founders of religion, Caesars, geniuses, lords and heroes of world history.

All this makes it clear why Christianity is now **no longer a different paradigm within Judaism but** finally and really **a different religion** (though with Jewish roots which it cannot give up) – since Jesus had now been rejected by the majority of the people of Israel as the Messiah of Israel. And that Christianity could become a world religion, but a world religion inconceivable without its Jewish roots, can be demonstrated in particular by that great struggle which burdened early Christianity and which Paul fought to a conclusion at the Apostolic Council and then in the quarrel with Peter: the dispute over the Jewish law.

6. Paul against the Jewish law?

It is clear to anyone confronted with Orthodox Judaism that the Pauline problem of the law was not only a Jewish problem of the time but is also a Jewish problem for today. As the Jewish theologian Shalom Ben-Chorin remarks, Paul can be rightly understood today by those who have made the attempt 'to put their lives under the law of Israel, to observe and practise the customs and precepts of the rabbinic tradition'. And he adds: 'I have attempted to take upon myself the law in its Orthodox interpretation without finding in it the satisfaction, that peace which Paul calls justification before God.'[19] What he is referring to here are **experiences of zeal for the law** and **falling short of the law**: 'Nowadays in Jerusalem we know this type of fanatical Yeshiva pupil from the Diaspora, though of course he no longer comes from Tarsus, but from New York or London. In demonstrations against those who are peacefully driving their automobiles on the Sabbath he is very often to be found among the zealots for the law who throw stones at cars and drivers – those Talmudic students from abroad. Presumably they would not react in this way to a formal desecration of the Sabbath in New York or London, but in Jerusalem they want to legitimate themselves as one-hundred-and-fifty-per-cent Jews. This is precisely how we must imagine the young Saul from Tarsus, who emphasizes that he surpassed many in Judaism in his conduct, that he was zealous for the law and that he delighted in the stoning of heretics (how similar it all is, how topical!). – However, we must now understand what it is to experience the iron discipline of the law, the halakhah, the *mizvot*, day after day, without experiencing any real proximity of God from it, without getting rid of the burdensome feeling of transgression, *averah*, sin... Does not the multiplicity of human commandments and precepts ensnare people?'[20]

That makes the question all the more pressing: did not Paul definitively 'abolish' the Jewish law, usher in its 'end' – and justifiably so? For centuries this was something that was regarded as settled in Christian exegesis. And particularly if one reads Paul through the spectacles of German exegesis, especially the exegesis inspired by Luther and impressively given systematic form by Bultmann in his *Theology of the New Testament*, then one's conviction is hardened that:

– With the death and resurrection of Jesus Christ, for Paul the Jewish law is finished once and for all. Now the gospel prevails instead of the law.

– For Christians, the Jewish law is insignificant, and all that matters is belief in Jesus Christ; instead of the law, faith is now what counts.

– Together with the Jewish law, in the end Judaism itself is now also superseded: the new people of God, the church, is now taking the place of the old people of God.

But can we be content with such exegesis and the totally antagonistic Lutheran scheme of 'law and gospel'? We cannot avoid some brief comments on this controversy over the validity of the law. Today it polarizes more than any other issue both Jewish and Christian exegetes of Paul, and also brings about a polarization among Christian exegetes. It is so complicated, not because Paul was a man of inconsistencies and contradictions, but because in his correspondence, which was written in Greek, he does not use the Hebrew word 'Torah' (even as a Hebrew loanword) but the Greek word 'nomos/law', which had been used generally for the word 'Torah' ('teaching', 'instruction') since the Greek translation of the Hebrew Bible, the Septuagint. But this has the disadvantage that we can never know whether in a particular passage in his correspondence Paul is using 'nomos' in the wider or narrower sense: in the **wider** sense as Torah, which in fact means the whole corpus of the five books of Moses, or in the **narrower** sense as halakhah ('Law'), the religious law of the rabbis, already grounded in the Torah and now increasingly permeating the whole of life, though at that time it was still not codified.

The disputed question is: may we say that for Paul the **Jewish law has ongoing validity**? Does the law still apply, or has it been abrogated? To be specific:
– According to Paul, have the Jews who are zealous for the law really perverted the law?
– May the Jewish law really no longer be observed by Jews who follow Christ? So is Jewish Christianity no longer a legitimate possibility alongside Gentile Christianity?
– Is Judaism, then, wrong not only because it rejects Jesus as the Messiah but also because and in so far as it still holds to the law?

It is important to differentiate in our answer.

7. *The Torah is still valid*

There is still widespread prejudice about Paul and his attitude to the Jewish law, not only among Jewish but also among Christian theologians. However, if we read the numerous Pauline texts on the law as far as possible without traditional schemes, whether Christian ('law and gospel') or Jewish ('abolition of the law'), it cannot be disputed that Paul takes it for granted that in so far as 'law' denotes the **Torah,** the law is and remains **God's** law, i.e. an expression of the will of God. Paul emphatically stresses that 'The law is holy and the commandment is holy and just and good.'[21] The law is to lead people 'to life'.[22] It is 'the embodiment of knowledge and truth',[23] it is 'spiritual'.[24] The 'giving of the law' is one of Israel's privileges.[25] Here 'law' for Paul clearly means the Torah in the sense of the five books of Moses, to which human beings have to be obedient as a demand of God.[26]

It follows from this that according to Paul, God's holy law, the Torah, is in no way abolished even after the Christ event, but remains relevant as the 'Torah of faith'.[27] Indeed, Paul explicitly says that it is **not 'overthrown'** (far from it!), but is 'upheld', 'established',[28] by faith. So it is clear that Paul's polemic is not directed against the law in itself, the Mosaic Torah, but against the **works** of the law, against a **righteousness** from the law. His slogan is not justification by faith 'without the law' (as though faith were something arbitrary and random and without any practical consequences), but 'without works of the law'. Paul does not oppose faith and law but faith and works. It remains the case that human beings are not justified before God here and now by what they do. God himself justifies human beings, and only one thing is expected from them: faith, unconditional trust. For both Jews and Christians it is true that 'no flesh will be justified before God on the basis of works of the law!'[29] If one were to want to use the law for one's own justification before God, this would be a 'dispensation of death', a 'dispensation of condemnation';[30] since 'the letter kills'.[31] But if the Torah stil holds, what does the freedom of which Paul boasts so much mean?

8. The most famous dispute in the early church

'Has Christ made us free for **freedom**'?[32] We can now reply that what Paul means is not simply freedom from the Torah and its ethical demands, but freedom from the works of the law. That is the freedom to which Christians are 'called',[33] which they 'have in Christ Jesus'.[34] To this degree those who now believe in Christ are 'no longer under the law, but under grace'.[35]

What follows from this for the question of the Torah? After all that we have heard, the answer can only be that when Paul speaks of freedom from the 'law' he is **by no means against the Torah in principle**; indeed, according to Abraham's example the Torah teaches justification by faith, and in his view its ethical commands even apply to the Gentiles. But what he is in fact doing – without already using this later terminology – is to speak **against the halakhah**, to the degree that this does not make ethical demands in general but calls for doing the '**works of the law**'. This means - as Jewish scholars also recognize today – those **works of the Jewish ritual law** (circumcision and the commands relating to cleanness, food and the sabbath) which are still an oppressive burden for many Jews even now and which according to Paul may not be laid upon the Gentiles. So what has lost its fundamental significance is not the Torah in the general sense of God's teaching or instruction but the Torah in the narrower sense. Paul rejects this ritual halakhah for Gentile Christians and makes it a fundamentally relative matter for Jewish Christians: for it is now to be understood according to the spirit that makes alive and not the letter which kills.[36]

So what does this now mean in practice for Christians? It means one thing for Jewish Christians and another for Gentile Christians:
– Christians of Jewish origin can observe the halakhah, but need not necessarily do so: what is decisive for salvation is no longer the doing of such 'works of the law' but faith in Jesus Christ; the works of the law are no longer to be understood literally, but according to the Spirit: **a life in the Spirit.**
– Christians of **Gentile origin** may have **only the ethical commands of the Torah** laid upon them (though Paul does not make a terminological distinction nor develop the question theoretically), and not the cultic and ritual commandments, which are developed in such breadth in the halakhah for the whole life of Jews. In other words they must not be compelled to adopt **the Jewish way of life**: circumcision, festivals, sabbath, commandments about purity and the sabbath.

The most famous **dispute in the early church**, in **Antioch**, the second great centre of Christian mission outside Jerusalem, was specifically on this last point, and particularly about kosher food (still an important question – who eats with whom?). It was a dispute between Paul, who was responsible for the mission to the Gentiles, and Peter, who was responsible for the mission to the Jews, as had been resolved at the Apostolic Council in Jerusalem.[37]

Peter was personally open to the Gentile mission. He had at first practised table-fellowship with the Gentiles in Antioch in the same way as Paul, but gave this up – out of toleration or cowardice? – after the arrival of followers of James from Jerusalem, who now stipulated kosher food and kept their own company.

Paul defends the freedom of the Gentile Christians passionately, specifically on this point of eating together. The account which he gives in Galatians is probably unintentionally biassed. But one thing is certain: Paul 'opposed Peter to his face'![38] From his perspective this was understandable: he had passionately to oppose the break in table-fellowship and eucharistic fellowship which had indeed destroyed the reconciliation of Jews and Gentiles in the one community of Jesus Christ. And what was more central for him than that? Even if Paul never denied his Jewishness and never forbade Jewish Christians to live in accordance with the halakhah, but affirmed it for his own sphere, this Jewish lifestyle was not to become a divisive factor over against the Gentile Christians. For the sake of a community made up of Jews and Gentiles, while he did not expect the Jewish Christians to deny the Torah of Moses, in this particular instance (not generally) he did expect them to deny the halakhah – which prohibited such table-fellowship by its ritual precepts – since those who believed in Christ were not to interpret it according to the letter but according to the spirit. For this is what the freedom brought by Christ has freed men and women for. Faith in Christ must also be fundamental for Jewish Christians.

In all this, it cannot be overlooked that in his criticism of the law Paul also reflects **the attitude of Jesus**. In quite specific instances – the sabbath, laws about food and cleanness – Jesus too spoke out for 'God's commandment' and against the application of the halakhah, the 'tradition of men' or 'the tradition of the fathers',[39] calling for an ethically determined cleanness of the heart in place of cultic and ritual purity (washing of the hands)![40]

Now is it true, as is often asserted, that with this decision of Paul's the fate of the Jewish Christians in the growing Diaspora church was really already sealed and that therefore the premature split into a Jewish-Christian and a Gentile-Christian church was preprogrammed? Was this an unavoidable conflict with a tragic outcome? No! An understanding would have been possible, indeed necessary, in the spirit of Jesus. For as Paul explicitly says, true freedom is never heedless: 'See that this freedom of yours does not become a stumbling-block for the weak.'[41] One is to serve others,[42] but without giving up one's own freedom: 'Do not become slaves of men.'[43]

Being open to others, being there for others, unselfish love: for Paul that is the supreme realization of freedom: 'For you were called to freedom, brethren; only do not use your freedom as an opportunity for the flesh, but through love be servants of one another. For the whole law is fulfilled in **one** word, "You shall love your neighbour as yourself."[44]

These fundamental statements by the apostle Paul all still apply today. Nevertheless we face the question: can Paul still be a practical model for Christianity over and above such fundamental statements?

9. A man of his time

Paul's remarks cannot simply be repeated and applied in a fundamentalistic way as an infallible word in our time, any more than any other texts of the Bible. They are all to be understood in terms of a time and translated into our time.

Take what Paul says about **women**. That woman was only a 'reflection of the man'[45] was a prejudice widespread in the Hellenistic world of his time. That while being married is good, being unmarried is better (though not to be insisted on)[46] is a statement made against the background of the Jewish expectation of an imminent end to the world, which Paul shared. The two cannot simply be taken over into our time. That 'women must be silent in church' and should 'submit'[47] is in any case according to present-day exegesis a subsequent insertion, since it contradicts the practice attested many times in Paul of the complete participation of women in liturgical life and in holding office in the communities. Paul even knows and praises women apostles like Junia, 'outstanding among the apostles'[48] (a later tradition, which can no longer imagine women apostles, has turned her into a male 'Junias'). And the list of greetings in Romans shows a whole series of women as collaborators, including Phoebe from Cenchreae, the missionary and community leader.[49]

What Paul says about the **state** is just as time-conditioned as what he says about women: the **state authority** which comes from God and to which everyone has to show 'due obedience'.[50] Christians today will naturally also affirm the right to resist a tyrannical state authority, and in extreme cases may even have to join the resistance.

Remarks about eating **meat offered to idols**[51] also seem to us out of date today. Nevertheless, this example in particular shows how much the principles developed in this instance about the strong in faith not despising the weaker ones and the weak in faith not censuring the stronger ones are still of significance. In other questions, too, Paul gives abiding stimuli for today: stimuli for individuals and their basic attitude to reality, stimuli to questions about the fate of Israel, and stimuli towards the structure of the Christian community.

10. The abiding stimuli for the individual, the people, the community

(a) What does Paul say about the secular **everyday life of Christians**? Paul is not an eccentric ascetic who despises all the good things in the world. On all occasions men and women are 'to test what the will of God is: the good and well-pleasing and perfect'.[52]

However, those who believe in Jesus Christ do not need a world of personal perfection or even to escape into a community of the perfect. Such people may and should do the will of God in the midst of the secular world. They need in no way give up all the good things of the world. But they must not devote themselves to them. The believer can give himself, herself away only to God. Paul had already recognized that no Christian need leave the world, but Christians must not fall victim to it. What is called for is not external, physical distance from the things of this world, but internal, personal distance. For those who are freed from the law the great saying is: 'All things are permissible for me.'[53] But at the same time: 'I must not allow myself to be dominated by anything.'[54] In the world 'nothing is of and in itself unclean'.[55] But I can lose my freedom to something in the world and allow myself to be dominated by it as if it were an idol. Then, while it is still the case that 'All things are permissible for me', it is also true that 'not everything is healthy'.[56]

And finally, at the same time one must ask: can what is both permissible and healthy for me nevertheless harm my fellow human beings? What then? Then, too, it is still the case that 'All things are permissible.' But at the same time, 'Not everything is edifying.' Therefore, 'Let no one seek his own, but that of the other.'[57] So freedom can become renunciation, renunciation above

35

all of domination: 'Although I am free towards others, I have made myself the servant of all.'[58] Here the freedom of the believer is not denied; on the contrary, it is claimed to the full. In the last instance the believer is never bound by the opinions and judgments, traditions and values of the other: 'For why should my freedom be judged by another's conscience?'[59] My own conscience, which knows the difference between good and evil, binds me.[60]

(b) What does the Jew Paul think of the greater part of the **Jewish people** which has not accepted Jesus as the Messiah? This is anything but a theoretical question for Paul. It is prompted by a wound which the one who had been brought up a Pharisee did not want to close in his lifetime. But despite all his sorrow and disappointment, Paul maintains that the election of Israel, the people of God, is binding, indispensable, irrevocable. God has not changed his promises, though after Christ their validity must be seen in a different light. The Jews are and **remain God's elect people, indeed his favourites**.[61] For, according to Paul, to the Jews – his 'brothers' by common descent[62] – still belong:
– the 'sonship': the appointment of the people of Israel as God's 'firstborn son' which already took place in Egypt;
– the 'glory': the glory of the presence of God ('Shekhinah') among his people;
– the 'covenants': the covenant of God with his people, constantly threatened and renewed;
– the 'giving of the law': the good ordinances of life given by God to his people as a sign of his covenant;
– the 'worship': the true worship of the priestly people;
– the 'promises': the abiding promises of God's grace and salvation;
– the 'fathers': the fathers of the former time in the community of the one true faith;
– the 'messiah': Jesus the Christ, born of Israel's flesh and blood, who in the first place does not belong to the Gentiles but to the people of Israel.[63]

How much the Jewish people and Christianity would have been spared had this theology of the apostle Paul, as it is presented above all in Romans 9-11, not been suppressed, indeed completely

36

forgotten! Paul's 'great sorrow' and 'incessant grief'[64] about the attitude of 'Israel' were transformed in the course of history into the unimaginable sorrow and cruel grief of Israel itself! In the name of the Jew Jesus and the Jew Paul, the people of the Jews was discriminated against beyond all bounds, persecuted and indeed exterminated.

Here it was not Paul who detached Christianity from Judaism: others did that after his death and the destruction of the Second Temple. Paul, the Jew who gave up being a Pharisee, **as a Christian in no way gave up his Jewishness.** Whatever one may say about him, though he was constantly attacked, misunderstood and defamed, he in no way felt that he was a transgressor of the law, an apostate, a heretic. The Christian Jew and apostle was simply fulfilling his Jewishness in a new, more comprehensive spirit, and in so doing thought that he had the Torah on his side: in the light of the God who had already beforehand acted in constantly new, unexpected ways and still did so, and of his Messiah. And Paul also believes in the salvation of the Jews, when Christ returns from Zion to judgment.

(c) How does Paul understand the **Christian community?** Were he to come again and see in particular the structure of the Catholic church, this church law worked out to the smallest detail, this monstrous hierarchy, above all the service of Peter endowed with a claim to infallibility and primacy, he would go to the barricades and once again resist 'to the face' anyone who 'deviates from the truth of the gospel'.[65] For 'holy rule', '*hier-archia*', was quite alien to Paul. He did not commend a hierarchical structure to his communities or build them up, but trusted in the charisma of all those who wanted to work together for the good of the community.[66] He was concerned with the 'democratic' interplay brought about by God. In his view, every member of the community has a particular task, a particular service, a particular charisma – and by this we should not just understand extra-ordinary phenomena like speaking with tongues and healing the sick. One cannot talk of enthusiasm in Paul any more than one can talk about clericalism. On the contrary, according to Paul **any** ministry which in fact is performed for the building up of the community (whether it is permanent or not, private or public) is charisma, **church** service, and as concrete service it deserves recognition and subordination. So **any** ministry, whether or not it is official, has authority in its own way if it is performed in love for the benefit of the community.

But can one keep **unity and order** in this way? Indeed, were not the Pauline communities in particular put in serious danger by rival groups, chaotic behaviour and morally dubious practices? Paul's correspondence with his communities is clear here: Paul did not want to produce unity and order by levelling out differences, by producing uniformity, hierarchy, centralization. Rather, he saw unity and order guaranteed by the **working of the one Spirit** which does not give all charismas to each person but gives each person his or her own charisma (the rule is: to each his or her own!), a charisma which is not to be used egocentrically, but for the benefit of the other (the rule is: with one another for one another); indeed it is to be used in submission to the one Lord (the rule is: obedience to the Lord!). Anyone who has not confessed Jesus and used his or her gifts for the benefit of the community does not have the Spirit of God. That is how spirits are to be discerned. The signs in the community of the Spirit of God which is identical with the Spirit of Jesus Christ are not clerical supervision and spiritual dictatorship, but consideration, recognition, behaviour in solidarity, collegial harmony, discussion, communication and dialogue in partnership.

(*d*) But in this perspective, is there still **authority in the church**? Could Paul exercise authority? Here too the answer is: Yes! Paul has an amazing authority, and he was not afraid in certain circumstances to use this apostolic authority forcefully. But Paul's practice of authority never became authoritarianism. The apostle never built up his authority - for example with a view to exercising a sacral jurisdiction. Rather, he constantly limited his authority voluntarily in the conviction that the apostles are not lords of faith but those who contribute to the joy of community members; that his churches do not belong to him but to the Lord, and therefore are free in the spirit: called to freedom and not to be slaves of others.

Certainly where Christ and his gospel are to be abandoned in favour of another gospel, in some circumstances Paul can even threaten the curse and exclusion. But whatever he may have done to an individual, temporary exclusion for betterment, he never did to a community even in the most serious cases of deviation. Rather, instead of issuing a prohibition he appealed to people's own judgment and responsibility; instead of exerting pressure he wooed them; instead of ordering them about he encouraged them; instead of talking about 'you' he talked about 'I'; instead of inflicting punishment he offered forgiveness; instead of oppressing freedom he challenged people to be free. That is apostolic ministry in concrete according to Paul! In moral questions, too, where it was not a matter of the Lord and his word, Paul wanted to give his communities freedom and not put a rope around their necks. And how many in our churches who think that they have Paul behind them in fact still have him before them, have still not really, have still not yet, understood what is really the nucleus of Christian freedom with which he was concerned!

To conclude: in all that I have said I have not grasped Paul, but simply come nearer to him. If one is to get to know all his themes – the preaching of the cross and the hope of resurrection, spirit and letter, the two wisdoms, the dialectic of weakness and power, the body of Christ and the sighing of the whole creation for redemption – then one must read Paul oneself. Then it is possible to understand why Paul, tested by suffering and militant, weak yet strong, was a great theologian, a great Christian thinker. It was because with body and soul, in pride and humility, he was utterly devoted to the cause, the Christian cause, the cause of Jesus Christ. His theology constantly admonishes us that it is not the apostle, whether Peter or Paul, who is the Lord. Jesus is the Lord: 'Jesus Kyrios'[67] – that is also Paul's confession of faith. And this Lord lays down the norm for his churches and for individuals, in whatever function.

No one knew better than Paul that he was no superman. No one was more aware of his humanity and his fragility, which mocks all claims to infallibility. He was an apostle who was always clear how far he came short of the cause of Jesus Christ himself without ever falling victim to despair or resignation, and without ever giving up hope: 'Not that I have already obtained this,' he writes to his favourite community in Philippi. And it is with a passage from his letter to that community that I would like to end: 'or am already perfect; but I press on to make it my own, because Christ Jesus has made me his own. Brethren, I do not consider that I have made it my own; but one thing I do, forgetting what lies behind and straining forward to what lies ahead, I press on toward the goal for the prize of the upward call in Christ Jesus.'[68]

Origen
The Great Synthesis of Antiquity and the
Christian Spirit

Chronology (following P.Nautin)

185	Born, probably in Alexandria.
201	Martyrdom of his father under Septimius Severus.
203-5	Continues his studies.
206-10	Time of persecution; instruction of those seeking baptism.
211	Emperor Caracalla: end of persecution; Origen opens a private school for grammar. 'Conversion': sells his library of profane literature and studies the Bible.
c.215	Travels to Rome for several months.
217-29	Returns to Alexandria; conversion of Ambrose, which makes it possible for Origen to have stenographers and copyists; beginning of his work on the 'Hexapla', the first commentary on the Bible; first minor works.
c.229	Travels to Arabia.
229-30	Alexandria: main systematic work, *De principiis*. Beginning of polemic against Origen; sermons in Caesarea and Jerusalem; return to Alexandria.
231-2	Journey to Antioch to the empress's mother Mammaea.
232	Short stay in Alexandria, travels to Greece via Palestine where he is ordained priest; protest actions from Bishop Demetrius of Alexandria.
233	Athens. Origen, informed of Demetrius's actions, responds with an autobiographical letter.
234	Returns to Caesarea.
235-8	Emperor Maximin the Thracian: renewed persecution of Christians; writes 'On martyrdom'.
239-45	Countless homilies and Bible commentaries.
245	Second journey to Athens.
245-7	Caesarea.
248	Stays with Ambrose in Nicomedia; letters of defence to Pope Fabian and Emperor Philip the Arab (murdered 249).
249	Caesarea: the apologetic work *Contra Celsum*; last Bible commentaries.
249-51	Emperor Decius: first general persecution of Christians; Origen arrested and tortured.
after June 251	Death of Origen.

1. The new challenge

When Origen was born around 185 CE, Christianity was still a small minority in the Roman empire. No one at that time could have guessed that around 150 years later it would already become an imperial church. For the imperial government which had initiated a local and temporary persecution of Christianity in the first century under Nero (to which Paul had fallen victim) was now to enter into a life and death struggle with the Christian community. Who would win? Around the end of the second century only a few doubted whether it would be the empire.

However, we should not be deceived: just because Christianity was a minority at that time does not mean that it was without influence. The English church historian Henry Chadwick has rightly pointed out that it was the Alexandrian philosopher **Celsus**, the one who still attempted to justify the traditional polytheistic Roman state religion once more in a comprehensive philosophical and theological tractate, who also seems to have been the first to recognize the strength of young Christianity: 'that this unpolitical, quietistic and pacifist community had the power to change the social and political order of the Roman empire'.[1]

Christianity as a subversive, revolutionary force? But at that time it took the most capable brain in the church to react adequately to the challenge of this renewed pagan philosophy. At that time the church had such a brain in the person of **Origen**, from Alexandria in Egypt, the city of learning. Origen – a brilliant, much-praised but also highly controversial theologian.

For centuries he was given only a secondary place in the history of theology. He was too much branded a heretic, he was condemned too much in the East, and in the West he was overshadowed by Augustine and Thomas Aquinas. In the German-speaking world it was Hans Urs von Balthasar who made an energetic plea that Origen should be set alongside Augustine and Thomas Aquinas and thus accorded his due place in history. And quite rightly so. Others, like the Protestant theologian Adolf von Harnack, had already long given him this place.

But why did Origen prove so fascinating for a Catholic theologian like Balthasar (who in the 1970s and 1980s unfortunately promoted a conservative, anti-conciliar Roman policy)? Because with this theology Balthasar, Henri de Lubac and their friends at the Jesuit College of La Fourvière in Lyons could undermine the almost complete domination of the Catholic church by Roman neo-scholasticism. None of the great figures, from the Cappadocians to Augustine, to Dionysius, Maximus, Scotus Eriugena and Eckhart, says Balthasar, could escape 'the almost magical attraction of the "man of steel", as they called him', and some had fallen completely under his spell. 'If we take the Origenistic shine from Eusebius, all that is left is a dubious semi-Arian theologian and a prolific historian. Jerome simply writes him off when he comments on scripture, still even when externally he had broken the chains harshly and angrily and denied the bonds which tie him to the master. Basil and Gregory of Nazianzus in enthusiastic admiration collected the most misleading passages from the innumerable works of one to whom they returned during their life, in the moments when they had some respite from the everyday struggle; Gregory of Nyssa fell victim to him even more deeply. The Cappadocian writings hand him on almost intact. Ambrose, who knows him at first hand, writes him off; yet some of his breviary readings (like those of Jerome and Bede) are barely altered texts of Origen.'[2]

Alexandria, city of learning, city of philosophy. When Origen was growing up there and beginning to think as a Christian, the **last great Greek philosophy** was beginning to develop: the Neoplatonism of **Plotinus**. Both the Christian Origen and Plotinus, a pagan who was around twenty years younger (c.205-70), had been disciples of the Platonist (or Pythagorean) Ammonius Saccas. But as far as we know, they never made each other's acquaintance. When Plotinus opened his Neoplatonic school of philosophy in Rome in 244, Origen had already been living for a good decade in Caesarea, the provincial capital of Palestine. How he would have liked also to work in Rome, where we know that he spent several months around 215, or in Athens, to which he travelled in 232 and 245!

What do we know about his person and work? We are better informed about Origen than about any other theologian before Augustine. Not only from autobiographical sources, from the evidence that Origen himself left behind, but also through theologians like Pamphilos, the Panegyric of Gregory (Theodore?)

and the church historian Eusebius[3] – though there are problems of chronology. However, for these one can confidently refer to the fundamental new work by Pierre Nautin.[4]

2. The thwarted martyr

The intellectual ground had already been prepared in Alexandria by Titus Flavius **Clemens**, who may have taught there since around 180. A much travelled man, with a classical education, already before Origen this free Christian thinker had found a way between Gnostic heresy and sterile orthodoxy. Clement was convinced that despite all their distance from paganism, despite all criticism of its philosophy and literature, Christians could learn much truth from Greek thought, especially from Plato and also from individual poets, despite all their frivolity.[5] Faith and knowledge, Christianity and Greek culture, need not be opposites. Rather, the 'Christian Gnostics' bound the two into a rational synthesis. Greek philosophy must not be rejected or simply commandeered, as by the apologists Irenaeus and Tertullian, to defend the Christian position. Rather, it was useful for clarifying thought and deepening Christian faith. Indeed, like the law for the Jews, for the Greeks **philosophy was the tutor to Christ**. Christian faith, which always remains the foundation, could go along with an illumination of the Christian message in the light of the Greek philosophical tradition.

But Clement of Alexandria wanted even more. He did not just want to write apologetic – like the Christian philosopher and martyr Justin at the beginning of the second century. He wanted to provide a positive theological elucidation of the Christian message, and he set this out in his book *Paidagogos*, which soon became a handbook of Christian ethics, highly prized by the laity, with practical instructions for a Christian attitude in all possible situations in life. **Christ is the great tutor of all the redeemed**. That is the basic thought of this book, which does not require an extreme ascetic ideal of Christians, but expresses a fundamentally affirmative attitude to creation and its gifts, including sexuality. At any rate, in the light of the Christian message everything can be put in the right proportion. But Clement soon had to leave

Alexandria. Perhaps he had to avoid a persecution of Christians under Septimius Severus in 202/3; perhaps he also had difficulties with his bishop. Be this as it may, Clement was compelled to emigrate to Jerusalem and Asia Minor, where he died before 215 – no one knows precisely where.

Clement's basic notions now also appear in **Origen**, who despite his Egyptian name ('son of Horus') came from a fairly well-to-do Christian family in Alexandria. But the basic mood of Origen is very much more serious than that of Clement. Why? Because at the age of seventeen Origen, the oldest of seven children, was traumatized by an event which was to determine his life once and for all. His father, who had made it possible for him to be trained in the sciences and had handed down to him a firm Christian conviction, was imprisoned for his faith. Indeed, he was tortured and publicly beheaded, and the family possessions were confiscated.

But Origen's misfortune had a silver lining. He was taken into the house of a rich Christian woman (whose orthodoxy was suspected by some) and was able to continue his education. After completing his literary studies, and with his mother and the rest of his family to feed, he opened a private school for grammar and studied philosophy again, now probably with the famous Ammonius. Between 206 and 210 there was another persecution, during which Bishop Demetrius and the greater part of the clergy of Alexandria made themselves scarce.

But not the young Origen: instead of also creeping away in fear, as 'the son of a martyr' he continued to teach undeterred. His pupils – candidates for baptism – were inspired by the martyrs to accept Christian faith. Origen kept up their morale, and cared for those arrested and condemned to death – he mentions them by name – so intensely that finally he himself had to go into hiding. Such decisive experiences shape a man for life: already in his early years Origen grew into not only a brilliant teacher but also a spiritual leader.

After the persecution Origen resumed teaching grammar and instructing in the faith in Alexandria, and the bishop on his return formally approved Origen's activity. However, after a kind of religious 'conversion' Origen closed his school of grammar and sold his library of *belles lettres*. Why? To devote himself wholly to teaching Christian philosophy and to the study of scripture. In his **Catechetical School**, which soon became famous, he reorganized teaching by dividing it into an elementary and an advanced course. All the human sciences, including logic, mathematics, geometry, astronomy and then ethics and metaphysics, were to be put at the service of theology and a more comprehensive understanding of the word of God. This was a truly ecumenical enterprise, which showed the breadth of Origen's thought and was open to Christians, non-Christians and Gnostics.

However, we must imagine Origen, stamped by his father's martyrdom, as what Hans von Campenhasuen has called a **'thwarted martyr'**.[6] This is manifested in his rigorous asceticism: celibacy, fasting, prayer, a spartan home, little sleep – in all this he differed completely from Clement. It is also manifested in his passionate theological commitment, which he probably saw as the only appropriate substitute for the martyrdom that he had escaped and now sublimated. How radically this Adamantius ('the man of steel') understood his Christian discipleship is clear from the way in which he followed Jesus' praise of those who are 'eunuchs for the sake of the kingdom of heaven'[7] by having himself secretly castrated by a doctor (already at that time a routine operation). Later this was to be used against him, even when he had gently distanced himself from such a literal interpretation of scripture.

Who was he, this Origen, whose heart burned with the hidden fire of scripture? An ecstatic? He never reported ecstatic experiences. A mystic? From all that we know, he was not a mystic in the strict sense, a man with a mystic experience of unity. But one thing is certain: he was a spiritualized, spiritual tutor to Christ – a theological 'spiritual director', as one might say. Through his life and his teaching of the inner, gradual ascent of the soul to God, he doubtless prepared the way for deep spiritual experiences. Here, since Origen, continence is no longer a post-marital matter for people of 'mature' age, but the ideal for a radical rethinking in youth. So Origen became the **model for ascetical monasticism**, which, as we know, did not begin with the earliest community in Palestine but only in the third and fourth centuries in the Egyptian desert with Antony and Pachomius. However, Origen is not hostile to science, like some monks after him. On the contrary.

3. The first model of a scientific theology

Origen also became the model for a scientific theology. His work was not 'academic', but pastoral, and aimed at the believer. He was not primarily interested in a method or a system, but in basic human attitudes before God and in life in the Christian spirit. Origen was a man with an insatiable thirst for learning, a comprehensive education and a tremendous creative drive. The bibliography made by Eusebius is said to have contained two thousand 'books'. His whole work had a clear aim: from the beginning he did theology passionately with the aim of achieving a definitive reconciliation between Christianity and the Greek world or, better, a **'sublation' of the Greek world into Christianity**, though a Christianization of Hellenism was the inevitable consequence of a Hellenization of Christianity. And so while Origen's theology does not represent a paradigm shift, **the Gentile Christian/Hellenistic paradigm already initiated by Paul achieves theological completion** in him. But what does completion mean?

Origen was a convinced Christian, but he remained a Greek through and through, as Porphyry, Plotinus's biographer, admiringly and bitterly confirms: Greek and Christian, Christian and Greek. He was a pacifist who rejected military service for Christians, but he was loyal to the state authorities (except in matters of faith). He now created, indeed embodied, **the first model of a scientific theology**, which moreover was to have tremendous effects throughout the old ecumene, in the East and also in the West. Indeed, we are fully justified in saying that Origen was the only real genius among the Greek church fathers. Professor and confessor at the same time, he was the admired model of a highly-cultivated Christian life and a spiritual leader. Critically yet constructively, this universalist who found value in everything worked through all previous theological approaches and materials, including those from Gnosticism.

So Origen proved to be a cultural mediator *par excellence*. He was not, as his predecessor Clement had ultimately been, still a brilliant dilettante, but the first scholar in Christianity to engage in methodical research; indeed he was the greatest scholar of Christian antiquity, and by the unanimous verdict of patrologists the inventor of theology as a science. So the French patrologist

Charles Kannengiesser rightly also says: 'He invented the appropriate **praxis** for this kind of theology, and the methodological **theory** which it needed. One wonders only if inventing a new paradigm need always entail as much innovation as Origen's creativity required.'[8]

Be this as it may, completely at home in the church community and yet at the same time in ongoing dialogue with Gentile and Jewish scholars of his time, Origen was able to open up a variety of new ways and express them in language which could be understood; he did so at a very early stage, and very boldly, in particular by an innovative way of **steeping the biblical message in systematic theology.** Presumably in response to criticism which had been expressed, he broke off work on a powerful commentary on Genesis to sum up his theological views in a major theological scheme: its idealism was inspired by Plato and its evolutionary character by the Stoa.

The work is called *On the Principles* (Greek *Peri archon*, Latin *De principiis*), and it deals with the basic principles of being, knowledge, Christian doctrine. However, because of some peculiar theses (for example on the pre-existence of souls) it made Origen an even more controversial theologian. Right up to his death it brought him the charge of heresy and ultimately condemnation – with devastating effects on his work as a whole, so that we have it only in fragments (his *Peri archon* above all in Rufinus's Latin translation). But Origen himself distinguished precisely between the *dogmata* of the church tradition which were to be maintained and the *problemata* which were to be discussed, i.e. the open questions in answering which already at that time he claimed and practised freedom of theological thought in the face of the bishops.[9] However, viewed historically, *Peri archon* is the impressive documentation of the completion of the Gentile-Christian/Hellenistic paradigm, a reconciliation of Christianity and the Greek world, which Origen embodies in a way unlike any before him. What does this reconciliation look like?

4. Reconciliation between Christianity and Greek culture: A vision of the whole

Loyal to the programme of his predecessor Clement, Origen attempted to reconcile Christian faith and Hellenistic education in such a way that **Christianity appears the consummation of all religions**. What is the foundation of his doctrinal system? It is Holy Scripture, but this is interpreted according to the tradition of faith of the apostles and the church. The result is less a first Dogmatics than a first 'Christian Doctrine',[10] in which the coherence of the discussion of various themes was for Origen a sign of truth. Precisely what is 'On the Principles' about? Here it is possible to mention only a few basic ideas.

The presupposition of Origen's theology is the Platonic-Gnostic scheme of fall and subsequent ascent and the thoroughgoing separation of eternal idea and temporal manifestation. We understand Origen only when we become clear that for him the question of the **origin** (and thus being) of Logos, spirit, spiritual being – one could call this the 'alpha' question – is in the foreground of his theological interest – as with the Gnostics, but without Gnostic sexual symbolism, mythologies and fantasies. That explains the four parts ('books') of his work, in which Origen presents the **whole of Christianity** in three great arguments: God and his unfoldings; the fall of the creaturely spirits; the redemption and restoration of the whole (Part 4 deals with the allegorical understanding of scripture). From the central 'elements and foundations' of Christianity Origen works out a 'coherent and organic whole':[11] a great synthesis which is not disowned but confirmed by Greek thought. Here are just the most important basic concepts.

1. **God.** Clearly the centre of theology, God is not understood anthropomorphically as a superman, but as the primal living One, the pure, absolutely transcendent, incomprehensible Spirit which can only be named in negatives or superlatives. He is the only One (against all polytheism), and he is the good creator God who directs everything through his providence (against Gnosticism and Marcion, who accept an independent demiurge below or even alongside the supreme God).

2. **Logos.** The Logos is God himself and at the same time a

separate 'hypo-stasis' (the Latin *sub-stantia* is open to misunderstanding). From eternity he is begotten constantly by God, the Father (Godself = *autotheos*), as Son, is his perfect image and at the same time the embodiment of the ideas and of all truth. However, the Logos remains clearly subordinate to Godself as 'second God' (*deuteros theos*), although 'of one being' (*homoousios*) with him; the Logos is not 'simply good' but the 'image of goodness'.[12]

3. **Holy Spirit.** The Holy Spirit proceeds from the Son, is less than him and remains subordinate to him: a third stage or hypostasis. So here in Origen for the first time we find talk of 'three hypostases' (in the West at the same time Tertullian was speaking of three 'persons') in the Godhead itself: the beginning of the doctrine of the Trinity proper.

4. **Spiritual being.** All the 'spiritual beings', called *logikoi*, are created by God in freedom, but they have all fallen from the primal light in a primal fall and are banished into material bodies for punishment and education. Those beings who only sinned slightly are banished to an ethereal body: they are the angels. Those who sinned gravely are banished to the densest body of all, the devils. Those in between are banished to an earthly body, as human beings. So it is not a lower divine being who is responsible for all the evil and wickedness in the world, as in some mythologies; the cause of this evil and wickedness is the misuse of freedom by creatures themselves.

5. **Redemption.** The redemption of all these spiritual beings, all of which are striving for the pure light world above, which is perpetually the same, comes about through the Logos made man, the 'God-man': he functions as a mediator for the return of beings to God; for the angels he is an angel and for human beings a human being.

6. **Soul.** The believing human soul, if it is inwardly united with Christ, may ascend stage by stage in freedom to perfection. Accordingly, the inner life is understood as a process of spiritual ascent from this earthly-material life, until the soul finally becomes one with the Godhead in the vision of God, indeed is divinized and becomes immortal.

7. **Apokatastasis.** Right at the end – Origen can imagine further periods and redemptions of the world – there takes place the

restoration of all things' (*apokatastasis ton panton*). Then God will finally be 'all in all'[13]: even the evil spirits will be redeemed, evil will disappear altogether, and everything (*ta panta*) will be restored to its original pure and identical spiritual state. The great cosmic circle between pre-existence, creation, fall, incarnation of all, ascent and reconciliation of all is closed. And is that not a grandiose solution to the problem of theodicy for Origen? God has triumphantly justified himself beyond all that is negative.

This is certainly a tremendous vision of the whole; many aspects of it may be alien to us today, but at the time it was fascinating for many people. In this way, along the lines of Clement, the history of humankind itself can be understood as a great **process of education** leading continually upwards through all breaks: **as God's pedagogy (*paideia*) with human beings!** In other words, the image of God in human beings, overlaid with guilt and sin, is restored by the providence and educational skill of God himself in Christ. So human beings are brought to perfection in accordance with a quite definite plan of salvation = an *oikonomia*, the word used by theologians more than a thousand years before it came to be used by economists. In Christ 'the union of the divine nature with the human took its beginning, so that the human nature itself might become divine through close union with the divine'.[14] According to this '*oikonomia*' the **incarnation of God** is itself the presupposition of the divinization of human beings.

Was it the idea of the reconciliation of all things, and thus the rejection of eternal punishment in hell and the redemption even of the devil, that now entangled Origen in a serious **dispute with his bishop Demetrius**? That is quite questionable. It is, though, certain that this scholar who meanwhile had become world-famous, who in 231 had even been invited to Antioch by the emperor's mother Julia Mammaea to give a lecture, was a burden for the Bishop of Alexandria. Probably Origen had too often criticized the ritualistic and hierarchical church in his interpretation of scripture and censured the all too worldly lifestyle of churchmen. In the meantime, in the Hellenistic-Roman metropolis of Alexandria the office of bishop had in fact changed from being a charismatic function of service into an institution of power and control which was often lacking in spirit and in love. Evidently the bishop preferred Origen's more pliant pupil and colleague

Heraclas to his spirited master: he ordained Heraclas presbyter, but refused ordination to Origen – allegedly because he had castrated himself (which was an impediment to ordination).

Origen did not accept this discrimination. On a journey to Greece in 232 he had himself ordained in Caesarea in Palestine by his friends the bishops of Caesarea and Jerusalem, without involving the Bishop of Alexandria. Demetrius reacted promptly: at two synods of presbyters the pioneer thinker of the Greek church was banished by his bishop, deprived of his office and at the same time denounced to the Bishop of Rome and other bishops: Heraclas became head of the school (and later even succeeded Demetrius). Origen was also condemned without a hearing by the Bishop of Rome – who was always concerned to have good relations with Alexandria. An evil omen! The first great conflict in church history was between a monarchical bishop and a free Christian teacher, between church power and spiritual authority, between an institutional church leadership and professional theology. It was a conflict in which the one attacked is criticized but cannot defend himself – and yet does not give way! But new possibilities of work opened up for the versatile Origen outside Alexandria and Rome.

5. How Origen read scripture

Origen continued his work, now supported by the bishops in Jerusalem and Caesarea. At the age of about forty-eight he founded **a new school** with a large library **in Caesarea**, the provincial capital of Palestine. Here he was able to do extremely fruitful work for almost two more decades. He had an enormous programme: extensive correspondence, various journeys, and numerous lectures and disputations before bishops and congregations, and at the same time the instruction of significant pupils who became theologians, men of prayer, saints, martyrs. He was a *homo spiritualis* who could speak in a simple style without rhetorical pomp, to educated and uneducated people alike. In his last decades, time and again Origen indefatigably expounded Holy Scripture book by book: for him this was the soul of any theology and spirituality. But in this intellectualy highly-developed

Hellenistic milieu, how could an often primitive and unphilo-
sophical scripture be understood?

Here Origen opened up new ways in **biblical textual criticism
and exegesis.** As one who always understood himself to be
primarily a scriptural interpreter and theologian he sees the
exegesis of Holy Scripture as his central task. His Bible commentaries do not fall far short of modern Bible commentaries in extent
and density. But his method is fundamentally different. Like the
Greek philosophers before him who interpreted the myths of, say,
Homer, and like the Jew Philo, who later, at the beginning of the
Common Era, interpreted the Five Books of Moses, now Origen
expounded the Old and New Testaments essentially not in a
historical way, but **allegorically,** in other words symbolically, in
different senses, spiritually, pneumatically. He did this not only
because a fundamentalist and literal exposition of scripture
would have produced something unworthy of God, immoral and
contradictory – a criticism which the Gnostic and heretic Marcion
had already advanced especially against the Old Testament. No,
Origen believed that only in this pneumatic way could the Bible
be plumbed in all its depth and mystery, as an inspired, spiritual
word of God, as the place of the presence of God. According to
him everything in Holy Scripture has a 'spiritual' meaning, but
by no means always a historical meaning. Just as the cosmos and
human beings themselves have three levels, body, soul and spirit,
so too in principle scripture has a **threefold meaning:**[15]

– the somatic-literal-historical sense: the somatic can see Christ
only as a human being;
– the psychical-moral sense: the psychical person sees Jesus only
as the historical redeemer of his world-age;
– the pneumatic-allegorical-theological sense: the pneumatic sees
in Christ the eternal Logos, who is already in God at the beginning.

Now already at that time, as still of course today, Origen was
accused of arbitrariness and fantasy because of his virtuoso
allegorical interpretation of scripture, since at many points he
only keeps to a pneumatic sense and rejects the literal sense. This
criticism is certainly not unjustified. But we should not forget that
Origen is also the greatest **philologist of Christian antiquity!** He
had learned Hebrew from a Jew, and his exegesis contains
numerous explanations of the literal meaning of the text, gram-

matical references and attempts at concordance. And because he wanted to have the authentic Greek text, particularly in discussions with rabbis, in a work which took him more than twenty years he produced the monumental five-volume *Hexapla*, the sixfold (= in six columns) Bible. In six columns he set out the Hebrew text: 1. in Hebrew writing and 2. in Greek transcription; then 3. the translations of Aquila, 4. Symmachus, 5. the Septuagint (here above all the important text-critical signs) and 6. Theodoret (in the meantime three further translations of Jewish origin had appeared). It was an unprecedented work. Existentially interested in the wording and literal meaning of the biblical texts, Origen himself even investigated Hebrew etymologies; indeed he attempted to identify the geography, and even carried out excavations in the river caves of the Jordan. So Origen was a systematic theologian and a biblical scholar in a comprehensive sense. And even more:

6. *Christian universalism*

For Origen, who so often preached, his commentaries and homilies (sermons) were even more important than all this scientific effort. However, he himself wrote hardly anything down; his rich pupil and convert Ambrose had made it financially possible for him to have everything (the homilies, though, only towards the end of his life) written out by six stenographers, who were supported by copyists and calligraphers. Through the spoken word, this philosophical theologian, who was always also a missionary and preacher, perceptively and with a good knowledge of people attempted to explain the spiritual meaning of scripture to his hearers and thus at the same time to communicate a Christian spirituality – in the face of widespread pagan criticism of Christianity. So Origen the systematic theologian and exegete proved also to be a perceptive apologist.

Indeed, Origen also **opened up new ways for Christian apologetics**: the one who attempted to integrate the values of Greece into his Christianity and was at the same time well aware of the weaknesses of paganism was a man of dialogue. As a clear-sighted, intrepid dialogue partner he disputed in a modest and superlative way simultaneously wth rabbis, pagan philosophers, and orthodox and heretical Christian theologians. Precisely on the basis of his theory of the divine Logos, who is at work everywhere, he advocates a **Christian universalism**, but does not exclude a discerning of the spirits – on the basis of the Christian message, which is and remains the decisive criterion for him.

So it should not surprise us that Origen – presumably just a few years before his death, wrote the most learned and perceptive **apologetic work** of Christian antiquity, *Contra Celsum*, against that philosopher Celsus about whom we heard at the beginning. Origen quotes him sentence by sentence (that is the only way we know about Celsus's work *The True Doctrine* at all), and then gently refutes it sentence by sentence. Jesus and the apostles are defended against the charge of deliberate deception, and Christianity generally is defended against the rationalistic charge that it calls only for blind faith and is opposed to any rational investigation. Nor does Origen fail to give a survey of Christian doctrines, beginning with the person and divinity of Christ and moving through creation and the nature of good and evil to the end of the world. Comparisons of statements by Plato with words from the Gospels, remarks about Satan, the Holy Spirit, the prophecies, the resurrection and the knowledge of God conclude the discourse.

What a life of ever new toil that was: sermons, dialogues, letters, journeys, literary production! And constantly this utterly pure man attempts to defend his orthodoxy to bishops, only towards the end of his life to have to resign himself to the fact that one should not rely on bishops. In particular in the great cities like Alexandria, they often behaved like autocrats. And as the persecutions of Christians had become increasingly rare by the middle of the third century, both the episcopate and the Christian communities could develop well in a period of peace. But this was a lull before the great storm.

7. *New persecutions and the success of Christianity*

In the middle of the third century – at a time of economic and political decline – there was an unexpected reversal. In particular, the millennary celebrations of the city of Rome in 248 became another occasion for loading frustration and hatred on to Christians and taking action against a church which, we must grant, had increasingly become a state within the state. On top of all this, the next year (249), the emperor Philip the Arab, who was well-disposed towards the Christians, was murdered. Under his successor Decius (249-251) there followed the **first general persecution of Christians**, which was continued by his successor Valerian (253-260). Specifically, that meant that a state law commanded all Christians in all provinces of the Roman empire, even women and children, to report to the authorities, perform a state sacrifice and obtain an official permit. The aim of these compulsory measures was not to execute as many Christians as possible but to persuade as many as possible to become apostates and thus break up the communities.

In 250 **Origen**, too, did not escape his fate. He was **imprisoned** and put in irons; in the torture chamber his feet were stretched all day long 'to the fourth hole'. But the threatened fiery death was not inflicted on this famous man: Origen was an unbroken confessor, but again a thwarted martyr. Had he died as a martyr at this time, this honourable death would presumably have spared him a number of charges of defective orthodoxy over the following centuries. But the martyr's son, who had himself longed for martyrdom at such an early age and had written an 'Admonition to Martyrdom', survived, and died – we do not know precisely where – between 251 and 254. He must have been approaching seventy.

When Origen died, Christianity – which so far had spread primarily in the eastern half of the empire and was Greek-speaking even in Rome – still formed a relatively small minority. In the third century, the most widespread religion was the cult of Mithras, which derived from the Indo-Iranian sphere; it was a sun cult which was compatible with the emperor cult, but not with Hellenism. Here Christianity had a quite different and ultimately successful capacity for adaptation: the forces and methods of Hellenistic philosophy were integrated. Many ideas from syncretistic Hellenistic piety were adopted – for example the understanding of baptism (now increasingly widely disseminated as infant baptism) and the eucharist (understood as a sacrifice).

And also borrowing from the empire, had not the church increasingly developed a strict discipline and compact organization?

Origen did not strive in practice for that kind of Christian theocracy in which the church would take over the political tasks of the state, as is claimed in our century. His allegory of, for example, Christ as the sun and the church as the moon is not focussed on the present church but on the future, eschatological church. But at a time of sun worship and the emperor cult, such an allegory could easily be understood by the Christian masses as the foundation for a new, Christian theocracy.[16] In fact for an increasing number of people the question increasingly arose whether Christianity was not perhaps the religion of the future, permeating the empire and binding it together. There is no doubt that with his combination of faith and science, theology and philosophy, Origen had attained that **theological turning point** which made possible the **cultural** turning point (the combination of Christianity and culture) which in turn made possible the **political** turning point (the alliance of church and state). It is in fact amazing that this should have been achieved just over fifty years after Origen's death – despite all the reactions of the pagan state.

However, first of all the persecutions by the emperors Decius and Valerian brought a decade of terror for Christianity. Valerian, too, had recognized the danger for the pagan state and attempted to exterminate Christianity with measures extending throughout the empire. Indeed his edict of 258 even intensified earlier decrees: immediate death penalty for bishops, presbyters and deacons; the death penalty also for Christian senators and *equites* if loss of rank and confiscation of possessions did not make them see the light; loss of possessions and perhaps banishment for well-to-do women; loss of possessions and forced labour on the imperial estates for imperial officials; confiscation of all church buildings and burial places. Much blood was shed over these years, involving figures like Bishop Cyprian of Carthage, the great defender of episcopal rights against the Bishop of Rome, who was claiming more and more power...

However, despite all the compulsory measures, the **persecutions** were a **fiasco** for the state, and Valerian's son Gallienus already found himself compelled in 260/1 to repeal the anti-Christian decrees. There followed round about forty years of peace, so that Christianity, which was tolerated in fact, if not by law, was able to spread more and more through Mesopotamia, Persia and Armenia, in North Africa and Gaul, even in Germany and Britain. It increasingly found access to educated and well-to-do people (even at the imperial court and in the army), as a more philosophical and spiritual form of worship – because it had no bloody sacrifices, statues of gods, incense and temples.

And this relative time of peace was one of the presuppositions for the coming hey-day of church theology, without which a broad discussion and a developed theology could hardly have come about. In particular at the centre, in christology, the momentous paradigm shift which had long been heralded was now to take place. Here Origen played a key role. But even now there is much discussion as to how his theology is to be evaluated. The question is:

8. Development or apostasy from the gospel?

If we look back at Origen's work, we can see how different everything is here from what was originally represented by Jewish Christianity – which was still alive at this time. There is no doubt about it: here we have a great new 'constellation of beliefs, values and techniques' with a **Hellenistic** formulation which is quite different from that of Jewish apocalypticism. It is what we would now call a 'modern' paradigm for this period of Hellenism: 'Exemplifying as an individual the unfettered access of Christian faith to the universal culture to which he belonged,' says Kannengiesser once again, 'Origen experienced, with the unique capacities of his genius, what was to become a paradigm for the whole church of future generations: the acceptance of 'modernity' in Christian theology.[17]

The characteristics of this new constellation are:
– the completion of the biblical canon;
– the church's tradition of faith;
– the monarchical episcopate;
– Middle- and Neo-platonic philosophical thought used in the interpretation of scripture.

All this also forms the hermeneutical framework for Origen's allegorical interpretation of scripture, which superelevates the wording of the Bible, and beyond question in many ways also reinterprets it. Moreover this spiritual-pneumatic interpretation of scripture established itself in the long run – in the face of the more sober Antiochene school, with its literal and historical interpretation – in the theology of both East and West. And instead of that model of the imminent apocalyptic expectation of Jesus Christ as the 'end of time' taken over from Judaism, there now first appears in full the Hellenistic, salvation-historical conception of Jesus Christ as the middle of time already prepared for in Luke's two-volume work, the Gospel and Acts: the **incarnation of God** in Christ is seen as the **hinge of world history**, understood as the drama of God and the world. We cannot fail to examine it critically here.

Certainly the new Hellenistic paradigm was historically unavoidable, because it was **necessary** if early Christianity did not want to *a priori* to renounce the inculturation of Christianity in the now quite different world of Hellenism (the kind of opportunity which is often missed nowadays). Without a comprehensive new spiritual and ecclesial self-understanding on the part of early Christianity as embodied in Origen, the coming cultural and political shift would not have been possible either. And how could theologians who thought and felt as Greeks, how could already Justin and Irenaeus, Clement and then Origen, have thought through the Christian message, how could this self-awareness have been realized, other than in Greek - i.e. in Middle- or Neo-platonic – categories and conceptions? This process of transformation is not decadence, but bears witness to the extremely lively dynamic of Christianity. A category like 'lapse from the gospel' certainly does not do justice to the completion of the paradigm shift!

However, the decisive question – which was already put by Harnack – remains whether with such a completion of the Hellenistic paradigm shift the **spirit of Hellenism did not penetrate too far into the Christian centre** and whether justice failed to be done to those central elements of the original Christian message which have been an indispensable part of it from the beginning. So the decisive question is whether the shift of focus in Christian theology does not also represent a shift of meaning in the original Christian message, the gospel.

9. A problematic shifting of the centre

So looking without prejudice at the development of theology in the third century, we cannot denounce this first paradigm shift as a 'lapse from the gospel'. Conversely, though, we cannot glorify it as an organic 'development of the gospel'. What then? What in fact took place was a highly problematic shift of focus and meaning in Christian thought under the influence of a Hellenism with a Neoplatonic stamp. This shift was already taking place from the time of the early apologists and their metaphysical understanding of the Logos, but now it became abundantly clear. Even if one does not want to go so far as Harnack, who wanted to see the 'triumph of the Logos christology in the rule of faith as a recognized part of the orthodox faith' as being 'the transformation of faith into the compendium of a Greek philosophical system',[18] one cannot avoid putting critical questions to Origen:

– For Origen, what is the fundamental problem with which human beings see themselves faced? It is the radical dualism between spiritual and material cosmos, between God and human beings, which is known in neither the Old nor the New Testament.

– And what is the central event of revelation in this salvation history for Origen's systematic thought? The overcoming of this infinite difference between God and human beings, spirit and matter, Logos and flesh by the God-man Jesus Christ in a way which is alien to the New Testament.

For what is the price? Under the influence of Hellenism the centre of Christianity is no longer unequivocally the cross and resurrection of Jesus, as it is in Paul, the evangelist Mark, still also in Matthew and Luke (with their infancy narratives) and even still in John. Now, the centre is more the 'incarnation', or more precisely the speculative problem of the eternal pre-existence and incarnation of the divine Logos and thus the overcoming of the Platonic gulf between above and below, between the true, ideal, heavenly world and the untrue, material, earthly world. By whom? By the 'God-man' (*theanthropos*) Jesus Christ. His picture must now be increasingly divinized, removed from the senses and the body. For while a God-man, son of the Virgin Mary – who later is called not only 'mother of Christ' but also 'mother of God' (*theotokos*) – may still eat and drink, he feels no needs and has no sexual urge. Measured by the original message, this is a grotesque caricature. Or, more precisely, it is a paradigm shift in Christianity with far-reaching consequences.

What are the precise characteristics of this paradigm shift which reached its first climax with Origen? The historians of dogma have stressed in a variety of ways what dogmatic theologians generally have hardly taken seriously. Here are three perspectives:

– Instead of thinking in an **apocalyptic-temporal** scheme of salvation with a forward direction (Jesus' earthly life – suffering, death and resurrection – coming again) people now think primarily from above downwards in a cosmic-spatial scheme of pre-existence – descent – ascent of the Son of God and Redeemer.

– Instead of being explained **in concrete biblical language** (logia of Jesus, narratives, hymns, baptismal confessions), the relationship of Jesus to God is now explained in the **essential, ontological concepts** of contemporary Greek metaphysics. Greek terms like *hypostasis, ousia, physis, prosopon,* or Latin terms like *substantia, essentia, persona,* dominate the discussion.

– Instead of further reflection on the **dynamic revealing activity** of God through his Son in the Spirit **in the history** of this world, the focal point of reflection shifts to a more static **contemplation of God in himself in his eternity** in his innermost 'immanent' nature, and thus to the problems of the pre-existence of three divine forms, hypostases, persons. The decisive theological problem is no longer, as in the New Testament, what is the relationship of this Jesus, the Messiah, to God? It is, increasingly, what is the relationship between Father, Son and Spirit already before all time?

To take just one example of the shift of perspective: the difference between the old (probably even pre-Pauline) confession of faith from the introduction to Romans and the famous christological formula of Ignatius of Antioch, about two generations later. Both talk of Christ as **Son of God**, but in clearly different ways.

The **Pauline** confession, like the famous passage from Peter's speech in Acts,[19] briefly gives a sketch of the story of Jesus by beginning from below with the man Jesus from the tribe of David, who from the resurrection is appointed Son of God: 'The gospel concerning his Son, who was descended from David according to the flesh and designated Son of God in power according to the Spirit of holiness by his resurrection from the dead, Jesus Christ our Lord.'[20]

By contrast, **Ignatius** already says quite naturally that Jesus Christ 'was from eternity with the Father and appeared at the end of the times'.[21] Indeed he already unhesitatingly identifies God and Jesus and speaks of Jesus as 'God come in the flesh', which then leads to paradoxical formulae like this: 'There is one physician, both fleshly and spiritual, begotten and unbegotten, come in flesh, God, in death, true life, both of Mary and of God, first passible and then impassible, Jesus Christ, our Lord'.[22]

We cannot overlook the fact that in the subsequent period the **exaltation christology** (the exaltation of the human Messiah to be Son of God, the two-stage christology) with an originally Jewish Christian stamp, beginning from below and centred on the death and resurrection, was in fact increasingly **suppressed by an incarnation christology beginning from above** (Logos christology), which ontologically intensified the lines of the Gospel of John or individual statements about pre-existence and creation in the hymns of Philippians, Colossians and Hebrews: the pre-existence and incarnation of the Son of God, his emptying and humbling, as a presupposition for his later elevation to God.

We can also say that in Old Testament terms, for the 'ascending' christology, to be Son of God means an election and acceptance in the place of son (exaltation, baptism and birth). It is now supplemented or even replaced by a 'descending' christology. For this approach, to be Son of God means less a dignity and position of power in the sense of the Hebrew Bible than an **essential begetting** of a higher nature – to be described increasingly more precisely in Hellenistic terms and concepts – his heavenly descent and origin. Terms like essence, nature, substance, hypostasis, person, union become more and more significant. Now people wanted to use them to describe the relationship between Father and Son (and eventually also Spirit). But how? A long dispute over that now began.

Indeed, what originally stood at the periphery of faith and confession now came to the centre and as a result was exposed to controversy. Christianity was now increasingly driven by a variety of speculative philosophical systems into a **crisis of orthodoxy** which was to have devastating consequences. For it was by no means the case that Origen exclusively dominated the theological scene at that time.

However, in particular in the second half of the third century after Origen the sources are extraordinarily sparse, and it is quite a dark period for historians. This is not only because we often have only very fragmentary evidence and do not know how far communities (larger or smaller) also stand behind particular names, but because:

1. Many independent theologians (like Paul of Samosata) were condemned as heretics although they were quite orthodox in their way, as their rehabilitation by historians in our century attests;

2. Most of the books of the 'heretics' (including some of Origen's after his condemnation) were destroyed, so that we are dependent on the often tendentious and selective quotations of their opponents;

3. The Hellenistic terms used at that time were ambiguous and often employed in contradictory ways: for example 'hypo-stasis' (in any case identical with the Latin *sub-stantia* only in its etymological significance) could be used both for God alone (thus only one divine hypostasis), for God, the Father, and the Son (two hypostases), or even also for the Holy Spirit (three divine hypostases).

Indeed who can count the names of those who were entangled in the course of the battles over the 'right faith', 'orthodoxy' – that unbiblical word which now become increasingly frequent in church terminology? The sorry conclusion is that as theology became increasingly scientific and intellectual – Origen and the consequences – it now increasingly ran into problems of orthodoxy, disputes over heresy, demarcations – and all this in the name of Jesus!

Only if we have understood this paradigm shift in christology can we understand:

– Why the messianic faith of Christians and Jews has drifted so far apart, as also the messianic faith of Gentile Christians and Jewish Christians;

– Why belief in Christ even within the Hellenistic Gentile Christian churches of the East led to splits in the church which have lasted to the present day; and

– Finally, why in the first millennium a deep gulf also opened up between the Eastern church and the Western church, which then led to a definitive schism in the second millennium. What emerges from this situation?

11. Christian self-criticism in the light of the future

To sum up: already with the early Greek fathers, the main interest of theology shifted from the concrete salvation history of the people of Israel and the rabbi of Nazareth to the great soteriological system. And in Origen it shifted from Good Friday (and Easter) – which were never kept silent about – to Christmas (Epiphany), indeed to the pre-existence of the Son of God, his divine life before all time. According to Origen, simple believers (the pistics) could hold to the earthly, crucified Jesus, but the advanced pneumatics (Gnostics) were now to rise to the transcendent Logos and divine teacher, whose relationship to God was now described in philosophical categories of Hellenistic ontology as the relationship between two or three hypostases.

But Harnack rightly asked about the original gospel. Today this question must be sharpened up against the background of a **markedly extended horizon of comparative religion**: today, more than ever, Christian theology has a responsibility to show ecumenical solidarity with other religions too. Questions arise.

– First of all with respect to **Christianity itself**: Are not the original message of Jesus and the New Testament proclamation of Jesus the Christ of God who was crucified and raised and is present in the Spirit distorted if in Christian theology, literature and piety the main interest has shifted from the cross and resurrection to the conception, birth and 'appearance' (Epiphany), indeed the pre-existence, of the Son of God and his divine life before all time? So has not the original gospel, the Pauline 'word of the cross', become *a priori* a triumphalist metaphysical doctrine, a 'theology of glory'?

– Then in respect of **Judaism**: Is it appropriate for Christian theologians, excessively heightening the Hebrew Bible's divine inspiration, to see the Old Testament as a book of deep Christian mysteries which they attempt to unveil with the help of the allegorical, symbolic method, so that they even think that they can discover a Trinity of Father, Son and Spirit in what becomes their 'Old Testament'?

– Finally, in respect of **Islam**: Is it in keeping with the Hebrew Bible, the Old Testament, when the salvation history narrated in the biblical books is forced more and more into an increasingly complicated dogmatic system which already split the church in the century after Origen and entangled it in increasingly complicated disputes, so that Islam could have such decisive success with its simple message – so close to Jewish Christianity - of the one God, the prophet and Messiah Jesus, and the 'seal' of the prophets, Muhammad?

Origen was firmly convinced that throughout his theology – in exegesis, apologetics and systematic theology – he had done no less than decipher his beloved Holy Scripture. But he was not aware how far he himself remained imprisoned in a quite definite philosophical world-view. That is why we have to speak at such length about these theological questions: to the present day in Eastern Orthodoxy people have maintained the all too natural conviction that the orthodox teaching of the church fathers is simply identical with the message of the New Testament, indeed that the Eastern churches and they alone stand in unbroken continuity with the early church – as though there had been no shift from the Jewish-Christian to the Hellenistic paradigm!

If we now look more closely at the development of Hellenistic christology and the formation of speculation on the Trinity, which makes a decisive beginning with Origen and which we shall soon be able to pursue further with Augustine, in connection with present-day preaching and present-day faith the need arises to consider more closely whether we can simply take over and repeat the christological formulations and notions of the time; whether, in this Hellenistic constellation, the biblical message was simply being interpreted for the abiding centre of the Christian faith, as traditionalist theologians assert, or whether the message of the New Testament was not being swamped by Hellenistic conceptuality and notions.

What is this **abiding centre**? What the Christian community believed from the beginning, what unites Paul and John, Matthew, Mark and Luke and all the rest of the New Testament witnesses:

– The man **Jesus** of Nazareth, the crucified one, has been raised to new life by God; appointed Messiah and Son, he rules as the exalted Lord;

– **God,** the one God of Abraham, Isaac and Jacob, is also the God who called Jesus his Father and our Father.

– The power of the **Spirit** who became powerful in and through Jesus is the Spirit of Godself, who not only permeates all creation but also gives power, comfort and joy to all who believe in Jesus as the Christ.

As a Christian one can hold firm to these indispensable basic elements; as a Christian one can speak of Father, Son and Spirit, without having to follow Origen in taking over the Middle Platonic/Neoplatonic doctrine of hypostases. That Origen attempted this in his time is his greatness. But we would be poor things if in our time we did not make the same attempt in our own way. Origen would have had the greatest understanding of this.

Augustine
The Father of All Western Latin Theology

Chronology (according to P.Brown)

354	Born in Tagaste.
371-3	Goes to Carthage for the first time. Death of his father Patricius; beginning of cohabitation with a woman; birth of his son Adeodatus.
383	Travels to Rome with wife and child.
384	Appointed teacher of rhetoric in Milan (autumn).
385	His mother Monica comes to Milan (late spring); separates from the woman.
386	Conversion to Christianity (end August); goes to Cassiciacum (September).
387	Returns to Milan (beginning of March); baptism; Ostia vision; death of Monica.
388	Moves from Ostia to Rome.
388-90	Returns to Carthage, then goes to Tagaste.
391	Moves to Hippo to found a monastery; ordained priest.
392	Debate in Hippo with the Manichaean Fortunatus.
394	First Synod of Carthage; reads about Romans in Carthage.
395	Successor to Bishop Valerius.
397-401	*Confessions*; debates with the Donatist bishop Fortunius.
399-419	The books *De Trinitate*.
410	Alaric enters Rome; Roman refugees come to Africa; Pelagius travels through Hippo; reversal of tolerance of Donatists.
411	Last great disputation with the Donatists; use of force.
413-25	The books *De civitate Dei*.
416	Provincial council of Miletus: condemnation of Pelagius and Celestius.
417	Innocent I condemns Pelagius and Celestius.
421	Eighteenth Synod of Carthage.
429	Vandals from Spain approach along the coast of Mauretania.
430	Devastation of Numidia by vandals; 28 August: death and burial of Augustine.

1. The father of a new paradigm

'Augustine is the only church father who even today remains an intellectual power. Irrespective of school and denomination he attracts pagans and Christians, philosophers and theologians alike by his writings and makes them come to terms with his intentions and his person. He also had an abiding indirect influence, more or less modified and broken, as a conscious or unconscious tradition in the Western churches, and through them in the general heritage of culture . . . Augustine was a genius – the only father of the church who can claim without question this pretentious title of modern personality-rating.'[1] Thus the Protestant historian Hans von Campenhausen in the Western tradition, for whom no praise is too high for Augustine.

But has Campenhausen – all too trapped in the Western perspective – deliberately or just unwittingly passed over Origen, that genius among the church fathers? At all events, it is true that the Christian West has dealt more graciously with Augustine's errors than the Christian East dealt with those of Origen. We need to be agreed on two things from the start:

– Augustine has **shaped Western theology and piety** more than any other theologian; in this way he became the father of the mediaeval paradigm.

– Augustine is **repudiated by the East** to a greater degree than perhaps any Western church father – a further indication of the shift in Christianity from the early church/Hellenistic paradigm to the Latin/mediaeval paradigm which in fact begins with him.

We shall be going on to talk about this in what follows: not about the wealth of Augustine's theological statements, which in any case are inexhaustible, but about his **paradigmatic significance** for the new Latin, Catholic paradigm, which is distinct from the Hellenistic, Greek paradigm. Eastern theology must not continue to ignore Augustine, but he may not be spared virtually all criticism, as he is in some Western accounts. A careful judgment should be passed on him as the **initiator of a new paradigm**. For any paradigm shift means not only progress, but also gain and loss. And in fact a new paradigm came about in theology when this originally extremely worldly man, this acute dialectician, gifted psychologist, brilliant stylist and finally passionate Christian began to work his extremely varied experiences into a powerful theological synthesis – as Origen had done a good century earlier.

2. Origen and Augustine – differences and common features

Like Origen, Augustine was a man of tremendous talent, passionate commitment, a unity of doctrine and life:
he attempted to reconcile Christian belief and Neoplatonic thought, the biblical and the Neoplatonic understanding of God;
he understood theology as a methodical reflection on Christian faith which may not allow any contradiction between faith and reason: theology as thoughtful discourse or an account of God.

Like Origen, Augustine worked through all possible philosophical approaches and material in a way which was both conservative and innovative:
he devoted himself to both Christian apologetic and biblical exegesis, the systematic penetration and the practical preaching of the Christian message;
he used the allegorical explanation of scripture, which at some points prefers a spiritual sense to the literal sense.

For Augustine, as for Origen, God as he has revealed himself in his Logos and his Son stands at the centre of theology;
the spiritual soul, which is in the possession of the body, is to find ascent to God through Christ;
religion is to be a matter of the heart instead of just a form of cult and community. One of Augustine's many famous sayings is: 'You have created us for yourself, and our heart is restless until it finds rest in you.'[2]

But the **differences** between Augustine and Origen are already evident here. We should reflect:
that Augustine was born almost one hundred years after Origen's death in what was now the Christian empire;
that while Origen from the start was an exegete and knew Greek philosophy, Augustine was a professor of rhetoric and an amateur philosopher;
that while Origen wrote in a taut, gripping style, Origen wrote with literary brilliance in a highly personal, existentially committed style;

that Origen remained a theologian who was critical of the hierarchy, while Augustine eventually became a Catholic bishop.

But Augustine could have been all this in the Greek East instead of in Rome, Carthage, Milan or Hippo. Still, these more external observations lead us to an inner difference: Origen was **Greek** through and through (with an outstanding knowledge of Hebrew), while from the start and with all his heart Augustine was **Latin**:

– Augustine was a Roman citizen and son of a city official in the Roman province of Numidia, present-day Algeria.

– His language, of which he had sovereign control, was Latin; he had no desire to learn Greek, and he was the only significant Latin philosopher who in practice did not know Greek.

– The heroes of his youth were not the African Hannibal or the Greek Pericles but Romans like Regulus and the Scipios.

– He studied the Latin classics, above all Virgil, and then as an orator of course Cicero, the orator and philosopher; he learnt Greek material, whether pagan or Christian, only from translations or imitations.

– He did not feel in solidarity with Carthage from the start, far less with Athens or Byzantium, but with Rome, for him still the capital of the world and now the centre of the church.

– Augustine hardly sought any contact with the great Greek church fathers of the East, the schools of Cappadocia, Antioch and Alexandria. In short, 'Augustine's education is grounded in Western language, if not wholly in Latin.'[3]

There is one more thing: whereas in a still pagan and hostile environment Origen went his way from youth onwards as a convinced Christian ready for martyrdom, as a young man in an environment which was already widely Christianized Augustine at first rejected Christianity. Only after many wanderings did he find the way from worldliness to being a Christian. So the fact that Augustine could initiate a new theological paradigm was due first to his Latin origin, education and culture. At the same time, however, we must see that any new paradigm, including a new Latin paradigm, arises out of a **crisis** which leads to a new constellation. And Augustine himself, although living in the 'golden age of the church fathers', had to surmount a threefold crisis: first the crisis of his life, then the crisis of the church, and finally the crisis of the empire.

3. A life in crisis

Aurelius Augustinus had grown up in Roman North Africa. The emperor Constantine had already been dead almost two decades when he was born in the little town of Tagaste in the high country of Numidia in 354, the son of a pagan father, Patricius, and a pious Christian mother, Monica. She introduced her child to the beginnings of Christian faith and had him given the rites of the catechumenate. Augustine was not baptized, but he did receive an intensive education, made possible by his father, who unfortunately was to die early.

Rhetoric, technically highly developed in the North African capital, Carthage – a good basis for becoming a lawyer or state official – was the ambitious aim of Augustine's studies and his goal: success, status, wealth and a good marriage. As a student among young careerists, as early as seventeen he lived with a woman. He does not mention her name in his later autobiographical *Confessions*, but she was to be his fate, since after a year, before he became a professor of rhetoric, she bore him a child (whom he called 'Adeodatus', given by God). In intellectual circles of the time a strictly monogamous sexual relationship without legitimate Roman marriage, evidently with the use of some form of birth control, was not unusual. Augustine's relationship to this woman lasted for thirteen years – until he abruptly broke off the relationship.

This is not the place to describe in detail the **spiritual Odyssey** of this man with his different 'conversions'; through his writings and letters, his *Confessions* and the contemporary biography by Possidius, Augustine is in any case the best-known man of antiquity. It might just be mentioned that his course lay from political rhetoric, at first under Cicero's influence (*Hortensius*), to a serious quest for **wisdom**; then from Cicero's philosophy, which was not religious enough for him, as a 'hearer' to that dualistic **Manichaeism** which explains evil (and sexuality) with the aid of an evil principle (eternally equal to the good God), whose 'elect' live a life of continence; then from Manichaeism, which after nine years proved to be a not very philosophical, fantastic mythology, to the **scepticism** of the 'Academics'... How were things to continue?

Augustine was almost thirty years old when in 383 he set out 'overseas' and after a short period of teaching in Rome took the post of a professor of advocacy in **Milan**. Milan was the imperial residence, later also that of Theodosius, the emperor of the East, who had shortly beforehand declared Christianity the state religion and banned all pagan cults. Augustine's mother, who had followed him, now forced him to make an appropriate marriage; it was against the law for him to marry his lowly-born concubine. Monica found a young heiress, only twelve, but from the best Milan family, who seemed to offer her son the prospect of an outstanding career. Thereupon Augustine's life-companion and mother of his son made a 'vow of continence' and travelled back to Africa, there presumably to put herself under the protection of the Christian community as a widow. But Augustine, offended, first of all consoled himself with a substitute lover, though this did not give him spiritual fulfilment. An arranged marriage, a conventional future as a married man and government official – was that now to be his life? His self-doubt reached a climax.

However, in Milan Augustine now met a brilliant advocate of the Christian cause, Bishop **Ambrose**. Ambrose's sermons, which were both rhetorically and theologically brilliant, and his allegorical interpretation of scripture inspired by Origen (at that time Origen had not yet fallen out of church favour in the East), removed Augustine's intellectual hesitations about Christianity. Now he saw a way of transcending the naive anthopomorphic notions of God and the offensive and contradictory features of the Bible. Another, acceptable form of Christianity showed him how Christian faith and ancient culture could be combined.

4. *The move to Christianity*

Through Ambrose and his intensive preoccupation with Neoplatonism, Augustine overcame scepticism, found access to the true world of the spiritual, and immediately experienced its intense joy. The connection between the Greek Logos and the Logos of the Johannine prologue dawned on him. Then it took only a thorough study of the letters of the apostle Paul, and in August 386 an account of the conversion of Antony and the monastic settlements in the desert, to spark off a new, dramatic and now **final conversion**: from worldly life and hedonistic habits to being a Christian in the spirit of renunciation and asceticism. As Augustine describes his conversion experience ten years later in his *Confessions*,[4] in deep turmoil, he understood the words of a child in a garden, 'Take and read,' as a personal address from God. On the spur of the moment he opened the letters of Paul and read: 'Not in riots and drunken parties, not in eroticism and indecencies, not in strife and rivalry, but put on the Lord Jesus Christ and make no provision for the flesh in its lusts.'[5]

Now Augustine, supported by his friends, resolved on conversion, which under the influence of Neoplatonism, and following the example of the monastic father Antony, he understood as a **radical break**: a decision against sexual pleasure and for perpetual continence, against a worldly career and for a life of seclusion with friends; against riches and for poverty; against sensual delights of all kinds and for asceticism. On Easter Eve 387 Augustine and his gifted son, who was to die early, were baptized by Bishop Ambrose; but from then on Augustine does not say a single word in his *Confessions* about the mother of his child.

Augustine did not become a monk as a result. But he did live a *vita communis*, first in Milan and then a year later – after a memorable farewell conversation his mother had died in Ostia on her journey home – in his native African city of Tagaste, where he sold his father's property. That means that from then on Augustine lived without private possessions, in the company of like-minded friends, a life in common study of the Bible and philosophy, in conversation and prayer, in fact a 'synthesis between the *bios philosophikos* of the Greeks, Cicero's *otium liberale* and the life of the Christian hermit'.[6]

However, after only three years, in which he wrote his works against scepticism and against the Manichaeans, there followed a further turn in the life of the ascetic layman. On a visit to the port of Hippo Regius (present-day Bône/Annaba in Algeria), the most important city after Carthage, this man of faith, who had meanwhile become famous, was recognized in church and literally dragged before old Bishop Valerius, a Greek by birth, in the choir of the church. The bishop was asked to make Augustine presbyter and Latin preacher in place of another candidate, and was prepared to do this. Augustine, at first putting up a vigorous resistance, agreed, and put his personal interests aside. So he was ordained priest and, five years later, in 395, now at the age of forty-one, he became co-bishop, and then successor to the Bishop of Hippo, who died shortly afterwards. This was a move which was to have great consequences for the politics of the church and theology.

Augustine was to remain bishop for thirty-five years, unlike the other bishops, who were mostly married, living until his death a strictly regulated 'common life' with his priests, deacons and other clerics, separated from the people by vows of celibacy and poverty and by the wearing of black robes (some of these companions later became bishops); the Middle Ages with its cathedral communities could see its model in the Augustinian community of priests. And as bishop, Augustine was now to become the chief figure in the two crises which not only shook the church of North Africa but also compelled Augustine himself to make new changes. These were finally to have an effect on the whole Latin church of the West. Here in Africa the form of the church of Europe was decided.

5. The dispute over the true church: Donatus and the consequences

As bishop, Augustine had a tremendous programme to get through: services and sermons, instruction of converts and baptismal candidates, administration and works of charity, judgments and petitions to authorities, sessions, synods, an enormous correspondence (extending as far as Gaul and Dalmatia) and endless journeys on horseback. The mediaeval fusion of state and church competence was heralded in the legal competence accorded by the emperor to bishops in civil trials. It was a life of action rather than one of contemplation, as it had been previously. But it was also a life of interpreting scripture, as is shown by Augustine's extensive commentaries, say, on Genesis and the Psalms, on the Sermon on the Mount and the Gospel of John.

Nevertheless, this man who kept several stenographers and writers busy found time over the years to write the majority – and most profound – of his theological works, now in middle age above all the *Confessions* of his spiritual development to conversion and baptism. This is a unique confessional work, written in the form of a prayer, as much psychological analysis as theological commentary, by one who had still not found rest; he wrote it for himself and a new spiritual and clerical elite, for both apologetic and a therapeutical purposes. After the *Confessions* came the *De Trinitate* and the *De Civitate Dei*, all in all an amazing theological conspectus, which keeps referring back to the Bible (well over 40,000 scriptural quotations have been counted in Augustine's work). Augustine was capable of patiently and consistently thinking through and working out in detail a great idea which had occurred to him.

However, this theology was deeply stamped by two crises in the church and theology which proved to be of significance for the whole of Western theology and the church. The first of these was the **Donatist crisis**, which was to have consequences for Augustine's emphatically **institutional and hierarchical understanding of the church and then that of the whole West**. The background is this. In the fourth century the Catholic church had become an already quite secularized church of the masses. But in North Africa in particular, some circles remembered very clearly the time of martyrdom and the strict church discipline, and the more pneumatic understanding of the church and the sacraments in Tertullian and Cyprian. According to these North Africans, baptisms and ordinations which had been performed by unworthy bishops and presbyters who had 'lapsed' in persecution (there seems to have been such a case earlier in Carthage as well) lacked the Holy Spirit and were therefore invalid; so they had to be repeated. There had already been a schism with the rigorists for around a century, even before the change under Constantine; the mainstream church was accused of laxity. Indeed, after the Constantinian change the majority of North African bishops were rigorists, and were now called **Donatists** after their leader Bishop Donatus (who died in 355).

All the negotiations, synod resolutions and persecutions over several decades were of little help: the Donatists regarded themselves as those who, compared with the great church, were a church unstained by anything unworthy, a pure and holy church whose bishops and priests alone possessed the Holy Spirit, so that they alone could dispense the sacraments validly. And when Constantine's son and successor Constans attempted to suppress Donatism by force, the opposition within the church fused with the social discontent and anti-Roman resentment of the Punic-Berber country population of North Africa, who were being increasingly impoverished by the large-scale agriculture of the Roman landlords. However, this social revolution was largely over when Augustine became bishop of the Catholics in Hippo, eighty-five years after the outbreak of the schism.

But the tensions within the church had not died away. And **the persecuted church** was now to become a **persecuting church**. How did this come about? After the Catholic church had been declared a state religion under Theodosius, and orthodoxy had been established, Theodosius's successor in the West, the emperor Honorius, decreed that the Donatists were to be brought back into the Catholic church by force. Only the Catholic church, whose authority Augustine had so admired since his conversion, would continue to be recognized by the state. Augustine would not have believed in the gospel, he had declared, had not the authority of the Catholic church moved him to it.[7] The subordination of the individual to the church as an institution, as the form of salvation, the means of grace – this was to become a characteristic of Latin Christianity.

The test case came soon, since from the start in Hippo Regius, where the majority were Donatists, Augustine had fought intensely for the **unity of the church**. As a Christian he was tormented by the broken unity of the African church, and as a Neoplatonist more than most he found the idea of unity a sign of the true and the good. No, for him the one true church could in no way be represented by a particular church which had split itself off, but only by the universal church – in communion with Jerusalem, Rome and the great Eastern communities: the great *Ecclesia catholica*, ever expanding and absorbing the world, endowed with sacraments and led by orthodox bishops, that church which Augustine called the 'mother' of all believers. Here, as Augustine stresses so strongly, the 'Catholic' becomes of the utmost significance for the paradigm of the Middle Ages.

But Augustine also knew that this one, holy, catholic church will never be perfect on this earth. Some belong to the church only in the body (*corpore*) and not in the heart (*corde*). The real church is a **pilgrim church** and will have to leave the separation of chaff and wheat to the final judge. To this degree the true church is the church of the saints, predestined, redeemed: a church contained in the visible church but hidden from human view. As for the **sacraments** of the church, a distinction must be made between validity on the one hand and legality and efficacy on the other. The decisive thing is not what is done by the bishop or priest (who is perhaps unworthy), but what is done by God in Christ. The sacraments are objectively valid (though they may not always be legitimate and effective), quite apart from the subjective worthiness of the one who dispenses them, provided that they are performed in order according to the church's understanding. *Ex opere operato*, people were to say in the Middle Ages: a sacrament is valid simply in the dispensation.

6. *The justification of violence in religious matters*

This great dispute without doubt led to fundamental clarifications, and in it Augustine largely gave to the whole of Western theology **categories, solutions and neat formulae for a differentiated ecclesiology and doctrine of the sacraments:** that the church can be understood as being at the same time visible and invisible, two entities which do not simply coincide; the understanding of the unity, catholicity, holiness and apostolicity of the church which follows from this; how word and sacrament go together; the word as audible sacrament and the sacrament as visible word; how in the theology of the sacraments a distinction can be made between the chief dispenser (Christ) and the instrumental dispenser (bishop, presbyter), and how the question of validity can be decided in that light.

And what about the **Donatists?** All the arguments, dialogues, sermons and more than twenty propaganda writings of Augustine, all the prohibitions of mixed marriages and gifts were of no avail. The situation came to a head: there were violent actions on both sides. In 411, on the orders of the imperial government, there was a last great disputation in Carthage, in which 286 Catholics and 279 Donatists took part. Augustine's superior arguments prevailed; at all events they served as a justification for the decision of the imperial commissioner (which had been settled from the start) now to implement the state orders through the police. This could not be done without violence and bloodshed.

Augustine and other bishops like Ambrose and Gregory of Nazianzus saw nothing un-Christian about this. They were convinced from the start that the state had the right to proceed against the heretics. But Augustine was to put this position more and more sharply over the years: in no way did he want hypocrites to populate the church. For him, initially compulsory state measures were a deterrent, and at first he protested against the imposition of the death penalty. But in the end, impressed by the success of crude police actions, he even justified the **use of force against heretics and schismatics** theologically. Indeed he did so with Jesus's saying from the parable of the great supper: '*Coge intrare*', in the emphatic Latin translation, 'Force (instead of compel) them to come in', those who are outside in the alleyways and hedgerows.[8]

And the success? Certainly Donatism had been broken. It had lost its bishops, church buildings and the support of the upper classes. The majority bowed to force. In this respect the Catholics had 'won'. But the price of this 'victory' was to be all too high in the long run. Historians today think that the forcible conversion of the Donatists ushered in the downfall of the African church which had once been so proud: that the former Donatists whose descendants were still causing trouble for Pope Gregory the Great at the end of the sixth century had no interest in defending the Catholic faith. So the African churches, even those of Carthage and Hippo, were overwhelmed by Islam in the seventh century without resistance and vanished without a trace into history.

Nevertheless, the mainstream church and the state (which of course was always interested in unity) did not succeed in completely eliminating all the schismatic and heretical subsidiary churches which kept reappearing. However, with his fatal arguments in the Donatist crisis, Augustine, the bishop and man of the spirit, who could talk so convincingly about the love of God and the love of human beings, was to be produced down the ages as the key witness: the key witness for the **theological justification for forcible conversions, the Inquisition and the holy war,** against deviants of all kinds; this was to become a characteristic of the mediaeval paradigm and was something for which the Greek church fathers had never argued. Peter Brown, who has written the most informed and most sensitive biography of Augustine, remarks: 'Augustine, in replying to his persistent critics, wrote the only full justification, in the history of the Early church, of the right of the state to suppress non-Catholics.'[9] Certainly Augustine could not exterminate the all too numerous non-Catholics in Hippo (as the Inquisition later exterminated the small sects), nor did he want to; he simply wanted to correct and convert. So – again according to Peter Brown – 'Augustine may be the first theorist of the Inquisition; but he was in no position to be a Grand Inquisitor.'[10]

7. *The dispute over grace: Pelagius and the consequences*

That Augustine, an indefatigable preacher and interpreter of scripture, had changed deeply on becoming a bishop – as so many were to do after him; that now more than before he tended towards institutional thinking, towards intolerance and pessimism, became even clearer in the second great crisis which his church had to undergo and in which he was again the main figure. This second great crisis is called the **Pelagian crisis.** It **sharpened and narrowed Augustine's theology of sin and grace,** but found decisive spokesmen not only in the Middle Ages but also in the Protestant Reformation and in Catholic Jansenism.

Pelagius, a highly respected ascetical lay monk and educated moralist from England, utterly opposed to Arianism, was active in Rome between 400 and 411, above all among lay people. He passionately attacked Manichaeism and the immoral paganism which was still widespread, and also the lax nominal Christianity of well-to-do Roman society. But in order to combat the evil, Pelagius, who had been inspired by Origen and his intellectualism

82

and optimism, and who wrote a commentary on Paul, attached great weight to **the human will and freedom**. He emphasized personal responsibility and practical action.

Certainly Pelagius also affirmed the necessity of the grace of God for all men and women, but he understood grace in a more external way, at all events not, like Augustine, as a force working within human beings, almost a material force. For Pelagius, grace was the forgiveness of sins, which for him, too, was the unmerited gift of God. Grace was also moral admonition and the example of Christ. And indeed, for Pelagius, too, the justification of men and women took place in baptism on the basis of faith without works and merits. But once a person had become a Christian – this was his concern – he or she had to make their way to salvation by their own actions – in accordance with the commandments of the Old Testament and the example of Christ.

So it was consistent that in contrast to Augustine, Pelagius should reject the notion of an 'original sin' which since Adam had been handed on to all human beings, a view which had already been put forward in a commentary on Paul falsely attributed to Ambrose (the author is now known as 'Ambrosiaster'). According to Pelagius, all human beings are born innocent; they fall by their own guilt. And with their own free will human beings can also repent and lead a new life. Pelagius was willing to recognize only a sinful bent in human beings, in voluntary imitation of the sin of Adam. When presented with Augustine's saying, 'Give what you command and then command what you will',[11] he rejected it as all too easy a way out. And his pragmatic Christianity found more admiration than criticism among the Romans, who were not interested in high dogmas but in law and morality. In some respects Pelagius was still advocating the old ideals of the past, of classical Stoic ethics. Augustine stood for ideas which were to belong to the future.

When Pelagius fled the West Goths, leaving Rome for North Africa, he did not come into contact with Augustine, and soon travelled on to Jerusalem. However, he had left behind his pupil in Carthage, the like-minded Celestius. And because Celestius now began openly to deny that infant baptism was also given for the forgiveness of sins, in 411 he was excommunicated at a synod of Carthage. Thereupon Augustine sent a personal messenger to

Jerome in Palestine also to obtain the condemnation of Pelagius in the East. However, Pelagius, who did not want a dispute, was able to justify himself: grace was necessary for good works, but there must also be a free act of the will for which human beings are really responsible. A synod of Eastern bishops, for whom the freedom of the will was no problem and the dispute over grace was more a product of Western scrupulosity, acquitted Pelagius in 415. This again caused indignation in Africa and prompted new activities on the part of Augustine who himself understood something else by 'grace', namely something inward; indeed, for Augustine, to assert an 'innocence of the newborn' was tantamount to a falsification of the relationship between God and human beings and a declaration that redemption was superfluous. So he could only feel that Pelagius's response was dishonest or deceitful.

In 416 Augustine therefore called a great synod of Numidian bishops in Milevis which, together with the Synod of Carthage, denounced Pelagius and Celestius to Pope Innocent I. The Pope then promptly excommunicated the two of them. And although Augustine was originally not a theologian fixated on the papacy (a papalist) but more a man of episcopal authority as Cyprian had been before him (an episcopalist), his comment on the action is said to have been 'Roma locuta, causa finita', 'Rome has spoken, the matter is settled' (the statement in this form does not appear in his writings).[12] But of course this causa, too, was by no means settled by the pronouncement of Rome. Pelagius was rehabilitated at two Roman synods, but a Carthaginian synod condemned him again. And it was again the intervention of Augustine and his friends, this time at the imperial court, which led to Pope Zosimus reluctantly – because of an imperial edict – condemning the two main advocates of this theology, Pelagius and Celestius.

But even then the 'cause' was not at an end. For to the end of his life Augustine had to grapple with a spirited defender of Pelagius's cause, **Julian**, the bishop of Eclanum. For Julian, of an aristocratic family and a generation younger than Augustine, the son of a bishop who married the daughter of a bishop but lived a long life of continence, was a brilliant dialectician who could cope with Augustine and could advance good arguments in Pelagius's favour. Furthermore, Julian turned the tables and accused Augustine of Manichaeism, because he condemned the act of sex, which was good in itself, and regarded sin as entanglement in the evil principle of dark matter, from which human beings could free themselves only through abstinence from marriage and the pleasures of the flesh. Furthermore, Julian, who because of his support for Pelagius had been banished from southern Italy in 419, could speak Greek well and in contrast to the 'African' (*Poenus*), as he constantly called Augustine, referred to the much more liberal **Greek tradition** on marriage, which regarded sex as indispensable for the majority of Christians and had no moral problems with sexual intercourse between married partners, or with the statement in scripture that God wants all human beings to be saved. Against this, even in his very last work, which he was unable to complete, Augustine put forward his rigorist position as Catholic doctrine: 'That is the Catholic view: a view which can demonstrate a just God in so many and great punishments and torments of small children.'[13]

But is that really the Catholic view? A more important difference between the Latin West and the Greek East opened up here. Augustine rejected any semblance of Manichaeism. But above all, Augustine felt that Pelagius's teaching touched a sore spot in his own personal experience and struck at the heart of his faith. Had not he, who more than anyone else in antiquity had the capacity for analytical self-reflection, through all the wearisome years before his conversion to Catholic Christianity, experienced and described in his *Confessions* how little human beings can do of themselves? How weak their wills are? How much the fleshly desires (*concupiscentia carnis*) culminating in sexual lust keep human beings from doing the will of God? How much human beings from the start constantly need grace – not just afterwards, to support their wills, but already for the willing itself, which in itself can be evil and perverted. Hence the Augustinian counterpoint:

8. The theology of original sin and predestination

Many pagans in antiquity were also convinced that a great sin lay behind all the misery in the world. But Augustine heightened this

85

view by historicizing, psychologizing and above all sexualizing the Fall. According to Augustine, from the start human beings are deeply corrupted by Adam's sin: 'In him all have sinned' (Romans 5.12). *In quo*: that is what Augustine found in the Latin translation of the Bible in his time, and referred this 'in him' to Adam. But the Greek text simply has '*eph'ho*' = 'because' (or in that) all sinned! So Augustine read from this statement in Romans not only a primal sin of Adam but even an **original sin** which every human being incurs right from birth, has as it were inherited – a reason why all human beings are poisoned in body and soul, are doomed to death.

But even worse, because of his personal experience of the power of sex and his Manichaean past, Augustine – in contrast to Paul, who does not write a word about it – connects this transmission of **'original sin' with the sexual act** and the 'fleshly' = selfish desires, concupiscence, which arise here. Indeed Augustine puts sexuality generally right at the centre of human nature. And what theologian in fact understood more about this than Augustine? Who could describe what goes on inside people better than he? All this influenced his biblical exegesis. For in contrast to most Greek and Syrian authors, Augustine understands the moment of sin after the first fall psychologically as a clearly felt sexual shame – punishment for sin! The inherited corruption of human nature since Adam's fall thus manifests itself particularly in the constant disruption caused by the sexual drive, which escapes the control of the will especially at the beginning and at the climax of the act, but also in sleep and in dreams.[14] Granted, it is not sexuality itself which is evil (as the Manichaeans believed), but the loss of control (thus Augustine). Even the newborn child is no innocent, but is rather a child born in sin who, if it is not to be damned eternally, needs liberation from original sin. And this act of liberation is baptism, so at all events this must be administered already to the newborn child. According to Augustine, not only the young man but also the older, married man has to strive for 'chastity' against sexual desires and take action against the sexual fantasies which constantly break in. Let us be clear about this: never before had an author in antiquity put sexuality so much under the spotlight of cool psychological analysis.

But this attempt at a solution raised a further question: if it is

God who brings about all good things in human beings (who are so corrupt in themselves), then the **problem of grace and freedom** arises. Where is human freedom, if everything takes place through God's grace, and the good will itself must be given by God's grace? Augustine was convinced that God's grace is not motivated through human freedom: on the contrary, the human will is first moved to freedom by God's grace. Grace is not acquired; grace is given. It is God's grace alone which brings about all things in human beings and which is the sole ground of human redemption. This freely given gift is constantly necessary for human beings until their end, but it requires their constant co-operation.

But in that case why are there so many people who are not saved? The more Augustine went into this controversy, the more his position hardened, as is clearest from his doctrine of **double predestination**, predestination to blessedness or to damnation.[15] To fill the gap brought about by the fall of the angels with other rational beings – here Augustine is manifestly taking up more a Manichaean than an Origenistic position – God has predestined a relatively small number of people, fixed in advance, to blessedness, and by contrast a great 'mass of damnation'.

– God's **mercy** is manifested in the **redemption** of human beings, which bestows eternal **bliss** without any legal claim (though envisaging human merits).

– However, God's **righteousness** is shown in the **rejection** of the majority of human beings. God does not will evil but does allow it (because of human free will), and thus lets human beings go on their way to eternal **damnation**. What a difference from Origen! This is a terrifying doctrine, which Calvin was to think through to the end. It raises a number of questions.

9. Critical questions to Augustine

There is no doubt that it is greatly to the credit of Augustine that he energetically directed Western theology, with its tendency toward righteousness by works, to **the Pauline message of justification**, which had lost all topicality with the disappearance of Jewish Christianity into Hellenistic Christianity, and thus indicated the **significance of grace**. Whereas Eastern theology continued to have a strongly Johannine stamp and largely neglected the Pauline problem of justification with its antitheses in favour of talk of the divinization of human beings, on the basis of his experiences and his deeper study of Paul Augustine made grace virtually the central theme of Western theology, and also found numerous neat Latin formulations in this sphere. Against the moralism widespread in the old Latin church which built all too much on human achievement, he demonstrated how everything is grounded in God's grace: 'What do you have that you did not receive?' So according to Augustine Christianity should present itself not as a religion of works and the law but as a religion of grace.

This great achievement of Augustine's has often been praised, and need not be emphasized further. Indeed, it is impossible here to come anywhere near assessing this epoch-making work and all the inspired and profound, brilliant and moving things he wrote about the human longing for happiness and the human situation in the world, under the rule of sin and the rule of grace, all his deep thoughts on time and eternity, spirituality and piety, surrender to God and the human soul. Within the framework of our paradigm analysis, our prime concern must be to work out the difference which gradually arose between Christian spirituality with a Hellenistic stamp and spirituality with a Latin stamp, and the change from the early church/Hellenistic paradigm to the Latin mediaeval paradigm. So what must occupy us here is not the whole breadth and depth of the theological content of Augustine's work but the paradigmatic shifts of this great theologian, which can be traced into the Middle Ages and their crisis, the Reformation, and on into modern times. And now there can be no doubt that the same Augustine who put forward the primacy of the will and love over against the Greek primacy of the intellect and wrote such a generous statement as '*dilige, et quod vis fac*', 'Love, and do what you will';[17] who could write so generously about the grace of God, is also responsible for highly problematical developments in the Latin church, at three decisive points:

1. The **suppression of sexuality** in Western theology and the Western church: more than other Latin theologians (e.g. Jerome),

Augustine stressed the equality of man and woman at least on a spiritual level (in respect of rational intelligence), because both are in the image of God. But at the same time he maintained the physical subordination of woman which was general at the time – according to Genesis 2 woman is made from man and for man.[18] In all this Augustine's theory of sexuality and sin remains problematical: it was so important to him that at the age of seventy he even wrote a letter to the patriarch Atticus of Constantinople, the successor to John Chrysostom (this letter has only recently been discovered), summarizing his position like this:

'An urge (what he means is the evil 'urge of the flesh') which burns quite indiscriminately for objects allowed and disallowed; and which is bridled by the urge for marriage (*concupiscentia nuptiarum*), that must depend upon it, but that restrains it from what is not allowed... Against this drive, which is in tension with the *law of the mind*, all chastity must fight: that of the married couple, so that the urge of the flesh may be rightly used, and that of men and virgins, so that, even better and with a struggle of greater glory, it should not be used at all. This urge, had it existed in Paradise, would, in a wondrous pitch of peace, never have run beyond the bidding of the will... It would never have forced itself upon the mind with thoughts of inappropriate and impermissible delights. It would not have had to be held upon the leash by married moderation, or fought to a draw by ascetic labour. Rather, when once called for, it would have followed the will of the person with all the ease of a single-hearted act of obedience.'[19]

From Augustine's perspective it was clear that ideally sexual intercourse should take place only for the procreation of children. Sexual pleasure purely for its own sake is sinful and is to be suppressed; it was inconceivable for him that sexual pleasure could even enrich and deepen the relationship between husband and wife. What a tremendous burden this particular Augustinian legacy of Augustine's, of the vilification of the sexual libido, was for the men and women of the Middle Ages, the Reformation and far beyond! And still in our own day a Pope has in all seriousness proclaimed the view that even in marriage a man can look on his wife 'unchastely', if he does so purely for pleasure...

2. The **reification of grace** in Western theology and piety.

Whereas in the East no idea of a 'created grace' corresponding to the Latin Western doctrine of grace developed, and interest was wholly focussed on the hoped-for divinization of human beings and their 'immortality' and 'transitoriness', Tertullian already understood grace not so much biblically, as God's disposition and decree of sins, but – following Stoic ideas – as a *vis* in human beings, a power more powerful than nature (*natura*: the contrast between nature and grace appears for the first time in Tertullian).

So for Augustine too, the 'grace of forgiveness' is merely the preparation for the 'grace of inspiration', which is poured into human beings as a healing and transforming dynamic substance of grace: *gratia infusa*, something like a supernatural fuel that drives the will (which of itself is impotent). By grace here Augustine no longer means the living God who is gracious to us, but a 'created grace' which is distinct from God himself, made independent and usually attached to the sacrament. There is nothing about this in the New Testament, but the Latin theology and church of the Middle Ages – a church of grace and the sacraments – was to concentrate on it, in complete contrast to Greek theology.

3. The anxiety about **predestination** in Western piety. Whereas the Greek church fathers maintained the human capacity for decision before and after the Fall and did not recognize any unconditional divine predestination to salvation or damnation, indeed partly even tended to the reconciliation of all things, like Origen and the Origenists, as he grew old Augustine, in an over-reaction to Pelagianism, took over a mythological Manichaean notion and in addition neutralized the universal significance of Christ; in a completely un-Pauline way he individualistically narrowed the statements in Romans about Israel and the church.[20] What kind of a God is it who has *a priori* destined countless human beings, including countless unbaptized babies, to eternal damnation (though perhaps in a milder form) for the sake of his 'righteousness'?

Augustine's contemporary John Chrysostom had explicitly emphasized that small children are innocent, since in his community some people believed that they could be killed by witchcraft and that their souls were possessed by demons. But Augustine also made quite a substantial contribution to fear of demons in the Western church. His doctrine of predestination, although already repudiated by Vincent of Lérins as an innovation (against the principle of the Catholic 'what has been believed everywhere, always, by all') and thus in no way fully received by the mediaeval church, instilled in many people, including Martin Luther, an anxiety about the salvation of their souls which does not match the message of Jesus and contradicts God's universal will to save. Even the French patrologist Henri Marrou, who generally interprets Augustine in such a generous way, cannot avoid stating: 'If serious errors have often distorted his real thinking, as the history of his influence shows, Augustine bears a great deal of the responsibility.'[21]

4. The **new conception of the doctrine of the Trinity**. Whereas Augustine did little to stimulate the Christian life of 'lay people' in the world or a cosmic piety, his theology does contain a good deal of speculation about God. For Augustine set completely new accents not only in matters of sexual morality or the theology of grace and the sacraments, but also in the doctrine of God, above all in rethinking the Christian tradition about the Trinity, where he goes far beyond what we heard previously from Origen about oneness and threeness in God. Summed up in all too brief statements, we may say:

– The Greeks thought in terms of the **one God and Father**; the Father is '**the** God', the one and only principle of the Godhead, which he also gives to the Son ('God from God and light from light') and finally also the Holy Spirit. They are like three stars one after the other: each gives the light to the next, but we only see one.

– Augustine now begins with the **one divine nature or substance**, the one divine essence, glory, majesty common to all three persons. The starting point and foundation of his doctrine of the Trinity is this one divine nature which for him is the principle of the unity of Father, Son and Spirit, within which these three differ only as eternal relationships (these are the foundation of life within God): the Father knows himself in the Son and the Son in the Father, and proceeds from this as the personified love of the Spirit. So Augustine asserts a twofold principle for the Spirit: the famous later Latin addition to the Nicene Creed, 'the Spirit, proceeding from the Father **and the Son** (*filioque*)', which to this day is rejected by the Greeks as nonsense.

So the **originally simple triadic confessional statements** of the New Testament about Father, Son and Spirit developed into an **increasingly demanding intellectual trinitarian speculation** on '3 = 1'. It was almost like a higher trinitarian mathematics, but despite all attempts at conceptual clarity, lasting solutions were hardly reached. We might ask whether this Graeco-Latin speculation, which, far removed from its biblical basis, boldly attempted to spy out the mystery of God in vertiginous heights, did not perhaps like Icarus, the son of Daedalus, the ancestor of Athenian craft, come too near to the sun with wings made of feathers and wax.

In the light of the New Testament, no more is required than that the relationship between Father, Son and Spirit should be interpreted in a critical and differentiated way for the present. The 'heart' of Christian faith is not a theological theory but belief that God the Father works in a revealing, redeeming and liberating way in us through his Son Jesus Christ in his Spirit. Any theological theory must not complicate this basic statement; rather, it must be seen simply as an instrument for clarifying it against differing cultural horizons.

Generally speaking, Augustine, unlike Origen, did not work out any comprehensive system, but put forward a unitary conception. And he had not yet completed his work on the Trinity, when as a bishop he was confronted with an event which now clearly indicated a crisis for the empire and a change in world history. How did his story go on?

10. The great threat to the empire

News of unprecedented terror ran through the empire. On 28 August 410, Rome, which had believed itself to be 'eternal' – even Christians called it *Roma aeterna* – had been stormed by King Alaric, leader of the Western Gothic army fighting for a homeland, and plundered for days. In North Africa refugees had told of horrific atrocities: numerous burnings, women raped, even senators murdered, the rich hunted, whole families exterminated, houses plundered, valuables of all kinds carted off by the barbarians, the old government and administrative centre of the Western world destroyed... Uncertainty and defeatism were abroad: if Rome, the **ancient capital**, could **fall**, what was still safe? How could things reach such a pitch? There were very different responses to the catastrophe:

1. The response of **pagan old Rome**, those educated pagan aristocrats (along with the peasants = *pagani*, the last pagans) who fled to Carthage was clear: it was the **vengeance of the gods of Rome**. The Christians were responsible for the fall of the Roman state. They had evacuated the political and religious idea of the Roman empire, rejected the emperor cult, and thus undermined the authority of the state, the law and the army. They had driven out the gods and replaced them with the cult of the Christian God, putting the state under the protection of Peter, Paul and so many martyrs. But these had evidently offered no protection against murder, plundering, rape, kidnap and extermination.

2. The response of **Christian new Rome**: this catastrophe was **God's punishment**. According to the Byzantines the old Rome had had the Messiah and Son of God crucified by its governor in Jerusalem, had for centuries subjected his disciples to a bloody persecution, and even when it had become Christian, had still tolerated paganism within its walls to the end. So the second, new, Rome, the Christian Byzantium, had long since replaced the old Rome. Its end was now well-deserved retribution for a mistaken policy and false belief.

3. **Augustine's response**. As an African and a Latin, he ignored the existence and myth of the Second Rome and so never paid due attention to the Christian empire as a whole. He gave his extremely sophisticated answer in his last giant work, on the 'City of God' (*De civitate Dei*; we should not forget that here the term 'city' is virtually equivalent to the modern 'state', a term not in existence at that time). For when his open letters and sermons had had too little effect even in Carthage, Augustine's friend Marcellus, tribune and notary in Carthage, had invited him to produce a more substantial work because of so much pagan criticism and so much helplessness and defeatism among Christians. Augustine took up this challenge and now carefully planned a major new work which

93

he published in several stages: the twenty-two books *De civitate Dei*, on which he spent a large part of his last two decades (413-426/7), during which he also composed most of his anti-Pelagian writings.

The first ten books, produced in haste, are devoted to **apologetic and polemic**. The pagans ought really to have seen that the old gods of Rome had always been incapable of keeping famine, epidemics and wars from Rome – one had only to think of the Punic wars or the Roman civil wars. The behaviour of the Christian Germans might be called moderate compared with the harsh conduct of the pagan Romans. Indeed, one can see the whole history of Rome from the beginning as a long chain of violent actions and accidents which begins with the fratricide of Remus by Romulus and in no way corresponds to the ideal of the state as Cicero describes it in *De re publica*, since it has no righteousness. The goal of the state is the preservation of peace in an order which rests on righteousness. There is no question that what Augustine offers here is a bold and unprecedented demythologizing of the history of Rome supported by numerous quotations from Roman authors.

But there is more: at the same time he produces a **demythologizing of the old gods** which sums up all previous apologetic. Not only are Christians not guilty of Rome's downfall, but the gods are not responsible for Rome's rise either. The virtues of the ancient Romans, ambivalent though they have been, were responsible for that. The gods are not only impotent; they do not exist at all; their competence is arbitrarily divided and self-contradictory. In other words, through Varro's distinction between a poetic religion (*religio fabulosa*), a political religion (*religio civilis*) and a natural religion (*religio naturalis*), Augustine carries out such a comprehensive critical destruction of all Graeco-Roman belief in gods that it made any further apologia superfluous in the future.

But Augustine also turns to the Christians, who in their propaganda to pagans had all too often inappropriately brought in the protection of the Christian God. The God in whom Christians believe nowhere promised to safeguard possessions and happiness on this earth in order to protect human beings from any external misfortune. Anyone who believes that does not really believe in God, nor does he understand the meaning of his life. That is recognized only by someone who is humble of heart before God: on their journey through life such persons may not always be able to ward off suffering, but they can endure it. First the end will bring freedom from all suffering and eternal peace. To this degree suffering can purge and thus contribute towards seeking God, not only for earthly advantages, but also for God's own sake. No, there was no argument that Augustine did not take up in the course of his work, in order to offer a large-scale **theodicy**, a justification of God in the face of all the indissoluble riddles of this life. And all this with the aim of strengthening unconditional trust, faith in God.

11. *What is the meaning of history?*

Augustine's concern is the destiny of human beings, indeed the destiny of humankind. And so in the last twelve books his apologia issues in a large-scale **interpretation of history**: the battle between the *civitas terrena*, the earthly state, the world state, world citizenship, and on the other hand the *civitas Dei*, the city of God, the state of God, the citizenship of God. The great controversy between world state and God's state is the mysterious foundation and meaning of history, which is at the same time a history of salvation and disaster. Augustine describes its origin and beginning, then its progress through seven ages, and finally its outcome and goal.

The origin of the two civil communities lies in primal times, when the apostasy of proud angels led to a second empire alongside God's state – the devil's state. Consequently there was a need to make good the gap torn open by the fall of the angels, from those predestined from the human race, until the full number of the citizens of God was attained again. However, through the primal sin of Adam, which thus includes the city of God and the city of this world in itself, the angelic sin of pride has repeated itself, so that now among human beings an earthly world state has developed as an opposite to God's state. Its first representatives were on the one hand Abel, the just, and on the other Cain, the builder of cities and fratricidal murderer; then Israel and the Gentile world; then Jerusalem the city of God, and Babylon the city of this world; and finally in the end time Rome, the new Babylon, and the Catholic church. So the city of God and the city of this world are different right from the beginning:

- Their Lord and Governor is different: on the one hand God, and on the other the gods and demons.
- Their citizens are different: the elect worshippers of the one true God – the repudiated worshippers of gods and the selfish.
- Their basic attitude is different: the love of God rooted in humility, going as far as despising the self – the self-love grounded in pride going as far as despising God.

So now both world history and the history of individuals runs in six periods, formed after the pattern of the week of creation, which in world history becomes a world week. Since its creation the world has gone through six great world ages. Thus for Augustine the transitoriness of cultures, the reality of breaks in eras and 'paradigm shifts', was already manifest from the Bible. With Jesus Christ, the Lord of the city of God has appeared corporeally in the world – the God-man as the climax of world history! Since then humankind has been living in the sixth day of the world week, in the end-time, at the end of which will come the Last Judgment. This is heralded in the downfall of the last world state, the Roman empire, which unmasked itself as the devil's state in the persecution of Christians, but now has the merit of having secured a peace from which God's state has also profited. But Augustine himself remains mistrustful of the Christian empire, as pagan forces are still at work in it. Augustine says hardly anything about the future of the Roman empire (whether Rome in the West or Rome in the East). By contrast, he is utterly certain that the kingdom of God in this earthly age has an empirical form: the **Catholic church**. It is the concrete embodiment, the manifestation, of the kingdom of God on earth. However, it is not simply identical with the city of God, since the city of this world is still at work in it. For Augustine, God alone knows the elect.

Of course Augustine is not a historian in the modern sense, but a theological interpreter of history; he is not primarily interested in the development of humankind, but in God's plan. And yet, unlike Homer and Virgil, he is concerned not with a mythology of history but with real history and its deepest ground. With the help of the Bible and ancient historians, Augustine wants to achieve two things: first, to present numerous historical details with all possible parallels and analogies, allegories and typologies; and secondly, precisely in this way to offer a **meaningful overall view of world history** as the great clash between faith and unbelief, humility and arrogance, love and striving for power, salvation and damnation – from the beginning of time until today. So it is Augustine who created the first monumental **theology of history** in Christianity – which had an influence deep into the whole of mediaeval Western theology and the theology of the Reformation, up to the threshold of the modern secularization of history. Before Augustine, in antiquity, there was neither a philosophy of history nor a theology of history. Augustine thus took seriously the fact that in the Jewish-Christian understanding – so completely different from the circular Hellenistic, Indian understanding – history is a movement towards an end, guided and directed by God: the eternal city of God, the kingdom of peace, the kingdom of God.

In this way the *magnum opus et arduum*, the 'great and difficult work', was completed.[22] But hardly two years had passed before Augustine, who in the meantime, because of the difficulties of his old age, had chosen a coadjutor with the right to succession, saw that the Arian Vandals, who in a single generation had come from Hungary and Silesia right through Europe to Spain and Gibraltar, were now marching along the Mauretanian coast of North Africa. In 430 Numidia too was devastated by the Vandals, and three months later now Hippo also was already under siege from them. Augustine, now seventy-five and a victim of fever, saw that his end had come. He had David's penitential psalms pinned to the wall and spent his time in prayer. The one who all his life had enjoyed having friends around him and never liked to be alone, wanted to die alone. Before the Vandals broke through the ring of defence, on 28 August 430 – precisely twenty years to the day after the conquest of Rome by the Goths – he died, the undisputed spiritual and theological leader of North Africa. Now Roman rule of the world had also collapsed here, but Augustine's theology was to make world history on another continent, that of Europe.

Down to our own days, this theologian and stylist, incomparable despite his limitations, reminds us not only of the meaning of history but also of the meaning of our life, when in the closing sentence of his *City of God* he conjures up that seventh world age, that indescribable and undefinable eighth day, on which God completes his creative work, the church achieves the goal of its pilgrimage, and the world recognizes its Lord: 'There we shall be still and see; we shall see and we shall love; we shall love and we shall praise. Behold what will be, in the end, without end! For what is our end but to reach that kingdom which has no end? (*Ibi vacabimus et videbimus, videbimus et amabimus, amabimus et laudabimus. Ecce quod erit in fine sine fine. Nam quis alius noster est finis nisi pervenire ad regnum, cuius nullus est finis?*).'[23]

Thomas Aquinas
University Science and Papal Court Theology

Chronology (according to J. A. Weisheipl)

1224/5	Born in Roccasecca.
1230/31–39	Benedictine Oblate in Monte Cassino.
1239–44	Student at the University of Naples; death of his father.
1244	Enters the Dominican order in Naples; abducted on the journey to Paris and taken to a family castle.
1245	Returns to the order.
1245–48	Paris: novitiate and study.
1248–52	Cologne: studies with Albert the Great; ordained priest.
1252–56	Returns to Paris: *sententiarius*.
1252	Becomes Magister of theology.
1256–59	Teaches as Magister of theology.
1259–64	The first great *Summa*: *Summa contra gentiles*.
1260–61	Stay in Naples.
1261–65	Teacher in Orvieto.
1266	Beginning of the second great *Summa*: *Summa theologiae*.
1267	Stay in Viterbo.
1269–72	Magister in Paris for the second time.
1270	10 December: condemnation of Averroism (Thirteen Propositions).
1272	Teaches as Magister of theology in Naples.
1273	6 December: Breaks off the *Summa theologiae*.
1274	February: invitation to the Council of Lyons. 7 March: dies on the journey in Fossanova.
1277	Condemnation of 219 propositions in Paris. 18 March: condemnation of propositions in Oxford.
1323	18 July: Beatification of Thomas by Pope John XXII in Avignon.

1. Another form of life in another world

Without the theology of Aurelius Augustine there would have been no theology of Thomas Aquinas. The Catholic fundamental theologian Heinrich Fries has rightly pointed to the great historical influence of Augustine's theology, which reaches deep into mediaeval theology and beyond: 'Augustine's theology influenced the whole of Western Christianity after him. He is the greatest theologian of the Christian West. One can say that the content and method of philosophy and theology up to the scholasticism of the thirteenth century was influenced by him. The *Sentences* of Peter Lombard, for centuries the textbook and handbook of theology, are primarily taken from Augustine's work. The programme of scholasticism, which is defined by Anselm of Canterbury's *Credo ut intelligam*, goes back to Augustine. And even when the work of Aristotle was received with Albert the Great and Thomas Aquinas, and theology methodologically took on a new form as a science, in the separation of knowledge and faith, philosophy and theology, in the distinction between nature and grace, Augustine's significance remained, as the work of Thomas Aquinas shows, as normative for mediaeval theology as that of Aristotle.'[1]

Aristotle – alongside Augustine, he is the second great figure without which the theology of Thomas Aquinas is inconceivable. His philosophy – which was rediscovered in the Christian Middle Ages – had a decisive influence in shaping Thomas's philosophy. In the thirteenth century in particular, Thomas's century, when the monasteries were replaced as centres of education by the universities with their sciences, this pagan philosopher was to have an epoch-making effect. We shall be seeing this in more detail later.

Thomas was born in 1225 (or at the end of 1224), the youngest son of the knight Landulf of Aquino, in the family castle of Roccasecca, precisely midway between Rome and Naples. At the early age of five he was taken to the powerful abbey of Monte Cassino as a *puer oblatus*. An 'offered' child – for what? For the service of God and thus for religious and intellectual schooling. However, because of the war between the pope and the emperor Frederick II – the powerful clan of Aquinos were among those on the imperial side – Thomas had to move his son to **Naples,** to the Studium Generale founded by Frederick, there to qualify in the propaedeutic studies in the arts faculty, which consisted of the seven *artes liberales*: grammar, rhetoric, dialectic (known as the trivium), and arithmetic, geometry, music and astronomy (known as the quadrivium).

What motivated Thomas to this study? He wanted to follow a **spiritual calling,** in other words not just to study Aristotle, though in Naples he got to know his natural philosophy and in all probability also his metaphysics at a time when these were still forbidden territory to Paris students. Thus prepared, at the age of nineteen Thomas made a decision which was to have great consequences for his life. In 1244 he entered the Dominican order. In so doing he opted for a life in accordance with the gospel. He had to fight for his choice – like Francis of Assisi – against the massive resistance of his powerful family: if he had to be a monk, they would rather have seen him as the abbot of the rich monastery of Monte Cassino. His brothers even abducted him on his journey to Paris and put him in a family castle. For about a year Thomas resisted not only a staged attempt at seduction by a courtesan but also the constant pressure of his relations.

He won. But he did not want to spend his life in personal sanctification, in a remote feudal monastery, where one was condemned to immobility by the vow of *stabilitas loci* and bound by the patriarchal authority of an abbot. Nor did he want to live a well-endowed, comfortable life as a canon, according to specific rules, in the shadow of a cathedral. Although born into a land-owning aristocracy, he had been attracted by the simple **'apostolic life' of the Mendicants,** a collective name for all the begging orders (from the Latin *mendicare*, beg), especially the Franciscans and the Dominicans. They formed a highly democratized international community of like-minded people, and it was evident that Thomas was seeking precisely that: another form of life in another world.

What kind of a world was this **other world**? Let us be clear that this was a time of transition: from a feudal type of **allegiance**, in which duty and an oath of allegiance bound people personally to their lord and landowner, to a common life, a **commonwealth**, in which the citizens of the towns had their own rights and freedoms within the framework of their guilds and corporations. In this situation the new anti-feudal orders which followed the mendicant movement offered quite different possibilities even to a young nobleman like Thomas; one could move in the midst of the great cities, the economic and scientific centres which were now forming, and involve oneself spiritually there. This was particularly true of the centres of the European spirit which came into being between the seventh and the middle of the thirteenth century from the city schools (not the conservative, monastic feudal schools, remote from the cities): the **universities**. Here private schools of scholars had joined together, and pupils from various regions flocked to hear famous teachers: for the first time there was a free community of teachers and taught, in which those being taught were sometimes even allowed to choose their rector.

Moreover very soon such universities sprang up in many European cities: in Bologna, Paris, Oxford, Cambridge, Padua, Naples and Salamanca, the constitution of whose faculty became the model for the universities which were soon also founded in the German empire: Prague, Krakow, Vienna, Heidelberg, Cologne and Leipzig. They had a strong legal position. For on the basis of imperial and papal privileges, as independent corporations the universities enjoyed autonomous statutes, the right to bestow academic awards, exemption from taxation, their own jurisdiction, safe conduct, freedom of teaching – all this, provided that they were not in conflict with church dogmas. For Thomas, now Paris, Cologne, Paris again, the Roman Curia, Paris a third time and finally Naples again were to be the stages of his life and teaching.

Thomas had resolved on a mendicant order which is also called the Order of Preachers, *Ordo fratrum praedicatorum*. Founded by the Spaniard **Dominic** (1170-1221) with papal approval, this order used 'sermons' in the style of the heretics (Albigensians, Catharists) both to attack these heretics and to deal with the wretched state of preaching in the church generally. Moreover, from the beginning the disciples of Dominic had a concern for solid university study, which was also Thomas's goal. He was attracted by a simple life of poverty, though without just making poverty absolute. For, as Thomas was to put it later, 'Perfection does not consist essentially in poverty, but in the discipleship of

Christ.'[2] That left scope for various forms of discipleship of Christ, of which the monastic-ascetic form was just one.

Of prime importance to the Order of Preachers was a concern for **Holy Scripture**, for revised editions of the Bible, a Bible concordance and Bible commentaries. Thomas Aquinas was also to combine his teaching activity with biblical exegesis and to write a whole series of commentaries on the Old and New Testaments.[3] All his life, he too saw himself primarily as a *doctor in divina pagina*, a teacher of Holy Scripture, which moreover he was constantly expounding in sermons. This makes it clear that the spiritual basis of his existence was not the study of Aristotle but the **discipleship of Christ**. This made Thomas capable of steeping himself fully in the philosophical thought of antiquity precisely for the sake of Christian faith: in a concern for a reconciliation of Christian faith not only with Neoplatonic thought, like his great predecessors Origen and Augustine, but also with the thought of Aristotle, which was very much less 'pious'. For this, Thomas was later censured by Luther and then by some Lutherans, who hardly knew Thomas on the basis of his original series of lectures. Were they right? Let us look more closely.

2. *Aristotle – the danger*

Brilliantly gifted as he was, Thomas was almost automatically drawn into the **second Renaissance** of the high Middle Ages which followed the early mediaeval Carolingian renaissance. By that we understand that movement of renewal inspired by the spirit of antiquity which in the twelfth century comprised not only literature (Ovid, Virgil), but also above all Roman law and politics. Now, in the second third of the thirteenth century, in Paris, the 'city of the philosophers' and the centre of European cultural life, it also reached a climax through the renewal of the *artes liberales*, philosophy and theology.

This became possible above all through the **reception of the whole of Aristotle**. Previously, Aristotle had been known to mediaeval scholars only as a logician and then mostly indirectly, but now his original thought developed tremendous power. Translations first from the Arabic and then also from the Greek, and knowledge through the intermediary of Arab Jewish philosophy – the most important transit points were Spain and Sicily – quickly made him known despite church bans on reading him, and Aristotle was soon **the** philosopher. Why? Because the discovery of his truly encyclopaedic thought amounted to a tremendous **extension of knowledge** for European scholars, particularly in the sphere of the natural sciences, medicine, anthropology and metaphysics. This in turn resulted in a further quest for knowledge, another spiritual atmosphere: a new university of interests, a new independence in thought, a new concern with natural science.

When Thomas, aged twenty, arrived at the study centre of his order in Paris – Notre Dame had just been completed – he had the inestimable good fortune to meet a uniquely learned teacher, around twenty-five years older, who rightly bore the title *Doctor universalis*. Three years later, Thomas was able to accompany this teacher for four years to **Cologne**, where he was ordained priest (he was nicknamed the 'dumb ox'). Thomas was so close to his teacher all his life that when Thomas was posthumously condemned by the church this elderly man rushed to Paris to defend his pupil. Who was he? The Swabian **Albert the Great**, from Lauingen near Ulm (1200-1280). Albert was the man who over twenty years had laboured to produce an encyclopaedia of Aristotelian thought. He had courageously sought to disseminate and evaluate the Aristotelian, Arabic and Jewish writings which had newly been discovered in the twelfth century. Since some of them were still banned at the time, Albert did not develop them further, but paraphrased them. He was courageous. But how so?

What we take for granted today was not at all the case at that time. For many people thought that a pagan philosopher like **Aristotle** was extraordinarily **dangerous** and disturbing. And with good reason. Did not Aristotle advocate the eternity of the world instead of a creation and thus the temporality of the world? The blind compulsion of history instead of a divine providence? The mortality of the soul tied to its body instead of its immortality? Generally speaking, did not this philosopher embody such a concentration on empirical and visible reality that heaven, God and his revelation seemed to be being neglected? As late as 1263 Pope Urban IV had once again banned the study of the writings of Aristotle – but in vain. For Aristotle, passed on through

Arabic scholars in Spain (Averroes!), also found his way into the intellectual centres of France and Germany.

I need not spend long explaining how both Aristotelianism and Arabism must have been a tremendous intellectual **challenge to the young Thomas** when at twenty-seven he returned to **Paris** in 1252 from Cologne, to prepare himself to teach theology as an assistant (*Baccalaureus*) at the Dominican study centre. What was his starting point? Already in Cologne he had to give an introduction to the Bible; now, in Paris, as *sententiarius* he had to expound the theological textbook of the Middle Ages: the *Four Books of Sentences* of Peter Lombard. This Paris professor and later bishop (he died in 1160) had made a collection of texts from the church fathers and above all Augustine, and systematically divided the material, using John of Damascus as a model, into the doctrine of God, the doctrine of creation, christology and the doctrine of redemption, the doctrine of the sacraments and eschatology – a structure and a sequence which have been maintained in theological curricula down to the present day. After four years, Thomas and the Franciscan Bonaventura were made **Magister of theology** in the University of Paris, in 1256. He was now *ordinarius* professor, and his task consisted in *legere* (lecturing), *disputare* (disputation) and *praedicare* (preaching).

This extraordinarily young Magister now faced the gigantic task of combining the new knowledge from ancient philosophy with scripture and traditional theology. But Thomas did not resort to antiquity for its own sake, so to speak out of philological and archaeological interest, but for the sake of people in the present, **with a theological and pastoral intent.** For as Étienne Gilson and Josef Pieper have shown, in so far as Thomas was a philosopher, he was a **Christian philosopher.** He was interested not in what Aristotle and other thinkers of antiquity had to say to the Athens and Rome of their day, but in what they had to say to the Paris of his day – presuming that they would have accepted Christian faith. To this extent we may not apply today's historical-critical criteria to Thomas's interpretation of Aristotle. The philosopher Thomas was a passionately **Christian theologian** and remained so. Certainly he wanted to understand Aristotle authentically, and therefore took the trouble to read translations and commentaries all his life. But at the same time, fusing the chronological horizons, he wanted to understand Aristotle better in Christian faith than Aristotle understood himself 1500 years earlier.

So Aquinas did not intend a revival of Aristotle but his transformation. However – *pace* Gilson and Pieper – he held firm to one thing: scientific and philosophical thought, empirical thought from below, was best learnt from the works of Aristotle himself. For this reason, Thomas took enormous trouble, in addition to his great theological works, to write extensive commentaries on Aristotle's most important works. Here, in the Aristotle commentaries, very much more than in the so-called 'philosophical' arguments of his theological works, we can grasp his philosophical thought. In particular his clear distinction between Aristotelian philosophical and Augustinian theological thought made it possible for him to give a new basis to theology.

3. Theology – now a rational university science

For Thomas it was clear, even if he did not say so, that traditional **Augustinianism**, which hitherto had governed everything, was **in a crisis**. In this new time one could no longer solely refer in questions of faith to the previous authorities – Bible, church fathers, councils and popes – which were often contradictory. Rather, one had to make much more use than before of reason and conceptual analysis to achieve clarity. At all events, Thomas did this both resolutely and boldly, with not a little objectivity and logical acuteness, but also often uncritically, and reinterpreting the statements of the authorities unhistorically – in the *expositio reverentialis*, respectful exposition, customary at the time.

However, we should be clear that Thomas's theology – unlike the more contemplative monastic theology of the church fathers and still that of Augustine – is quite essentially a **rational university theology**, composed by professors in the *schola*, the school, and intended primarily not for the people and pastoral care, but for students and colleagues in theology. All the works of Thomas Aquinas – whether the *Summas* or the questions for disputation, the commentaries on Aristotle, Pseudo-Dionysius, Peter Lombard and Boethius or those on a variety of Old and New Testament books, or finally the various opuscula – are utterly stamped with the 'scholastic' approach to learning. They are all exclusively **composed in Latin** (Thomas did not learn either German in Cologne or French in Paris); all are very clear, terse and compact, but impersonal and monotone compared with Augustine, because their procedure is constantly analytic, with numerous divisions and subdivisions, with sharp definitions of concepts and formal distinctions, with objections and answers, with all the means of grammar, dialectic and disputation.

But there is no doubt that for all his tremendous use of highly-developed and often over-developed scholastic technique, Thomas Aquinas never lost sight of the great task of his life. Right at the beginning of his first great personal work, the *Summa contra gentiles*, he formulated as his lifelong task: 'I am aware that I owe it to God as the first task of my life to let him speak in all my discourses and senses.'[4] So for Thomas, the university professor, as for Augustine, the bishop, 'theo-logy' was responsible talk of God.

With this basic theological and pastoral intention, Thomas created **a new philosophical and theological synthesis** for the new time: brilliant, constructed with methodological rigour and didactic skill, of an unprecedented unity. And it was presented in two *Summas*, one philosophical and theological, against the 'Gentiles' (*Summa contra gentiles*), and one theological and philosophical, for Christian faith (*Summa theologiae*). Why, one might ask, this division, which neither Origen nor Augustine would have allowed?

4. The discovery of the power of reason

The influence of Aristotle is particularly evident from the fact that Thomas gave, had to give, knowledge gained by **human reason quite a different value** from what was usual in the theological tradition. For there was no disputing the fact that reason has its independence, its own right, its own sphere, over against faith. The new desire for knowledge, for science, had to be taken seriously. Earlier theologians had had things easier here: they proved as it were the justification for reason alongside faith. But as he shows in the introductions to his two *Summas*, Thomas felt compelled to prove the justification for faith alongside reason (*rationem fidei*). This was a completely new challenge, which forced him to think through the relationship between faith and reason in a new, fundamental way. How?

For Thomas, there is no question that philosophy exists in its own right alongside theology. Not by permission of the church, but because of the nature of the order of creation. The creator God himself has endowed human beings with understanding and reason. Science is a 'daughter of God' because God is the 'Lord of the sciences' (*Deus scientiarum dominus*). If one takes this seriously, the result is a liberating **shift for all theology**:
– a shift towards the creaturely and empirical,
– a shift towards rational analysis,
– a shift towards scientific research.

To be more precise: more than any other theologian of his time, Thomas understood that in view of the new significance of reason, in view of Aristotle and Averroes, it was no longer appropriate to seek to combine the whole of reality without distinction into one great philosophical and theological union of reason and faith. Augustine's thought, which did not know any independent philosophical system, was no further use here, important though it remained in other spheres. No, in this new time, no thought was publicly defensible in which philosophical truth was not *a priori* one with revealed truth, in which philosophical arguments could not be used for the interpretation of the Bible and, conversely, biblical quotations could not be used as a basis for philosophical thought. So what was required? Another, purer **method** which created an utterly **rational basis** for theology.

So we understand Thomas only if we have understood his basic hermeneutical methodological decision. It consists in a fundamental **distinction** between the modes of knowledge, levels of knowledge and thus the sciences:
– There are two different human **modes of knowledge** (directions of knowledge): it is important to analyse precisely what natural reason is capable of and what comes from faith through grace.
– There are two different human **modes of knowledge** (perspectives of knowledge): it is important to distinguish precisely what human beings know as it were 'from below', within the limits of their horizon of experience, from what they know

'from above', from God's own perspective through inspired Holy Scripture: in other words, what belongs on the lower level of natural truths and what belongs on the upper level, that of revealed, supernatural truth.

– So there are two different **sciences**: a precise distinction must be made between what philosophy can know in principle and what theology can know. What are we to learn from Aristotle, 'the philosopher' (hence the commentaries on Aristotle), and what are we to know from the Bible (hence the Bible commentaries)?

So according to Thomas, **human reason** is given a wide sphere in which it can be independently active in knowledge. For even the existence and properties of God, God's work as creator and God's providence, the existence of an immortal soul and many ethical insights, are natural truths which human beings can know, indeed demonstrate by reason alone, without revelation. And **faith**? Faith in the strict sense is necessary for the acceptance of certain higher truths of revelation. These include the mysteries of the Trinity or the incarnation of God in Jesus of Nazareth, and also the primal state and the last state, the fall and redemption of human beings and the world. These truths transcend human reason; they cannot be proved rationally but are beyond reason, though they should not be confused with irrational 'truths', which can be refuted rationally.

5. *Two* Summas – *a formal principle*

Because of this twofold possibility of knowing God, and the twofold mode of knowing the truth about God, while **philosophy** (including the philosophical doctrine of God) and **theology** are not to be separated, since they speak of the same God, they are to be distinguished, since they speak differently of God. Here philosophy proceeds rationally 'from below', from the creation and creatures, while theology proceeds in faith 'from above', from God. Nevertheless, reason and faith, philosophy and theology, should support each other since, being both rooted in the one truth of God, they are compatible. In this theology, *intelligo ut credam*, 'I know in order to believe', rather than Augustine's *credo ut intelligam* ('I believe in order to know'), stands in the foreground.

The very first part of the *Summa theologiae* – beginning with twelve long chapters on the one God, his life, knowledge and will,[5] and going on to sixteen equally long chapters on the threefold God[6]! – makes it clear that the starting point is to be two spheres, two levels of knowledge, metaphorically **two storeys**, which are clearly distinguished but not simply separated: one of higher certainty, the other fundamental and rationally clearly superior, both of which are in the last resort not contradictory but in fundamental accord. The First Vatican Council in 1870, 600 years later, was to define the relationship between faith and reason in a similar Neoscholastic, Neothomistic way.

Thus beyond question Thomas Aquinas **created for theology the mature, classical form of the mediaeval Roman Catholic paradigm.** His restructuring of all theology includes an evaluation:
– reason as compared with faith,
– the literal sense of scripture as compared with the allegorical-spiritual sense,
– nature as compared with grace,
– the natural law as compared with a specifically Christian morality,
– philosophy as compared with theology; in short,
– the human as compared with the distinctively Christian.

Moreover, it was quite coherent and in no way inconsistent for Thomas to work out **two different *Summas*,** two overall accounts for two different purposes, although in both he deals with the same God, the same world and the same human beings, and in both also uses **the same cyclical formative principle, understood primarily in spatial terms** which come from Neoplatonism: the scheme of departing and returning. In their first halves, both of Thomas's schemes deal with the *exitus*, the issuing of all things from God (God as origin), and in the second with the *reditus*, the return of all things to God (God as goal) – however, they do so without the cosmic determinism of the Neoplatonists. All things are to be understood from God, their supreme ground of being and their ultimate goal. So why two *Summas*, despite the same basic pattern? Because the two *Summas* serve different purposes and could operate at different levels.

1. The *Summa* against the Gentiles. It was written for Christians who found themselves arguing with Muslim (and also Jewish and heretical) opponents, whether with Muslims in Spain, Sicily and North Africa, or Jews and heretics in Christian Europe. In the thirteenth century, Islam, which was advanced culturally, was not only a political and military but also an intellectual and spiritual challenge. Therefore an alternative had to be provided to the Graeco-Arab world view. This was the aim of the *Summa contra Gentiles*: an overall view of Christian convictions with an apologetic, missionary and scientific purpose. But precisely because it is aimed at convincing non-Christians, except in the fourth apologetic part it largely operates at the level of **natural reason**. Scriptural statements are at best used in isolation to confirm it. In the introduction Thomas says that one cannot discuss about God, creation and the moral life (the three themes of the first three parts) on the basis of the Old or New Testaments, 'so it is necessary to resort to the natural reason, to which all are compelled to assent'.[7]

2. The *Summa theologiae*. This is intended for theologians, indeed for 'beginners' in theology (a typical professorial overestimation of the capacities of students). The theological *Summa* is a handbook with a clear pedagogical and scientific aim within the church, which is meant to provide a systematic survey of the whole of 'sacred doctrine'. Here, despite all the rational arguments, in principle the biblical message and thus **Christian faith** is constantly presupposed, though here too, often, as already in the doctrine of God and also in the ethical section, the procedure is on two levels. But Thomas succeeds impressively in interpreting personal language about God, the Father who speaks and can be spoken of, with concepts from Greek philosophy: God as the supreme being (*summum esse*), being itself (*ipsum esse*), the greatest truth (*maximum verum*), the truth itself (*ipsa veritas*), the supreme good (*summum bonum*).

6. *A new theology – at first regarded as heresy*

With his two *Summas*, Thomas set a high standard for theology, and moreover with him this literary genre of theology breaks off.

But his *Summa theologiae* in particular, his *magnum opus*, has shown him to be a master among theologians for all time. However, this was a late insight. For how could someone like him, who at that time changed the hermeneutical and methodological premises so radically compared with the tradition and at the same time presented a variety of novel theories, like the doctrine of transubstantiation for the eucharist (which unfortunately was defined at the Council of Trent), remain an uncontroversial theologian? Had he not delivered over the gospel to the conceptuality of Aristotelian philosophy?

Moreover Thomas was regarded by the traditionalist (Augustinian) theologians of his time as the advocate of a 'new theology' (Aristotelian and Averroistic). No wonder that he was increasingly contested as a modernist and branded a **heretic**: in 1270, theses of Siger of Brabant and probably also Thomas Aquinas were condemned by the Bishop of Paris (an early chancellor of the university); at any rate Thomas was so sharply attacked in a formal academic session by a young Franciscan colleague, the brilliant John Pecham (who was later to become Archbishop of Canterbury), that the Bishops of Paris appointed a commission of theologians to investigate the radical Aristotelianism which had evidently broken out here. In 1272 – after only three and a half years, his most fruitful – Thomas was given a new post in Italy by the general of his own order. But the agitation in Paris continued. Finally in 1277, on precisely the third anniversary of his death, a whole series of theses of Thomas Aquinas were formally **condemned** by the Bishop of Paris, within whose jurisdiction Thomas was, and also by the Bishop of Oxford (a Dominican!).[8] This condemnation meant that (outside the Dominican order) the neo-Augustinianism advocated by Bonaventure had conquered at least for the next fifty years; it would later issue in Scotism (the teaching of the Franciscan Duns Scotus), which was at first to play a more significant role than Thomism at the Counter-Reformation Council of Trent.[9]

So it is understandable that – although forty-nine years after his death he was beatified by a pope in Avignon and therefore eighteen months later was acquitted of his condemnation and excommunication by the Bishop of Paris – Thomas Aquinas was far from being a classical Catholic. It is understandable that after his death a period of apologia for Thomas and the *Defensiones* had to follow. It was only at the end of the fifteenth century that the first commentaries on the *Summa theologiae* appeared. The whole *Summa* was first commented on by the classic interpreter of Thomas, Cardinal Cajetan de Vico, who was to preside over a hearing of Martin Luther at the Reichstag in Augsburg in 1518.

It was 1567 before Thomas was formally elevated to the status of teacher of the church – by the Dominican pope Pius V, an early Grand Inquisitor. But it then took another three hundred years, until the first Vatican Council and afterwards, for popes to promote Neo-Thomism (rather than Thomas!) with all the power at their disposal: encyclicals on Thomas, naming Thomas the authentic teacher of the church and patron of Catholic schools, a new critical edition of Thomas, the commitment of Catholic theology to twenty-four normative basic philosophical theses, and indeed finally the legal regulation in the *Codex Iuris Canonici* of 1917/18 that philosophy and theology were to be treated in Catholic education institutions 'according to the method, teaching and principles of the *Doctor Angelicus* (the angelic teacher)'.[10] Up to 1924 one can count no less than 218 commentaries on the first part of the *Summa theologiae* and 90 on the whole *Summa*. It is true that Thomas Aquinas played virtually no role at the Second Vatican Council, which was concerned with *aggiornamento* and the problems and hopes of Christianity which had recently appeared; since then, moreover, there has not been a Thomistic school. But in the new 1983 *Codex Iuris Canonici* he is again 'especially' commended, and in the traditionalist Roman World Catechism which was published in 1993, of all the post-biblical church writers – apart from Augustine (88 times) and John Paul II (137 times) – he is quoted by far the most frequently.

Today even opponents no longer dispute that Thomas Aquinas created a grandiose new theological synthesis for his time. But the question must be asked: did Thomas also create a really new paradigm for theology? The answer is 'No'. Why that is the case should become clear in the following sections.

7. A problematical dependence on Augustine

Why could not Thomas – unlike Augustine – create a new paradigm, make possible a new overall constellation? Why did he not become – as Luther did later – the initiator of a paradigm shift in theology and church history, although he did not lack either a new milieu (the university), nor knowledge, perceptiveness and courage? The answer is that while with his philosophical theological system Thomas Aquinas quite substantially **modified Augustine's Latin paradigm**, he did not replace it. Indeed, despite its encyclopaedic (but ultimately fragmentary) greatness – his theology has its indisputable **limitations** and **defects**.

However much Thomas may have corrected Augustine in some details, modified him and sometimes even ignored him, at the level of the truths of faith he remained essentially **bound to the prevalent Augustinian theology**. Certainly as a philosopher Thomas was no Augustinist, but as a theologian he was - loyal to the distinction in his system. Thomas largely retained the second 'storey', the theological superstructure, the sphere of the 'supernatural' and the mysteries of salvation, in the Neoplatonic Augustinian tradition. Certainly he constantly pointed out that the theology of Augustine and the church fathers used Platonic conceptuality. But neither in the doctrine of the Trinity nor in christology, in soteriology nor in the doctrine of the church and the sacraments, did he fundamentally investigate behind the patristic positions. He reflected these with his Aristotelian conceptuality, in order to bring them up to date, refine them and confirm them; but only rarely, and then sometimes more tacitly, as in the doctrine of predestination, did he fundamentally correct them.

But in so doing Thomas also shares the fundamental **weaknesses** of Augustine's theology. For Thomas does not see through either the one-sidednesses and defects of Augustine's 'psychological' **doctrine of the Trinity** (starting from the one divine nature) or the narrowing of the **doctrine of redemption** (which was accentuated by Anselm of Canterbury's doctrine of satisfaction). He does not criticize Augustine's notion of an **original sin** which has been handed down since Adam to all human beings through the sexual act. Against the Greeks he defends the doctrine of a **purgatory**, which was similarly developed by Augustine. And he takes the reification of the understanding of grace (a concentration on 'created grace') considerably further, though at the same time, within the framework of his doctrine of grace,[11] he happily develops a *quaestio* of his own on the 'justification of the sinner'.[12] But he neglects 'grace' as God's disposition, benevolence, graciousness[13] – as his teacher Albert the Great already did. Instead, with the help of Aristotelian physiology and psychology, he analyses the different kinds of that *gratia creata* (which cannot be found in the New Testament), that 'created grace' or 'gift of grace' (to be understood as something like a supernatural fluid or fuel) and its effects on the substance of the soul, the intellect, the will, before, during and after the act of knowing and willing. Thus typical scholastic distinctions of grace come into being: active and cooperative, prevenient and subsequent, habitual and actual grace. These were all very impersonal, over-complex distinctions which would already be obsolete in Luther's time. And there is a further factor: his dependence on the ancient world-view.

8. *An ancient world-view: a test case – the place of women*

Most of the Neo-Thomists would not see that although at that time Thomas boldly confronted an immense wealth of new and specifically scientific knowledge which came to him from Aristotelian and Arab philosophy, his new philosophical-theological system remained deeply rooted in the **world-view of Greek antiquity**. This is not an accusation, but a statement.[14] For there can be no authentic understanding of Thomas's theology without an understanding of his metaphysics, and no understanding of his metaphysics without an understanding of his physics, chemistry and biology. Anyone who reads the two *Summas* attentively will make a discovery which is at first perplexing: that Thomas draws his models of theological explanation not so much from metaphysics as from Aristotelian science, e.g. gravitation, light, heat, chemical process and properties, biological procreation and growth, the physiology of the senses and emotions. Even the most important metaphysical concepts like being as such, act and potency, relation, *actus purus*, rest on insights from science and natural philosophy.

It is therefore undeniable that Thomas has taken over almost unchanged the world-view of Greek antiquity – including the notion of a begetting of human beings in the interplay between human beings and the sun. He unhesitatingly affirms it all: that all mixed bodies consist of four elements; that the seven planets are moved and guided by seven pure spirits (angels); that there are three heavens. For him the world is a perfect order, immutable from beginning to end, a cosmos in which being is more powerful as it ascends, a strictly hierarchical, geocentric and anthropocentric cosmos.

Indeed, with the aid of the Platonic concept of an unchangeable, static order (*ordo*), Thomas constructs an all-embracing interpretation of the world from Christian faith, which at the same time represents a thoroughgoing interpretation of faith in terms of the geocentric view of the world. That means that the Bible is understood cosmologically and the cosmos biblically. Christian faith guarantees the world-view, and conversely the world-view guarantees Christian faith. It is a perfect harmony of theology and cosmology, the order of salvation and the world order. Not only is knowledge of God possible from the order of creation, but astrology too is largely acceptable; so too is an angelic hierarchy corresponding to the heavenly spheres, and even (we are reminded of Origen) the number of the elect (to replace the fallen angels).

But even more, Thomas justifies from the Bible and reason the composition and origin of human beings with body and soul; the primal state of paradise and original sin; then the descent of Christ from heaven to earth and the underworld and his subsequent ascent; then grace and the seven sacraments, the hierarchical order of church and state, an ethic of order and obedience: and lastly precise notions about the end of the world and the bodies of those who are resurrected. There is no doubt that down to the last detail this mediaeval theology is dependent on the world-view of Greek antiquity; indeed it is an amalgam of the Middle Ages and antiquity. And we can now already guess what must happen to the content of this theology once its physical, chemical, biological, medicinal and cosmological presuppositions collapse – following the Copernican revolution and the victory of mathematics and experimentation, to which Aristotle and, of course also Thomas, completely fail to do justice. A test case is the position of women.

By way of excuse, it has been said that for all his universality, Thomas Aquinas did not understand three things: art, children and women. Because of his monastic way of life, of course he had been surrounded almost only by males. But did he not say quite basic and historically influential things about women and their nature? Defenders of Thomas point out that he only dealt with women here and there throughout his work, as it were incidentally. But at two crucial points even in the *Summa theologiae* there are quite basic statements about women: within the doctrine of creation a whole *quaestio* with four articles on the 'bringing forth (*productio*) of the woman (from Adam)',[15] and within the framework of the doctrine of grace an important article on the right of women to speak in church.[16]

Now it must be said straight away that for Thomas Aquinas there was no doubt:

– that **woman**, like man, is **created in the image of God**;
– that woman therefore in principle has the same dignity and the same eternal destiny for her soul as man;
– that woman was created by God not only for procreation but also for a shared life.

No, Thomas Aquinas may not be depicted as a dark mediaeval misogynist. But is that a reason for playing down his other statements? In matters relating to the theology of the feminine did not Thomas **accentuate** and refine many of **Augustine's remarks** and as a result not tone down but intensify the contempt for women? In all seriousness he asserts that:

– man is the starting point (*principium*) and goal (*finis*) of woman;
– woman was not created from head of the man (so that she should not rule over him), nor from his feet (so that she should not be despised), but from his rib, so that man and woman should remain together inseparably all their lives;
– by 'nature' woman is subjected to man, since in man the rational power of discernment is present more abundantly and so the woman falls short of the man in power and dignity;
– in relation to the whole of creation, while woman is among its good things, individually woman is '**something deficient and**

unsuccessful' (*aliquid deficiens et occasionatum*) compared with the man.[17]

There is no disputing the fact that for Thomas Aquinas, on closer inspection a woman is a man who by chance is defective and unsuccessful, a *mas occasionatus*. This finding from the doctrine of creation explains why **women** had absolutely no say at all in the **mediaeval church**. Granted, in the light of the Old Testament they could not in principle be denied the gift of prophecy. But the ordination of women as priests? While Thomas was not able to discuss this in more detail in the *Summa*, since he broke off working on it in his younger days he had come to a negative decision on this question in the commentary on the *Sentences*.[18] Not only the illegitimacy but even the invalidity of such an ordination is asserted here, and moreover this view was promptly taken up in the posthumous supplements to the *Summa* (*Supplementum*) as Thomas's valid position.[19]

The same holds for **women's preaching**. In view of the heretical movements, lay preaching at that time was in any case a provocative topic. And what about a preaching and teaching office even for women, a 'grace of the discourse of wisdom and knowledge', exercised publicly? No, Thomas excludes this with special arguments:[20]

– Above all because it is the condition of the female sex to be subject to the male: teaching as a public office in the church is a matter for those set over others (*praelati*) and not subordinates, which now essentially include the women precisely because of their sex (and not accidentally like the simple priest, who is at any rate a man);

– The senses of males are not to be stimulated to lust by women preaching (lust = *concupiscentia* or *libido* was a widespread theme after Augustine);

– Women were generally not so distinguished in matters of wisdom that one could appropriately entrust a public office of teaching to them.

But anyone who on the basis of all these negative statements should immediately want to pass a definitive verdict (in the negative) on Thomas should remember three things. First, Thomas is anything but original in many of his sayings; rather, in many cases he simply expresses what people (men) thought at that time.

Secondly, in many of his statements Thomas is simply basing himself on the Bible, on the Old Testament (for example women inherit only when there are no male descendants; no men in women's clothes) or the New Testament (for example, woman created for the sake of man, women to keep silent in church). And in his knowledge of women Thomas simply followed the greatest scientific and philosophical authority of his time, **Aristotle**. It was Aristotle who in his treatise 'On the Procreation of Living Beings' provided the biological basis for a fatal 'sexual metaphysics' and 'theology of sex' by attributing all the activity in the act of procreation to the male sperm (the female ovum was discovered only in 1827!). None of this excuses him (Galen, the most famous doctor of Roman antiquity, had assumed an active biological share of the woman in the origin of the foetus), but it does explain some things. But yet another weakness is intrinsic to Thomas's theology.

9. Despite everything, a court theology: the papacy safeguarded

One can easily overlook these weaknesses if one first (rightly) emphasizes the innovative power of Thomas's theology and even refers to his history of conflict with the magisterium of the church. But they cannot be concealed, sobering though that may be for Thomas's admirers. For in his understanding of the church and above all the papacy, Thomas Aquinas differs both from Origen, who as a theologian remained critical of the hierarchy, and Augustine, who even as a bishop was anything but fixated on the pope (a papalist), but more an episcopalist like Cyprian. In the end – and this must be said quite clearly – Thomas became the great **apologist of the centralist papacy** in the spirit of Greogry VII and Innocent III and remains so today. He put his theology at the service of dogmatic papolatry. He became a court theologian like others. This is understandable, since for nine years, from 1259 to 1268, he taught colleagues in the order in the Roman Curia (in Anagni?, at all events in Orvieto and Viterbo) and in Rome (S.Sabina), and had a close friendship with Popes Urban IV and Clement IV. That is also understandable, for though he was personally quite unpretentious (the Pope vainly offered him the archbishopric of Naples), he belonged to an order which was directly under papal authority. So he was *de facto* a court theologian.

Certainly Thomas was the one who claimed a **magistral** teaching office for theologians, which in contrast to the **pastoral** teaching office of the bishop was not to proceed authoritatively but by argumentation, and to rest on the academic competence of the Magister. But at the same time he was able to incorporate the new political and juristic development towards an absolutist papalism in the second half of the thirteenth century into the dogmatic system of theology. To what extent? One might compare him with Augustine. Whereas Augustine still does not think in terms of any primacy of jurisdiction for Peter, this primacy is at the centre of Thomas's view of the church. If for Augustine Christ himself and belief in him is the foundation of the church, for Thomas this foundation is the person and office of Peter. Whereas for Augustine the ecumenical council is the supreme authority, for Thomas this supreme authority is the Pope. In contradiction to the paradigm of the early church and still to Augustine, this is a Gregorian **view of the church, completely derived from the papacy**: a papalist ecclesiology in the framework of a theological systematics which at all points provides ideological backing for the new absolutist church system and both the ecclesiastical and secular claims of the papacy. Against the view of the Greek church (and the early church), he demonstrates the thesis that the Pope 'has the fullness of power in the church',[21] 'that it is for the Pope to define what faith is', indeed 'that it is necessary for salvation to be subordinate to the Roman Pope'.[22] All this is an ideological preparation for Pope Boniface's bull *Unam sanctam*, the classical document of the mediaeval papacy.

We cannot avoid the conclusion that if we leave aside the philosophical substructure and see Thomas's system from the perspective of his theology, and above all his ecclesiology, Thomas Aquinas has a new theology only to a limited degree. What we find in him is a systematic and speculative shaping of the Roman Catholic paradigm which had been initiated above all by Augustine and Pope Leo in the fifth century, achieved with Aristotelian categories and arguments, but above all a **cementing**

of this paradigm in dogma. So on the whole this is more a reinforcement, accentuation and completion of the traditional paradigm than an overcoming of it. The speculative scholastic system had first to reach crisis point – in late mediaeval nominalism (Ockhamism) it had become increasingly remote from the Bible and had neglected the basic truths of faith and its existential character simply by virtue of its rational conclusions – for a new starting point to be created for a paradigm shift: the paradigm shift in the direction of the Reformation.

Otto Hermann Pesch, the specialist on Thomas, is therefore right in seeing as 'the objective basic error of Neo-Thomism' that it started from '**directly** regarding Thomas as relevant without examining his work and in advance of all detailed questions'; Thomas can be rightly understood today only 'through a fundamental experience of his alien character'.[23] So with a departure from the Thomistic claims to absoluteness, it has rightly become established that 'Thomas's theology is to be seen as a model, not so much in its material content as in the public nature and courage of the questions it asks'.[24]

10. Dialogue with Islam and Judaism?

Indeed, who would dispute that with no little courage and great openness Thomas Aquinas also accepted the challenge of non-Christian thinkers, whether these were 'pagan' philosophers of antiquity like Aristotle, or Muslim and Jewish philosophers of his time like Averroes and Moses Maimonides. So there is no doubt that Thomas Aquinas was involved in **living discussion of the challenge of Judaism and Islam.** Nor did he content himself with the ignorance that was customary in the early Middle Ages and ugly polemic against Islam and the Qur'an. Indeed his *Summa contra gentiles* cannot be understood unless we sense the pressure that must have burdened some Christian intellectuals of the time: is not Islam both spiritually and culturally far in advance of Christianity? Does it not have the better philosophy? How can the option for Christianity rather than Islam and Judaism be justified?

Granted, 'Thomas did not travel to Morocco nor to the land of the Mongols, and he did not utter a single remark about the Crusades' – thus, once again, M-D.Chenu, who continues: 'But he always had the works of the great Muslim philosophers on his desk, and he measured the dimensions of a Christianity which, having hitherto been included within the geographical and cultural frontiers of the Roman empire, now suddenly became aware that it embraced only a part of humankind and discovered the immeasurably secular condition of the cosmos.'[35] That is admirably put, but it is correct only if once again at precisely this point we also take note of the limitations of Thomas Aquinas.

The limitations do not so much lie in the fact that Thomas 'did not travel to Morocco nor to the land of the Mongols'; Spain and Sicily would have been far enough. Rather, the problem is that Thomas did not know any Muslims personally, and did not engage in personal dialogue with any of them. But it is more suspicious that Thomas 'did not utter a single word about the Crusades', though Dominicans were also active in Palestine and though it had already proved that the Crusades were not having the hoped-for effect upon the Muslims. And it is most suspicious that Thomas knew Islam at best from the 'works of the great Muslim philosophers', who in any case were more philosophers than Muslims, but not from the Qur'an itself, which was now already available in more than one Latin translation as a result of the initiative of Petrus Venerabilis (died 1156), the last significant abbot of Cluny. Thomas evidently did not study this translation – at the cost of having only a very **rudimentary knowledge of Islam**. He had no access to the self-understanding of Muslims, who regard the Qur'an as the definitive revelation of God. His main informants may have been Christian missionaries, who evidently had had difficulties arguing against Islam. Whereas the Franciscans only attempted to influence the Muslims by simple preaching and practical example, at a very early stage the Dominicans also engaged in intellectual argument with them.

Precisely because of this method, we can no longer regard the *Summa contra gentiles* today as a model of Christian apologetic against Islam. Granted, in contrast to most of the early apologists of Latin or Byzantine origin Thomas argued in a way which was pleasantly neither polemical nor argumentative, and attempted to adapt to the horizon of his conversation partner's understanding as far as possible. But all this was not an *apologia ad extra* but at best an *apologia ad intra*, i.e. for those already converted. At that time only isolated individuals thought of an authentic inter-religious dialogue, indeed in twelfth-century Paris the dialogue with the Jews which was still going on had now been interrupted as a result of the Crusades, the expulsion of the Jews, pogroms and all their atrocities.

11. *The mysterious breaking off of the* Summa

In retrospect we can say that Thomas Aquinas would have been the last person to strive for any form of 'canonization' or even 'absolutization' of his theology. Within certain limits he was well aware of the contextuality of statements of faith and thus of their relativity. More than anyone else he embodied **a contemporary theology**, a theology in living exchange with the great spiritual trends of its time, a theology which can only make its distinctive statement in this way. If we take the 'spirit' and 'nature' of the theological work of this great thinker seriously in this way, even today theology has to stand on the spiritual fronts which move a time – equipped with the whole range of critical methods without which scholarly work since then is quite unthinkable: historical criticism, hermeneutics, comparative and interdisciplinary studies. A theology which masters this academic 'technique' is truly theology in the spirit of Thomas Aquinas. But a Thomism which repeats theses in a sterile way does not provide any stepping stones on to which the spirit can leap.

Even now it remains a biographical enigma why **Thomas broke off work on the *Summa theologiae*** in the middle of the third part, in his discussion of the sacrament of penance. It is attested beyond all doubt that on 6 December 1273, Thomas Aquinas, who according to his contemporaries studied, taught, wrote and prayed all the time and hardly wasted a moment, declared to his faithful companion Reginald of Piperno after morning mass that he could no longer go on. Why? 'I can do no more, for all that I have written seems to me like straw!'[26] *Omne foenum* – all straw? What had happened? Even now people puzzle over this self-assessment and over what had happened at that service: did this man with a notoriously massive body have a stroke? Did this man who was not yet fifty but had already written more than forty extensive works have a breakdown of health? Or an ecstatic experience? Or both together? A visionary experience of heavenly glory or insight into the transitoriness of his two-storey theological system? All straw?

The only certain thing is that from that hour on Thomas did not write or dictate any more (like Origen and Augustine he often even had several secretaries and himself wrote almost illegibly on small pieces of paper). At any rate, he had four months still to live, but did not produce another single line. Still, he accepted Pope Gregory X's invitation and made his way to the Council of Lyons, which among other things was to be concerned with negotiations for union with the Greeks. He wanted to take a copy of his work *Against the Errors of the Greeks* with him. However, exhausted after a few hours' journey he asked if he could stop and stay with his niece Francesca, Countess of Ceccano, at Maenza castle. When his state deteriorated there, Thomas asked to be taken to the nearby Cistercian abbey of Fossanova. Here, on 7 March 1273, he passed peacefully away. It was noted at the time with disapproval that no Superior of the Dominican order from Naples or Rome was present at the burial. After some extremely macabre manoeuvres over his body in Fossanova, he was finally laid to rest almost a century later (1369), in Toulouse, where the founder of his order had brought the first Dominican house into being.

Thomas Aquinas's gigantic work represents a tremendous piece of thought, an abiding obligation for all theology for all time. At the same time, though, for all his intellectualism Thomas also constantly remained aware of the **limits of his own understanding of God**. Indeed for him any definition transferred from human beings or the world to God at the same time called for a negation: the negation of any human-worldly limitations and imperfection. For Thomas, too, God's real being remained hidden, inaccessible to human reason. To this degree he can agree with Pseudo-Dionysius, whom he also regarded as a pupil of Paul: 'Therefore this is the last (*ultimum*) of human knowledge of God; that he (the human being) knows that he does not know God (*quod sciat* *se Deum nescire*), and that in so far as he knows, what God is transcends all that we understand of him (*illud quod Deus est, omne ipsum quod de eo intelligimus, excedere*).'[27]

Martin Luther
Return to the Gospel as the Classical Instance
of a Paradigm Shift

Chronology (according to R.Schwarz)

1483	10 November: Luther born in Eisleben.
1505	Enters the monastery in Erfurt.
1510	Travel and pilgrimage to Rome.
1512	Gains his doctorate in theology.
1513	First lectures on the psalms to the University of Wittenberg.
1515/16	Produces his work *Ein Theologia Deutsch*.
1517	95 theses on indulgences: 'Sermon on Indulgences and Grace'.
1518	Interrogation before Cardinal Cajetan in Augsburg.
1519	Charles V elected emperor: Leipzig disputation.
1520	'To the Christian Nobility of the German Nation' (June).
	15 June: Leo X's bull *Exsurge Domine*; threat of excommunication, call for repentance and burning of all his writings.
	17 June: Luther appeals to a general council: *De captivitate Babylonica ecclesiae praeludium* (late summer).
	'The Freedom of a Christian' (autumn). *Adversus execrabilem Antichristi bullam* (November).
	10 December: burning of the papal bull and of the papal church law in Wittenberg.
1521	January: bull *Decet Romanum Pontificem*. 18 April: appearance before the Reichstag in Worms.
	26 May: Emperor Charles V places Luther and his followers under the imperial ban (Edict of Worms).
1521/22	Wartburg: translation of the Bible, unrest in Wittenberg; Luther's return.
1524/5	Parts company with the enthusiasts.
1525	Peasants' War; marriage; break with Erasmus.
1526-30	Territorial extension of the Reformation.
1528	Dispute with the Swiss theologians.
1529	Reichstag at Speyer; protest of the 'Protestants'. Religious dialogue in Marburg with Zwingli and Bucer.
1530	Reichstag at Augsburg (*Confessio Augustana*); failure over reconciliation; foundation of the Schmalkald League of Protestant German princes.
1531-39	The Reformation safeguarded politically by the empire.
1521	Jean Calvin establishes his church republic in Geneva.
1546/47	Schmalkald wars.
1546	18 February: Luther dies in Eisleben.

1. Why there was a Lutheran Reformation

Hardly a single one of Luther's reform concerns was new. But the time had not been ripe for them. Now the moment had come, and it needed only religious genius to bring these concerns together, put them into words and embody them personally. Martin Luther was the man of the moment.

What had been the **preparation** for the new paradigm shift in world history immediately before the Reformation? Briefly:[1]

– the collapse of papal rule of the world, the split in the church between East and West, then the twofold, later threefold, papacy in Avignon, Rome and Pisa along with the rise of the nation states of France, England and Spain;

– the lack of success by the reform councils (Constance, Basel, Florence, Lateran) in 'reforming the church, head and members';

– the replacement of the natural economy by a money economy, the invention of printing and the widespread desire for education and Bibles;

– the absolutist centralism of the Curia, its immorality, its uncontrollable financial policy and its stubborn resistance to reform, and finally the trade in indulgences for rebuilding St Peter's, which was regarded in Germany as the pinnacle of curial exploitation.

However, even north of the Alps, as a result of the Roman system, some of the abuses were quite blatant:

– the retrograde state of church institutions: the ban on levying interest, the church's freedom from taxation and its own jurisdiction, the clerical monopoly of schools, the furthering of beggary, too many church festivals;

– the way in which church and theology were overgrown with canon law;

– the growing self-awareness of university sciences (Paris!) as a critical authority over against the church;

– the tremendous secularization even of the rich prince bishops and monasteries; the abuses caused by the pressure towards celibacy; the proletariat, which comprised far too many uneducated and poor people:

– the radical critics of the church: Wycliffe, Hus, Marsilius, Ockham and the Humanists;

– finally a terrifying superstition among the people, a religious nervousness which often took enthusiastic-apocalyptic forms, an externalized liturgy and legalized popular piety, a hatred of work-shy monks and clerics, a malaise among the educated people in the cities and despair among the exploited peasants in Germany... All in all this was an abysmal crisis for mediaeval theology, church and society, coupled with an inability to cope with it.

So everything was ready for an epoch-making paradigm shift, but there was need of someone to present the new candidate for a paradigm credibly. And this was done by a single monk, in the epoch-making prophetic figure of Martin Luther, who was born on 10 November 1483 in Eisleben in Thuringia. Although as a young monk and doctor of theology Luther certainly did not understand himself primarily as a prophet but as a teacher of the church, intuitively and inspirationally he was able to meet the tremendous religious longing of the late Middle Ages. He purged the strong positive forces in mysticism, and also in nominalism and popular piety, confidently centred all the frustrated reform movements in his brilliant personality, which was stamped with a a deep faith, and expressed his concerns with unprecedented eloquence. Without Martin Luther there would have been no Reformation in Germany!

2. The basic question: how is one justified before God?

But when did things get this far? As a result of acute fear of death during a violent thunderstorm and constant anxiety about not being able to stand in the final judgment before Christ, at the age of twenty-two, in 1505, Luther had entered a monastery against the will of his father (who was a miner and smelter by trade). But when did the Augustinian monk who loyally obeyed the rules and was concerned for righteousness by works become the ardent Reformer of 'faith alone'? Historians argue over the precise point in time of the 'breakthrough to the Reformation'.

Be this as it may, there is no disputing the fact that Martin Luther, who had a very similar scholastic training in philosophy and theology to Thomas Aquinas, was in deep crisis over his life. Being a monk had not solved any of his problems, but had accentuated many of them. For the works of monastic piety like choral prayer, mass, fasting, penitence, penance to which Luther submitted himself with great earnestness as an Augustine eremite could not settle for him the questions of his personal salvation and damnation. In a sudden intuitive experience of the gracious righteousness of God (if we follow the 'great testimony' of 1545), but presumably in a somewhat longer process (if we look at his earlier works more closely), in his crisis of conscience a new understanding of the justification of the sinner had dawned on Luther. Whenever precisely the 'breakthrough to the Reformation' took place (more recent scholarship is predominantly for a 'late dating' to the first half of 1518[2]), the '**shift to the Reformation**' happens here.

So the starting point of Luther's reforming concern was not any abuses in the church, not even the question of the church, but the **question of salvation**: how do human beings stand before God? How does God deal with human beings? How can human beings be certain of their salvation by God? How can sinful human beings put right their relationship with the just God? When are they **justified** by God? Luther found the answer above all in Paul's Letter to the Romans: human beings cannot stand justified by God, be justified by God, through their own efforts – despite all piety. It is God himself, as a gracious God, who pronounces the sinner righteous, without any merits, in his free grace. This is a grace which human beings may confidently grasp only in faith. For Luther, of the three theological virtues faith is the most important: in faith, unrighteous sinful human beings receive God's righteousness.

That was the decisive theological factor. But there was a second one: starting from a new understanding of the event of justification Luther hit upon a new understanding of the **church**. This was a radical criticism of a secularized and legalized church which had deviated from the teaching and praxis of the gospel, and of its sacraments, ministries and traditions. But in this criticism had not Luther broken completely with the Catholic tradition? With his understanding of justification was he not *a priori* un-Catholic? To answer this question, for all the discontinuity one must also see the great continuity between Luther and the theology which preceded him.

3. The Catholic Luther

An **interrupted train of tradition** binds Luther to the church and theology of the preceding period precisely in his understanding of justification. We must look briefly at four lines of historical continuity, all of which are important for Luther's understanding of Reformation and which in part overlap: the Catholic piety which Luther encountered in the monastery; in connection with that, mediaeval mysticism; then Augustine's theology; and finally late mediaeval nominalism in the form of Ockhamism.

Catholic piety? Granted, the traditional Catholic piety caused a crisis for Luther in the monastery. And so all his life, for him the monastic way of perfection remained the way of legalistic works and wanting to be something before God, which did not bring him peace of mind and inner security, but anxiety and desperation. Nevertheless, Luther salvaged the best of Catholic piety through his crisis. For the doctrine of justification it is particularly significant that it was Luther's superior in the monastery, Johannes von Staupitz, a man with a concern for reform, who diverted him from his heart-searchings over his own predestination and pointed him to the Bible, to God's will for salvation and the picture of the crucified Jesus, before whom all anxiety about whether or not one is elected disappears.

Mediaeval mysticism? Granted, the pantheizing features of mysticism and its tendency to blur the line between the divine and the human were quite remote from Luther. Nevertheless, it is known that Luther had knowledge of the mysticism of Dionysius the Areopagite and Bernard of Clairvaux. Moreover, he discovered the mystical work *Die Theologia deutsch*, studied it with enthusiasm and brought out an edition in 1515/16 (completed in 1518). Furthermore he called the mystic Tauler one of the greatest theologians and continued to commend him. There is no doubt that Luther's sense for being humble, small, nothing before God, to whom alone honour belongs; his insight that piety by works leads to vanity and self-satisfaction and away from God; and finally his faith in the suffering Christ, particularly as he took this from the words of the Psalter – all these ideas which were decisive for his understanding of justification are traditional material of mediaeval mysticism.

Augustine's theology? Granted, it was not least the doctrine of predestination and the understanding of the perfect love of God as developed by the old anti-Pelagian Augustine which were responsible for Luther's crisis. And all his life Luther understood grace differently from Augustine, in a more personal way. Nevertheless, insight into the deep corruption of sin as human selfishness and a distortion of the self remained decisive for Luther's understanding of justification, as did insight into the omnipotence of the grace of God, which he learned above all from Augustine. So Luther remained tied to one of the basic components of mediaeval theology, the theology of Augustine, whose *Confessions* and great treatises *On the Trinity* and *The City of God* he had studied at a very early stage, Augustine, who was not only dominant in pre-Aristotelian early scholasticism and in the high scholasticism of Alexander of Hales and Bonaventure, but who also could not be overlooked in Thomas Aquinas and his school (though there he had clearly been forced into the background) and finally also in the late Middle Ages. The continuity was much stronger than Luther himself realized, not only in the doctrine of the Trinity and christology, but also in the theology of grace. It dawned on Luther that Romans 1.17, the passage about the 'righteousness of God', which was decisive for his breakthrough to the Reformation, does not speak of the inexorable judgment of God's righteousness, before which no sinner can stand, but of his righteousness as a gift. The passage was understood in this way not just by Augustine, as Luther thought, but, as Catholic scholars have demonstrated,[3] by the majority of mediaeval theologians.

Ockhamism? Granted, in his doctrine of justification Luther reacted most vigorously against the Pelagianism of the late-Franciscan Ockhamist school which is found both in Ockham himself and in his great pupil Gabriel Biel, and also in Bartholomew Arnoldi of Usingen, Biel's pupil and Luther's teacher. Nevertheless, there is also a way from Ockham and Biel to Luther's doctrine of justification. The Thomistic school was certainly not right in slating late mediaeval theology in general and Ockhamism (nominalism) in particular as a disintegration of mediaeval theology. But on the other hand Protestant Reformation scholarship has been equally wrong in treating late mediaeval theology only as the dark background against which Luther's doctrine of justification could shine out particularly brightly. Attention must not be limited, as it usually is in the Protestant sphere, to Luther's dependence on Paul and Augustine; his positive connection with Ockham and Biel must also be considered: for example in respect of particular aspects of his concept of God (the absolute sovereignty of God), his view of grace as favour, the acceptance of human beings by free divine choice which has no ground in humankind.

What follows from this fourfold connection with the tradition? That it is *a priori* impossible for Catholics **sweepingly to condemn** Luther. The mediaeval Catholic tradition has far too much in common with Luther's great theological concentration. However, it is important not to lose sight of what is particularly characteristic of Luther. What is this? We can demonstrate it from the famous dispute over indulgences.

4. *The spark of Reformation*

The **dispute over indulgences** was neither the internal cause nor the fortuitous external cause for the Reformation, but the catalyst, the factor which sparked it off. Should, can, may the Pope grant indulgences? May he grant to the living and even to the dead (in purgatory) partial or total remission of the temporal punishments for sin which God may have imposed before entry into eternal life? At that time this was not only a highly theological but also a highly political question. Luther had taken it up in view of an unprecedented campaign for indulgences which had been staged in Germany on the orders of Pope Leo X, with all available means of propaganda, for the rebuilding of St Peter's in Rome.[4] The Commissioner General for these so-called Peter's indulgences was the Archbishop of Mainz, Albrecht of Brandenburg.

Penance – what is it? Luther gave a theologically radical answer to this question. For Christians, penance is not limited to the sacrament of penance; it should embrace the whole of life. And the decisive thing is that forgiveness of guilt is God's concern alone; at best the Pope can confirm by a subsequent declaration that a sin has already been remitted by God. At all events, the authority of the Pope is limited to this life and ends with death.

To think that the salvation of souls could be bought by expensive indulgence certificates created to pay for an ostentatious papal church: what a perversion of the great notion of the free gift of God to the sinner!

But at the same time this attack meant that at a stroke Luther had not only robbed the whole business of indulgences of its theological legitimation but at the same time shattered the authority of those who had set up this trade in their own favour: the Pope and the bishops. Luther summed up his position in **ninety-five** theses, sent them to Archbishop Albrecht of Mainz under whose jurisdiction he was, and at the same time made them known to the academic public. It may be a legend that, as is so often depicted in pictures, he personally affixed these theses to the door of the Schlosskirche in Wittenberg on 31 October (or 1 November) 1517 (it goes back to a remark made by Melanchthon, Luther's most capable and loyal companion; however, Melanchthon was still teaching at the University of Tübingen at the time and made this remark only after Luther's death).[5]

Be this as it may, at all events we can say that to begin with Luther was in no way 'boldly steering towards a break with the church'; in fact he 'became a Reformer unintentionally', as the Catholic church historian Erwin Iserloh writes. Iserloh concludes from this: 'However, that puts even greater responsibility on the bishops concerned.'[6] Another thing is certain: Luther's theses were rapidly disseminated everywhere, with Luther making his own contribution. He commented on them through Latin 'Resolutions'[7] and popularized their main ideas in a 'Sermon on Indulgences and Grace',[8] deliberately speaking increasingly direct to the people in German, their mother tongue. The deep and widespread discontent with the indulgences and the curial fiscalism now exploded in a storm of indignation.

Counter-action soon followed. A **heresy investigation** into Martin Luther had already opened in Rome, his accusers being the Archbishop of Mainz and the Dominican order. In spring 1518 Luther was summoned before the **Reichstag at Augsburg** and interrogated for three days by the papal cardinal legate. The legate was Cajetan, the leading Thomist of his time, who shortly beforehand had written the first commentary on the whole *Summa theologiae* of Thomas Aquinas. However, the hearing did not lead to any agreement, so Cajetan ultimately gave the stubborn Augustinian monk the choice: recant – or be imprisoned and burnt. His prince, Frederick of Saxony, was asked to hand Luther over, but Luther had secretly left Augsburg.

Two completely different perspectives, indeed two different 'worlds', two different worlds of thought and language, **two different paradigms,** met in Luther, the Reformer, and in Cajetan, the Thomist and papal legate. The result was only to be expected: total confrontation, a hopeless debate, understanding impossible to reach. Essentially the church authorities, who were unwilling for reform, had only one thing to set against Luther's call for reform: a demand for capitulation and submission to the papal and episcopal magisterium. And now with Luther the whole nation faced the hitherto unprecedented alternative: **recant and 'return' to the old** (to the mediaeval paradigm), **or convert to the new** (to the Reformation-gospel paradigm). An unprecedented polarization began which soon divided the whole church into friends and enemies of Luther. 'Reformation' was for some the great hope for a renewal of the church – for others the great apostasy from Pope and church.

Luther, who appealed to the gospel, reason and his conscience, and so would not and could not recant, had fled from Augsburg and appealed against the Pope to a general council. But instead of investigating the reform ideas, the church authorities attempted to deal with Luther theologically, in order finally to quench the flame of dispute. In the summer of 1519 there was a **disputation in Leipzig** lasting for three weeks. Luther's main Catholic opponent was now Johann Eck, who adopted skilful tactics. Instead of taking up Luther's criticism of the church, he concentrated the whole problem on the question of papal primacy and infallibility. Luther did not in fact want to continue to recognize the primacy as a divine institution necessary for salvation, but saw it as an institution of human law. So a trap had been laid, and it snapped to when the question of **the infallibility of councils** was raised, above all that of the Council of Constance, which had condemned and burnt Hus. There was nothing left for Luther than to concede the possibility that even councils could err, since in the case of Hus the council had even condemned some statements which were in accord with the gospel. But with that

Luther had left the ground of the Roman system. And without Rome having had to go into his demands for reform, Luther was now finally branded a heretic, publicly unmasked as a Hussite in disguise. For his part, Luther, who at first had not rejected the authority of Pope, episcopate and councils, but relativized them historically, was now completely convinced: his opponents were incapable and unwilling even to consider a reform of the church in the spirit of scripture.

The **heresy investigation** was moving to a fatal conclusion. After an unusually long postponement by the Roman Curia because of the election of the emperor (in which the prince of Saxony had an important vote), on 15 June 1520 – a year after Leipzig – Luther was confronted with the papal bull *Exsurge Domine*.[9] This papal document not only designated forty-one of Luther's statements, selected without any understanding, as 'heretical', but threatened Luther with excommunication and the burning of all his writings if he did not recant within sixty days. Instead of relevant theological argumentation, Luther now felt the whole power of papal jurisdiction (the Roman body set over him consisted almost entirely of canon lawyers). Luther reacted by appealing once again on 17 November to a general council[10] (as the Sorbonne had done shortly beforehand, despite two papal prohibitions of such an appeal). Furthermore, he wrote the work *Adversus execrabilem Antichristi bullam* ('Against the accursed bull of the Antichrist')[11] against the Pope, whom, because of his usurpation of all scriptural exegesis and rejection of any reform, he increasingly saw as the Antichrist.

Now the crisis came to a dramatic head; when Luther got hold of a printed copy of the bull and learned of the burning of his books in Louvain and Cologne ordered by the nuncio Aleander, he responded on 10 December 1520 in Wittenberg with a spectacular act: accompanied by colleagues and students, he burned not only the papal bull but also the books of papal church law (the Decretals): a clear sign that he no longer recognized Roman jurisdiction and the legal system built up on it, since they condemned his teaching – which was in keeping with the gospel. This amounted to raising a banner for the whole nation, and three weeks later, at the beginning of January 1521, Rome sent the bull containing Luther's excommunication ban (*Decet Romanum*

Pontificem). At first little note was taken of it in Germany, but the die in the 'Luther case' was now finally cast. The Reichstag at Worms in the same year, 1521, to which Luther was invited by the young emperor Charles on the prompting of his cautious prince Frederick the Wise, was not to change matters.

5. The programme for Reformation

1520, the year of the breakthrough in church politics, was also a year of theological breakthrough for Martin Luther. The great programmatic writings for the Reformation were composed. And while Luther was hardly a man with a deliberately planned theological system, he was a man who could confidently make theological proposals to suit the situation and carry them through effectively:

– The **first writing** of this year was the long sermon 'On Good Works' (beginning of 1520), addressed to the churches, written more in an edifying than a programmatic way.[12] It is theologically fundamental, in that here Luther dealt with 'his' basic question, which is **the** question of Christian existence: the **relationship between faith and works**, the innermost motive of **faith** and the practical consequences which follow from it. Using the Ten Commandments, he demonstrated that faith which gives God alone the glory is the foundation of Christian existence; only from faith can and should good works follow.

– The **second writing**, addressed to the emperor, princes and other nobility, took up the *gravamina* (objections) of the German nation and is also a passionate call for the **reform of the church**, similarly written in the vernacular: *To the Christian Nobility of the German Nation Concerning the Reform of the Christian Estate* (June 1520).[13] Here Luther launches the sharpest attack so far on the papal system, which is preventing a reform of the church with its three pretensions ('walls of the Romanists'): 1. spiritual authority stands above worldly authority; 2. the Pope alone is the true interpreter of scripture; 3. the Pope alone can summon a council. At the same time, a programme for reform, as comprehensive as it is detailed, is developed in twenty-eight points. The first twelve demands relate to the reform of the papacy: a renunciation to claims to rule over world and church; independence of the emperor and the German church; the abolition of the many forms of curial exploitation. Then it deals with the reform of church life and secular life generally: the monasteries, priestly celibacy, indulgences, masses for souls, feasts of the saints, pilgrimages, mendicant orders, universities, schools, care of the poor, abolition of luxury. Here already we have the programmatic statements on the priesthood of all believers and ministry in the church, which, according to Luther, rests on a commissioning for public exercise of the priestly authority which is common to all Christians.

– The **third writing** in the late summer of 1520 is addressed to scholars and theologians and is therefore written in Latin in a formal academic way: *The Babylonian Captivity of the Church*.[14] This work, probably the only work of strict systematic theology that Luther the exegete wrote, is devoted to the sacraments – highly explosive, because it was about the foundation of Roman church law. According to Luther the **sacraments** themselves are constituted by a promise and a sign of Jesus Christ himself. If here we take the traditional criterion 'institution by Jesus Christ himself' really seriously, then only two sacraments, baptism and the Lord's Supper remain – three at most, if one adds penance: the other four sacraments (confirmation, ordination to the priesthood, marriage, final unction) are therefore pious church customs, but not instituted by Christ. Luther again makes many practical proposals for reform of the sacraments and customs – from communion with the cup for laity to the remarriage of innocent parties in divorces.

– The **fourth writing**, *On the Freedom of a Christian*,[15] published in the autumn, develops the thoughts of the first work and offers a summary of Luther's understanding of justification on the basis of I Cor.9.19 in two statements: 'A Christian is a perfectly free lord of all, subject to no one' (in faith, according to the inner man), and 'a Christian is a perfectly dutiful servant of all, subject to all'[16] (thus in works, according to the outer man). It is faith which makes someone a free person who may serve others in their works.

In these four writings we have the foundation stone of the Reformation. And now we can also answer the questions relating to Martin Luther's ultimate concern, what moves him in all his writings, what motivates most deeply his protest, his theology, and indeed his politics.

6. *The basic impulse of the Reformation*

Despite his enormous political explosive force, Luther remained a man of deep faith, a theologian who out of existential need struggled over the grace of God in the face of human fallenness. It would be quite superficial to think that he was concerned only with the fight against indescribable church abuses, especially the indulgences, and the liberation of the papacy. No, Luther's personal impetus towards Reformation and his tremendous historical explosive effect came from the same thing: **a return of the church to the gospel of Jesus Christ** as it was experienced in a living way in **Holy Scripture** and especially in **Paul**. In concrete, this means (and here the decisive difference from the mediaeval paradigm clearly emerges):

– Against all the traditions, laws and authorities which have grown up in the course of the centuries Luther sets the **primacy of scripture**, 'scripture alone' (*sola scriptura*).

– Against all the thousands of saints and tens of thousands of official mediators between God and human beings, Luther sets the **primacy of Christ**: 'Christ alone' (*solus Christus*).

– Against all pious religious human achievements and efforts ('works') to achieve the salvation of the soul, Luther sets the **primacy of grace and faith**, 'grace alone' (*sola gratia*), of the gracious God as he has shown himself in the cross and resurrection of Jesus Christ and unconditional human faith in this God, unconditional trust in him (*sola fide*).

But at the same time, much as Luther originally came to know the private pangs of conscience of a tormented monk and aimed at the conversion of the individual, his theology of justification went far beyond the creation of privatistic peace for the soul. Rather, the theology of justification forms the basis for a **public appeal to the church for reform** in the spirit of the gospel, a reform which is aimed not so much at the reformulation of a doctrine as at the renewal of church life in all areas. For it was the religious practice of the church which was forcing itself between God and human beings; it was the Pope who had in fact in his authority put himself in the place of Christ. In these circumstances a **radical criticism** of the papacy was unavoidable. However, Luther was not concerned with the Pope as a person, but with the institutional practices and structures encouraged and legally cemented by Rome, which manifestly contradicted the gospel.

For its part, the Roman church thought that it could quickly either force this heretical young monk in the far north to recant, or (as in the cases of Hus, Savonarola and hundreds of 'heretics' and 'witches') bring him to the stake with the state's help. So from a historical perspective there can be no doubt that Rome **bears the main responsibility** for the way in which the dispute over the right way to salvation and practical reflection on the gospel very quickly turned into a fundamental dispute over authority in the church and the infallibility of Pope and councils. For in Rome – and also in the German episcopate – people at that time could not and would not publicly hear this call to repentance and conversion, to reflection and reform. Think of what would have to have changed there! There was too much at stake for Rome, taken completely by surprise by the 'new' message (and politically involved in dealings in Italy, with the Turks and the church state): not only the tremendous financial needs of the Curia in rebuilding St Peter's, which was to be paid for by indulgences and levies, but above all the principle 'in the end Rome is always right', and thus the whole mediaeval Roman Catholic paradigm.

That is also how things looked to the Spanish Habsburg, brought up a strict Catholic, who at the age of twenty-one became the emperor Charles V. He was the one who at his first **Reichstag** held on German soil, **at Worms**, sat in judgment over Luther at the memorable session of 18 April 1521. This was a session at which Luther, as a professor of theology – facing the emperor and the imperial staff – showed unique theological courage when despite the tremendous pressure he did not deviate from his conviction of faith, appealing to scripture, reason and his conscience.[17]

Charles V made unmistakeably clear what was at stake for Luther here: the following day he had his personal, very impressive confession on the tradition of Catholic faith read out in German.

And at the same time he declared that while granting Luther free conduct he would without delay initiate proceedings against him as a notorious heretic. Moreover in the **Edict of Worms** on 26 May Charles V put Luther and his followers under the imperial ban. All Luther's writings were to be burned and an episcopal censorship of books was to be introduced for all religious works appearing in Germany.

As Luther was in extreme personal danger, his prince had him hidden away on the Wartburg. As 'Knight George', in his ten months there he completed his translation of the New Testament – on the basis of Erasmus's Greek and Latin edition – the masterpiece of High German. The Bible was to be the foundation of gospel piety and the new community life. And Luther's Reformation paradigm, totally constructed on the Bible, was now to be the real, great alternative to the mediaeval Roman Catholic paradigm.

7. *The Reformation paradigm*

The return to the gospel in protest against the false development and wrong attitudes in the traditional church and traditional theology was the starting point for the new **Reformation paradigm**, the **Protestant-evangelical paradigm of church and theology**. Luther's new understanding of the gospel and the completely new status of the doctrine of justification in fact gave the whole of theology a new orientation and the church a new structure; this was a **paradigm shift** *par excellence*.[18] In theology and the church too, from time to time such **processes of paradigm shift** take place not just in limited micro- or meso-spheres of individual questions and tractates but also in the macro-sphere: the shift from mediaeval to Reformation theology is like the shift from the geocentric to the heliocentric view:

– Fixed and familiar terms change – justification, grace, faith, law and gospel – or are abandoned as useless: Aristotelian terms like substance and accidents, matter and form, act and potency;

– Norms and criteria which determine the admissibility of certain problems and solutions shift: holy scripture, councils, papal decrees, reason, conscience;

– Whole theories like the hylomorphic doctrine of the sacraments and methods like the speculative deductive method of scholasticism are shattered.

Not least, the attractive language of the new paradigm was decisive for countless clergy and laity of the time. From the beginning many were quite fascinated by the internal **coherence**, the elemental **transparency** and pastoral **effectiveness** of Luther's answers, with the new simplicity and creative linguistic force of Lutheran theology. Moreover, the art of printing books and a flood of printed sermons and pamphlets, along with the German hymn, proved to be essential factors in the rapid popularization and extension of the alternative constellation.

Thus the model of interpretation changed, along with the whole complex of different concepts, methods, problem areas and attempted solutions as hitherto recognized by theology and the church. Like the astronomers after Copernicus and Galileo, so the theologians after Luther got used as it were to **another way of seeing,** of seeing in the context of another macro-model. That means that some things were now perceived which had not been seen earlier and possibly some things were overlooked which had been seen earlier. Martin Luther's new understanding of word and faith, God's righteousness and human justification, the one mediator Jesus Christ and the universal priesthood of all believers led to his revolutionary **new biblical-christocentric conception** of all theology. From his rediscovery of the Pauline message of justification there followed for Luther;
– a new understanding of **God**: not a God abstractly 'in himself', but a God who is quite concretely gracious 'for us';
– a new understanding of **human beings**: human beings in faith as 'at the same time righteous and sinful';
– a new understanding of the **church**: not as a bureaucratic apparatus of power and finance but renewed as the community of believers on the basis of the priesthood of all believers;
– a new understanding of the **sacraments**: not as rituals which worked in a quasi-mechanical way, but as promises of Christ and signs of faith.

Western Christianity had got itself into a hopeless situation: for traditional Roman Catholicism the Reformation represented apostasy from the true form of Christianity, but for those inclined towards the gospel it represented the restoration of its original form. The latter abandoned the mediaeval paradigm of Christianity with joy. Rome might be able to go on to excommunicate the Reformer Luther, but it could not stop the radical reshaping of church life in accordance with the gospel by the Reformation movement, which progressed and stirred up all Europe. The **new Reformation constellation of theology and the church** was soon solidly established. From 1525 the Reformation was carried through in countless German territories, and after the failure at reconciliation at the Augsburg Reichstag in 1530 (the *Confessio Augustana*) the Schmalkald League of Protestant German princes was formed, which perfected the combination of Lutheran Reformation and political power.

It was thus clear that to the great schism between East and West a no smaller schism had been added between (roughly speaking) North and South – an event of prime importance in world history, with incalculable consequences also for state and society, economics, science and art, which (with all their ambivalence) have extended even to North and South America.

Indeed it has taken a long time, almost 450 years, for Catholics and Protestants to find a way out of their polemical confrontations and approach one another. Today the question is: have the churches still not got clear of the old controversial questions raised by Luther? How can they finally come together again? By what criterion can they establish their unity?

8. *The criterion of theology*

We have already seen how the mediaeval understanding of justification was not simply out of keeping with the gospel, and how Luther's understanding was not simply un-Catholic. Only a differentiated and nuanced assessment does justice to both sides. And this differentiated and nuanced assesment will not harmonize, but at the same time see discontinuity in all the continuity: Luther's decisive new beginning.

The decisive **theological** argument, which is primarily to be put forward not by the church historian but by the systematic theologian, may not simply be carried on with the 'Catholic'

Luther – with a Luther who was still Catholic or remained Catholic.[19] It must be carried on with the **Reformation Luther**, who with Paul and Augustine attacked scholasticism generally and Aristotelianism in particular. It is Luther's distinctive Reformation doctrine which needs to be taken seriously, not just historically and psychologically, i.e. what it meant for the history of the church and theology and for Luther personally, but also theologically.

By what **criterion**? Unfortunately Catholic church historians have seldom reflected on this decisive question. Moreover, their judgments on Luther's theology are often less historical than dogmatic evaluations. As a criterion for their judgment they have often taken the Council of Trent, whose basic theological weaknesses they have overlooked (thus the conciliar historian Hubert Jedin), or the theology of high scholasticism, the Catholicity of which has not been critically investigated (e.g. by the Catholic Reformation historian Joseph Lortz), or Greek and Latin patristics, the distance of which from scripture has manifestly not been seen (thus French theologians).

Here it must be said that anyone who does not want to suspend theological judgment cannot avoid a purely **exegetical** study of Luther's theology and especially his understanding of justification. As we have seen, Luther's doctrine of justification, his understanding of the sacraments, his whole theology and his explosive effect on world history are grounded in one thing: in the return of the church and its theology to the gospel of Jesus Christ as originally attested in Holy Scripture. So can one really argue with the most distinctive features of Luther if in the last resort one avoids this battleground, on which schism and church union are ultimately decided, whether out of superficiality, convenience or incompetence?

No, neo-scholastic theology, Trent, high scholasticism and patristics are all only secondary criteria compared with this **primary, fundamental and permanently binding criterion: scripture,** the original Christian message to which both the Greek and Latin fathers and the mediaeval theologians, the fathers of Trent and the neo-scholastic theologians appealed, and before which of course Luther himself also has to answer. In other words, it is not decisive whether this or that saying of Luther in this form or that can already be found in a pope, in Thomas Aquinas, in Bernard of Clairvaux or Augustine, but whether or not it has behind it the original Christian message on which all subsequent tradition, including the Gospels, depends.

9. *Where Luther can be said to be right*

Does Luther have the New Testament behind him in his basic approach? I can venture an answer which is based on my previous works in the sphere of the doctrine of justification.[20] In his basic statements on the event of justification, with the 'through grace alone', 'through faith alone', the 'at the same time righteous and a sinner', **Luther has the New Testament behind him,** and especially Paul, who is decisively involved in the doctrine of justification. I shall demonstrate this simply through the key words:

– 'Justification' according to the New Testament is not in fact a process of supernatural origin which is understood physiologically and which takes place in the human subject, but is the verdict of God in which God does not impute their sin to the godless but declares them righteous in Christ and precisely in so doing makes them really righteous.

– 'Grace' according to the New Testament is not a quality or disposition of the soul, not a series of different quasi-physical supernatural entities which are successively poured into the substance and faculties of the soul, but is God's living favour and homage, his personal conduct as made manifest in Jesus Christ, which precisely in this way determines and changes people.

– 'Faith' according to the New Testament is not an intellectualist holding truths to be true but the trusting surrender of the whole person to God, who does not justify anyone through his or her grace on the basis of moral achievements but on the basis of faith alone, so that this faith can be shown in works of love. Human beings are justified and yet always at the same time (*simul*) sinners who constantly need forgiveness afresh, who are only on the way to perfection.

So Catholic theology today will be able to **take note** more openly than a few decades ago of the **evidence of scripture** and thus also Luther's doctrine: first, because Catholic exegesis has made considerable progress; secondly, because the time-conditioned nature of the Council of Trent and its formulations have been demonstrated to everyone by the Second Vatican Council; thirdly, because the anti-ecumenical Neo-scholastic theology which was so dominant between the councils clearly manifested at Vatican II its inability to solve today's new problems; fourthly, because the changed atmosphere since the Council has opened up incalculable and formerly undreamed-of possibilities for ecumenical understanding; fifthly, because while the discussion over justification carried on in recent years has shown great differences in the interpretation of the doctrine of justification, it has not brought out any **irreducible differences** between the Protestant and the Catholic doctrines of justification **which would split the church**. A number of officially agreed documents from both sides have confirmed that the doctrine of justification no longer divides the churches.[21]

Of course all this does not mean that there were not already differences between Paul's and Luther's doctrines of justification simply on the basis of their different starting points; Protestant scholars themselves often note them, in particular too individualistic an orientation on Luther's part. Nor does it mean that in some statements of his doctrine of justification Luther did not lapse into one-sidedness and exaggeration; some formulations with *solum* and works like *De servo arbitrio* and *On Good Works* were and remain open to misunderstanding and need supplementation and correction. But the basic approach was not wrong. This approach was right, as was its implementation – despite some defects and one-sidedness. The difficulties and problems lie in the further conclusions drawn, above all in questions of understanding the church, ministry and the sacraments; these, too, have largely been resolved in theory today but are awaiting practical realization.

So, welcome though it is that even Rome now recognizes that in abstract theological terms the doctrine of justification no longer splits the churches, this cannot disguise the fact that Rome has not drawn the consequences which followed for Luther for the structure of the church. Indeed the present clerical, unspiritual dictatorship of Rome again mocks the basic concern of the

Reformation, which is also a good Catholic concern (the Pope is not above scripture). Rome still has little understanding of what Luther wanted in the light of the gospel.

But – here a counterpoint is due – for all our assent to Luther's great basic insight in keeping with the gospel, who could overlook the fact that in its results the Lutheran Reformation remained divided, was two-faced.

10. The problematical results of the Lutheran Reformation

The Lutheran movement developed a great dynamic and was able to spread powerfully not only in Germany but beyond, in Lithuania, Sweden, Finland, Denmark and Norway. Parallel to the events in Germany, in Switzerland, which had already begun to detach itself from the empire since the middle of the fifteenth century, an independent, more radical form of Reformation had been established by Ulrich Zwingli and later Jean Calvin which, with its understanding of the church, was to make more of an impact than Lutheranism in both the old world and the new. But it was Luther himself at any rate who in the 1520s and 1530s succeeded in establishing the Reformation movement within Germany.

Indeed, Germany had **split into two confessional camps**. And in view of the threat to the empire from the Turks, who in 1526 had defeated the Hungarians at Mohács and in 1529 had advanced as far as Vienna, Luther had even asked which was more dangerous for Christianity, the power of the papacy or the power of Islam; he saw both as religions of works and the law. At the end of his life Luther saw the future of the Reformation churches in far less rosy terms than in the year of the great breakthrough. Indeed in the last years of his life, although he was indefatigably active to the end, Luther became increasingly subject, on top of apocalyptic anxieties about the end of the world and illnesses, to depression, melancholy, manic depressions and spiritual temptations. And the reasons for this growing pessimism about the world and human beings were real – not just psychological and medical. He was not spared great disappointments.

First, the original **Reformation enthusiasm** soon **ran out of**

steam. Congregational life often fell short of it; many who were not ready for the 'freedom of a Christian' also lost all church support with the collapse of the Roman system. And even in the Lutheran camp, many people asked whether men and women had really become so much better as a result of the Reformation. Nor can one overlook an impoverishment in the arts – other than music.

Secondly, the Reformation was coming up against **growing political resistance**. After the inconsequential Augsburg Reichstag of 1530 (the emperor had 'rejected' the conciliatory 'Augsburg Confession' which Melanchthon had the main part in drafting), in the 1530s the Reformation was able at first not only to consolidate itself in the former territories, but also to extend to further areas, from Württemberg to Brandenburg. But in the 1540s the emperor Charles V, overburdened in foreign politics and at home constantly intent on mediation, had been able to end the wars with Turkey and France. Since the Lutherans had refused to take part in the Council of Trent (because it was under papal leadership: Luther's work *Against the Papacy in Rome, Founded by the Devil*, 1545),[22] the emperor finally felt strong enough to enter into military conflict with the powerful Schmalkald League of Protestants. Moreover the Protestant powers were defeated in these first wars of religion (the Schmalkald wars, 1546/47), and the complete restoration of Roman Catholic conditions (with concessions only over the marriage of priests and the chalice for the laity) seemed only a matter of time. It was only a change of sides by the defeated Moritz of Saxony – he had made a secret alliance with France, forced the emperor to flee through a surprise attack in Innsbruck in 1552, and so also provoked the interruption of the Council of Trent – which saved Protestantism from disaster. The confessional division of Germany between the territories of the old faith and those of the 'Augsburg Confession' was finally sealed by the religious peace of Augsburg in 1555. Since then what prevailed was not religious freedom, but the principle *cuius regio, eius religio*, i.e religion went with the region. Anyone who did not belong to either of the 'religions' was excluded from the peace.

Moreover the Protestant camp itself was unable to **preserve**

unity. At a very early stage Protestantism in Germany split into a 'left wing' and a 'right wing' of the Reformation.

11. *The split in the Reformation*

Luther had roused the spirits, but there were some that he would only get rid of by force. These were the spirits of **enthusiasm**, which while certainly feeding on mediaeval roots, were remarkably encouraged by Luther's emergence. A great many individual interests and individual revolts began to spread under the cloak of Luther's name, and soon Luther found himself confronted with a second, 'left-wing' front. Indeed Luther's opponents on the left (enthusiastic turmoil, riots and an iconoclastic movement as early as 1522 in his own city of Wittenberg!) were soon at least as dangerous for his enterprise of Reformation as his right-wing opponents, the traditionalists orientated on Rome. If the 'papists' appealed to the Roman system, the 'enthusiasts' practised an often fanatical religious subjectivism and enthusiasm which appealed to the direct personal experience of revelation and the spirit ('inner voice', 'inner light'). Their first agitator and Luther's most important rival, the pastor Thomas Münzer, combined Reformation ideas with ideas of social revolution: the implementation of the Reformation by force, if need be with no heed to existing law, and the establishment of the thousand-year kingdom of Christ on earth!

But **Luther** – who politically was evidently trapped in a view 'from above' and has been vigorously criticized for that from Thomas Münzer through Friedrich Engels to Ernst Bloch – was not prepared **to draw such radical social conclusions** from his radical demand for the freedom of the Christian and to support with corresponding clarity the legitimate demands of the peasants (whose independence was manifestly threatened and increasingly exploited) against princes and the nobility. Despite all the reprehensible outbursts, were not the demands of the peasants also quite reasonable and justified? Or was it all just a misunderstanding, indeed a misuse, of the gospel? Luther, too, could not deny the economic and legal distress of the peasants.

But a plan for reform would by no means *a priori* have been an illusion. Why not? Because the democratic order of the Swiss confederacy, for the peasants of southern Germany the ideal for a new order, could have been a quite viable model. However, all this was alien to Luther, trapped in his Thuringian perspective and now with his conservative tendencies confirmed. Horrified by news of the atrocities in the peasant revolts, he fatally took the side of the authorities and justified the brutal suppression of the peasants.

12. The freedom of the church?

As well as the left-wing Reformation there was the right wing. And here we must note that the **ideal of the free Christian church**, which Luther had enthusiastically depicted for his contemporaries in his programmatic writings, was **not realized** in the German empire. Granted, countless churches were liberated by Luther from the domination of secularized bishops who were hostile to reform, and above all from 'captivity' by the Roman Curia, from its absolutist desire to rule and its financial exploitation. But what was the result?

In principle Luther had advocated the dotrine of state and church as the 'two realms'. But at the same time, in view of all the difficulties with Rome on the one hand and with enthusiasts and rebels on the other, he assigned to the local rulers (and not all of them were like Frederick 'the Wise') the duty of protecting the church and maintaining order in it. As the Catholic bishops in the Lutheran sphere had mostly left, the princes were to take on the role of 'emergency bishops'. But the **'emergency bishops'** very soon became 'summepiscopi' who attributed quasi-episcopal authority to themselves. And the people's Reformation now in various respects became a princes' Reformation.

In short, the Lutheran churches which had been freed from the 'Babylonian captivity' quickly found themselves in almost complete and often no less oppressive dependence on their own rulers, with all their lawyers and church administrative organs (consistories). The princes who even before the Reformation had worked against peasants and citizens for the internal unification of their territories (which had often been thrown together haphazardly) and a coherent league of subjects had become excessively powerful as a result of the secularization of church land and the withdrawal of the church. The **local ruler** finally became something like a **pope in his own territory**.

No, the Lutheran Reformation did not directly prepare the way (as is so often claimed in Protestant church historiography) for the modern world, freedom of religion and the French revolution (a further epoch-making paradigm shift would be necessary for this), but first of all for princely absolutism and despotism. So in general, in Lutheran Germany – with Calvin, things went otherwise – what was realized was not the free Christian church but **the rule of the church by princes**, which is questionable for Christians; this was finally to come to a well-deserved end in Germany only with the revolution after the First World War. But even in the time of National Socialism, the resistance of the Lutheran churches to a totalitarian regime of terror like that of Hitler was decisively weakened by the doctrine of two realms, by the subordination of the churches to state authority which had been customary since Luther, and the emphasis on the obedience of the citizen in worldly matters. It can only be mentioned in passing here that in the sermons before his death Martin Luther had spoken in such an ugly and un-Christian way against the Jews that the National Socialists did not find it difficult to cite him as a key witness for their hatred of Jews and their antisemitic agitation.[23] But these were not Luther's last words, nor should they be mine.

I would like to close with three great statements which are utterly characteristic of Luther.

First, the dialectical conclusion of his work 'The Freedom of a Christian': 'We conclude, therefore, that a Christian lives not in himself, but in Christ and in his neighbour. Otherwise he is not a Christian. He lives in Christ through faith, in his neighbour through love. By faith he is caught up beyond himself into God. By love he descends beneath himself into his neighbour. Yet he always remains in God and in his love... As you see, it is a spiritual and true freedom and makes our hearts free from all sins, laws and commands. It is more excellent than all other liberty which is external, as heaven is more excellent than earth. May Christ give us liberty both to understand and to preserve.'[24]

Then Luther's summary plea before the emperor and the Reichstag at Worms: 'Unless I am convinced by the testimony of the Scriptures or by clear reason (for I do not trust either in the Pope or in councils alone, since it is well known that they have often erred and contradicted themselves), I am bound by the Scriptures I have quoted and as my conscience is captive to the Word of God, I cannot and I will not retract anything, since it is neither safe nor right to go against the conscience. God help me. Amen.'[25]

And finally, the last thing that Luther wrote: 'Nobody can understand Virgil in his *Eclogues* and *Georgics* unless he has first been a shepherd or a farmer for five years. Nobody understands Cicero in his letters unless he has been engaged in public affairs of some consequence for twenty years. Let nobody suppose that he has tasted the Holy Scriptures sufficiently unless he has ruled over the churches with the prophets for a hundred years. Therefore there is something wonderful, first, about John the Baptist; second, about Christ; third, about the apostle. "Lay not your hand on this divine Aeneid, but bow before it, adore its every trace." We are beggars. That is true.'[26]

Friedrich Schleiermacher
Theology at the Dawn of Modernity

Chronology (according to M.Redeker)

1768	21 November: born in Breslau.
1783	Enters the Paedagogium of the Brethren community in Niesky, Oberlausitz.
1785	Enters the theological seminary of the Brethren community in Barby, Elbe.
1787	Studies at the University of Halle.
1790	First theological examination in Berlin; tutor in the house of Count Dohna in Schlobitten, East Prussia.
1794	Passes second theological examination and is ordained; auxiliary preacher in Landsberg.
1796	Pastor at the Charité in Berlin; enters the circle of friends of the Berlin Romantics (Henriette Herz, Friedrich Schlegel).
1799	*On Religion*. Unhappy relationship with Eleonore Grunow.
1800	*Monologues*.
1802	Court preacher in Stolp, Pomerania.
1804	Professor of theology and university preacher in Halle.
1805	*Christmas Eve*.
1806	University of Halle closed in the course of the Napoleonic wars.
1807	Moves to Berlin. At first freelance work.
1809	Preacher at the Trinity Church. Marries Henriette von Willich.
1810	Professor at the new University of Berlin and first dean of the new theological faculty.
1813	Political involvement as the editor of the *Preussischer Korrespondent*.
1814	Secretary of the Berlin Academy of Sciences; suspected of being a political reactionary; dismissed from the Department of Education.
1815	Rector of the University of Berlin.
1817	Plays leading role in the union of the Prussian state church.
1821-22	*Magnum opus, The Christian Faith described according to the Principles of the Protestant Church*
1824-25	Climax of church-political disputes with the Prussian king.
1833	Travels to Sweden, Norway and Denmark.
1834	12 February: death and burial in Berlin.

1. Beyond pietism and rationalism

'The first place in a history of the theology of the most recent times belongs and will always belong to Schleiermacher, and he has no rival.' So says Schleiermacher's most vigorous opponent, who was to drive him from his pinnacle, and continues: 'It has often been pointed out that Schleiermacher did not found any school. This assertion can be robbed of some of its force by mention of the names of his successors in Berlin, August Twesten, Karl Immanuel Nitzsch of Bremen, and Alexander Schweizer of Zürich. But it is correct in so far as Schleiermacher's significance lies beyond these beginnings of a school in his name. What he said of Frederick the Great in his Academy address entitled "What goes to make a great man" applies also to himself: "He did not found a school but an era".' So spoke the one who saw to it that Schleiermacher, 'the church father of the nineteenth century', did not also become the church father of the twentieth century: Karl Barth in his *Protestant Theology in the Nineteenth Century*.[1]

Friedrich Daniel Ernst Schleiermacher was the offspring of two Reformed clergy families (both his grandfather and father were theologians, and his mother was the daughter of the Berlin chief court preacher Stubenrauch). He was born in Breslau in 1768 and took the name by which he was called from Frederick the Great, under whom his father had served as a Prussian military chaplain for soldiers of the Reformed confession. He was a highly talented young man, and because of the possibilities open to him could go several ways, though of course hardly into Lutheran orthodoxy – which was still strong in some circles.[2]

For already his **grandfather** Daniel Schleiermacher had been a **Pietist**. As a Reformed preacher he had been active in a radically pietistic community of apocalyptists and finally after disturbances in this sect (which was accused of magic and witchcraft) had to move to Holland.

His **father**, Gottlieb Schleiermacher, was also a Pietist; he too was at first the member of a Pietist community, but was to be alienated from it for a long time: it was only at the age of fifty that finally he felt at least inwardly that he belonged to the Herrnhuter Community of Brethren.

Moreover the young Friedrich could also have become a pietist when at the age of fourteen he saw his mother (who was soon to die) and his father (who was soon to remarry) for the last time, and was handed over to the care of the Brethren community, first at boarding school in Niesky, near Görlitz. Then, at the age of seventeen, he **studied theology** at the strict theological seminary of **Barby** near Magdeburg. Here the religion was one of the heart, which centred less on feelings of repentance and penitence as it did in pietistic Halle than on joy at redemption.

However, the young Schleiermacher hunted in vain at that time for the supernatural feelings and familiar converse with Jesus that the pious milieu required. Instead of this he found himself drawn to forbidden books, like Kant's *Prolegomena to a Future Metaphysics* (1783). The result was what might have been expected, for Schleiermacher now began increasingly to see the world no longer with pietistic eyes but with the eyes of the rational Enlightenment. Moreover after two years of theological study the student, now nineteen, wrote to his father (2 January 1787): 'I cannot believe that he was the true eternal God who only called himself the Son of Man; I cannot believe that his death was a vicarious atonement, because he never explicitly said as much and because I cannot believe that it was necessary, for it was impossible that God should have wanted to punish for ever men and women whom he evidently did not create for perfection but for striving towards it, because they had not become perfect.'[3] This letter must have prompted bad memories for his father, and now it was only with some reluctance that he allowed Friedrich to study in **Halle**. For:

Friedrich's father, the pastor, had himself long been a **rationalist**, and indeed was a freemason stamped by the Enlightenment. Moreover in a letter to his son he explicitly confessed that 'for at least twelve years' he had 'preached as a real unbeliever'.[4]

Moreover they were also rationalists at the University of **Halle**, founded barely a century beforehand in the pietistic spirit of August Hermann Franke: it was now a **bastion of the Enlightenment**. The leading German Enlightenment philosopher Christian Wolff had worked here and established numerous schools. Moreover the theological faculty had become open to the spirit of the Enlightenment. Its leading figure was Johann Salomo Semler (died 1791), who in his treatise on the free investigation of the canon had founded the historical-critical exegesis of the Bible in Germany and thus introduced a shift from the old orthodox theology to enlightened 'neology', to 'new teaching'.

So it seemed most likely that Friedrich Schleiermacher would also become a rationalist. For at the age of nineteen he now – we are still talking of 1787 – moved to this University of Halle, there to spend the next two years studying theology. He lived in the home of his uncle on his mother's side, Samuel Ernst Timotheus Stubenrauch, an enlightened Reformed theologian who became almost a second father to him. Indeed in his four semesters in Halle (until 1789) Schleiermacher studied not so much theology – he even had a pronounced antipathy to dogmatics – as philosophy, under Wolff's pupil Johann August Eberhard.

Schleiermacher the student wanted to create for himself the philosophical foundations for his own view of the world. And to this end he steeped himself in the Greek classics, above all Plato, and wrote his first academic work on Aristotle's *Nicomachean Ethics*. To this end he steeped himself further in the main works of **Immanuel Kant**, which had been appearing in rapid succession since 1781; he also devoted most of his early, almost exclusively philosophical, works to Kant. No wonder that all this reinforced his scepticism towards traditional Lutheran orthodox dogmatics. Indeed, reading Kant would shape him for life; in his epistemology Schleiermacher remained a Kantian all his days. For him, too, pure reason has no competence outside the horizon of human experience.

And yet, specifically in matters of ethics and religion, Schleiermacher would **not follow Kant.** Kant's moral proofs for God and immortality seemed to him to have too little foundation, despite everything. How could God be the regulative principle of our knowledge if he is not at the same time the constitutive principle of our being? Schleiermacher remained convinced that in the world of thoroughgoing natural laws there is a last mystery which human beings have to respect. Here may be the deepest reason why Friedrich Schleiermacher, the passionate philosopher, in the last resort remained a theologian. Although he kept his love of philosophy to the end of his life, although he initiated modern Plato scholarship (in his obituary he was called a 'Christian Plato') with a translation of Plato's works (with introductions to all the Dialogues), and although, like Kant, Schelling, Hegel and Hölderlin, he became a tutor after his studies (for more than six years, first at the castle of Count Dohna in **East Prussia**, from where he also visited Kant in his old age), Schleiermacher did not become a professional philosopher – unlike the Tübingen theologians Schelling and Hegel. Moreover Schleiermacher ended his theological study with the two ordination examinations (getting good to excellent marks in everything but the dogmatics whch he hated) and finally became a preacher in the remote little town of **Landsberg**. Here he preached regularly in the spirit of the Christian Enlightenment, commending a reasonable faith, incessant moral striving and Jesus as the model of a right way of life; in addition he had already translated several volumes of English sermons. And a preacher he was to remain, indefatigable and loyal to his life's end.

However, in 1796 there was a decisive new move in Schleiermacher's life. He received a post in **Berlin**. At the age of twenty-eight he now became Reformed preacher at the great German hospital, the Charité, where he was to spend the next six years (until 1802). These were to be decisive, formative years, which were to give Schleiermacher the characterististics which distinguished him later. He had bidden farewell to both pietism and rationalism and yet had retained the legacy of both. As he once put it later, after all he had 'again become a Herrnhuter', but now 'of a higher order'.[5] Indeed during this Berlin period Friedrich Schleiermacher, this physically rather small, neat and slightly deformed man, but with great liveliness and agility, became **the** modern theologian, a man in whom piety and modernity were combined in an exemplary way.

2. *A modern man*

Schleiermacher's post as hospital chaplain in Berlin, where he had to preach to simple people, left him time to himself. He made use of this time. The man who hitherto had argued with modernity only in silence and solitude (conversations above all with philosophical books) now entered the social life of a modern city. He moved in the salons of educated Berlin society, where people talked about poetry and art, history, science and politics. It was an exciting time, still deeply marked by the French Revolution, though a counterpoint was already emerging. How much had changed in culture and society, in the sciences and in everyday life, as a result of the philosophical and literary Enlightenment and the political upheavals! Were not important corrections also due in the sphere of theology? Schleiermacher followed everything with a lively mind – without ecclesiastical blinkers and moralistic Christian prejudices.

A new period in church history did not begin with Schleiermacher, as was said in a communication to the students after his death, but it did come to theological maturity in him. Here the theological paradigm shift from the Reformation to **modernity** virtually takes on bodily form: Schleiermacher no longer lived like Martin Luther (and Melanchthon), still largely in a pre-Copernican mind-set, in a mediaeval world of angels and devils, demons and witches, borne along by a basically pessimistic and apocalyptic attittude, intolerant of other confessions and religions. It would never have occurred to him to have someone burned for having problems with a dogma of the early church, as Calvin did with the anti-trinitarian Servetus. Nor did he have difficulties with modern science, with Copernicus and Galileo, as did the Roman popes imprisoned in the mediaeval paradigm; in the nineteenth century the writings of the modern scientists remained on the Index of books forbidden to Catholics alongside the Reformers and modern philosophy (from Descartes to Kant). No, Schleiermacher, who even as a professor still went to lectures on science, remained convinced by Kant all his life that there is a thoroughgoing regularity in nature, which allows no 'supernatural' exceptions. A supernaturalism in theology? That was not Schleiermacher's affair.

So in Schleiermacher we meet a theologian who is a **modern man** through and through. That means:

He knows and affirms the modern **philosophy** with which he had grown up and which had reached its challenging heights with Kant, Fichte and Hegel; as a classical philologist he had also gained the respect of classical scholars by his masterly translation of Plato.

He affirmed historical **criticism** and himself applied it to the foundation documents of the biblical revelation; in the great dispute over the fragments of Reimarus he would have certainly been on Lessing's side against Goeze, the chief pastor of Hamburg; at any rate, later he inaugurated historical criticism of the Pastoral Epistles with a critical study of I Timothy, which he said could not come from the apostle Paul; later he attributed the writings of Luke to the community life of earliest Christianity and its oral tradition; he demonstrated the presence of a collection of sayings in the Gospel of Matthew; the writings of the New Testament were to be treated like any others; his hermeneutics (introduction to the understanding of texts) became a basic work for theological, philosophical and literary interpretations.

He affirmed and loved modern **literature, art and social life** above all. He himself played an active part here through his close links with the Berlin Romantic circles which were striving to get beyond the Enlightenment, above all with their leader, the twenty-five-year-old Friedrich Schlegel, who lived with him for almost two years, and Henriette Herz, the beautiful and witty thirty-two-year-old wife of Marcus Herz, the highly respected Jewish doctor who had been a pupil of Kant; he visited their salon almost every day, where the spirit of Goethe and Romanticism replaced that of the Enlightenment. So he was a theologian in the closest contact with writers, poets, philosophers, artists and political enthusiasts of every kind. That is how we are to imagine the young Friedrich Schleiermacher. Only now does his thought and writing achieve a broad horizon and finally succeed in combining the Romantic religion of feeling with scientific culture.

3. Belief in a new age

So it is not surprising that Schleiermacher also had works published in the key journal of early Romanticism, the *Athenaeum*, edited by the Schlegel brothers. In addition to other anonymous fragments, he wrote, for example, the 'Idea for a Rational Catechism for Noble Ladies.'[6] The first commandment? It runs: 'You shall have no lover but him; but you shall be able to be a friend without playing and flirting or adoring in the colours of love.' Or the seventh to tenth commandments? They run: 'You shall not enter into any marriage which would have to be broken. You shall not want to be loved where you do not love. You shall not bear false witness for men; you shall not beautify their barbarity with your words and works. Let yourself long for men's education, art, wisdom and honour.' He was truly a theologian who simply in his attitude to **women** and **their emancipation** is far removed from the mediaeval and the Reformation paradigm, from their paternalism and sexism, and who not least had a living experience through women of the ethos of a spiritualized, interiorized Christianity.

However, the fact must not be concealed that in Berlin Schleiermacher finally fell passionately in love with Eleonore Grunow, the deeply religious wife of a Berlin pastor. Her marriage was an unhappy one, but although she loved Schleiermacher in return, she would not leave her husband even when in 1802, well advised by the anxious church authorities, Schleiermacher went into 'exile' in the small Pomeranian town of **Stolp,** a community of about 250 Reformed Christians. There he hoped that he would be able to marry Eleonore inconspicuously – to no avail, as the next three years were to prove. In his unhappiness Schleiermacher kept his sanity by translating Plato and producing the outlines of a critique of moral theory to his day (that of Kant and Fichte). Five years later, at the age of forty-one, he was then to marry Henriette von Willich, the twenty-year-old widow of a pastor friend who had died early. She was certainly a good housewife, but a less good partner (as she later fell completely under the influence of a clairvoyante and a revivalist preacher). Schleiermacher later revoked his seventh rational commandment for noble ladies, which could be understood as an invitation to divorce, in a sermon on the Christian household.

That Schleiermacher was also anything but conventional in his thinking about **children** – he himself had three daughters and a highly-gifted son who to his abiding sorrow died at the early age of nine – is shown in the same context by his fifth commandment: 'Honour the idiosyncracies and whims of your children, that all may go well with them and they may live a mighty life on earth.' Moreover Schleiermacher was to become a **pioneer of modern education.** Through his planning and organization he later not only left his stamp on Prussian **schools** but was also a co-founder of Berlin University and a decisive figure in establishing the Berlin Academy of Sciences. He was truly a theologian who in an astonishing way quite naturally took a place at the centre of modern life and played an active part in shaping it.

What did Schleiermacher believe in this new time? The spiritual foundation of all his activities was a new extended **ideal of humanity**. And he once formulated his 'faith' like this:

'1. I believe in **infinite humanity** which was there before it took the guise of masculinity and femininity.

2. I believe that I am not alive to be obedient or to dissipate myself, but to be and to become; and I believe in the **power of the will and education**, again to approach the infinite, to redeem me from the fetters of miseducation and to make me independent of the limitations of gender.

3. I believe in **enthusiasm and virtue**, in the worth of art and the attraction of science, in friendship among men and love of the Fatherland, in past greatness and future nobility.'[7]

Belief in infinite humanity, in the power of the will and education, in enthusiasm and virtue: should we make all this grounds for censuring Schleiermacher, as Karl Barth did? Should he be criticized for feeling responsible for the intellectual and moral foundations of society? For being concerned for the elevation, development and ennobling of individual and social life? For not only being interested in culture but also being increasingly involved in it – as preacher, writer, teacher, researcher and organizer? Indeed, for virtually embodying this modern culture as a man with a thorough intellectual and moral education? Indeed, we might ask back: how else should Schleiermacher have done theology in the Berlin of his time? On the basis of other, pre-modern presuppositions, as they had been worked out by philosophy, history and science in his time? Should he have remained, like others, in the mediaeval or Reformation paradigm instead of resolutely doing theology in the new modern paradigm, in his quite decisive concern for culture and therefore for **education**? But here a fundamental question arose for many of his contemporaries.

4. *Can one be modern and religious?*

The young Schleiermacher primarily had contact with the **educated** among his contemporaries. And when on the occasion of his twenty-ninth birthday he was asked by those celebrating it to write a book by his thirtieth birthday (on the topic of how religion could be expressed in a new way today), he took up the challenge and in fact expressly addressed only the educated classes (he thought that one should **preach** to the uneducated). Of course Schleiermacher was well aware of how ambivalent the picture of religion was, particularly among these educated people, how it wavered between affirmation and rejection, assent and mockery, admiration and contempt. So while he addressed his book to the educated, he explicitly addressed it above all to the educated among the **despisers of religion**, who were at least to know what they either despised, or did not know properly because of their prejudices. Thus came into being his famous first work, *On Religion. Speeches to its Cultured Despisers*[8] which appeared in 1799, when Schleiermacher was in his thirty-first year.

There is no doubt that all was not well with religion and theology at this time. Moreover, in these years some of Schleiermacher's most famous contemporaries – Fichte, Schelling, Hegel and Hölderlin – had moved from theology into philosophy (or poetry). Certainly they had not given up 'religion' completely, and had incorporated it into their speculative metaphysical system – as philosophical thinkers who certainly cannot be said to have denied religion completely (above all not the 'piety of thought' claimed by Hegel); however, they themselves lived and thought on the basis of genuinely philosophical roots. Many of Schleiermacher's new friends showed only an incomprehension of religion.

It needed someone of the stature of Schleiermacher to adopt a counter-position here that was worth taking seriously. Moreover, generally speaking there was no one on the church theological scene who in these stormy times between revolution and restoration, Enlightenment and Romanticism, could ask the question 'What about religion?' as urgently, credibly and effectively in public as he could.

So this was Schleiermacher's concern on the threshold of a new century: a bold and original attempt to **recall to religion, after the**

Enlightenment, a generation which was weary of religion and to which religion was alien and 'to reweave religion, threatened with oblivion, into the incomparably rich fabric of the burgeoning intellectual life of modern times'.[9] Or were only poetry and literature, holy philosophy and the sciences and the humanities, to determine the hopeful century that was dawning? Had not the poets and seers, the artists and orators, already always been mediators of the eternal and the most high, 'virtuosi of religion'? Was a 'sense of the holy' to be the mark only of ordinary people, and not also of the educated? No, the topic of religion was a live one, because it was raised by the whole human disposition and was therefore undeniable. But everything depends on what one understands by 'religion'.

5. What is religion?

Religion is not science, nor does it seek 'like metaphysics to determine and explain the nature of the universe'. Nor is religion morality, nor action: having an influence on the universe by moral action, 'to advance and perfect the Universe by the power of freedom and the divine will of man'.[10] Not that religion has nothing to do with understanding and morality. What 'religion' is about is something independent, original, underivable, immediate.

The peculiar feature of religion is a mysterious **experience**; it is **being moved by the world of the eternal**. So religion is about the heavenly sparks which are struck when a holy soul is touched by the infinite, a religious experience to which the 'virtuosi of religion' give direct expression in their speeches and utterances and which is communicated by them also to ordinary people. To be more precise, religion seeks to experience the universe, the totality of what is and what happens, meditatively in **immediate seeing and feeling** (these categories come from Fichte): 'It is neither thinking nor acting, but intuition and feeling. It will regard the Universe as it is. It is reverent attention and submission, in childlike passivity, to be stirred and filled by the Universe's immediate influences.'[11]

One can also say that religion is a religion of the heart: in it human beings are encountered, grasped, filled and moved in their innermost depths and their totality – by the infinite which is active in all that is finite. No, religion is neither praxis nor speculation, neither art nor science, but a 'sense and taste for the infinite'.[12] This living relationship to the eternal, the infinite, represents the original state of each individual 'I', but this must be aroused. Religious experiences are countless, and patience is called for. So in the religious consciousness the two limits, individuality and the universe, make contact. From a historical perspective this means that religion is:

– no longer as in the Middle Ages or even the Reformation a departure, transition into something beyond the world, supernatural;

– nor as in Deism and in the Enlightenment a departure into something behind the world, metaphysical;

– rather, in a modern understanding, it is the intimating, the seeing, the feeling, the **indwelling of the infinite in the finite**. The infinite in the finite or God as the eternal absolute being that conditions all things – this, we can say, is the modern understanding of God and not (as Schleiermacher adds in the second edition at the end of the excursuses on the idea of God) 'the usual conception of God as one single being outside of the world and behind the world'.[13] Like Kant, Fichte, Schelling and Hegel, Schleiermacher with philosophical strictness rejects any anthropomorphizing of God. God in the modern understanding is the immanent-transcendent primal ground of all being, knowledge and will.

This feeling is not to be understood in a restricted psychological sense as Romantic enthusiastic emotion, but in a comprehensive, existential way: as human beings being encountered at the centre, as immediate religious self-awareness (Ebeling compares this function with that of the conscience in Luther). Schleiermacher will later himself make this notion more precise, will withdraw the term 'contemplation' of the universe, which is open to misunderstanding (with the senses or spiritually?), in favour of the term 'feeling' and, as we shall see, speak more precisely in his *The Christian Faith* of religion as the **feeling of absolute dependence**.

6. The significance of 'positive religion'

Now if religion is the feeling of 'absolute dependence', then is not a dog the best Christian?[14] – thus one of the most malicious *bon mots* about Schleiermacher's thought, made by Georg Friedrich Wilhelm Hegel, from 1818 his Berlin colleague in philosophy as successor to Fichte? No, witty and spiteful as this *bon mot* is (Schleiermacher ignored Hegel's polemic), it does not get to Schleiermacher's position. It is unjust, because it ignores not only the total, spiritual nature of 'feeling' but above all Schleiermacher's understanding of God with its emphasis on Christian freedom as compared with any religious servitude. So in 'feeling' before their God Christians are not as 'dependent' as dogs on their master.

No, on the contrary Schleiermacher is concerned with the inner **freedom** of the moral person – the source of eternal youth and joy – moreover freedom is also a key word in the *Monologues*, the second major work which Schleiermacher published after the *Speeches* (as a New Year's gift at the begining of 1800) and in which he attempted to describe his religious view of life and the world in the form of a 'lyrical extract from a permanent diary'.[15] And in complete contrast to Hegel, already in the *Speeches* Schleiermacher is decidely against the state church. For him, as a Reformed Christian, this is the source of all corruption. He called passionately for the separation of church and state following the French model, and in his fourth Speech on Religion virtually developed the programme for a radical reform of the church in which the parish communities would be replaced by personal communities (of the kind that he was later to have himself).

Anyone who thinks that in his *Speeches* Schleiermacher is simply practising 'natural theology' (something abhorred by many since Karl Barth) should note that he makes it emphatically clear over against the whole theology of the Enlightenment that for him there is **no such thing as 'natural religion'**. This would in fact be a rational matter with a moral orientation, so that everything going beyond such a religion of reason would have to be rejected as 'superstition'. No, for Schleiermacher such a natural religion or rational religion was an artificial product of philosophical reflection without that life and immediacy which characterize an authentic religion. So from the beginning, part of

Schleiermacher's concern is that religion can be understood rightly only if it is not simply considered 'in general' but in the individual, living, concrete, 'positive' religions (Judaism, Christianity, Islam, etc.).

So the *Speeches* end in a reflection on the 'positive' element in the religions. The basic notion is this. There is no 'Infinite' in itself, in pure abstraction. The infinite can always be grasped only in the finite: it empties and manifests itself in an infinite variety of forms. The view of the universe is always an individual one, and none of these countless views can be excluded in principle. So 'religion' must individualize itself in different religions. As a result, anyone who wants to understand 'religion' must understand the different religions. The individual religions may have lost their original lives and be identified with particular formulae, slogans and convictions; in the course of their long history they may have been distorted and deformed; nevertheless, they are authentic and pure individualizations of 'religion' if and to the extent that they make possible an experience of the infinite in the human subject, to the extent that they make a particular view of the infinite their central point, their central view, to which everything in this religion is related.

Thus in his *Speeches* Schleiermacher took great pains not only generally to disperse all the prejudices of his modern contemporaries about religion, but also to make them open to the **positive element in religions**, the positive element ('the given') in all religions. However, here we should note that in Schleiermacher the individual religions by no means all stand on the same level: Schleiermacher takes it for granted that what religion is has individualized itself most in Christianity. **Christianity** is thus **relatively the best of all religions** in human history. Christianity need not fear comparison with other religions.

Here we can only regret that Schleiermacher did not have more precise knowledge of the **non-Christian religions** (apart from Greek religion). Though with his stress on religious experience he had also brought out an important aspect of 'religion', in later years he never had so broad a knowledge of the history of religion as, say, his later Berlin colleague and rival Hegel. Hegel in his lectures on the philosophy of religion treated the religions of humankind in a quite concrete way: as the great historical forms of the absolute Spirit revealing itself in the human spirit – beginning with the nature religions (the deity as a natural force and substance) in Africa, China, India, Persia and Egypt through Judaism, Greek and Roman religion, the religions of spiritual individuality, to Christianity, which, as the highest form of religion, includes in itself all its previous forms.[16]

And yet there is no denying that no theologian was to give such a boost to the future history, phenomenology and psychology of religion; no theologian worked it out intellectually to such a degree as Schleiermacher. If there is so much talk of **experience** in religious studies and theology, this is essentially because of him. If religion is no longer understood as mere private religion but in communal terms, this again is largely due to Schleiermacher. If Christianity can be understood as the best and supreme individualization of religion and so can be included in the comparison of religions, this too finds its legitimation, at least in principle, in Schleiermacher.

7. *The essence of Christianity*

For Schleiermacher, the easiest way of finding access to the spirit of religions is to have one oneself. And this is certainly particularly important for the one who 'approaches the holiest in which the Universe in its highest unity and comprehensiveness is to be perceived':[17] Christianity. Nor can it be disputed, despite all criticism, that Schleiermacher made an essential contribution towards providing a constructive answer to the question of the **essence of Christianity**, which had been posed by the Enlightenment. His view is that the essence of every religion must be seen in a 'basic vision', its 'vision of the infinite'.[18]

So what is the central vision, the original being, the spirit of **Christianity**, which can be defined despite all the historical distortions, despite all disputes over words and despite all the bloody holy wars? Schleiermacher sees the relationship between the finite and the infinite in Christianity as differing from that in Judaism. It is not determined by the idea of retribution, but as a relationship of **corruption and redemption, hostility and mediation**. Christianity is polemic through and through, to the degree that it recognizes the universal corruption and proceeds against the irreligion outside and inside itself. However, Christianity has the aim of pressing through to an ever-greater holiness, purity and relationship to God: everything finite is to be related everywhere and at all times to the infinite.

So Christianity represents religion in a higher potency, even if as a universal religion it should not exclude any other religion and any new religion. It does not have its origin in Judaism, but underivably and inexplicably in the one **emissary** on whom first dawned the basic idea of universal corruption and redemption through higher mediation. What does Schleiermacher admire in Jesus Christ? Not simply the purity of his moral doctrine and the distinctiveness of his character, which combines power and gentleness; these are human features. The 'truly divine' in Christ is the 'glorious clearness to which the great idea he came to exhibit attained in his soul. This idea was, that all that is finite requires a higher mediation to be in accord with the Deity.'[19] What does this 'higher mediation' mean?

All that is finite needs the mediation of something higher for its redemption, and this 'cannot be purely finite. It must belong to both sides, participating in the Divine Essence in the same way and in the same sense in which it participates in human nature.'[20] Therefore he is not the only **mediator** but the **unique** mediator, of whom it is rightly said, 'No one knows the Father but the Son and the one to whom he wills to reveal it': 'This consciousness of the singularity of his religion, of the originality of his view, and of its power to communicate itself and to awake religion, was at once the consciousness of his office as mediator and of his divinity.'[21] It is beyond question that such a formulation of the significance of Jesus Christ even at that time made more than the orthodox frown.

8. A modern faith

From the beginning, Schleiermacher's **christology of consciousness** was sharply attacked: does not the revelation of God here become a mode of human knowing and feeling? Does not belief in Christ become an illuminating universal human possibility? Does Jesus Christ here still remain an objective historical entity which is distinct from pious feeling? Or is christology dissolved into psychology, a universal christological psychology instead of a concrete historical christology? And in all this is not the deity of Christ ultimately left out of account?

After the *Speeches* and *Monologues*, Schleiermacher clarified his christological position in a poetical-theological work, *Christmas Eve*[22], composed as a 'conversation', which appeared in 1805. A year previously Schleiermacher had been rescued from his exile in Stolpe by a call to the University of Halle as *extraordinarius* Professor of Reformed Theology and University Preacher. In his 'conversation', which is set at a family Christmas celebration with music, songs and food, in imitation of Plato's 'Dialogues', various conversation-partners, all of whom he presents sympathetically with inner understanding, show how differently they understand the experience of Christmas and the person of Christ. Even now there is discussion as to which conversation-partner Schleiermacher identifies himself with, if he identifies himself with any of them. So we shall have to wait for Schleiermacher's 'Dogmatics' to get a clear answer to the question of his christology.

However, in the following years there was not much time to clarify his christology. In 1806 Napoleon inflicted a lightning defeat on the Prussians at Jena, also occupied Halle and closed the university. Schleiermacher, originally enthused by the French Revolution, changed under the pressure of events from being a Romantic cosmopolitan to being a **Christian Prussian patriot**; now he worked with the leaders of Prussian reform (above all with Freiherr vom Stein on a new constitution for the Prussian church), went off on secret missions, recruited volunteers, and in all this hoped for a fundamental change in political conditions under the leadership of Prussia – but in vain, as was soon to prove. However, the combination of Christianity and patriotism which he expressed even in sermons was not to benefit German Protestantism.

When Halle was attached to the kingdom of Westphalia which was founded by Napoleon, in 1807 Schleiermacher moved to **Berlin**, where he first gave private lectures on history and philosophy for a pittance, continued his lectures for educated people, went on working for the Patriotic Party, was active as a journalist, and took part in the discussions on the refounding of the University of Berlin (the model for German university reform in the nine-teenth century): in his view, in its constitution it should be marked by autonomy, freedom of spirit and independence from the state.[23] Then in quick succession followed the **honorary appointments** which mark out the framework of his Berlin activity: in 1809 preacher at Trinity Church and marriage; 1810 professor at the university; 1811 a member of the Prussian Academy of Sciences. Several times in the next years he was dean of the theological faculty: at that time he wrote his *Brief Outline of Theological Study in the Form of Introductory Lectures* (1811).[24] From 1810 to 1814 he worked as a member of the Education Commission in the Ministry of the Interior on the reform of Prussian schools. But in the restoration he was suspected by the reactionaries as being a revolutionary, and in 1814 he was dismissed because he argued for a constitutional state.

Schleiermacher's lectures in Halle and Berlin had now been sufficient preparation for him to write his theological *magnum opus*, which was to become the **most significant Dogmatics of modern times.** However, he deliberately avoided the word 'dogmatics', and instead of this chose the title *The Christian Faith* – but now with the significant addition 'described consecutively in accordance with the Principles of the Protestant Church'.[25] It is a systematic theology with an artistic structure, which for its ingenious uniqueness and otherness can certainly be set alongside the *Summa* of Thomas Aquinas and Calvin's *Institutes*. It sought to be believing and pious, critical and rational, all at once – in its own way.

Schleiermacher's modern doctrine of faith thus differs both from mediaeval *Summas* and from any orthodox Reformation dogmatics which thinks of faith primarily as holding particular objective facts of revelation or truths of faith to be true.

By contrast, Schleiermacher's work:
– **has a strictly historical construction:** for it, dogmatic theology – and this is said against both biblicism and rationalism – is not the science of an (allegedly) timeless, unchanged Christian doctrine, but is 'the science which systematizes the doctrine prevalent in a Christian church at any one time' (§19);
– **has an ecumenical form:** the reference to a 'church' does not of course mean the authority of a magisterium but the confessional

writings of the churches and their prime document, Holy Scripture. Here Schleiermacher did not think that the controversies between Lutheran and Reformed doctrine (unlike the opposition between Protestantism and Catholicism) split the church; Schleiermacher argued more than anyone else for the Lutheran-Reformed Union, introduced in Prussia at the Feast of the Reformation in 1817 with joint eucharistic celebrations; he understood his *Christian Faith* as a dogmatics of union;

– **is related to experience**: as was his wont, Schleiermacher begins from religious experience, the disposition or consciousness of Christians, the piety of the church community, in short from pious human consciousness (which, however, is collective and communal). The dogmatic statements in scripture and tradition certainly cannot be proved, but Schleiermacher can rightly claim to stand in the Christian tradition. For he explicitly does theology from the community of faith, from the church; not, though, to prove its faith but to make its innermost essence understandable in a critical and constructive way. So both the sayings of Anselm on the title page of his *The Christian Faith* are not just decoration from the tradition but express a consciousness of the tradition: 'I do not attempt to know in order to believe, but I believe in order to know. For anyone who does not believe will not experience, and anyone who does not experience will not know.'[26]

But what is the **essence of Christianity** according to Schleiermacher's *The Christian Faith*? The famous definition runs: 'Christianity is a monotheistic faith, belonging to the teleological type of religion, and is essentially distinguished from other such faiths by the fact that in it everything is related to the redemption accomplished by Jesus of Nazareth' (§11).

If we are to understand this definition of essence, which while simple is not all that easy to understand, we must remember four things:

– In the three stages of religious development presupposed by Schleiermacher, fetishism – polytheism – **monotheism** (universally advocated in the Enlightenment) – Christianity stands at the uppermost level, not only as an 'aesthetic' religion (a religion of nature or destiny), but as a religion which corresponds to human nature in a 'teleological' way – i.e. is determined by a goal and thus is an ethical, active religion.

– The 'distinctive' feature of Christianity, which sets it apart from all other religions, does not lie in its natural rational character but in its **redemptive character**: for everything is governed by the basic opposition of sin and grace and precisely in this way related to the 'mediator' Jesus of Nazareth.

– Its **christocentricity** is emphasized by the prominent position of christology already in the 'Introduction': in Schleiermacher, christological statements stand at the point where in orthodox dogmatics there was a discussion of Holy Scripture. The central position of the person of Jesus Christ in Christianity is indispensable for Schleiermacher!

The fundamental methodological starting-point in the consciousness of faith is maintained: Schleiermacher does not begin from the objective story of Jesus of Nazareth, but from our pious Christian '**consciousness**', the consciousness of the church community, of redemption through the person of Jesus Christ.

That brings us back to the question which we had to raise in connection with *Christmas Eve*: is the pious consciousness of the person of Jesus Christ related to a **particular**, concrete reality which thus is defined and definable, or is this particular figure included in a **universal** essence and meaning of history, and thus levelled down?

9. Christ – truly human

One difficulty about Schleiermacher's consciousness-christology was that the pious consciousness always only circles around itself, that it does not have any real object. This difficulty seems to me to be answered in *The Christian Faith*: Schleiermacher's christology is without doubt not just a postulate of the pious consciousness, is not the complex imagination of subjective faith. For we cannot overlook the fact that:

Christian consciousness, Christianity generally, is inconceivable without the historical figure of Jesus of Nazareth as its **historical origin**.

So at the centre of Christianity stands not a general notion or a moral doctrine, but a historical figure and his redemptive effect on human beings and history after him. The christocentricity of

The Christian Faith (and the picture of Christ in Schleiermacher's sermons) is thus not the result of Schleiermacher's speculation, but a consequence of the history of Jesus Christ himself and what followed from it.

In Schleiermacher the historical figure does not remain an abstract 'saving event'; rather his **history** can be **narrated**. Moreover it is no coincidence that Schleiermacher wrote a *Life of Jesus*, which depicts Jesus of Nazareth with his unshakeable consciousness of God and his concern for suffering human beings. Certainly it is idealistic, all too orientated on the Gospel of John and the Greek ideal of 'noble simplicity and silent greatness', but nevertheless it is in no way simply in conformity with the ideals of the bourgeois society of Schleiermacher's time.[27] At the same time, by taking up the criticism of the Enlightenment, but applying it in accordance with religious and not purely rational criteria, in his *The Christian Faith* Schleiermacher carried out a large-scale **demythologizing**: not only of the Old Testament narratives of an original existence of the first human couple in paradise, a primal fall and original sin, angels and devils, miracles and prophecies, but also a demythologizing of the New Testament narratives of Jesus' virgin birth, nature miracles, resurrection, ascension, and the prophecy of his return.

So there is no doubt that Schleiermacher holds firm to the **vere homo**, the 'truly man', of the classical christological confession of the Council of Chalcedon (451). But what about the **vere Deus**, the truly God, who is said to be there in Jesus?

10. *Christ – also truly God?*

Schleiermacher, too, did not want to go back to heretical solutions in christology. Moreover for his conception he distinguished his approach *a priori*: not only from **docetism** (towards which **supernaturalism** was now tending) on the right, which can see only a phantom existence in Jesus' human nature, but also from Nazoraeism (Ebionitism, to which **rationalism** now came close) which reduces the existence of the redeemer to the level of ordinary humanity.[28] Particularly in christology, Schleiermacher is a

'Herrnhuter of a higher order' when he attempts to transcend these oppositions.

It was a difficult task – why? Because the classical christological formula 'Jesus Christ is one (divine) person in two natures (one divine and one human)' had come under sharp criticism above all from the 'neologians' in the process of the Enlightenment. Jesus of Nazareth now appeared to many people as nothing but an ordinary man, as a more or less revolutionary Jewish improver of doctrine and the law, who to others could seem a teacher and model of moral and religious perfection. But that was too little for Schleiermacher; for him it was a quite 'meagre' 'empirical' view of redemption! And the alternative?

Was one, like the supernaturalists, to put forward what in fact was a 'magical' conception of redemption in which the punishment for human sin was as it were magicked away by the miraculous act of a satisfaction and a sacrifice of the Son of God, and Jesus was understood simply as the heavenly high priest mediating grace? There could be no question of that either. But what then? How was redemption to be interpreted meaningfully through Christ? And then above all: how was the relationship of Jesus of Nazareth to God to be described? In Schleiermacher's view the whole of Christianity stands and falls with the answer to this question.

Faithful to his starting point, here too Schleiermacher begins with the pious Christian consciousness – a 'mystical' view only in an inauthentic sense. What takes place there? Answer: in their consciousnesses, Christians can experience:
– that they are utterly dependent on the world-historical impulse which Jesus produced: Jesus is both the historical starting point and the abiding source of a new relationship with God;
– that the power of Jesus (which influences all movements of spirit, will and disposition) mediates consciousness of God in a redemptive and reconciling way;
– that in this way a new kind of personal life, indeed historical 'total life', has entered history, which is not in the grip of the consciousness of sin but – under the emanation of Christ's consciousness of God – produces a consciousness of grace.

Despite all the demythologizing, the **difference** between Schleiermacher's christology and **the Jesuology of the Enlightened**

rationalists is clear. According to Schleiermacher, it follows from an analysis of the pious Christian consciousness,

– that Christ is the active one and human beings are recipients: it is Christ who overcomes the power of sin through his grace;

– that Christ makes possible a living community with human beings and a new higher life in humankind;

– that what is decisive for this is not individual features (which are possibly dubious), but the overall impact of his ongoing personality;

– that this historical personality bears in itself a primal perfection, so that it is not only a model which human beings are to imitate but a **primal image of the consciousness of God**, which grasps and forms human beings.

So who was this Jesus Christ in his uttermost depths? The old Herrnhuter struggled passionately for the answer to this question. For a long time he had worked on new answers to old questions which were deeply religious and at the same time clear and simple. Now -- in *The Christian Faith* – he can reply: Christ is for all human beings **the same**! To what extent? 'In virtue of the identity of human nature.' Christ is **different from all human beings**! To what extent? 'By the constant potency of his God-consciousness, which was a veritable existence of God in him.'[29]

A **veritable existence of God** in Christ? Schleiermacher leaves no doubt: whereas other people have only a general religious disposition and an 'imperfect and obscure' God-consciousness, Jesus's God-consciousness was 'absolutely clear and determined each moment, to the exclusion of all else'.[30] This can be regarded 'as a continual living presence, and withal a real existence of God in him', in which at the same time his 'utter sinlessness' is given – and, as a presupposition of this, his innocence from the beginning.[31] That means that in Christ 'the being of God' is there unbroken 'as the innermost fundamental power within him from which every activity emanates and which holds every element together'[32] (to use an illustration: just as the intelligence as the basic force in human beings orders and holds together all other forces). The eternal infinite is present in Jesus' consciousness with its unconditioned power and force without annihilating it; rather, it controls this consciousness and shapes the whole of Jesus' life so that he becomes an instrument, model and primal image. And this is decisive, for without a divine dignity in the redeemer there can be no redemption, and vice versa. So the new communion of life with Christ, the beginning of new life and the renewal of the disposition which is constantly necessary, is made possible – a process which takes part utterly in grace: that is the particular concern of Schleiermacher the theologian and above all the preacher.

So has the christological question been answered in Schleiermacher? *Vere Deus?* Truly God? Yes, Jesus is formed by the divine primal ground in a way unlike any other. Certainly, God is present everywhere in the finite as **the** one who is active, but in Christ the God-consciousness is the principle which shapes the personality. His God-consciousness must be understood as a pure and authentic revelation, indeed as the true and authentic indwelling of the being of Christ in the finite. This is no supernatural miracle, and yet it is something quite unique and miraculous in this world dominated by sin. Here the believer does not postulate God's being, but becomes one with the divine which has a living influence on history with Christ – Schleiermacher's great concern since the *Speeches*.

Was all this 'orthodox'? Schleiermacher specifically states that with this interpretation of the divinity of Christ he is departing from 'that language of the Schools as used hitherto'[33] (the doctrine of the two natures). He was all the more aware of doing this since, having given lectures on almost all the writings of the New Testament, he believed that his view could be grounded in the Bible; it was grounded 'in the Pauline God was in Christ and on the Johannine the Word became flesh'[34]! So Schleiermacher understood his own Christianity 'not as an imitation of an ethical ideal, which was the approach of the Enlightenment theology of the time, nor as an obedient acceptance of incomprehensible dogmatic doctrinal statements, but as a completely inward determination by the historical Jesus and the God present in him'.[35]

But is Schleiermacher on the other hand a 'pluralist'? Schleiermacher would turn against any pluralist theology of religion which simply establishes different 'saviours' in the world and in so doing thinks that it has solved the problem of the religions' claim to truth. He was convinced that Christ 'exclusively' has the 'being of God', so that only in connection with him can it be said

that 'God has become man'.[36] 'The Word became flesh' is for
Schleiermacher 'the basic text of the whole of dogmatics'.[37]

11. *Critical questions*

Of course from a present-day perspective dogmatic theologians
can ask whether in his christological statements Schleiermacher
reached the 'heights' of the christological councils of the fourth
and fifth centuries. But Schleiermacher would reply that he
regarded these conciliar christological statements – in the perspective of the New Testament and the present – as superseded, as
'transcended'. Is not Jesus of Nazareth an authentic human
person? Instead of being from eternity a second divine person
who entered into human existence? Instead of a truly human
person with a human will, are there then to be two natures and
two wills and contradictory theories about the divine and the
human in Christ? And on top of that, three persons in one divine
nature? Is all this biblical, original? Is it all comprehensible and
acceptable to modern men and women? There was good reason
why in his *The Christian Faith* Schleiermacher put forward
the programmatic thesis: 'The ecclesiastical formulae about the
person of Christ need an ongoing critical treatment.'[38] Moreover
in an unparalleled piece of theological thinking he developed a
modern christology not only beyond the two-natures doctrine of
the early church, which was obviously time-conditioned, but also
beyond the meagre Jesuology of the Enlightenment.

Of course Schleiermacher's doctrine also needs 'ongoing critical
treatment' – as he himself would certainly agree. And this 'ongoing
critical treatment' – soon two centuries will have passed since
Schleiermacher's epoch-making achievement – will have much to
criticize. For me, the most important questions to ask, especially
about the christology which was also central for Schleiermacher,
are these:

First, in Schleiermacher's consciousness theology there is certainly room for telling the story of Jesus; after all, he himself gave
lectures on the life of Jesus. To this degree he is open to a 'narrative
theology'[39] (of the kind which today is simply called for in
slogans). Nevertheless, there is a danger in Schleiermacher's

approach and the subordinate role of the Bible in his *The Christian Faith* that our own experience of redemption will control the telling of the story of Jesus all too much, instead of constantly not only being newly inspired by the story of Jesus, but also being radically criticized and corrected by it. After all, the Christ of Christians is the abiding criterion and constant corrective of Christianity.

Secondly, the modern starting point of the human subject, from the **consciousness of the community of faith,** is to be affirmed in principle, even if one can find fault with Schleiermacher's definition of religion ('the feeling of absolute dependence') as an overextension of the results of his analysis of the consciousness. But there is a danger which needs to be taken more seriously that as a result of Schleiermacher's generally philosophical and theological remarks about religion and the definition of the essence of Christianity in his 'Introduction' a prior decision has been taken as to 'what content is left for christology if it is to be different from anthropology'.[40]

Thirdly, Schleiermacher's idealistic interpretation of reality and harmonious basic mood hardly take the **real experiences of negativity** seriously with the necessary urgency: the alienation and fragmentation of human beings; suffering, guilt and failure; and the contradictions and disasters of history – all this seems to be taken up and transcended in the unity of the divine plan of redemption. Schleiermacher also interpreted Jesus' unshakeable consciousness of God idealistically in the light of the Gospel of John, and thus largely got round and interpreted away the darkness of God and the tribulation, despite all the divine inwardness.

Fourthly, in his great systematic work Schleiermacher certainly described the prophetic, high-priestly and royal office of Jesus. But in so doing he did not give a central place to the **scandal of the cross** and the **hope of resurrection** which are fundamental to the New Testament writings. So he remained incapable of taking Jesus' abandonment by human beings and God really seriously (not to mention his flirting with the hypothesis of a pseudo-death); in contrast to the synoptic evangelists, he sees death and resurrection as a seamless transition of an ideal figure of cheerfulness and pure love from the physical to the spiritual present, which makes possible direct access to him for all those who live after him.[41]

All these are questions which have finally pushed this modern theology into the twilight: a theology of modernity which in some respects has delivered itself over too much to the spirit of modernity.

12. Nevertheless: the paradigmatic theologian of modernity

Schleiermacher died in the sixty-sixth year of his life, of inflammation of the lungs, on 12 February 1834, after celebrating the eucharist with his family. To the end he was a controversial man in his church. Just a decade earlier he had been cited three times to Berlin police headquarters for his support for a constitutional state, greater freedoms for the people, and for the students; there was a threat that he would be removed from his professorship. His very different opponents from the revival movement, conservative confessionalism and Hegel's camp to some degree pursued him even after death with their sharp repudiation.

However, his friends and supporters secured triumphs for him which he was still able to enjoy in the last years of his life – something not granted to everyone. Shortly before his death Schleiermacher was awarded an order and other honours, and in his last years he drew greater audiences than any other theologian or churchman, whether at lectures or sermons (ten volumes of sermons in the first complete edition of his work). His fearless attacks on any despotism and his concern to arouse a social concern among the upper classes (for example, shortening working hours) made him popular far beyond educated circles.

Given this influence, it is no surprise that **Schleiermacher's funeral** in February 1834 at Trinity Church in Berlin became an impressive demonstration of solidarity in which people of all classes and professions gathered together. If we follow the account of the historian Leopold von Ranke, between 20,000 and 30,000 people must have followed the coffin: 'I recall what an impression it made on me when we buried Schleiermacher, and there was weeping all down the long street from every window and from every door', an impression which is confirmed by other participants: 'Perhaps Berlin never saw such a funeral. Everyone followed the coffin and the procession wound endlessly through the streets... Generals and former ministers, the committees of the ministry and the clergy, both Catholic and Protestant, teachers from the university and the schools, students and pupils, old and young – one might even say friend and foe. It was a recognition of a spirit such as is seldom seen.'[42]

History has meanwhile often confirmed the verdict of such contemporaries. This Berlin professor of theology and academic philosopher; this interpreter of Plato and proclaimer of the gospel; this exegete, dogmatic theologian, ethicist; this critic and theologian of culture with a universal education, a passionate quest for truth and the ability to achieve public enthusiasm, was indeed a 'rare', outstanding spirit. He was an existential thinker with an amazing capacity for work, who has left behind him unmistakeable, deep traces wherever he worked. He was a many-sided scholar of the utmost precision and at the same time a brilliant writer and preacher for the cultural elite, who was convinced that the Reformation was continuing there and then. In the nineteenth century his *The Christian Faith* occupied and influenced all theologians, including the theology of his opponents.

But this Friedrich Schleiermacher, endowed with a sharp, ironic and witty spirit, continued to be remembered by his contemporaries not only for his advocacy of the truth in truthfulness but also for his concern to be a convincing Christian. Faithful to his ideal of an educated individuality, to the end of his life he was not only involved in university and academy but also in church and state, in the pulpit as well as at the lecture desk and above all in the study. He was an ardent patriot who fought for freedom, justice and reform, and at the same time an outstanding church teacher who followed his inner mission, and who also later always argued for the greatest possible independence of the church from the state (not a state church but a people's church with a synodical constitution), who against the king's will passionately attacked his liturgical reform from above and intrepidly made a stand against the king's right in internal matters and against an order of service which he had worked out personally. All in all this was a paradigmatic theologian, freely human and bound to God in a Christian way, **the** paradigmatic theologian of modernity.

As is well known, the most credible praise often comes from opponents. So let us leave the last word on Schleiermacher (like the first) to Karl Barth, who almost precisely a century after Schleiermacher's death, in the first volume of his *Church Dogmatics*, was to present a great theological alternative to Schleiermacher in the twentieth century: 'We have to do with a hero, the like of which is but seldom bestowed upon theology. Anyone who has never noticed anything of the splendour this figure radiated and still does – I am almost tempted to say, who has never succumbed to it – may honourably pass on to other and possibly better ways, but let him never raise so much as a finger against Schleiermacher. Anyone who has never loved here, and is not in a position to love again and again, may not hate here either.'[43]

Karl Barth
Theology in the Transition to Postmodernity

Chronology (according to E.Busch)

1886   10 May: born in Basel; spends his youth in Bern.

1904-08   Studies theology in Bern, Berlin, Tübingen and Marburg.

1909-11   Assistant pastor in Geneva.

1911-21   Pastor in the industrial town of Safenwil (Aargau, Switzerland).

1913   Marries Nelly von Hoffmann.

1919   *Romans* (second completely revised edition 1922).

1921   Called to be honorary Professor of Reformed Theology in Göttingen.

1925-29   Professor of Dogmatics and New Testament Theology in Münster.

1930   Begins as Professor of Systematic Theology in Bonn.

1932   Begins his (incompleted) *magnum opus Church Dogmatics*.

1934   First Confessing Synod of Barmen.

1934   '*No!*' to Emil Brunner.

1934   Suspended by the Nazis and forced to retire in June 1935; later ban on all Barth's works in Germany.

1935   Begins as Professor of Dogmatics in Basel.

1948   Speech to the World Council of Churches in Amsterdam.

1959   Last completed volume of the *Church Dogmatics* (IV/3).

1961-62   Last series of lectures, 'Introduction to Evangelical Theology'.

1962   First visit to the USA.

1966   Last visit to Rome.

1967   Breaks off the *Church Dogmatics* with the fragmentary volume IV/4.

1968   Death and burial in Basel.

1. A controversial Protestant in the World Council of Churches

The year is 1948. Karl Barth is sixty-two years old and – as a result of the eventful world history of the first half of the century – already has an eventful life behind him. He studied theology in Bern, Berlin, Tübingen and Marburg between 1904 and 1909; from 1909 to 1921 he was first assistant minister in Geneva and then pastor in Safenwil, in Switzerland; from 1921 to 1935 he was professor of theology in Göttingen, Münster and Bonn; all this after a single book (*The Epistle to the Romans*) which appeared in 1919 had made this Swiss provincial pastor a theologian famous throughout the whole German-speaking world. In 1935 he was driven from his Bonn chair by the Nazis, and since then had taught theology at the University of Basel, as a passionate 'Swiss voice' taking part to the end in the church struggle of German Protestantism against the barbarity of Hitlerism.

But now, after the war, in 1948, Karl Barth had been invited by his Reformed friend and fellow Reformed believer, the great Dutchman Willem Visser't Hooft, the powerful and wise spiritual director of the ecumenical movement, to take part in the **First Assembly of the World Council of Churches in Amsterdam**, which marked the foundation of the World Council of Churches (with Visser't Hooft as General Secretary). Previously Barth had taken hardly any part in the ecumenical movement. But here in Amsterdam, in conversation above all with Michael Ramsey, later to become Archbishop of Canterbury, and the Orthodox theologian Georges Florovsky, he learned that in academic theology there must also be something like an 'ecumenics', alongside 'dogmatics' and 'symbolics'. This makes it possible for an examination by competent theologians of the different churches of 'disagreements within the agreement' and 'agreements within the disagreement', so as to come a step nearer to union.

But Rome, the Pope, had refused to take part in this ecumenical gathering, as too had the Russian Orthodox Church. And what was Barth's reaction? It was typical of him. In Protestant freedom and Helvetic warmth, in his great speech he simply proposed that people should get on with the agenda. One has to hear his original words to understand how he stood, spoke and argued: 'May this freedom (for the one Lord Jesus Christ **despite** these separated eucharists) also mean that the sighing or the indignation over the refusals that we have received from the churches of **Rome** or **Moscow** occupy as little space as possible in the discussions of our first section! Why should we not simply recognize the mighty hand of God over us in these refusals! Perhaps God is giving us a sign through which he wants to take any boasting from us, as if here we could build a tower the summit of which reached to heaven. Perhaps God is showing us here how miserable our light was hitherto, as it evidently cannot even shine out into these other, yet allegedly also Christian, spheres. So perhaps God is preserving us from conversation partners with whom we could not even be a community in an imperfect way here, because – albeit for different reasons – they did not want to take part in the movement of all the churches to Jesus Christ without which Christians of different origin and nature cannot speak to one another or hear one another, let alone come together. And perhaps God is thus putting us in a very **good** place, by virtue of the fact that **Rome** and **Moscow** in particular seem to be united in wanting to have nothing to do with us. I suggest that we now praise and thank God specifically for this, that it pleases him to get in the way of our plans so clearly.'[1]

Karl Barth – an anti-Catholic rabble-rouser? That is what it might seem like to a superficial onlooker. But the polemic of published Catholic opinion at that time against an evidently anti-Catholic Barth – after all, this was the heyday of Pius XII, the last pre-conciliar Pope – was now drowned by the Catholic indignation over the revelations in Hochhuth's play *The Representative* (1962), which was to lead to street demonstrations in Basel in front of the Stadttheater.

2. A critic of Roman Catholicism

But Barth's criticism of Roman Catholicism went theologically deeper and much further back in time. In the five important years of his second professorship (after Göttingen) in Münster, 'that nest of Papists and Anabaptists':

– There Catholic dogmatics was present in the person of the Neo-Thomist Franz Diekamp, whom Barth often quoted later;

– There he studied Anselm of Canterbury and Thomas Aquinas intensively;

– There (an innovation) he invited a Catholic theologian to a seminar discussion and to personal conversations. This was the Jesuit Erich Przywara, who in an uncommonly knowledgeable and skilful way had developed a similarity of being, an **analogia entis,** between God and human beings, along the line of Augustine's, Thomas Aquinas's and Scheler's ideas of 'God in us and God over us'.

However, Przywara only confirmed Karl Barth in his conviction that while Catholic theology and the church had preserved more of the substance of Christianity than the 'Neoprotestantism' of Schleiermacher, they were flawed with the same **basic error.** They too seized God's revelation, had taken control of grace, in such a way that God could no longer be God and human beings could no longer be human beings – an issue which for him was the prime concern of 'dialectical theology'. To this extent 'Roman Catholicism' was 'A Question to the Protestant Church', as Barth entitled his controversial theological lecture of 1928,[2] because Catholicism reflected problems which were also recognizable within Protestantism. In sharp confrontation with this, Barth therefore argued for a Protestantism which had strictly to concentrate on its evangelical concern. And this means that world is world, and human beings are human beings, but God is God, and reconciliation is only in Jesus Christ!

But Catholic theology began to take note of Barth. Already in the 1920s and 1930s, first Karl Adam of Tübingen and then Erik Peterson of Bonn, and then after Erich Przywara above all Gottlieb Söhngen began to grapple with the early Barth (*Romans* and the following writings). When around 1940 German voices had to fall silent as a result of the war, French-speaking Catholic theologians could be heard: the Jesuits Louis Malevez, Henri Bouillard and the Dominican Jerôme Hamer (nor should we forget the Dutchman Johannes C. Groot). But most of these works took little note of the Barth of the monumental *Church Dogmatics,*[3] which had only been taking shape since 1940: after the *Prolegomena* (Volumes I.1-2) in 1932 and 1938, Barth's

Doctrine of God (II/1-2) appeared only in 1940/42, then his *Doctrine of Creation* (III/1-4) in the years 1945-1951. The *Doctrine of Reconciliation* (IV/1-4) and the *Doctrine of Redemption* or eschatology were to remain uncompleted. The discussion which he had by correspondence after Amsterdam with the French Jesuit Jean Daniélou – one of the main representatives of the 'nouvelle théologie' in France who was suspected of heresy, later conformed and became a cardinal – proved ultimately unproductive. 'Too much is required of both of us', Barth told him abruptly with reference to Rome's refusal to come to Amsterdam 'for us to be able to take your unconditional claim to superiority seriously and to have longed for your presence!'[4]

3. *Catholic attempts at understanding*

Another theologian, a pupil at the same time of Przywara and Henri de Lubac, who since 1940 had, like Barth, lived in Basel, Hans Urs von Balthasar from Lucern, was the one to write the book which for Catholic theology brought a breakthrough to a **sympathetic understanding of Barth's theology**.[5] Balthasar had left the Jesuit order because he felt called to found a 'lay order' with his spiritual friend Adrienne von Speyr. Looking back from Barth's mature work, Balthasar attempted to distinguish a 'period of dialectic' in the early Barth (*Romans*, 1919, second edition 1922), then a 'move to analogy' (*Christian Dogmatics in Outline*, 1927), which was finally extended by Barth to the full form of analogy (from *Church Dogmatics*, Volume II).

It was Balthasar who drew attention to the **artistic architecture** and intellectual and linguistic force of Barth's theology – comparable only with Schleiermacher and inspired by Schleiermacher: how creation and covenant were dovetailed on a radical christological foundation, how it arrived at a new understanding of human beings as God's partners, a new doctrine of sin and reconciliation. But Balthasar had been fascinated above all by Barth's new interpretation of predestination, which 'sublated' the Augustinian-Calvinistic dualism (part of humankind predestined to bliss, another part to hell) in a Christian universalism almost reminiscent of Origen: the Christ-centre mediates with an all-oneness of redemption. There was a **christocentricity** which was now also to make possible a new definition of the relationship between faith and knowledge, nature and grace, judgment and redemption – for Protestants and Catholics alike. But what does that mean?

In the preface to the first volume of the *Church Dogmatics* of 1932 there is the famous and notorious sentence, without any reference to Przywara: 'I regard the *analogia entis* as the invention of Antichrist, and I believe that because of it it is **impossible** ever to become a Roman Catholic, all other reasons for not doing so being to my mind short-sighted and trivial'.[6] We can understand this polemic against the analogy of being which puts God and human beings on the same level as tantamount to the Antichrist only if we recognize the **two fronts** which it is attacking.

On the right wing, Barth is primarily protesting against that Roman Catholicism which, following scholasticism and the First Vatican Council, put God and human beings on one level and thus established an interplay between human beings and God, nature and grace, reason and faith, philosophy and theology. How pernicious this 'damned Catholic **and**' was emerged for Barth above all from the Catholic mariological dogmas ('Jesus **and** Mary') and the Catholic understanding of scripture **and** tradition, of Christ **and** the infallible Pope. 'In the doctrine and worship of Mary there is disclosed the one heresy of the Roman Catholic Church which explains all the rest,'[7] wrote Barth, and his criticism of the 'Roman Catholic error'[8] which ultimately 'even declares itself identical with God's revelation' could not have been sharper.[9] But all this had to do with what in his eyes was the pernicious way in which **Catholicism put God and human beings on the same level** by its concept being (both 'are'). Barth believed that he had to protest against this in the name of a wholly other God, in the name of God as **God**.

On the left wing Barth was fighting at the same time no less against that **liberal Neoprotestantism** which, following Schleiermacher, had oriented itself completely on pious, religious human beings instead of on God and his revelation. It was no coincidence for Barth that on the basis of a 'natural theology' which levelled out to such a degree both Roman Catholicism and liberal Neoprotestantism had come to an **arrangement** in uncritical assimilation to the **ruling political systems** of their time: first with the Kaiser's empire and its war policy, and then again with National Socialism. Because of this equating of God and man, had not the Protestant 'German Christians' seen National Socialism as something like a new revelation and Adolf Hitler even as a new Luther – binding together Christianity and Germanhood – even a new Christ? Because of this analogy of being between God and human beings, had not even prominent representatives of Neoscholastic Catholic two-storey theology (Karl Adam and Michael Schmaus) found that National Socialism was to be affirmed because it wanted on the natural level what Catholic Christianity was bringing about on the supernatural level: order, unity, discipline, the Leader principle? No, here Barth could see the whole political danger of the 'Christian' natural theology which showed its true face in 1933. A stand had to be made against it because it was politically serious. The Barmen Synod of the 'Confessing Church' – in essence theologically inspired by Barth – is the most visible sign of this.

However, the irony of history is that the most important theological result of von Balthasar's book was that the whole diastasis of the analogy of being or analogy of faith which Barth stressed so strongly was seen as a **false expression of the problem**. Whatever was practised in popular Catholic piety, both Catholic theology and the Catholic church did not want simply to level out the difference between God and humankind, and could not and would not seize hold of revelation, the grace of God. Caught theologically by von Balthasar with difficult distinctions within the concept of nature, Barth finally also had to concede this. When in 1955 as a young man I returned from Rome after seven years there and – like many Catholic theologians moved by these problems – talked about this controversy with Barth in our first conversation, he proved to be a man not only of holy wrath but also winning humour: 'In theology one never knows: does he have me or do I have him?' And in connection with the much-disputed *analogia entis*, for the sake of which alone one cannot become a Catholic, he merely said, 'Now I've buried that!' And in fact after that Barth never used the expression again – though without actually pointing this out. But this has not prevented confessionally inclined Catholic and Protestant theologians who want to see the division between the churches quite personally grounded and secured in the Holy Spirit, Jesus Christ or even in God the Father rather than in pope, church and sacraments, from seeing and cherishing the *analogia entis* as what really divides the churches.

I grant without further ado that without Balthasar's book on Barth my own work on Barth would have been impossible. I learned from Balthasar that the Catholic and the Protestant can be reconciled at the very point where they are most consistently themselves. And above all I learned from him that Karl Barth, precisely because he embodied the most consistent development of Protestant theology, came closest to Catholic theology: in Protestant, evangelical fashion completely focussed on Christ as the centre and precisely in this way reaching out in a universal, catholic way – the possibility of a new **ecumenical theology**.

4. *Ecumenical understanding*

In connection with our portrait of Luther we heard that since the time of the Reformation and the Council of Trent the doctrine of the **justification of the sinner** has been regarded as *articulus stantis et cadentis Ecclesiae*, as the article of faith by which the church stands and falls, and thus as the fundamental obstacle to an understanding between Catholics and Protestants. It would be a considerable achievement towards doing away with the split in the church if it were possible to demonstrate a convergence, indeed a consensus, here.

My book *Justification*[10] sought to show precisely this: that in the doctrine of justification seen as a whole, a fundamental agreement could be recognized between the teaching of Karl Barth and the teaching of the Catholic church, rightly understood, and that in the light of this there was no longer any ground for a schism between Protestants and Catholics. Cunning as he was, Karl Barth cautiously wrote in his letter that went with my book: 'If what you infer from Holy Scripture, the old and new Roman Catholic theology and moreover "Denziger" and indeed the texts of the Council of Trent really is and is confirmed to be the teaching of your church (perhaps confirmed by a consensus over your book), **then**, having twice gone to the church of Santa Maria

Maggiore in Trent to commune with the *genius loci*, I may very well have to hasten there a third time, to make a contrite confession: *patres peccavi*, "Fathers, I have sinned".'[11] And what happened?

My book was not put on the 'Index' of forbidden books by the Roman censors, as some had hoped and some had feared. In 1958 a new Pope was elected and a new development began. Finally, in 1971, on the Mediterranean island of Malta, it proved possible for a study commission of the Lutheran World Federation and the Roman Catholic church to work out, after careful preparations, a joint document. This **Malta Document** states the consensus: 'Today there is a far-reaching consensus on the interpretation of justification. On the question of justification, Catholic theologians also emphasize that no human conditions attach to God's gift of salvation for believers. Lutheran theologians emphasize that the event of justification is not limited to individual forgiveness of sins and do not see it as a declaration of the righteousness of the sinner which remains purely external. As a foundation of Christian freedom over against legal conditions for the reception of salvation, the message of justification must constantly be expressed anew as an important explication of the centre of the gospel.'[12] So here was confirmation from Rome on the issue of the message of justification. However, Karl Barth no longer had occasion to make a pilgrimage to Trent. For three years he had no longer been among the living.

Of course the message of justification 'as a foundation of Christian freedom over against legal conditions for the reception of salvation' has radical consequences: not only for the individual but for the church, which only has meaning as a community of believers that constantly needs to live anew by God's grace, forgiveness and liberation: *ecclesia semper reformanda*!

Barth was making a programmatic statement against liberal and also Kierkegaardian individualism when he replaced the original title *Christian Dogmatics* (the false start of 1927) with **Church Dogmatics**. He was not only attacking any facile use of the word 'Christian' but above all – despite the 'laments accompanying the general course of my development' making it clear that dogmatics cannot be an absolutely 'free' science but must be 'a science bound to the sphere of the church, where alone it is possible and meaningful'.[13] So there are long ecclesiological chapters already in the Prolegomena (on church proclamation, on the hearing and the teaching church) and then in the doctrine of God and election (the election of Israel and the church), and of course above all in the three volumes of the doctrine of reconciliation. All that is said here about the gathering, building up and mission of the church through the power of the spirit of God who raises to faith, enlivens in love and calls to hope; all that is said here about the *ecclesia una sancta, catholica et apsotolica*, is the strongest development of Protestantism and the closest approach to the Catholic: a catholic and thus truly ecumenical ecclesiology concentrated on the gospel.

Ecumenical understanding on both sides became difficult only when there was talk about the **organizational structure** and **practical policy of the church**: the significance of the sacraments and above all of the theological understanding of church ministry, the ministries of priest and bishop and (of course above all) the papacy.[14] Karl Barth was fascinated by the tremendous ecumenical possibilities of the papacy, but put off by its concrete form and praxis: 'I cannot hear the voice of the Good Shepherd from this chair of Peter', he used to say. That was under Pius XII.

5. The Second Vatican Council

The pontificate of John XXIII, which lasted only five years but was epoch-making, above all the Second Vatican Council and the **double paradigm shift** that it introduced – an integration of both the Reformation and the modern paradigms into the Catholic church and theology – also moved Karl Barth deeply. It had been Barth who had challenged me, as a Catholic theologian brought up a Roman, to speak publicly about something as primally Protestant and therefore at the time suspect to Catholic ears as *Ecclesia semper reformanda*: at a lecture to 'his' university in 1959 – literally six days before the utterly surprising announcement of the Council.

Subsequently Barth took a lively interest in my programme of conciliar reform then sketched out in my book *The Council and Reunion*[15]; indeed he had even proposed its precise title. The

Council then took up what was allegedly so Protestant a statement of the need for constant reform (*Ecclesia semper in reformatione*) into its Constitution on the Church and also put it into practice: by taking up numerous concerns on the one hand of the Reformers (the revaluation of the Bible and preaching, and of the laity to the point of giving them a say in the liturgy), and on the other of modernity (freedom of faith, conscience and religion, toleration and ecumenical understanding, a new attitude to the Jews, the world religions and the secular world generally). Karl Barth began to be amazed at the movement of the Spirit which had come about at that time in the Catholic church, which seemed to contrast with a widespread fossilization in Protestantism. Moved profoundly, not simply by the human side but also by the deeply evangelical side of the council Pope, now he did not hesitate to say of John XXIII: 'Now I can hear the voice of the Good Shepherd.'

However, for all that he did not become a Catholic. In any case he had not thought of conversion to another church; his concern was the constantly new conversion of all churches to Jesus Christ. But the new situation in 1966 at any rate attracted him to make a **journey to Rome.** He called it a *peregrinatio ad limina Apostolorum*, a pilgrimage to the tomb of the apostles – ill-health had prevented him from accepting an invitation to the Council which I had conveyed to him. In Rome – after conversations with various Roman authorities – he found his generally positive impression of conciliar Catholicism confirmed: 'The church and theology there has moved to a degree that I could never have envisaged.'[16] However, Roncalli's successor, Paul VI, gave him the impression of being a man worthy of respect, indeed lovable, but somehow to be pitied; he told Barth in an almost touching way how difficult it was to bear and use the keys of Peter which had been entrusted to him by the Lord. That was still before Paul VI's fateful encyclical against 'artificial' birth control; but the aporias that would follow the council – the consequences of ongoing curial obstruction and the compromises made at the council – were already emerging.

We do not know what Karl Barth thought of the next two popes who – as an expression of both compromise and aporia – both combined the names of their predecessors, John and Paul, two such different men. A few months after his visit to Rome he finally broke off work on the *Church Dogmatics* (he had already exhausted his creative powers long before his death); all he wanted to see published was a lecture fragment of the fourth part of the doctrine of reconciliation, on ethics. It was to be his last major publication. The great thirteen-volume work remained an **unfinished symphony** like the *Summa* of Thomas Aquinas, the *magnum opus* which, as we heard, Thomas had enigmatically stopped working on some months before his death. The faith of the fathers always had to be listened to in the church, wrote Karl Barth in his last incomplete draft lecture: 'God is not a God of the dead but of the living.' 'In him they all live, from the apostles to the fathers of the day before yesterday and yesterday.' These were the last sentences that Barth, now eighty-two, was to write. The next morning, on 10 December 1968, his wife found that he had peacefully gone to sleep for ever.

In his last years Karl Barth often felt 'out of date', and then he would tell me: 'Now I would like to be as young as you again – then I would go back to the barricades.' Karl Barth again on the barricades? On the barricades of the 1970s, the 1980s? I have often asked myself in the last two decades where and how he would have gone on the barricades, what he would have done had he not been a Barthian but really a truly rejuvenated Karl Barth. And I would like to reflect a little on this question, now that I have spoken about Karl Barth's shift from confrontation with Catholic theology, through attempts to come to terms with it, finally to an ecumenical understanding with it. So we move from then to now; not, however, in arbitary hypothetical speculations, 'what ifs', but looking at the substance of Barth's theology and constructively taking it further. What now?

6. *Why the paradigm of modernity has to be criticized*

The first question is the question which nags at any theologian: where and how is Karl Barth to be put in the history of theology? Is he monumentally 'neo-orthodox?' (and hardly read as a whole), which is how he is classified almost all over America and often also in the Bultmann school – and written off? Or is he the unsurpassable theological innovator of the century, which is how he is glorified in Germany far beyond the Barth school – and blocked?

My comprehensive Catholic thesis against both antagonists who disqualify Barth and followers who glorify him is: Karl Barth is the **initiator** of what I would now call a **'modern' paradigm of theology.** By that I mean two things:

– I would like to make it clear to those who despise Barth that Karl Barth is really an initiator, indeed the **main initiator,** of a 'postmodern' paradigm of theology which was already dawning at that time.

– But, for uncritical admirers of Barth: Karl Barth is an initiator **and not a perfecter** of such a paradigm.

It is easy to demonstrate three things from Barth's writing and his career as it has been described in an exemplary way by Eberhard Busch 'from his letters and autobiographical texts'.[17]

First, Barth was **a decisive follower of modern theology:** originally from the middle-class world (from poetry and music through beer and student association life to the military), at a very early stage he was enthused by Schiller's idealism and Richard Wagner's Tannhäuser 'proclamation'. Soon Kant and of course Schleiermacher were the leading lights of the thought of the theological student who already in his first semester was familiarized with the historical-critical method. So he became the pupil of the great liberal masters: first Harnack (in Berlin) and then, even more importantly, Wilhelm Herrmann (in Marburg), who could combine Kant and Schleiermacher with a marked christocentricity. As editorial assistant to Martin Rade at the liberal *Christliche Welt* Barth had dealings with the intellectual products of all the eminent liberals, from Bousset and Gunkel to Troeltsch and Wernle.

But **then** Barth turned into the **sharpest critic of the modern Enlightenment paradigm** which, after a phase of strict Lutheran and Calvinist orthodoxy, had already developed in the seventeenth century, established itself in the eighteenth century and finally in the nineteenth century taken on its classical form with Schleiermacher, achieving a leading position with the liberal theology that followed him: a paradigm, as we saw, wholly orientated on humanity. Barth's ten-year experience as **pastor of Safenwil,** an increasingly industrialized Swiss farming community with all the social problems of that time, made him doubt already before the First World War the bourgeois optimism over progress and the assimilationist tendencies of culture Protestantism, and indeed made him a Socialist committed to the cause of the workers. He saw that in the oppressive crisis over preaching – empty pews, ineffective confirmation instruction – all the modern critical knowledge of the Bible was no help to him. For preaching, instruction and pastoral care he needed quite a different theological foundation, which was not primarily concerned with human beings but with God. Despite all his respect for modern liberalism, Barth sensed that historical relativism, combined with religious individualism, had increasingly evacuated Christianity.

It was the outbreak of the **First World War** in 1914 which for Barth proved a radical crisis for the modern paradigm.

– On the one hand the modern tendency of liberal theology towards assimilation had been shown up completely when ninety-three German intellectuals including almost all Barth's famous theological teachers, foremost among them Harnack and Herrmann, identified themselves in a public manifesto with the war policy of Wilhelm II and the attack on neutral Belgium.

– But on the other hand European Socialism, too, had failed in the face of the war ideology and had supported the war almost everywhere.

So Karl Barth's personal theology developed into a 'theology of crisis', which was given a highly dramatic background in 1918 with the final downfall of the German empire along with the control of the churches by local princes, with the United States in Europe, the Russian Revolution and the social unrest in Germany. Was this the collapse of an epoch – modernity with its belief in reason, science and progress – but also the birth of a new, postmodern epoch?[18]

7. Initiator of the postmodern paradigm of theology

In fact Barth became the **principal initiator of a postmodern paradigm of theology**. In the complex crisis which threatened everything it had become abundantly clear to him that Christianity cannot in any way be reduced to a historical phenomenon of its time which is to be investigated critically, and a present-day inner experience of a predominantly moral kind. In the face of the epoch-making collapse of bourgeois society and culture, its normative institutions, traditions and authorities, after the War Barth more than anyone else mobilized the critical power of faith and – in connection with *The Epistle to the Romans*[19] – along with his friends Emil Brunner, Eduard Thurneysen, Friedrich Gogarten and Rudolf Bultmann 'between the times' (the name of a new journal which they founded) called programmatically for a move to a '**theology of the Word**' (often called 'dialectical theology').

And that means that there was no going back behind Schleiermacher, but **progress forward beyond Schleiermacher**:
– away from modern anthropocentricity to a new theocentricity;
– away from a historical-psychological self-interpretation of the 'religious' person and theology in terms of history and the humanities to God's own Word attested in the Bible, to revelation, the kingdom and action of God;
– away from religious talk about the concept of God to the proclamation of the Word of God;
– away from religion and religious feeling to Christian faith;
– away from human religious needs (the modern man-God) to God who is the 'wholly other', manifest only in Jesus Christ (the 'God-man' understood biblically).

In the general political, economic, cultural, spiritual revolution after the catastrophe of the First World War the theology of Karl Barth – with Barth himself as a model of 'theological existence' – powerfully introduced the paradigm shift from the modern liberal to what we can now call in retrospect a postmodern paradigm, though at that time only pale outlines of it could be recognized. To this degree it is Barth – and not Ritschl, Harnack, Herrmann or Troeltsch – who is called the 'church father of the twentieth century'.

In the face of the crisis of the modern paradigm, Karl Barth called for and encouraged a **fundamentally new orientation of theology**. Earlier than others – in a theological critique of ideology – his theology saw through the despotic and destructive forces of modern rationality, relativized the claim of Enlightenment reason to absoluteness, and showed Enlightenment reason where it was deceiving itself; in short, earlier than others, his theology recognized the 'dialectic of the Enlightenment' and worked for an Enlightenment beyond the Enlightenment. Barth countered the liberal diffusion of Christianity into the universally human, the historical, with a new christological concentration on salvation in Christ. Over against the assimilation to social and bourgeois trends in culture Protestantism he emphasized the political and social provocation of the gospel. It remains amazing how already at that time Barth spoke out resolutely against any nationalism and imperialism, the corrupt heritage of modernity, taken over and carried to absurd extremes by totalitarian systems in our century. It is amazing how already at that time he committed himself forcefully to a policy of world peace and social justice and to a critical prophetic attitude of the church against all political systems.

Barth's fundamentally new theological involvement showed its political power in 1934 at the **Synod of Barmen,** against the Nazi pseudo-religion: in the clear confession, conceived by Barth, of Jesus Christ as the 'one Word of God' alongside which the church cannot recognize 'yet other happenings and powers, images and truths as divine revelation'.[20] Not blinded like other theologians who saw Nazi Fascist totalitarianism as the necessary great culmination of the modern development, Barth saw it more as the terrifying relic of a 'modernity' which urgently had to be transcended: the 'end of modernity', as Romano Guardini was to call it after the Second World War.

So we have not understood Barth (at any rate not the young Barth) if we brand him neo-orthodox. On the contrary, it seems to me that even today in theology we must hold to the **great intentions of Karl Barth:**

– The biblical texts are not mere documents of philological-historical research but make possible an encounter with the 'wholly other'; the utterly human testimonies of the Bible are concerned with **God's** Word, which men and women can acknowledge, know and confess.

– Men and women are thus called to more than neutral contemplation and interpretation: their penitence, conversion and faith is required, a **faith** which always remains a venture; human salvation and damnation are at stake here.

– It is the task of the church to express uncompromisingly in society, through its human words, this word of God on which men and women can always rely in trust.

Both church preaching and church dogmatics have to be utterly concentrated on **Jesus Christ,** in whom for believers not just an exemplary 'good man' has spoken and acted, but God himself; Jesus Christ is the decisive criterion of all talk of God and human beings.

That is all good, more than good. But a question must finally also be put to this theology, too. **How** are these great theological intentions to be realized in a new time? Is Barth's *Church Dogmatics*, which as a theologian he did not want to be revered, but read and taken further, already the theology that is called for in the postmodern paradigm? It seems to me that here a clear counterpoint must be set – and for that we must go back once again to the beginning of Barth's theology, the beginning of the 1920s.

8. Not the perfecter of the postmodern paradigm

In order to create the essential presuppositions for his lectures, the pastor of Safenwil who as yet had no doctorate and had now been appointed Göttingen Professor of Reformed Theology (happily the University of Münster gave him an honorary doctorate) went back to the Reformation heritage, to Calvin and the Heidelberg catechism. But that was not enough. Should we see it as chance or fate that after his first two years, in 1924, when he had to prepare his lectures on dogmatics, the newly launched professor hit upon an 'out-of-date' 'dusty' book which was to be his destiny: *The Dogmatics of the Evangelical Reformed Church* by Heinrich Heppe, from the year 1861,[21] which gave him the answers to all the dogmatic topics between heaven, earth and hell? Whose answers? Those of **old Reformed orthodoxy.**

So in Barth's first lectures on dogmatics there was a **shift** which, while not uncritical, was remarkable, since it was towards dogmas disputed in the modern world, from the Trinity, through the virgin birth and the descent into hell, to the ascension: a shift not only to old Protestant orthodoxy but also – where did this ultimately get its wisdom from? – to mediaeval scholasticism and the patristics of the early church. And what about the other brains of 'dialectical theology'? None of them went along with this move of Barth's, but all watched it, shaking their heads. However, it was not the reference back to the tradition of the early church, the Middle Ages and the Reformation in itself which was the problem (there was a good deal to be learned here) but the way in which Barth did this – simply ignoring and often defaming important results of modern exegesis, history and theology.

Of course Barth did not become an orthodox Calvinist, Lutheran confessionalist or even mediaeval scholastic as a result. His own theological approach and his own specific theological epistemology, which he further radicalized after the discontinued *Christian Dogmatics in Outline*, was too original for that. The key work here was his book on Anselm of Canterbury, *Anselm: Fides Quaerens Intellectum*.[22] What does Anselm's *credo ut intelligam* mean? For Karl Barth there is no question about that: 'I believe in order to understand.' 'Faith' has the priority in everything. Right from the beginning, according to Barth, a Christian has to take a leap into the subject-matter itself. It is not, as in Schleiermacher, a matter of first wanting to understand (the historical, philosophical, anthropological and psychological presuppositions of faith) in order then to believe. Rather, it is the opposite, first believe in order to understand by subsequent fathoming of the 'possibilities' of faith.

Barth defines faith as knowledge and affirmation of the word of Christ, but then – and this is where the problem emerges – this is very quickly identified with the church's creed, with the confession of faith which has come into being historically in a long history. This was now **Barth's approach** in the light of Anselm: on the presupposition **that** it is true that God exists, is a being in three persons, became man, there is now further reflection on how far all this is true. So now the emphatically *Church (!) Dogmatics*, published after the *Christian Dogmatics in Outline*, becomes reflection on the **creed which has been said and affirmed beforehand**. Hardly anyone can really be astonished, then, that already in the 'Prolegomena' to the Dogmatics (not what is to be said beforehand but what is to be said first), there are two hundred pages on the doctrine of the Trinity, which is not developed from the New Testament but from the church doctrine of the fourth century. This is not grounded, but made comprehensible, in a brilliantly developed conceptual dialectic – on the presupposition that it is accepted in faith. So now Karl Barth's fundamental thesis on revelation is utterly trinitarian (§8): 'God's Word is God Himself in His revelation. For God reveals Himself as the Lord and according to Scripture this signifies for the concept of revelation that God himself in unimpaired unity yet also in unimpaired distinction is Revealer, Revelation, and Revealedness',[23] or, in a biblical formulation: Father, Son and Spirit.

One can best make this procedure clear through a **comparison**: Barth's radicalized and intrinsically volatile theology of the Word is structurally reminiscent – for all the manifest differences in content – of Hegel's philosophy of the Spirit (Barth had always had a 'certain weakness' for him) in so far as this, similarly circling round itself and moving forward dialectically in three stages, presupposes the whole of truth, calls for a similar leap into the subject-matter, and presents a similar alternative:

– **Either, Hegel** would say, one raises oneself above all that is empirical and abstract to truly concrete speculative thought, and then in reflection the truth of the Spirit dawns automatically – or one does not elevate oneself to this speculative level and is then not really a philosopher.

– **Either, Barth** would say, one subjects oneself, untroubled by all historical, philosophical, anthropological and psychological difficulties, to the Word of God as it is attested in scripture and proclaimed by the church and then, indeed then, on reflection the truth of revelation will dawn of its own accord – or one does not believe and then is not really a Christian!

And for Christians – so Karl Barth now says in the *Church Dogmatics* with the utmost christological concentration but also **exclusiveness** – for Christians Jesus Christ is now the word of God made flesh, the **one**, the **only** light of life, alongside which there are **no** other lights, nor can there be, no other words of God, no revelation.

9. The abiding challenge of 'natural theology'

Many theologians trained by Barth (like the right-wing Hegelians of their time) see no difficulties here. One is in the circle and *a priori* thinks on the high dogmatic level that is called for. For myself, while I personally can move on this 'height' of theology myself, I cannot forget my contemporaries 'down in the valley', cannot conceal the fact that I have difficulties here and that in the light of the great Catholic tradition (which here too has largely lagged behind the Reformation tradition) I had them from the beginning. No, Barth's theology is too important for us to be able to avoid confronting its substance here.

We cannot limit ourselves to a purely immanent paraphrase of Barth, worthwhile though that may be in the interest of bringing Barth's theology alive for the present-day generation of theologians.[24] A good seventy-five years after Barth's *Romans* and a good sixty years after the first volume of his *Church Dogmatics* we cannot be content with a mere internal correction of a conventional picture of Barth while otherwise largely agreeing with him. It seems to me that criticism of Barth, too, must be more critical of Barth's theology.

So we must ask:

If **God's creation** is no longer, as the young Barth thought in his early phase, the point of contact for the grace of God falling vertically from above, and if God's creation now in the late Barth can be taken quite seriously as God's good work, so that it is now possible to write four volumes of *Church Dogmatics* about it; if all that is the case, then why should this not have consequences for a true **knowledge of God** from creation – in principle not only for Christians but for all men and women?

– If God, in terms of the **substance of theology**, beyond doubt stands at the beginning of all things and thus certainly has the primacy, why must it be **methodologically illegitimate for theology** to begin with the questions and needs of present-day people and then to ask behind them to God, on the understanding that the order of being and the order of knowing are not simply identical? Has not Barth in principle conceded this to Schleiermacher?

– If the **biblical message** is beyond question the decisive criterion of any talk of God for Christians, why should any talk of God be dependent on the Bible?

– And finally, if the **negative statements of the Bible** about the error, darkness, lie, sin of the non-Christian world are taken seriously as an invitation to conversion, why should one keep silent about, suppress or obscure the fact that the God of the Bible – also according to the testimony of the New Testament – is the God of all people and as such is near to all people, so that even non-Christians (already according to the testimony of Romans and even more so according to the testimony of Acts) can recognize the real God?

Confronted with these and similar questions, a long time ago now Karl Barth referred me to the **third volume** of his **Doctrine of Reconciliation**, then in preparation, where he discusses Jesus the light of the world. And indeed subsequently all too little note was taken of the fact that in the last completed volume of the *Church Dogmatics* (1959) there are **new theological accents**. Granted, here the old Karl Barth returns to his first and repeated harsh exclusivist thesis: Jesus Christ is 'the one, the only, light of life'. However, then (granted, with many dogmatic cautions and without open *retractationes*, as in Augustine) he concedes that now finally alongside the one light Jesus Christ there are also **'other lights'**; there are also 'other true words' alongside the one Word.[25] Granted, contrary to all empirical evidence Barth wants dogmatically to maintain that the other lights are only reflections of the one light of Jesus Christ (is the Buddha only a reflection, which only shines in the light of Jesus Christ?). Nevertheless, it is evident that in Barth's late theology a revaluation of knowledge of God from the world of creation and natural theology is in the making, a revaluation also of philosophy and human experience generally, indeed in an indirect and concealed way also a revaluation of natural law, natural religion, indeed the world religions, all of which – including the religions of grace and faith of the Indian Bhakti and Japanese Amida Buddhism[26] – Karl Barth had formerly just disqualified as forms of unbelief, indeed of idolatry and righteousness by works.[27] This revaluation also underlies the questions of the old Karl Barth to Friedrich Schleiermacher, which significantly remain 'open'.[28]

All this means that in the end the *Church Dogmatics*, which after the completion of the paradigm shift from modernity to postmodernity reached back in a second phase behind modernity (back past modern criticism to Protestant orthodoxy, scholasticism and patristics) and involuntarily led to a kind of neo-orthodoxy, that in the end this **dogmatic edifice** conceived on such a large scale, stringently constructed and carefully built, had at least in principle (though most Barthians hardly noticed) been **blown up**! Barth's 'positivism of revelation' which Dietrich Bonhoeffer criticized in his letters from a Nazi prison had fundamentally been robbed of its basis.

That may have demonstrated clearly that Karl Barth, who already at the beginning of the 1920s, after the completely revised *Epistle to the Romans*, and then again at the beginning of the 1930s, after rejecting and then completely revising the first volume of the *Dogmatics*, had said that he could and wanted to say the same thing as before but now he could no longer say it as he had once said it – this Barth, I am convinced, would say the same thing again if in the 1980s and 1990s he could return to the barricades as a young man. As he said then: 'What option had I but to begin at the beginning, saying the same thing, but in a very different way?'[29] So he might perhaps do what **Paul Tillich** also emphasized in his last lecture before his death as something greatly to be desired: he would attempt to work out a Christian theology in the context of the world religions and the world regions.[30]

Towards the end of his life – now emphasizing more the humanity of God than his divinity – Karl Barth was reconciled with his old sparring partner **Emil Brunner**, a man with whom he had broken quite unnecessarily, simply because Brunner thought that he had to speak of a 'point of contact' in human beings for God's grace (*No!*[31] was the title of Barth's work against Brunner's *Nature and Grace*,[32] published in 1934). The question is certainly not an idle one. Would not perhaps the same Karl Barth today, a rejuvenated Karl Barth, even have been reconciled with his great opponent Rudolf Bultmann, since his earlier programmatic attempt at understanding, *Rudolf Bultmann: An Attempt to Understand Him*,[33] had completely failed? Might he have become reconciled with the Bultmann who on the one hand affirmed his basic theological intentions (God as God, God's Word, proclamation and human faith) but on the other hand did not simply want to give up the important concerns of liberal theology; who therefore wanted to hold on unconditionally to the historical-critical method in exegesis and the need for demythologizing and an interpretation of scripture orientated on human understanding?

10. *The abiding challenge of Rudolf Bultmann*

No, today there can be no question of going over from Barth to Bultmann or conversely replacing Barth with Bultmann. That is quite wrong: both great Protestant theologians must be taken with the utmost seriousness in their own way; each has his strengths and weaknesses. And Karl Barth saw **Bultmann's weakness** clearly from that day, probably as early as 1929 in Göttingen, when Bultmann read out to him the lectures of Martin Heidegger which he had heard in Marburg and written down, to the effect that theology now had to move in an existentialist direction and also to deal with the gospel documented in the New Testament in this light. Barth did not criticize the view that scripture was to be interpreted in an 'existential' way, in terms of human existence; he did that himself in his own fashion. But he did criticize the fact that Bultmann, fettered to the early Heidegger, prescribed an **existentialist reduction** and (a criticism that Bultmann's distinguished pupil Ernst Käsemann also made):[34]
– that he bracketted out the cosmos, nature, the environment in favour of human existence;
– that he reduced real world history to human historicity, and the authentic future to human futuricity;
– that he neglected concrete society and the political dimension in his theology of being-in-the-world.
Conversely, at a very early stage Bultmann saw and noted **Barth's weaknesses:**
– that Barth liked to avoid discussions of hermeneutics, in order to go on working 'as thetically as possible';
– that after his shift to Protestant orthodoxy and to Anselm in 1930, Barth even refused to deliver a lecture on the burning topic of natural theology which he had promised to give to the 'old Marburgers', to the great annoyance and disgust of his friend

Bultmann, and thus dropped the long-expected discussion of the difference which had grown up between them in the meantime.

– that Barth argued increasingly resolutely that he could practise a 'theological exegesis', without denying historical-critical exegesis, but also without seriously bothering about it;

– that Barth also largely dropped the critical history of dogma in favour of a principle of tradition which in fact tied Christians for all times to the Hellenistic conceptualization of the relationship between Father, Son and Holy Spirit (although when he wanted to, he was capable of making conceptual corrections to the classical doctrine of the Trinity – 'mode of being' instead of 'person');

– that finally Barth, contrary to his intentions, in the Dogmatics which were so emphatically 'Church' Dogmatics, with the help of the church tradition had brought about a **conservative restructuring of pre-modern dogmatics**, large parts of which were not backed up by exegesis; in its tie to a 'past world-view' and lack of relevance to experience, this could hardly succeed in 'making the Christian proclamation so comprehensible to people today that they become aware that *tua res agitur* (it's your concern)'.[35]

So it is not wrong for writers today to speak of 'an excessive concern for a foundation' in Barth's theology, as Eberhard Jüngel does, or of a questionable 'dogmatic over-complexity' which endangers the original intent, as Karl-Josef Kuschel does.[36] Indeed in the face of the provocation of modern exegesis and the history of dogma, Karl Barth at that time (like the Swiss army in the Second World War) shut himself up in the Alpine redoubt of the orthodox dogmatics of the sixteenth/seventeenth or fourth/fifth centuries and with such a defensive strategy was prepared, for the sake of the freedom and independence of God from all human experience, if need be even to surrender the most fertile parts of the land. And how would things be today? I think that if Barth, by a miracle rejuvenated, wanted to complete in postmodern terms a theology which had begun in postmodern terms, he would not be Karl Barth if he did not once again begin from the beginning and from the regained centre and, with better strategical and hermeneutical safeguards, attempt to advance all over again.

In other words – without all this military poetry: once again he would begin from the beginning much more radically and say the same thing again quite differently. He would start from the evidence of the Bible as gained from historical criticism – not only in respect of purgatory and marian and papal dogmas, for which he criticized the Catholics harshly, but also in respect of original sin, hell and the devil, indeed in respect of christology and the Trinity; in a word, he would have attempted to work out a **responsible historical-critical dogmatics** in the light of an **exegesis with a historical-critical foundation,** in order in this way to translate the original Christian message (in accordance with Bultmann's demand, but without Bultmann's existentialist narrowing) for the future that had dawned in such a way that it was again understood as a liberating address from God. He would again speak of God in relation to human beings, even of that 'theanthropology' which the old Barth had in his sights, the Barth who in his youth had denounced anthropology as the mystery of modern theology – so applauded by Feuerbach. And here the 'historical Jesus', without whom, according to Ernst Käsemann, the 'Christ of dogma' becomes a myth that can be manipulated at will,[37] might, it seems to me, again become of the utmost importance and urgency – quite differently from his role in Barth and Bultmann – for example in respect of true human liberation in individual life, in society and in the church.

No, there is no going back: either to Schleiermacher or to Luther, to Thomas or to Augustine or to Origen. Rather, with Origen, Augustine and Thomas, with Luther and Schleiermacher, the way must be forwards, with Barth's intrepidity and resolution, concentration and consistency.

11. *Towards a critical and sympathetic re-reading against the postmodern horizon*

'We have no awareness of our own relativity,' Barth once critically remarked,[38] and he could say of his own work: 'I do not understand the *Church Dogmatics* as the conclusion but as the opening of a new joint discussion.'[39] Today, of course, this discussion, under changed theological and social conditions, would have to involve a **critical-sympathetic re-reading** of the *Church Dogmatics*. Such a re-reading against the post-modern horizon, for all its criticism, would have to bring the great themes and the tremendous fullness of this theology constructively into the present and treat it again in the context of the religions and regions of the world. Truly, what overflowing riches there are in this theology, in its doctrine of God, creation and reconciliation, a theology which sought to be neither Reformation nor Lutheran theology, but ecumenical theology, and the more ecumenical the more it went on! What systematic power and depth there is in the quite independent and original penetration of central theological topics like the dialectic of the divine properties, the connection between creation and covenant, time and eternity, Israel and the church, christology and anthropology, taken further in concrete terms in an ethic of freedom before God, in community, for life, within restrictions. Radical liberation theology before any theology of liberation!

And at the same time, for all its overflowing complexity, for all the wealth of material which cannot be tamed (9185 pages in the German edition of the *Church Dogmatics* alone), this theology never lost its centre. What Karl Barth could write about the 'great free objectivity' of Wolfgang Amadeus Mozart, the one musician whom he loved, here too in an inclusive way, he could have said, did say, about himself. His portraits of Mozart, both in the Church Dogmatics[40] and in his brief 1956 work on Mozart,[41] are also something like self-portraits of his theology in a nutshell. What he heard in this music he also wanted to resound in his theology. Mozart's music, he said, was 'free in a quite unusual way... free of all exaggerations, of all fundamental breaks and clashes. The sun shines, but it does not blind, consume or burn. The heaven spans the earth, but it is no burden on it, does not oppress it or swallow it up. So the earth is and remains the earth, without having to assert itself in a titanic revolt against heaven. Darkness, chaos, death and hell can be seen, but they may not for a moment gain the upper hand. Mozart makes music, knowing everything, from a mysterious centre, and so he knows and preserves the limits to right and to left, upwards and downwards... There is no light which does not also know darkness, no joy which does not also include sorrow, but conversely, there is no terror, no anger, no lament which does not have peace at a greater or lesser distance from it. So there is no laughing without weeping, but also no weeping without laughing.'[42]

Indeed, Barth's theology also comes from this **mysterious centre,** which for him was the God who shows his **gracious concern for men and women in Jesus Christ.** And because the God made visible in the crucified and risen Jesus was the centre, this theology, too, can preserve the limits, can let God be God and human beings be human beings; this theology, too, knows the darkness, the evil, the negative, the nothingness in the world, and yet at the same time is written in the great trust that the good and merciful God will keep the last word for himself. Indeed, in the theology of Karl Barth more breaks through than the demonic and tragic in the world; it too, like Mozart's music, avoids extremes, knows 'the wise confrontation and mixing of the elements', so that every No continues to be borne up by a great Yes. Those who hear this music, indeed who study this theology, 'may understand themselves to be subject to death and yet still alive, as we all are, and feel themselves called to freedom'.[43]

Epilogue

Guidelines for a Contemporary Theology

Paul, Origen, Augustine, Thomas, Luther, Schleiermacher, Barth: what each reader has learned from these great Christian thinkers, their strengths and weaknesses, their insights and limitations, will be different. I myself have learned most from studying their persons and their work. But I do not want to end by attempting a résumé, nor can I: any comprehensive comparison would be too complex. So there will now be no artificial closing septet of all too different voices, but simply a short epilogue – in academic prose: guidelines for a contemporary theology.

If one has been preoccupied all one's life with these great Christian thinkers (and with others too); if one has attempted constantly to learn something new from all of them and yet not drop any of them, the question arises: **what theology** is desirable today, what theology should one do today? I shall limit myself to three perspectives – the ethos, style and programme of theology – which have become important for my own theologizing over the course of the decades.[1]

First, it seems to me that the **ethos** of all theologizing today needs to be:
– a theology which is not opportunist and conformist but **truthful**: a thoughtful account of faith which investigates and speaks the Christian truth in truthfulness;
– a theology which is not authoritarian but **free**; a theology which pursues its task without hindrance from administrative measures and sanctions on the part of the church authorities and which expresses and publishes its well-founded convictions to the best of its knowledge and conscience;
– a theology which is not traditionalist but **critical**; a theology which knows that it is freely and truthfully obligated to the scientific ethos of truth, the methodology of the discipline and a critical examination of all its problems, methods and results;

213

– a theology which is not confessionalist but **ecumenical**; a theology in which each theology sees the other no longer as an opponent but as a partner, and which is concerned for understanding rather than separation – in two directions: **inwards**, for the sphere of ecumenism within Christianity and between the churches; and **outwards**, for the sphere of the world ecumene outside the churches and outside Christianity, with its different regions, religions, ideologies and sciences.

As for the **style** of theologizing, the following 'ten commandments' should apply in our time:

– No secret science for those who already believe, but **comprehensibility** also for non-believers.

– No premium on 'simple' faith or defence of a 'church' system, but uncompromising concern for the truth in a strictly **scientific approach**.

– Ideological opponents should neither be ignored nor branded as heretics, not theologically commandeered, but interpreted in the best light **in critical sympathy** and at the same time exposed to fair, relevant discussion.

– **Interdisciplinary** work is not only to be called for but to be practised: dialogue with the other sciences involved and concentration on one's own cause belong together.

– There should be no hostile opposition, nor any *laissez-faire* co-existence either, but a **togetherness in critical dialogue**, especially between theology and philosophy, theology and the sciences and humanities, and theology and literature: religion and rationality belong together, but so do religion and poetry.

– Problems of the past should not have priority, but rather the wide-ranging and complex **problems** of human beings and human society **today**.

– The norm of a Christian theology which governs all other norms cannot again be any church or theological tradition or institution, but only the gospel, the **original Christian message** itself: theology orientated on the gospel, but understood historically and critically.

– There should be no talk either in biblical archaisms and Hellenistic scholastic dogmatisms or in fashionable and theological jargon, but as far as possible in **language which can easily be understood** by modern men and women; no effort is to be spared to achieve this.

– Credible **theory** and **praxis** that can be lived out, dogmatics and ethics, personal piety and reform of the institutions, liberation in society and liberation in the church cannot be separated; rather, note must be taken of the unbreakable connection between them.

– There must be no confessionalistic ghetto mentality, but **ecumenical breadth** which takes account both of the world religions and the modern ideologies: the greatest possible tolerance of those outside the churches, of the universally religious, of the *humanum* generally on the one hand, and working out what is specifically Christian on the other, belong together.

Finally, the **programme** of a theology, a **critical ecumenical theology**. Such a theology must sustain the tensions in every new age and again **at the same time** (here, regardless of the Reformation 'alone', an 'and' is called for!) at the same time attempt to be:

– **catholic**, constantly concerned for the whole, universal church;
– and at the same time **evangelical**, strictly related to scripture, to the gospel;
– **traditional**, constantly responsible to history – **and** at the same time **contemporary**, taking up the relevant questions of the present;
– **christocentric**, resolutely and distinctly Christian;
– and at the same time **ecumenical**, orientated on the ecumene, the whole inhabited earth, all Christian churches, all religions, all regions;
– **theoretical and scientific**, concerned with doctrine, with the truth – and at the same time **practical and pastoral**, concerned with life, renewal and reform.

But enough of programmatic words! Does this programme for a contemporary theology have any prospect of being realized? Am I not perhaps the voice of one crying in the wilderness of a sometimes boring, confessionally narrow and inward-looking blind theology of the present, which seems to sense little of the breath of our seven great Christian thinkers? It is for others to judge that. But I know that I am at one with many people, not least my two Tübingen colleagues and friends, Eberhard Jüngel and Jürgen Moltmann, to whom I have dedicated this book, in criticism of a sterile, bloodless science fixated only upon itself, at one also in the ideal of a theology which is obligated to the spirit of ecumenism and the critical audience of our time.

In the more than forty years during which I have dared to do theology I have attempted to keep to the guidelines that developed over time from the process of my research and teaching which I have set out in this theological programme. And if at the age of sixty-six one is more markedly aware than previously of how limited the time remaining is, one would want at least to express the hope that younger theologians will take forward this programme critically and creatively. So *'vivant sequentes'*, 'Long live those who are to come!'

Bibliography and Notes

Literature on Paul

The basis for this chapter is H.Küng, *Judaism* (1991), London and New York 1992, 2 B, V.1-2, 'The Controversial Paul. The Sympathetic Transformation'. For research into Paul see the early important articles by R.Bultmann, K.Holl, H.Lietzmann, A.Oepke, R.Reitzenstein, A.Schlatter, A.Schweitzer, collected by K.H.Rengstorf, *Das Paulusbild in der neueren deutschen Forschung*, Darmstadt 1964. For an orientation on scholarly research, which is almost beyond surveying, cf. the account by B.Rigaux, *St Paul et ses lettres. État de la question*, Paris 1962; H.Hübner, 'Paulusforschung seit 1945. Ein kritischer Literaturbericht', in *Aufstieg und Niedergang der Römischen Welt. Geschichte und Kultur Roms im Spiegel der neueren Forschung*, ed. W.Haase and H.Temporini, II.25.4, Berlin 1987, 2649-840 (this also includes extended articles on the latest state of the interpretation of individual letters of Paul); O.Merk, 'Paulusforschung 1936-1985', *Theologische Rundschau* 53, 1988, 1-81. For an introduction to the person and work of the apostle Paul, in addition to the introductions to the New Testament, see among more recent critical works especially M.Dibelius, *Paul*, ed. W.G.Kümmel, London 1953; P.Seidensticker, *Paulus, der verfolgte Apostel Jesus Christi*, Stuttgart 1965; G.Bornkamm, *Paul* (1969), London and New York 1975; E.Käsemann, *Perspectives on Paul* (1969), London and Philadelphia 1971; O.Kuss, *Paulus. Die Rolle des Apostels in der theologischen Entwicklung der Urkirche*, Regensburg 1971; K.Stendahl, *Paul among Jews and Gentiles*, Philadelphia 1976; F.F.Bruce, *Paul, Apostle of the Free Spirit*, Exeter 1977; E.P.Sanders, *Paul and Palestinian Judaism*, London and Philadelphia 1977; id., *Paul, The Law and the Jewish People*, London and Philadelphia 1983; id., *Paul*, Oxford 1991; J.C.Beker, *Paul the Apostle. The Triumph of God in Life and Thought*, Edinburgh 1980; K.H.Schelkle, *Paulus. Leben – Briefe – Theologie*, Darmstadt 1981; G.Lüdemann, *Paul: Apostle to the Gentiles* (1980), London and Philadelphia 1984; id., *Opposition to Paul in Jewish Christianity* (1983), Minneapolis

1989; W.A.Meeks, *The First Urban Christians. The Social World of the Apostle Paul*, New Haven 1983; H.Räisänen, *Paul and the Law*, Tübingen 1983; G.Theissen, *Psychological Aspects of Pauline Theology* (1983), Edinburgh 1987; F.Watson, *Paul, Judaism and the Gentiles. A Sociological Approach*, Cambridge 1986. For Paul from the Jewish side and in Jewish-Christian dialogue, from the more recent literature see S.Sandmel, *The Genius of Paul. A Study in History*, New York 1958; H.-J.Schoeps, *Paul. The Theology of the Apostle in the Light of Jewish Religious History* (1959), London 1961; S.Ben-Chorin, *Paulus. Der Völkerapostel in jüdischer Sicht*, Munich 1970; M.Barth et al., *Paulus. Apostat oder Apostel? Jüdische und christliche Antworten*, Regensburg 1977; F.Mussner, *Tractate on the Jews* (1979), Philadelphia 1984; P.Lapide and P.Stuhlmacher, *Paulus – Rabbi und Apostel. Ein jüdisch-christlicher Dialog*, Stuttgart 1981; P. von der Osten Sacken, *Grundzüge einer Theologie im christlich-jüdischen Gespräch*, Munich 1982; id. *Evangelium und Tora. Aufsätze zu Paulus*, Munich 1987; F.W.Marquardt, *Die Gegenwart des Auferstandenen bei seinem Volk Israel. Ein dogmatisches Experiment*, Munich 1983; E.Biser et al., *Paulus – Wegbereiter des Christentums. Zur Aktualität des Völkerapostels in ökumenischer Sicht*, Munich 1984; L.Swidler – L.J.Eron – G.Sloyan – L.Dean, *Bursting the Bonds? A Jewish-Christian Dialogue on Jesus and Paul*, New York 1990; A.F.Segal, *Paul the Convert. The Apostolate and Apostasy of Saul the Pharisee*, New Haven 1990.

Notes on Paul

1. F.Nietzsche, *The Antichrist*, Complete Works, Vol. 6, London 1911, 178.
2. Ibid., 184.
3. Acts 8.3.
4. Phil.3.5f.
5. Cf. Acts 22.25-29.
6. Cf. Phil.3.5f.
7. Cf. Gal.1.13, 23; I Cor.15.9; Phil.3.6.
8. Cf. Gal.1.13f.
9. Cf. I Cor.1.17-31; Gal.3.1-14.
10. Cf. Acts 9.3-9.
11. Cf. I Cor.9.1; 15.8-10; Gal.1.15f.; Phil.3.7-11.
12. II Cor 11.23-26.

13. For belief in the resurrection see H.Küng, *Credo*, ch.IV.

14. Cf. Rom.15.9.

15. Not only the central message (the kerygma) of the crucifixion and resurrection (I Cor.15.3-8) but also the tradition of the Last Supper (I Cor.11.23-25), attitudes to marriage and divorce (I Cor.7.10f.), the instruction to provide the preacher's wherewithal to live (I Cor.9.14), the pre-eminent position of the commandment to love (I Thess.4.9; Gal.5.13; Rom.13.8-10; I Cor.13); and finally also the Davidic descent of Jesus (Rom.1.3), Christ according to the flesh from Israel (Rom.9.5), being a son of Abraham (Gal.3; Rom.4), human birth and subordination under the law (Gal.4.4), being human, humbling himself, being obedient to death (Phil.2.6-8), weakness (II Cor.13.4), poverty (II Cor.8.9), the passion (I Cor.11.23). I Cor.4.12; 13.2 and Rom.16.19 can also be added.

16. Cf. I Cor.3.11.

17. Phil.2.21: 'For all seek their own advantage and not the things of Jesus Christ.' Cf. I Cor.7.32-34, 'The things of the Lord'.

18. E.Käsemann, 'Wo sich die Wege trennen', *Deutsches Allgemeines Sonntagsblatt*, 13 April 1990.

19. S.Ben-Chorin, *Paulus. Der Völkerapostel in jüdischer Sicht*, Munich 1970, 11.

20. Ibid., 57.

21. Rom.7.12.

22. Rom.7.10; cf. 10.5; Gal.3.12.

23. Rom.2.20.

24. Rom.7.14.

25. Rom.9.4.

26. The complex problem of the law in Paul is discussed in detail and at length in H.Küng, *Judaism*, Part Three, Chapter B III, 'For the Sake of Human Beings'.

27. Rom.3.27.

28. Rom.3.31.

29. Rom.3.20; cf. Gal.3.10.

30. II Cor.3.7, 9.

31. II Cor.3.6.

32. Gal.5.1.

33. Gal.5.13.

34. Gal.2.4.

35. Rom.6.14; cf. 7.5f.

36. Cf. II Cor.3.6.

37. Cf. Gal.2; Acts 15.1-34.

38. Gal.2.11.

39. Cf. Mark 7.8; 7.4.
40. Cf. Mark 7.1-23.
41. I Cor.8.9.
42. Cf. I Cor.9.19; Gal.5.13.
43. I Cor.7.23.
44. Gal.5.13f.; cf. I Cor.13.1-13.
45. I Cor.11.7.
46. Cf. I Cor.7.1-7.
47. I Cor.14.34; the insertion extends from 14.33b to 14.36.
48. Rom.16.7.
49. Cf. Rom.16.1-2.
50. Cf. Rom.13.1-7.
51. Cf.Rom.14.1-23.
52. Rom.12.2; cf. Phil.1.10.
53. I Cor.6.12.
54. Ibid.
55. Rom.14.14; cf. Titus 1.15, 'To the pure all is pure'.
56. I Cor.6.12.
57. I Cor 10.23f.
58. I Cor.9.19.
59. I Cor.10.29.
60. Cf. I Cor.8.7-12; 10.25-30.
61. Cf. Ex.4.22.
62. Cf. Rom.9.3.
63. Cf. Rom.9.4f.
64. Cf. Rom.9.2.
65. Cf. Gal.2.14.
66. It is to the lasting credit of E.Käsemann, 'Ministry and Community in the New Testament', in *Essays on New Testament Themes*, London and Philadelphia 1964, 63-94, that he has brought to light again the significance of the charisma in criticism of the church in the twentieth century.
67. I Cor.12.3.
68. Phil.3.12-14.

Literature on Origen

The earlier literature can be found in B.Altaner, *Patrology*, London 1960, § 55. Cf. also A.von Harnack, *Der kirchengeschichtliche Ertrag der exegetischen Arbeiten des Origenes*, Teil I-II, Leipzig 1918/19; id., *Geschichte der altchristlichen Literatur bis Eusebius*, second enlarged edition, Leipzig 1958, I/1, 332-405; II/2, 26-54; J.Daniélou, *Origen*, London and New York 1955; H.de Lubac, *Histoire et Esprit. L'intelligence de l'Écriture d'après Origène*, Paris 1950; id., *Recherches dans la foi. Trois études sur Origène, Saint Anselme et la philosophie chrétienne*, Paris 1979; H.von Campenhausen, *The Fathers of the Greek Church*, London 1963; H.Crouzel, *Théologie de l'Image de Dieu chez Origène*, Paris 1956; id., *Origène et la 'Connaissance mystique'*, Paris 1961; id., *Origène et la philosophie*, Paris 1962; id., *Origène*, Paris 1985; M.Harl, *Origène et la fonction révélatrice du Verbe incarné*, Paris 1958; H.Kerr, *The First Systematic Theologian. Origen of Alexandria*, Princeton, NJ 1958; R.P.C.Hanson, *Allegory and Event. A Study of the Sources and Significance of Origen's Interpretation of Scripture*, London 1959; P.Nemeshegyi, *La Paternité de Dieu chez Origène*, Tournai 1960; W.Jaeger, *Early Christianity and Greek Paideia*, Cambridge, Mass. 1961; G.Gruber, *ZOE. Wesen, Stufung und Mitteilung des wahren Lebens bei Origenes*, Düsseldorf 1963; H.Chadwick, *Early Christian Thought and the Classical Tradition. Studies in Justin, Clement and Origen*, Oxford 1966; J.Rius-Camps, *El dinamismo trinitario en la divinización de los seres racionales según Origenes*, Rome 1970; P.Kübel, *Schuld und Schicksal bei Origenes, Gnostikern und Platonikern*, Stuttgart 1973; W.Gessel, *Die Theologie des Gebetes nach 'De Oratione' von Origenes*, Paderborn 1975; P.Nautin, *Origène. Sa vie et son oeuvre*, Paris 1977; L.Lies, *Wort und Eucharistie bei Origenes. Zur Spiritualisierungstendenz des Eucharistieverständnisses*, Innsbruck 1978; id., *Origenes' Eucharistielehre im Streit der Konfessionen. Die Auslegungsgeschichte seit der Reformation*, Innsbruck 1985; U.Berner, *Origenes*, Darmstadt 1981.

Notes on Origen

1. H.Chadwick, *The Early Church*, Harmondsworth 1967, 75.
2. H.U.von Balthasar, *Origenes. Geist und Feuer. Ein Aufbau aus seiner Schriften*, Salzburg 1938, 11.
3. Cf. Eusebius, *Church History*, VI.
4. Cf. Nautin, *Origène*.
5. Cf. above all Clement of Alexandria, *Protreptikos* = Admonition to the Greeks.
6. Cf. von Campenhausen, *Fathers of the Greek Church*.
7. Cf. Matt.19.12.

8. C.Kannengiesser, 'Origen, Augustine and Paradigm Changes in Theology', in *Paradigm Change in Theology*, ed. H.Küng and D.Tracy, Edinburgh 1989, 113-29: 126.

9. Cf. Origen, *De principiis*, Preface.

10. H.Görgemanns and H.Karpp, *Origenes, Vier Bücher von der Prinzipien*, 17.

11. Origen, *De principiis*, Preface, 10.

12. Cf. id., *Contra Celsum*, V.39; *De Principiis*, I, 2, 13.

13. Cf. I Cor.15.27f.

14. Origen, *Contra Celsum*, III.28.

15. Cf. id., *De principiis*, IV.2,4-6.

16. Thus rightly (against K.L.Schmidt), A.A.T.Ehrhardt, *Politische Metaphysik von Solon bis Augustin*, II, *Die christliche Revolution*, Tübingen 1959, 204-26.

17. Kannengiesser, 'Origen, Augustine and Paradigm Changes' (n.8), 123.

18. Harnack, *History of Dogma* II, London 1900 reissued New York 1961, 380.

19. Cf. Acts 2.14-40.

20. Rom.1.3f.

21. Ignatius of Antioch, *To the Magnesians*, VI.1.

22. Id., *To the Ephesians*, VII.2.

Literature on Augustine

The earlier literature can be found in B.Altaner, *Patrology*, London 1960, §102. In addition to earlier handbooks of dogma (A. von Harnack, F.Loofs, R.Seeberg) which are still important, and more recent ones (C.Andresen, K.Beyschlag, J.Pelikan, M.Schmaus, A.Grillmeier), see the following more recent monographs and general accounts: É.Gilson, *Introduction à l'étude de saint Augustin*, Paris 1929, [4]1969; H.I.Marrou, *Saint Augustin et la fin de la culture antique*, Paris 1938, [4]1958; id., *Saint Augustin et l'Augustinisme*, Paris 1955, [8]1973; F.van der Meer, *Augustinus de Zielzorger*, Utrecht 1947; A.Zumkeller, *Das Mönchtum des heiligen Augustinus*, Würzburg 1950, [2]1968; T.J.van Bavel, *Recherches sur la christologie de saint Augustin. L'humain et le divin dans le Christ d'après saint Augustin*, Fribourg 1954; J.J.O'Meara, *The Young Augustine. The Growth of St Augustine's Mind up to his Conversion*, London 1954, [2]1980; R.W.Battenhouse (ed.), *A Companion to the Study of St*

Augustine, New York 1955; M.Löhrer, *Der Glaubensbegriff des hl.Augustinus in seinen ersten Schriften bis zu den* Confessiones, Einsiedeln 1955; A.D.R.Polman, *Het woord gods bij Augustinus*, Kampen 1955; R.Schneider, *Seele und Sein. Ontologie bei Augustin und Aristoteles*, Stuttgart 1957; G.Strauss, *Schriftgebrauch, Schriftauslegung und Schriftbeweis bei Augustin*, Tübingen 1959; H.von Campenhausen, *The Fathers of the Latin Church*, London 1964, ch.6; C.Eichenseer, *Das Symbolum Apostolicum beim heiligen Augustinus, mit Berücksichtigung des dogmengeschichtlichen Zusammenhangs*, St Ottilien 1960: C.Andresen (ed.), *Zum Augustin-Gespräch der Gegenwart*, I-II, Darmstadt 1962/81; P.Brown, *Augustine of Hippo. A Biography*, Berkeley and London 1967; A.Mandouze, *Saint Augustin. L'aventure de la raison et de la grâce*, Paris 1968; C.Boyer, *Essais anciens et nouveaux sur la doctrine de saint Augustin*, Milan 1970; R.A.Markus, *Saeculum. History and Society in the Theology of St Augustine*, Cambridge 1970; E.Te Selle, *Augustine the Theologian*, London 1970; J.Brechtken, *Augustinus doctor caritatis. Sein Liebesbegriff im Widerspruch von Eigennutz und selbstlose Güte im Rahmen der antiken Glückseligkeits-Ethik*, Meisenheim 1975; W.Geerlings, *Christus Exemplum. Studien zur Christologie und Christusverkündigung Augustins*, Mainz 1978; W.Wieland, *Offenbarung bei Augustinus*, Mainz 1978; A.Schindler, 'Augustin', *Theologische Realenzyklopädie* IV, Berlin 1979, 645-98; H.Fries, 'Augustinus', in H.Fries and G.Kretschmar (ed.), *Klassike der Theologie* I, Munich 1981, 104-29.

Notes on Augustine

1. von Campenhausen, *Fathers of the Latin Church*, 183, 185.
2. Augustine, *Confessions* I.1 (1).
3. Marrou, *Saint Augustin et la fin de la culture antique*, 489-5 (for further details); the quotation comes from p.495.
4. Cf. Augustine, *Confessions* VIII, XII (28ff.).
5. Rom.13.13f.
6. Marrou, *Saint Augustin et l'Augustinisme*.
7. Augustine, *Contra epistolam Manichaei* 5 (6).
8. Id., *Sermo* 112.8.
9. Brown, *Augustine of Hippo*, 235.
10. Ibid., 240.
11. Augustine, *Confessions* X, XXXI (45).

12. Cf. id., *Sermo* 131, 10.

13. Id., *Opus imperfectum contra Julianum* II.22.

14. Cf. id., *Sermo* 151: *Contra Julianum Pelagianum*, above all book IV.

15. Cf. Augustine, *Ep.* 217 v.16; *Enchiridion* XXIII, XXIX.

16. I Cor. 4.7.

17. Augustine, *In primam epistolam Ioannis* VII, 8.

18. Cf. K.E.Børresen, *Subordination et Equivalence. Nature et rôle de la femme d'après Augustin et Thomas d'Aquin*, Oslo 1968, esp.I. 1-3.

19. Quoted in P.Brown, *The Body and Society. Men, Women and Sexual Renunciation in Early Christianity*, New York and London 1988, 424 (which is a good study of Augustine and sexuality before and after his conversion).

20. Cf. Rom.9-11.

21. Marrou, *Saint Augustin et l'Augustinisme.*

22. Augustine, *De civitate Dei* I, Preface.

23. Ibid., XXII, 30.

Literature on Thomas Aquinas

Recent literature is based on the careful researches of Neo-Thomists like J.Berthier, P.Castagnoli, H.Denifle, F.Ehrle, M.Grabmann, P.Mandonnet and A.Walz. The best historical introduction to Thomas's work is still that of M.-D.Chenu, *Introduction a l'étude de saint Thomas d'Aquin*, Paris 1950; cf. also id., *Saint Thomas d'Aquin et la théologie*, Paris 1959. The American J.A.Weisheipl's *Friar Thomas d'Aquino. His Life, Thought and Works*, New York 1974, is a thorough critical biography based on the most recent historical research. The German theologian and former Dominican O.H.Pesch has produced the most illuminating recent theological introduction against today's horizon: *Thomas von Aquin. Grenze und Grösse mittelalterlicher Theologie. Eine Einführung*, Mainz 1988, ²1989. For further important recent literature cf. J.Pieper, *Hinführung zu Thomas von Aquin. Zwölf Vorlesungen*, Munich 1958; S.Pfürtner, *Luther und Thomas im Gespräch. Unser Heil zwischen Gewissheit und Gefährdung*, Heidelberg 1961; J.B.Metz, *Christliche Anthropozentrik. Über die Denkform des Thomas von Aquin*, Munich 1962; M.Seckler, *Das Heil in der Geschichte. Geschichtstheologisches Denken bei Thomas von Aquin*, Munich 1964; E.Gilson, *Le thomisme. Introduction à la philosophie de saint Thomas d'Aquin*, Paris

1965, ⁶1983; U.Kühn, *Via caritatis. Theologie des Gesetzes bei Thomas von Aquin*, Göttingen 1963; H.Vorster, *Das Freiheitsverständnis bei Thomas von Aquin und Martin Luther*, Göttingen 1965; L.Oeing-Hanhoff (ed.), *Thomas von Aquin 1274/1974*, Munich 1974; W.Mostert, *Menschwerdung. Eine historische und dogmatische Untersuchung über das Motiv der Incarnation des Gottesohnes bei Thomas von Aquin*, Tübingen 1978; E.Schillebeeckx, 'Der Kampf an verschiedenen Fronten: Thomas von Aquin', in H.Häring and K.J.Kuschel (ed.), *Gegenentwürfe. 24 Lebensläufe für eine andere Theologie*, Munich 1988, 53-67; A.Zimmermann (ed.), *Thomas von Aquin. Werk und Wirkung im Licht neuerer Forschungen*, Berlin 1988.

Notes on Thomas Aquinas

1. H.Fries, 'Augustinus', in H.Fries and G.Kretschmar (eds.), *Klassiker der Theologie* I, Munich 1981, 126.

2. Thomas Aquinas, *Summa theologiae* II-II, q.188, a.7; cf.q.185, a6, ad I.

3. OT: commentaries on Isaiah, Jeremiah, Job, Psalms; NT: commentaries on the Gospels of Matthew and John and the Pauline epistles.

4. Thomas Aquinas, *Summa contra gentiles*, I.2.

5. Cf. id., *Summa theologiae* I, q.1-26.

6. Ibid., q.27-43.

7. Id., *Summa contra gentiles*, I.2.

8. Cf. Chenu, *Thomas d'Aquin*.

9. For the circumstances of this condemnation (above all for Thomas himself) cf. Schillebeeckx, 'Kampf', 58-67; Weisheipl, *Friar Thomas*, 302-18.

10. *Codex Iuris Canonici* (1917), canon 1366, 2.

11. Cf. Thomas Aquinas, *Summa theologiae* I-II, q.109-114.

12. Cf. ibid., q.113.

13. Cf. ibid., q.110 a.1; cf. q. 116.

14. Cf. N.M.Wildiers, *Wereldbeeld en teologie*, 1972.

15. Thomas Aquinas, *Summa theologiae* I, q. 92, a, 1-4.

16. Cf. ibid., II-II, q.177, a 2.

17. Ibid., I q.92, a.1.

18. Id., *Commentary on the Sentences*, IV d.25, q 2. qla, 1. ad 4.

19. Id., *Summa theologiae* I, Supplementum q.39, a.1.

20. Id., *Summa theologiae* II-II q.177, a.2.

21. Cf. id., *Contra errores Graecorum*, Pars II, cap 32-35.

22. Cf. ibid., cap.36.

23. Cf. Pesch, *Thomas von Aquin*, 26f.

24. Cf. ibid., 34.

25. Chenu, *Thomas d'Aquin*.

26. Cf. the report and commentary on the last phase of Thomas's life from 6 December 1273 to 7 March 1274 in Weisheipl, *Friar Thomas*, 293-302.

27. Thomas Aquinas, *De potentia*, q.7, a 5 ad decimumquartum.

Literature on Martin Luther

For Martin Luther and the Reformation in Germany, in addition to important earlier works (especially H.Grisar, R.Hermann, K.Holl, J.K.Köstlin and G.Kawerau, O.Scheel), see J.Lortz, *Die Reformation in Deutschland*, I-II, Freiburg 1940; E.H.Erikson, *Young Man Luther. A Study in Psychoanalysis and History*, London 1958; H.J.Iwand, *Gesammelte Aufsätze*, I-II, Munich 1959/80; F.Lau, *Luther*, Berlin 1959; M.Lienhard, *Martin Luther. Un temps, une vie, un message*, Paris 1959, ²1991; J.Delumeau, *Naissance et affirmation de la Réforme*, Paris 1965; E.W.Zeerden, *Die Entstehung der Konfessionen. Grundlagen und Formen der Konfessionsbildung im Zeitalter der Glaubenskämpfe*, Munich 1965; id., *Konfessionsbildung. Studien zur Reformation, Gegenreformation und katholischen Reform*, Stuttgart 1985; R.Friedenthal, *Luther. Sein Leben und seine Zeit*, Munich 1967; E.Iserloh, J.Glazik and H.Jedin, *Reformation. Katholische Reform und Gegenreformation*, Freiburg 1967; R.Stupperich, *Geschichte der Reformation*, Munich 1967; H.Bornkamm, *Luther. Gestalt und Wirkungen. Gesammelte Aufsätze*, Gütersloh 1975 (which contains extensive criticism of Erikson's thesis); id., *Martin Luther in der Mitte senes Lebens. Das Jahrzehnt zwischen dem Wormser und dem Augsburger Reichstag*, ed. K.Bornkamm, Göttingen 1979; P.Chaunu, *Le temps des Réformes. Histoire religieuse et système de civilisation. La Crise de la chrétienté. L'Eclairement (1250-1550)*, Paris 1975; id., *Eglise, culture et société. Essais sur Réforme et Contre-Réforme(1517-1620)*, Paris 1981; H.A.Oberman, *Werden und Wertung der Reformation. Vom Wegestreit zu Glaubenskampf*, Tübingen 1977; id., *Luther. Mensch zwischen Gott und Teufel*, Berlin 1981; id., *Die Reformation. Von Wittenberg nach Genf*, Göttingen 1986; H.Lutz, *Reformation und Gegenreformation*,

Munich 1979; R.H.Bainton, *Here I Stand. A Life of Luther*, New York 1950; E.Iserloh, *Geschichte und Theologie der Reformation im Grundriss*, Paderborn 1980; id., *Kirche – Ereignis und Institution. Aufsätze und Vorträge II: Geschichte und Theologie der Reformation im Grundriss*, Münster 1985; B.Lohse, *Martin Luther. Eine Einführung in sein Leben und sein Werk*, Munich 1981, [2]1983; M.Brecht, *Martin Luther*, I-II, Stuttgart 1981-7; W.von Loewenich, *Martin Luther. Der Mann und das Werk*, Munich 1982; O.H.Pesch, *Hinführung zu Luther*, Mainz 1982; J.M.Todd, *Luther. A Life*, London 1982; H.Junghaus (ed.), *Leben und Werk Martin Luthers von 1526 bis 1546*, I-II, Berlin 1983; H.Löwe and C.J.Roepke (eds.), *Luther und die Folgen. Beiträge zur sozialgeschichtlichen Bedeutung der lutherischen Reformation*, Munich 1983; G.Vogler (ed.), *Martin Luther. Leben, Werk, Wirkung*, Berlin 1983: R.Schwarz, *Luther*, Göttingen 1986; for Luther's life I have followed this work by the distinguished Luther scholar, which sums up his earlier researches.

Notes on Martin Luther

1. This was worked out first in an unprejudiced way on the Catholic side by Lortz, *Reformation in Deutschland*, I, 1-144. There is a recent comprehensive account in Chaunu, *Le temps des Réformes*, esp. chs.IV-V.

2. For the discussion cf. Pesch, *Einführung*, Ch. V ('The Move towards Reformation').

3. Cf. H.Denifle, *Die abendländische Schriftausleger bis Luther über justitia Dei (R 1,17) und Justificatio*, Mainz 1905.

4. In the Roman Curia the contribution was estimated at the horrendous sum of 50,000 gold ducats. Half of this was to be sent to Rome by the Fuggers, who were acting as bankers, and the other half to the Margrave Albrecht of Brandenburg – at the age of twenty-three Archbishop of Magdeburg (and Halberstadt) and then also Archbishop of Mainz – so that the Margrave could repay to the Fuggers the loan raised to pay for a dispensation which would allow him, against the regulations imposed by Rome, to hold a plurality of offices, and to do so below the minimum age.

5. Cf. H.Volz, *Martin Luthers Thesenanschlag und dessen Vorgeschichte*, Weimar 1959; E.Iserloh, 'Luthers Thesenanschlag. Tatsache oder Legende?', *Trierer Theologische Zeitschrift* 70, 1961, 303-12, expanded version, *Luther zwischen Reform und Reformation. Der Thesenanschlag fand nicht statt*, Münster [3]1968; id., 'Martin Luther und der Aufbruch der

Reformation (1517-1525)', in Iserloh, Glazik and Jedin, *Reformation*, 3-114, esp. 49f.

6. Thus the Catholic Reformation historian E.Iserloh, *Geschichte und Theologie der Reformation*, 33.

7. Cf. M.Luther, *Resolutiones disputationum de indulgentiarum virtute* (1518), English translation in Luther's Works: American Edition (henceforth cited as LW), Vol.31, 77-252.

8. Cf. id., 'A Sermon on Indulgences and Grace' (1517), in *D.Martin Luthers Werke. Kritische Gesamtausgabe* (= WA), I, 239-46.

9. Cf. H.Denziger (ed.), *Enchiridion symbolorum definitionum et declarationum de rebus fidei et morum* (1854), Freiburg [31] 1960, nos.741-781.

10. Cf. M.Luther, *Appellatio D.Martini Lutheri ad concilium a Leone X, denuo repetita et innovata* (1520), in WA VII, 74-82.

11. Cf. id., *Adversus execrabilem Anichristi bullam* (1520), LW 32, 5ff.

12. Cf. id., *On Good Works* (1520), LW 32, 106ff.

13. cf. id., 'To the Christian Nobility of the German Nation', LW 44, 123-217. Cf. id., 'On the Babylonian Captivity of the Church' (1520), LW 36, 11-126.

15. Cf. id., 'The Freedom of a Christian' (1520), LW 31, 333-77; also in *Martin Luther's Basic Theological Writings*, ed. T.F.Lull, Minneapolis 1989, 585-629.

16. *Basic Theological Writings*, 596.

17. Cf. the 'Colloquy with D.Martin Luther at the Reichstag at Worms', WA VII, 814-87, esp.838; the famous statement 'Here I stand, I can do no other' is not authentic.

18. Cf. S.Pfürtner, 'The Paradigms of Thomas Aquinas and Martin Luther. Did Luther's Message of Justification mean a Paradigm Change?', in H.Küng and D.Tracy (eds.), *Paradigm Change in Theology*, Edinburgh 1989, 130-160.

19. O.H.Pesch, 'Zwanzig Jahre katholische Lutherforschung', *Lutherische Rundschau* 16, 1966, 392-406, already pointed this out over against the Loretz school (and Jedin).

20. Cf. Hans Küng, *Justification*; id., 'Katholische Besinnung auf Luthers Rechfertigunslehre heute', in *Theologie im Wandel. Festschrift zum 150-jährigen Bestehen der Katholisch-Theologischen Fakultät an der Universität Tübingen 1817-1967*, Munich 1967, 449-68.

21. That the doctrine of justification is no longer something that divides the churches was first confirmed by the agreement between the Lutheran World Federation and the Roman Secretariat for Unity, *The Gospel and the Church* (Malta Report), 1972, in H.Meyer, H.J.Urban

and L. Vischer (eds.), *Dokumente wachsender Übereinstimmung. Sämtliche Berichte und Konsenstexte interkonfessioneller Gespräche auf Weltebene 1931-1982*, Paderborn 1983, 248-71, esp.nos.26-30.

22. Cf. M.Luther, *Against the Roman Papacy, an Institution of the Devil* (1545), LW 41, 263-376.

23. Cf. H.Küng, *Judaism* (1991), London and New York 1992, Ch.I C V 2, 'Luther, too, against the Jews'.

24. M.Luther, *The Freedom of a Christian, Basic Theological Writings*, 623.

25. *Colloquy with D.Martin Luther at the Reichstag of Worms* (Luther's plea summing up his speech), WA VII, 838.

26. M.Luther, *Table Talk*, LW 54, 476.

Literature on Friedrich Schleiermacher

For Friedrich Schleiermacher cf. W.Dilthey, *Leben Schleiermachers* I, Berlin 1870, ²1922 (ed. H.Mulert); the work was revised, extended and republished under the editorship of M.Redeker in two half-volumes, Göttingen 1966/70, using material from Dilthey's literary estate; E.Hirsch, *Geschichte der neueren evangelischen Theologie* IV, 490-82; V, 281-364, Gütersloh 1949, ²1960; id., *Schleiermachers Christusglaube. Drei Studien*, Gütersloh 1968; Karl Barth, *Protestant Theology in the Nineteenth Century* (1952), ET London ²1972, 452-73; P.Seifert, *Die Theologie des jungen Schleiermacher*, Gütersloh 1960; T.Schulze, 'Stand und Probleme der erziehungswissenschaftlichen Schleiermacher-Forschung in Deutschland', in *Paedagogica Historica* I, 1961, 291-326; H.-J.Birkner, *Schleiermachers christlicher Sittenlehre im Zusammenhang seines philosophisch-theologischen Systems*, Berlin 1964; id., 'Theologie und Philosophie. Einführung in Friedrich Schleiermacher', in M.Greschat (ed.), *Gestalten der Kirchengeschichte* 9,1, Stuttgart 1985, 87-115; F.Hertel, *Das theologische Denken Schleiermachers untersucht an der ersten Auflage seiner Reden 'Über die Religion'*, Zurich 1965; F.W.Kantzenbach, *Friedrich Daniel Ernst Schleiermacher in Selbstzeugnissen und Bilddokumenten*, Reinbek 1967; M.Redeker, *Friedrich Schleiermacher, Leben und Werk (1768-1834)*, Berlin 1968; H.Gerdes, *Der geschichtliche biblische Jesus oder der Christus der Philosophen. Erwägungen zur Christologie Kierkegaards, Hegels und Schleiermachers*, Berlin 1973; D.Lange, *Historischer Jesus oder mythischer Christus. Untersuchungen zu den Gegensatz zwischen*

Friedrich Schleiermacher und David Friedrich Strauss, Gütersloh 1975; id. (ed.), *Friedrich Schleiermacher 1768-1834. Theologe – Philosophe – Pädagoge*, Göttingen 1985; E.H.U.Quapp, *Barth contra Schleiermacher? 'Die Weihnachtsfeier' als Nagelprobe, mit einem Nachwort zur Interpretationsgeschichte der 'Weihnachtsfeier'*, Marburg 1978; G.Moretto, *Etica e storia in Schleiermacher*, Naples 1979; E.Schrofner, *Theologie als positive Wissenschaft. Prinzipien und Methoden der Dogmatik bei Schleiermacher*, Frankfurt 1980; U.Barth, *Christentum und Selbstbewusstsein. Versuch einer rationalen Rekonstruktion des systematischen Zusammenhanges von Schleiermachers subjektivitätstheoretischer Deutung der christlichen Religion*, Göttingen 1983; B.A.Gerrish, *A Prince of the Church. Schleiermacher and the Beginnings of Modern Theology*, Philadelphia 1984; J.O.Duke and R.F.Streetman (ed.), *Barth and Schleiermacher. Beyond the Impasses?*, Philadelphia 1988; M.Junker, *Das Urbild des Gottesbewusstseins. Zur Entwicklung der Religionstheorie und Christologie Schleiermachers von der ersten zur zweiten Auflage der Glaubenslehre*, Berlin 1990; A.Weirich, *Die Kirche in der Glaubenslehre Friedrich Schleiermachers*, Frankfurt 1990; R.D.Richardson (ed.), *Schleiermacher in Context. Papers from the 1988 International Symposium on Schleiermacher at Herrnhut, The German Democratic Republic*, Lewiston 1991.

Notes on Friedrich Schleiermacher

1. Cf. K.Barth, *Protestant Theology in the Nineteenth Century*, 425.

2. For the biographical details see M.Redeker, *Friedrich Schleiermacher*.

3. F.Schleiermacher, letter to J.G.A.Schleiermacher, 21 January 1787, in F.D.E.Schleiermacher, *Kritische Gesamtausgabe*, ed. H.-J.Birkner et al., Berlin 1980ff. (in the following notes cited as KGA), V.1, 49-52: 50.

4. J.G.A.Schleiermacher, 'Letter to F.Schleiermacher of 7 May 1790', in KGA V.1, 198f.

5. F.Schleiermacher, 'Letter to G.Reimer of 30 April 1802', in *Aus Schleiermachers Leben. In Briefen*, ed. L.Jonas and W.Dilthey, Vol.I, Berlin 1858, 309.

6. Cf. id., 'Idee zu einem Katechismus der Vernunft für edle Frauen' (fragment), in KGA I.2, 154.

7. Id., 'Der Glaube' (Fragment), in KGA I.2, 154.

8. Cf. id., *On Religion. Speeches to its Cultured Despisers* (1799), reissued with a preface by R.Otto, New York 1958.

9. R.Otto in his Introduction to *On Religion*, vii.

10. Schleiermacher, *On Religion*, 277.

11. Ibid.

12. Ibid., 101.

13. Ibid.

14. Cf. G.W.F.Hegel, Preface to Hinrichs' *Religionsphilosophie* (1822), in *Werkausgabe* XI, Frankfurt 1970, 42-67, esp.58.

15. Cf. Schleiermacher, *Monologen. Ein Neujahrsgabe* (1800), KGA I, 3, 1-61.

16. Cf. H.Küng, *The Incarnation of God. An Introduction to Hegel's Theological Thought as Prolegomena to a Future Christology* (1970), Edinburgh 1987.

17. Schleiermacher, *On Religion*, 238.

18. Ibid., 235.

19. Ibid., 246.

20. Ibid., 247.

21. Ibid.

22. Cf. ibid., *Christmas Eve. A Dialogue on the Incarnation* (1806), Richmond, Va. 1967.

23. Cf. id., *Gelegentliche Gedanken über Universitäten im deutschen Sinn. Nebst einen Anhang über eine neu zu errichtende*, Berlin 1808.

24. Cf. id., *A Brief Outline of the Study of Theology* (1811), Richmond, Va 1966.

25. Cf. id., *The Christian Faith* (1821-22, second revised edition Berlin 1830-31), English translation, Edinburgh 1928.

26. Anselm of Canterbury, *Proslogion* I; id., *De fide trinitatis et de incarnatione verbi*, II.

27. Cf. F.Schleiermacher, *Life of Jesus* (1832), Philadelphia 1975.

28. *The Christian Faith*, §22.

29. Ibid., §94, p.385.

30. Ibid., 397.

31. Ibid.

32. Ibid.

33. Ibid.

34. Ibid.

35. D.Lange, 'Neugestaltung christlicher Glaubenslehre', in id. (ed.), *Friedrich Schleiermacher*, 85-105: 101.

36. F.Schleiermacher, *The Christian Faith*, 397.

37. Cf. id., 'Über die Glaubenslehre. Zweites Sendschreiben an Lücke', in KGA I, 10, 743.

38. Id., *The Christian Faith*, §95, p.389.

39. I myself have presented one in my *On Being a Christian*.

40. Cf. M.Junker, *Das Urbild des Gottesbewusstseins. Zur Entwicklung der Religionstheorie und Christologie Schleiermachers von der ersten zur zweiten Auflage der Glaubenslehre*, Berlin 1990, 210f.

41. Cf. Lange, *Historischer Jesus*, 170.

42. Both quotations come from Kantzenbach, *Friedrich Schleiermacher*, 146.

43. Karl Barth, *Protestant Theology in the Nineteenth Century*, 427.

Literature on Karl Barth

Important articles on Karl Barth's early period (by R.Bultmann, E.Peterson, E.Przywara, G.Söhngen) are listed in E.Jüngel, 'Karl Barth', *Theologische Realenzyklopädie* V, Berlin, 1980; cf. also James M.Robinson (ed.), *The Beginnings of Dialectical Theology*, Richmond, Va. 1968. For the period after the Second World War see J.C.Groot, *Karl Barth en het theologische kenproblem*, Heiloo 1946; J.Hâmer, *Karl Barth. L'Occasionalisme théologique de K.Barth. Etude sur sa méthode dogmatique*, Paris 1949; O.Weber, *Karl Barth's Church Dogmatics. An Introductory Report on Volume I.1 to III.4*, Philadelphia and Edinburgh 1953; H.U.von Balthasar, *The Theology of Karl Barth*, New York 1972; E.Riverso, *Intorno al pensiero di Karl Barth, colpa e giustificazione nella reazione antiimmanentistica del Römerbrief barthiano*, Padua 1951; id., *La Teologia esistenzialistica di Karl Barth. Analisis, interpretazione e discussione del sistema*, Naples 1955; A.Ebneter, *Der Mensch in der Theologie Karl Barths*, Zurich 1952; H.Fries, *Bultmann, Barth und die katholische Theologie*, Stuttgart 1955; B.Gherardini, *La parola di Dio nella teologia di Karl Barth*, Rome 1955; G.C.Berkouwer, *The Triumph of Grace in the Theology of Karl Barth*, Grand Rapids 1956; H.Bouillard, *Karl Barth. Parole de Dieu et Existence Humaine*, I-II/2, Paris 1957; H.Küng, *Justification. The Doctrine of Karl Barth and a Catholic Reflection* ([4]1964), London and New York 1965; E.Jüngel, *The Doctrine of the Trinity. God's Being is in Becoming*, Grand Rapids and Edinburgh 1976; id., *Barth-Studien*, Zurich 1982; id., 'Umstrittene Theologie. Zum 100 Geburtstag Karl Barths', *Neue Zürcher Zeitung*, 10/11 May 1986; H.Gollwitzer, *Reich Gottes und Sozialismus bei Karl Barth*, Munich 1972; F.-W.Marquardt, *Theologie und Sozialismus. Das Beispiel Karl Barths*, Munich 1972; E.Busch, *Karl*

Barth. *His Life from Letters and Autobiographical Texts*, London and Philadelphia 1976; W.Kreck, *Grundentscheidungen in Karl Barths Dogmatik. Zur Diskussion seines Verständnisses von Offenbarung und Erwählung*, Neukirchen 1978; S.W.Sykes (ed.), *Karl Barth. Studies of His Theological Method*, Oxford 1979; M.Beintker, *Die Dialektik der 'dialektischen Theologie' Karl Barths*, Munich 1987; C.Frey, *Die Theologie Karl Barths. Eine Einführung*, Frankfurt 1988; K.-J.Kuschel, *Born Before All Time? The Dispute over Christ's Origin*, London and New York 1992.

Notes on Karl Barth

1. K.Barth, 'Die Unordnung der Welt und Gottes Heilsplan', *Evangelische Theologie* 8, 1948/49, 181-8: 185.
2. Cf. id., 'Roman Catholicism: a Question to the Protestant Church', in *Theology and Church* (1928), London and New York 1962, 307-33.
3. Cf. id., *Church Dogmatics* I/1-IV/4 (1932-67), Edinburgh 1936-1968. (henceforth cited as CD).
4. Id., 'Answer to Fr Jean Daniélou', in Karl Barth. *Offene Briefe 1945-1968*, ed. D.Koch, Zurich 1984, 171-5: 174.
5. H.U.von Balthasar, *The Theology of Karl Barth*.
6. CD I/1, xiii.
7. CD I/2, 143.
8. CD I/2, 688.
9. Cf. CD I/2, 687ff.
10. Cf. H.Küng, *Justification. The Doctrine of Karl Barth and a Catholic Response*.
11. Karl Barth in his 'Letter to the Author', ibid, xviii.
12. 'Das Evangelium und die Kirche. Bericht der evangelisch-lutherisch/römisch-katholischen Studienkommission', *Herder-Korrespondenz* 25, 1971, 536-44: 539.
13. CD, I.1, xiii.
14. Cf. J.Brosseder, 'Consensus in Justification by Faith without Consensus in the Understanding of the Church? The Significance of the Dispute over Justification Today', in K.-J.Kuschel and H.Häring (eds.), *Hans Küng. New Horizons for Faith and Thought*, London and New York 1993, 138-51.
15. Cf. H.Küng, *The Council and Reunion* (US: *The Council, Reform and Reunion*, 1960), London and New York 1961.
16. Barth, *Letters 1961-1968*, Edinburgh and Grand Rapids 1981.
17. Cf. Busch, *Karl Barth*.

18. For more detail see H.Küng, *Global Responsibility* (1990), London and New York 1991, A 1, 'From Modernity to Postmodernity'.

19. Cf. K.Barth, *The Epistle to the Romans* (second edition, 1922), Oxford 1933.

20. 'The Barmen Declaration', in *Creeds of the Churches*, ed. John H.Leith, Atlanta, Ga ³1982, 520.

21. Cf. H.Heppe, *Dogmatics*, London 1950 (with a preface by Karl Barth).

22. Cf. K.Barth, *Anselm: Fides quarens intellectum (1931)*, London and Richmond, Va 1960.

23. CD I/1, 295.

24. Cf. F.-W.Marquardt – D.Schellong – M.Weinrich (eds), *Karl Barth: Der Störenfried?*, Munich 1986.

25. CD IV/3, 38-164.

26. CD I/2, 280-97.

27. CD I.2, 300-25.

28. Cf. K.Barth, postscript to *Schleiermacher-Auswahl*, ed. H.Bölli, Munich 1968.

30. Cf. P.Tillich, 'The Significance of the History of Religions for the Systematic Theologian', in *The Future of Religions: Memorial Volume for Paul Tillich*, ed. J.C.Brauer, New York and London 1966, 80-94.

31. Cf. K.Barth, *Nein! Antwort an Emil Brunner* (1934, the English translation is entitled *Natural Theology*, London 1946).

32. Cf. E.Brunner, *Natur und Gnade. Zum Gespräch mit Karl Barth*, Zurich 1934 (included in *Natural Theology*, see n.31).

33. Cf. K.Barth, 'Rudolf Bultmann. An Attempt to Understand Him' (1952), in *Kerygma and Myth* II, London 1962, 83-162.

34. Cf.E.Käsemann, 'Those who Hunger and Thirst for Righteousness', in id., *Jesus Means Freedom*, London and Philadelphia 1969, 130-43.

35. Bultmann to Barth, 11-15 November 1952, in *Barth-Bultmann Letters, 1922-1966*, Edinburgh and Grand Rapids 1982.

36. Cf. K.-J.Kuschel, *Born Before All Time? The Dispute over Christ's Origin* (1990), London and New York 1992, 123. In his fine article ' "Jesus Christ is the Decisive Criterion": Beyond Barth and Hegel to a Christology "From Below"', in *Hans Küng. New Horizons for Faith and Thought* (n.14), 171-97, Kuschel has shown how much in my theology I have kept the substance of Barth's basic concern (despite all the differences in method and content).

37. Cf. E.Käsemann, 'Blind Alleys in the "Jesus of History" Controversy', in *New Testament Questions of Today*, London and Philadelphia 1969, 23-65. For a reply cf. R.Bultmann, 'Antwort an Ernst Käsemann',

in id., *Glauben und Verstehen. Gesammelte Aufsätze* IV, Tübingen 1965, 90-8.

38. K.Barth, *Die Woche*, 1963, no.4.

39. Id., *The Christian Century*, 1963, 1, 7ff.

40. CD III/3, 298f.

41. Id., *Wolfgang Amadeus Mozart 1765/1956* (1956), Grand Rapids 1986.

42. Ibid., 53f. (I have preferred my own translation.)

43. Ibid., 54f.

Notes on the Epilogue

1. I develop the following fundamental statements in connection with my books *On Being a Christian* and *Does God Exist*. Cf. H.Küng, *Theology for the Third Millennium* (1987), San Francisco and London 1991, 202ff.

TRAVELERS

TRAVELERS

A Novel

HELON HABILA

W. W. NORTON & COMPANY

Independent Publishers Since 1923   New York | London

Permission granted by Ayebia for Helon Habila's quote from his poem "Three Seasons" from *Fathers & Daughters: An Anthology of Exploration* Ed. Ato Quayson (2008): © Ayebia Clarke Publishing Limited, Banbury, Oxfordshire, UK.

For information about permission to reproduce selections from this book, write to Permissions, W. W. Norton & Company, Inc., 500 Fifth Avenue, New York, NY 10110

For information about special discounts for bulk purchases, please contact W. W. Norton Special Sales at specialsales@wwnorton.com or 800-233-4830

Manufacturing by Lake Book Manufacturing
Book design by Chris Welch
Production manager: Lauren Abbate

Library of Congress Cataloging-in-Publication Data

Names: Habila, Helon, 1967– author.
Title: Travelers : a novel / Helon Habila.
Description: First Edition. | New York : W. W. Norton & Company, [2019]
Identifiers: LCCN 2018059858 | ISBN 9780393239591 (hardcover)
Classification: LCC PR9387.9.H26 T73 2019 | DDC 823/.92—dc23
LC record available at https://lccn.loc.gov/2018059858

W. W. Norton & Company, Inc., 500 Fifth Avenue, New York, N.Y. 10110
www.wwnorton.com

W. W. Norton & Company Ltd., 15 Carlisle Street, London W1D 3BS

1 2 3 4 5 6 7 8 9 0

For Sharon, Adam and Edna

And for Sue

I cannot rest from travel . . .
—ALFRED, LORD TENNYSON, "ULYSSES"

It is part of morality not to be at home in
one's home.
—THEODORE ADORNO, *MINIMA MORALIA:*
REFLECTIONS FROM DAMAGED LIFE

Acknowledgments

My gratitude, first and foremost, to the voices whose stories animate this book—thanks for trusting me with your stories. In your travels, may you find the home you look for.

Thanks to my friends who made the time to read various versions of these stories and made suggestions, especially with the German language: Pascale Rondez, Branwen Okpako, Funmi Kogbe, Zainabu Jallo, Panashe Chigumadzi and Kai Hammer.

Johanna Meier, thanks for being my guide in Berlin.

Thanks to my agents, David Godwin and Ayesha Pande for your undying support and encouragement, and for taking care

of business. To my editors, Simon Prosser and Alane Mason, it's been a long journey over the years; thanks for making me a better writer.

The excellent *Tears of Salt: A Doctor's Story* by Pietro Bartolo and Lidia Tilotta was quite helpful in making me understand other dimensions of the refugee crisis in Europe.

The video installation referenced in Book 1 is by Branwen Okpako.

Thanks to the DAAD Fellowship for that magical year in Berlin. This book wouldn't have been possible without your support. To Flora Veit-Wild and Susanne Gherrmann at the Institute for Asian and African Studies, Humboldt University, Berlin, thanks for your friendship and support.

Finally, to those not mentioned here, you are always in my heart. Knowing you has changed me forever.

Book 1

ONE YEAR IN BERLIN

We came to Berlin in the fall of 2012, and at first everything was fine. We lived on Vogelstrasse, next to a park. Across the road was an *Apotheke*, and next to that a retirement home, and next to that a residential school for orphans. The school was once a home for single mothers, but eventually the mothers moved on and only the children were left. The school is made up of two cheerless structures—one noticeably newer than the other—behind waist-high cinder-block walls and giant fir trees. In the evenings the children ran in the park, jumping on trampolines and kicking around balls, their voices cutting through the frigid air clear as the bell ringing. In the mornings they sat in the courtyard behind the short

fence to craft wooden animals and osier baskets under the watchful eyes of their minders. Once, out early with Gina, one of the boys, anywhere between the ages of eight and ten, sighted us and rushed to the low wall, he leaned over the top, almost vaulting over, his face lit-up with smiles, all the while waving to us and shouting *"Schocolade! Schocolade!"* I turned away, ignoring him. Gina stopped and waved back to him. "Hello!" How his eyes grew and grew in his tiny face! Surprise mingled with pleasure as he ran back to his mates. He repeated this whenever he saw us, and Gina always indulged him, but I never got used to it. I never got used to the thin, eager voice, and how the other children, about a dozen or so, stopped and raised their eerily identical blond heads and blue eyes to watch him waving and calling *"Schocolade!"* as if his life depended on it.

•

I first met Mark when he came to the house with one of Gina's flyers in his hand. "I am here for this," he said, waving the yellow flyer. It said Gina was working on a series of portraits she called *Travelers*, and she was looking for real migrants to sit for her. Fifty euros a session, to be paid for by the fellowship. I pointed him to the guest room she had converted into a studio. Soon their voices carried to the living room, hers polite but firm, his questioning, arguing. He was being turned down, and I could have told him not to press, Gina would never change her mind. Later, when I asked her why, she said he wasn't right and didn't elaborate, but I guessed he looked too young, his face was too smooth and lacking the

character only time and experience brings. Last week she had drawn a lady and her four-year-old daughter. I met the lady in the living room waiting for Gina to set up her easel, still wearing her outdoor coat, an old woolen affair, and when I asked her if she wanted me to take the coat she shook her head, I turned to the daughter, did she want a drink, she pulled the child closer to her. The week before that it was a man, Manu, who told me he was a doctor in his former life, now he worked as a bouncer in a nightclub, waiting for the result of his asylum application. His face was lined, prematurely old, and I knew Gina would love those lines, each one of them an eloquent testimony to what he had left behind, to the borders and rivers and deserts he had crossed to get to Berlin. She would also love the woman's hands that tightly clutched her daughter's arm, they were dry and scaly, the nails chipped, no doubt ruined while working in some hotel laundry room, or as a scullery maid.

Mark came out of the studio and stood by the living room door, a wry smile on his face, his red jacket in one hand, still holding the yellow flyer in the other hand. Behind him Gina, in her paint-splattered overalls, was already back at her painting, dabbing away at the easel, her face scrunched up.

"I'll walk you to the bus stop," I offered. I had been indoor all day reading, I needed to stretch my legs, or perhaps I felt sorry for him, coming all the way for nothing, or I might have sensed something intriguing about him, something unusual that maybe Gina had sensed as well, and for that reason had

turned him away. That same thing that made her send him away had the opposite effect on me, it drew my attention. Right now he looked dejected, as if he had already made a budget for those fifty euros, which he was now realizing he would never see. I asked him if he had ever sat for a painter before. He hadn't. Who had, apart from professional models, but he thought what she needed were ordinary people, real people, and wasn't he real enough?

I walked ahead of Mark, down the stairs to the ground floor and out the door. My intention was to leave him at the bus stop and continue on across the road to the little lake where I sometimes went for a walk, but the bus was pulling away as we arrived and I decided to wait for the next bus with him, and when the bus failed to come on time he said he'd go by foot and on a whim I said, "Let's walk." It was spring and the sun lingered in the west, unwilling to set, its slanted rays falling unseasonably warm and bright. Perfect weather. We joined the flow of after-train crowd past the wurst stand, past the strawberry-colored strawberry stand. Berliners sat alfresco eating ice cream beneath beach umbrellas, *Eis*, the sign said. Ahead of us a chubby diminutive lady in a red jacket was shouting into her phone, *Nein! Nein!* as she paced back and forth on the sidewalk, staring down passersby. And the more people stared the higher her voice rose; for a moment she was famous. "*Nein! Ich weiss es nicht!*" she shouted, basking in the sunrays of her notoriety.

We passed a Roma couple on a bench next to a Kaiser's store, their dull, beady eyes focused on their daughter, who stood by the sidewalk with a pan in her hand. Mark walked with his head bowed, muttering to himself.

"It is a lovely day," I said. He nodded. I'd walk with him, but it wasn't my duty to cheer him up. Two ladies walked just ahead of us, at the same pace as us, always a few steps ahead, and it was a pleasure to watch their slim and shapely bodies beneath their identical jean jackets, and their blond hair bouncing with each step, hand in hand. They belonged to this day. One was older, in her forties perhaps, the other looked to be in her twenties; mother and daughter, or sisters, or friends, or lovers; there was a gentleness to their clasped hands, especially next to the rude screeching of tires and the blaring of horns from the motor road.

On both sides of the road neon signs on storefronts blared out: *McFit, McPaper, McDonald's*—a very American top layer over the more traditional back streets and side streets and sleepy quarters that still throbbed on, timeless, like the tram tracks buried beneath the concrete and tarmac. In our first couple of months in Berlin, Gina and I had walked these back streets that led away from Kurfürstendam and on and on and narrower and narrower to the front windows of artisans' workshops and soup kitchens and *Blumen* stores and family homes with children and parents seated at the table eating dinner. Just a few months ago these streets were empty and snow-covered, with garish Christmas lights strung from every leafless tree and storefront like charms to ward away winter's malevolent spirits. At George-Grosz-Platz the two women disappeared into a beauty store. Mark and I sat in the square and watched the yellow double-decker buses stop and start, and stop again, the people coming off and on. We sat, not talking, just enjoying the last sunrays of the day. Mark looked round at the people seated in front of the roadside

cafés drinking coffee and smoking cigarettes and said, "This could be Paris." After about thirty minutes he sighed and stood up, waved and walked away with slow steps toward Adenauerplatz station. I wondered what his story was, if I'd see him again.

I continued to sit in the dying sunlight, wrapped up in my thoughts. A fat-jowled man ran awkwardly after a M29 bus, but he was too late. He stopped and waved his arms in frustration as the bus pulled away, his open trench coat flapping about him, but when he turned I saw it wasn't a man but a woman, her thick, porcine jowls clenched in annoyance. A young lady in high heels came off the M19 and sat on a bench next to me. She took out a lipstick and a mirror. When she returned the lipstick and mirror to her bag, she looked up and our eyes met, she smiled, and then she was gone, walking at that surprisingly fast clip people here have. I could have started a conversation, I could have said "Hi," and we might have sat, and talked, elegant like Parisians. We might talk of George Grosz, after whom the square was named, painter, intellectual, rebel, who survived the First World War, and defied the Nazis in the Second, and fled to America only to be driven back to Berlin by nostalgia; he fell down a flight of stairs after an all-night bout of drinking.

"A beautiful death," she might have said. But as I watched her go, I felt the already unbridgeable gap between me and this city widen. Even if I spoke her language, the language the city spoke, would she understand me? A month ago I had gone to the post office to post a letter, and the lady behind the counter, a flaxen-haired battle-ax, had stared at

me, refusing to speak English, and we had stood glaring at each other as the line behind me grew and grew, she kept shouting German words at me, and I kept answering back in English, I wanted to buy stamps, I wanted to post my letter, till finally a lady from the back of the line stepped forward and interpreted. It was a tense standoff while it lasted, and I was sweating when I came out. A week later I started taking German classes.

"You must come, darling," Gina said to me a year ago in our home in Arlington, "I can't do it without you." She had been offered the prestigious Berlin Zimmer Fellowship for the Arts. One year in Berlin. Perhaps this was what we needed, a break from our stagnating life and routine. Every year the Zimmer selected ten artists—writers and painters and movie directors and composers—from around the world, and this year Gina was one of two artists from the USA. She was an assistant professor at a local university, while I was teaching ESL to Korean immigrants in a back room in the local library. I was also a TA in my school, it paid for my tuition, but teaching was something I did with circumspection. Whenever I

stood in front of the expectant young faces I felt like a fraud. Would they take everything I told them as the gospel truth, and what right did I have, what knowledge, what experience, to place myself before them as an authority? I was only thirty-five; perhaps if I were fifty, if I had traveled a little more, lived a little more . . .

"It is only a job, darling," Gina, always pragmatic, told me. "You are being overconscientious."

Or maybe it was my fear of commitment—Gina mentioned this, referring not just to my uncompleted PhD dissertation, but also to the fact that we had promised to get married after graduating. She had graduated, I hadn't. We had lived together for three years in her tiny student apartment overlooking a parking lot. But no, I told her, it was only my immigrant's temperament, hoping for home and permanence in this new world, at the same time fearful of long-term entanglements and always hatching an exit plan.

But we did get married, and it was a good marriage, stable, we had our routines, like most married people, we woke up together, we went to work, in the evenings we sat on our narrow balcony overlooking the parking lot sharing a bottle of wine, sometimes we went to the movies, or to dinner, and perhaps that was why I hesitated to say yes to Berlin: What if we went and things changed between us? What if Berlin transformed us beyond where we wanted to go? It was obvious to me that part of the reason she applied for the Zimmer, apart from its prestige and its importance to her career, was because my dissertation was on nineteenth-century African history, on the 1884 Berlin Conference specifically, and what better way to encourage me to resume my research than by spending

a year in Berlin? Still I hesitated because I knew every departure is a death, every return a rebirth. Most changes happen unplanned, and they always leave a scar.

Two months after our marriage Gina got pregnant. We hadn't planned on that, and we certainly hadn't foreseen losing the pregnancy after just seven months. Devastating for both of us, but something shifted in Gina. She stopped going out; she cried all day; she stopped eating. There wasn't much I could do; I sat by her side, held her hand, I reminded her we were still young and there'd be opportunities to try again. I read her poems, something I used to do a lot before we got married. Her middle name was Margaret, and I would recite Hopkins's "Spring and Fall" to her: *Margaret, are you grieving / Over Goldengrove unleaving* . . . It always cheered her up, and she'd smile and shake her head; but not this time. She turned her face to the wall and curled into a ball, making herself smaller, like a tiny fetus. Gina had always been strong, maybe stronger than I was, certainly more resourceful than me, and this was the first time I was seeing her so helpless. How suddenly and unexpectedly everything had changed, one moment we were a normal married couple, young, with our future before us, the next moment we were stricken by misfortune, prone and helpless.

One day she went to visit her parents in Takoma Park and didn't come back; the next day her mother came and threw Gina's things into a bag and said Gina needed to rest, to recover, she added, her demeanor hinting that I was to blame for her daughter's breakdown. I got along better with the father, a retired professor who had spent a year in Nigeria on a Fulbright scholarship in the 1980s, and who always looked

back to that year with great fondness. Alone in our two-room apartment, every morning I put in a call to Gina to see how she was doing, and to find out when she was coming back, and after that, with nothing more to do but sit and twiddle my thumbs in front of the TV, I began to drink. I drank in the nights at first, then in the afternoons, then in the mornings. I was sliding down a precipice, but I was unable to stop.

Gina stayed at her parents' for six months, and it was while she was there that she applied for the Zimmer. Exactly six months to the day she left, she walked into our tiny apartment, her eyes shining with hope and excitement as she showed me the Zimmer fellowship email. That night she didn't go back to her parents'. We lay in one another's arms all night long. Berlin. Maybe this was what we needed. A break from our breaking-apart life.

Even in Berlin I miss Berlin, Mark loved to say. He lived in Kreuzberg with his three friends, Stan, Eric, and Uta, in an abandoned church building next to the river Spree. The church was tilted, as if a fingertip push could topple it, one of those crumbling buildings you occasionally saw around Berlin, spared by the war, and overlooked by the demolition ball, looking odd next to the newer structures. A baroque façade with a twisted spire faced the street behind a thick wire fence that cut off the building from the neighboring houses and the passing cars. Most of the doors and windows were gone. In the courtyard the wind, like a restless spirit, drove pieces of paper and beer cans over the unruly grass in the driveway.

Mark and his friends had inherited the dwelling from another group of "alternatives" who had moved on to Stockholm in search of stiffer anti-establishment challenges when Berlin grew too tame for them.

"I had to deconsecrate it when we moved in," he said. "There was a spirit living in the walls. I have a sense for these things." It was one of his outlandish yet casually uttered comments that would have sounded crazy coming from another person, but from Mark it sounded normal, even reasonable. I met him again toward the end of spring, in a gallery. Gina was sleeping all day after working through the night—she wouldn't wake up till late afternoon when she'd emerge looking drawn and ethereal only to grab a sandwich from the fridge and go straight back to work—and I was left alone to stumble from place to place, mostly art galleries and libraries. I had learned about this particular exhibition from the emails sent to Gina by the Zimmer people. The gallery was exhibiting apartheid-era portraits by South African photographers. A young lady at the entrance handed me a pamphlet which proclaimed in bold Helvetica the bombastic title of the exhibition: *Apartheid, Exile, and Proletarian Internationalism*. There were also photographs and video installations from local black artists. I drifted from room to room, reading the texts below the portraits—the photographs were mostly of South African exiles in East and West Berlin in the 1970s and 1980s. I looked at the unsmiling faces, thinking how ironic history was, that they'd come for succor here, escaping persecution and apartheid, this place that a few decades earlier had been roiling with its own brand of persecution under the Nazis. How did they cope with the food, the new

language, with being visibly different, with the bone-chilling winter of exile? Most of them had returned to South Africa, those who had survived exile's bitterness, and were now their country's new leaders, replacing their white oppressors, most of whom had in turn been relegated to exile in the dark and dusty chapters of history.

I soon tired of viewing the identically gray and cheerless faces on the first floor and moved to the video installations in the basement. Apparently, I had the whole room to myself, and it felt a bit eerie, standing in the center of the room, surrounded by multiple flickering TV monitors showing people opening and closing their mouths wordlessly. I sat in a booth nearby and put on the headphone and suddenly the mute faces became vocal. They were speaking German. I almost jumped when a hand touched mine. I turned. A figure had crystalized out of the dark space next to me. In the gloom his red jacket had coalesced with the red couch we were seated in and I had failed to see him. Now he was offering me his hand. The hand was slim and soft, and for a moment I thought it was a girl. He noticed my momentary disorientation and smiled, as if he was used to being mistaken for something he wasn't. His hand still in mine, he said, "I am Mark."

It was him, the would-be portrait sitter, turned down by Gina. He recognized me at about the same time. The silence lingered for a while, then I pointed at the TV monitors. "What's this about?"

The TV monitors formed a triptych, one on our left with a woman on it, one on our right with a man on it, and one in front showing an old movie. The two faces on the left and right appeared to be discussing the movie in real time as it

played. But it was all in German. "The movie is *Whity*, by Rainer Werner Fassbinder. And these two are commenting on its handling of race." I knew of Fassbinder, but I had not seen *Whity* before.

"The lady," Mark said, pointing to the curly-haired woman, "she made this installation. She is half-Nigerian." Mark, I discovered later, was a film student, or used to be a film student—with Mark nothing was straightforward. We sat in the dark booth for a while, staring at the movie, the German words from the headphones bouncing around meaninglessly in my skull. Mark took off his headphone and offered to recap the movie plotline for me, I listened, impressed by his intensity. When he finished I thanked him and asked if he'd like a beer at the bar. He put down his headphone and put on his baseball cap. The bar was in the basement, next to the viewing room, and at the moment it was empty except for a couple seated by themselves on a couch in a corner. We ordered beers.

"Where are you from?" he asked.

"Originally, Nigeria."

"Your wife is also Nigerian?"

"No, American."

He was Malawian but had lived in Germany for over five years.

"Well, cheers," I said, raising my glass.

"To Africa," he said.

"To Africa."

I tried to guess his age. He looked between twenty-five and thirty. The baseball cap covered the upper part of his face, and since he was shorter than me, I had to constantly lean down

to make eye contact. He had lived a rather peripatetic life, moving from Stockholm, to Stuttgart, to Potsdam, and now Berlin. He loved Berlin most of all.

"Even in Berlin I miss Berlin," he told me that day. He was only technically speaking a student, his registration had expired—something to do with school fees, and this had, or soon would, also affect his visa status—which was why he was squatting with friends in the old church in Kreuzberg. For pocket money he freelanced for crew.com, an organization for out-of-work actors and film technicians. But it had been a while since he had done anything for crew.com. He didn't tell me all this that day at the gallery, of course, but afterward, over several meetings. He looked a bit of a mess, almost feral, his black Converse sneakers were dirty and worn out, but there was an ease about him that I responded to.

"Come and meet my friends," he said, after my second beer, his third, when I told him I had to go, "we live close by."

I followed him out of the bar and into the night. He walked with a swagger, at one point he casually stepped into the road and crossed to the other side, weaving between cars, raising his hand like a matador to halt a car that came close to hitting him, ignoring loud curses from incensed drivers. He stood at the other side, unperturbed, waving me over impatiently. I waited for the light to turn before crossing, not sure if I was impressed or alarmed by his reckless self-assurance.

"This is a church," I said when he pushed open the little gate and waved me in. My comment was half question, half statement.

"We live here for the moment, yes. Temporarily."

His three housemates were all there, Eric, Stan, and Uta. I

nodded and sat down next to Mark. When Mark told them I
was a "fellow African," Uta immediately told me her mother
was Cameroonian, her father German. She was lying on
the couch, her legs in Stan's lap—he was half-seated, half-
reclining next to her, his long dreadlocks falling over the back
of the couch and over his shoulders. We were in what they
called the living room, in the basement, which used to be
a Sunday school classroom. There was a blackboard on one
wall, and a wooden lectern in front of it. There were bottles
of beer on a redwood table with scratched and grime-dulled
wood grain. Mark opened a beer for me. Eric was holding
a joint in one hand and browsing through a laptop with the
other hand.

"So, what do you do?" Uta asked in her tentative English.

"I teach, back in the States. And here as well." I gave English classes to some of the non-English-speaking Zimmer fellows, once a week. Uta was a student at the Free University
and was currently working on a novel.

"A novel?"

"The novel is dead," Mark declared. "Cinema is the present
and the future."

"You think so?"

"The cinema does everything the novel does, but without
being boring."

I took a pull on the joint that had made its way into my
hand. I felt light-headed.

The conversation drifted from subject to subject, lulling
into a contemplative silence that never felt awkward, and then
resuming, veering off in a totally new direction. Now Eric
was talking about the last protest march they had participated

in. They had been to Davos, and several G20 meetings all over the world.

"What are you protesting?" I asked.

They all stared at me, their faces showing their surprise at my question.

"Everything, man," Stan said.

"Everything?"

"We believe there should be an alternative to the way the world is being run now," Eric said.

"Too much money in too few hands," Uta said.

"Millions exploited in sweatshops in Asia. Wars in Africa," Stan said.

"This is the twenty-first century, no child should be dying from hunger or disease," Uta said.

I nodded. I had met others like them here in Berlin, at readings, on the train, young men and women, in threadbare sweaters and tattered jeans, mostly living in communes in abandoned buildings, purveyors of an alternative way of life, often not agreeing on what exactly that alternative should be, just an alternative to the status quo, otherwise what was the point? I drank, and smoked, and listened. At a point Mark stood behind the altar and read from a passage from the Bible; his father was a preacher and he was mocking his father's preaching style. He stood with hands raised, eyes rolling, voice thundering: *The summer is ended, the harvest gathered, and still we are not saved* . . .

The others clapped. I looked on, uncertain if it wasn't self-mockery and even real pain in Mark's voice and face as he bowed to the applause before returning to his chair. They told

me he had deconsecrated the church when he first moved in a month ago. "The place was haunted. I could feel the spirits lurking all over."

"How do you deconsecrate a church?" I asked.

"With alcohol. Pour alcohol in the corners and read secret passages from the Bible."

Even in my tipsy, sedated state, I sensed how ephemeral this moment was. How long before they saw the world as it is, vile and cruel and indifferent, and there is really no changing it; how long before they moved out of their crumbling ivory tower and joined the rest of humanity swimming in what Flaubert described as a river of shit relentlessly washing away at the foundation of every ivory tower ever built? One day they'd start shaving and become bankers or middle managers and drive BMWs and Mercedes-Benzes; they'd start a family and surround themselves with the empty accoutrements of position and power, the same things they now derided. But now, right now, they were free and pure as morning dew on a petal, and something in me wanted to lean in and sniff the fragrance from that bud.

So I kept returning to that slanted, run-down church building in Kreuzberg. I kept returning even when I discovered they were a far cry from the downtrodden proletariats they so identified with: Uta's parents were both doctors from the former East Berlin; Stan was a PhD student at Humboldt, he grew up in Senegal where his father worked for a multinational food company, his mother was a painter. Nor were they as

young as they appeared. None of them was under thirty—Mark was the youngest at exactly thirty, Uta was thirty-one even though she looked twenty-five, Stan was thirty-two, and Eric was thirty-five and married, though currently separated from his wife, who lived with their daughter in Mannheim.

Then it was May. Mark and his friends invited me to the May Day demonstrations. "You'll like it," Mark said. The first of May protests were a tradition I had to experience, they told me, young men and women breaking down store doors and government buildings and flipping over cars on the high streets, sometimes setting them ablaze, denouncing the status quo.

That day in Kreuzberg, from Hermannplatz to Moritzplatz, the police began their patrol early. They came in riot gear and bulletproof vests, they cordoned off streets with their trucks and wagons, and only documented residents were allowed in or out. I arrived earlier at the church to avoid the cordon.

I found them by the door, all dressed up in boots and jeans and ready to go. Mark was talking to a girl I had never seen before. His girlfriend, Lorelle. I stopped myself from staring openly at the pins and rings in her lips and nostrils and cheeks and eyebrows, the stud in her tongue, making her face look like a pincushion. It must hurt. I imagined more piercings in hidden places beneath her lumpy sweatshirt. There was a mandala tattoo on her left cheek, in pink and blue colors, bringing her face alive like a neon light. Her hair, one side shaved off completely, was a mix of blue and pink over blond roots. I shook her hand.

"Well, nice to meet you," she said, "I have heard so much about you from Mark."

Her handshake was firm. Her voice was nothing like her appearance, it was warm, and soft, with a strong American accent. She was American, but born in Heidelberg. Her parents were military, now back in the US; but she had remained, preferring life here. She, like Mark, was a student at the film school.

We passed through parks and back streets, avoiding the cruising police vans and large congregations. Our destination was the Berlin-Turkish café, whose owner had been turning away black people, claiming they were all illegal immigrants and drug dealers. A surprisingly large crowd had already gathered in front of the café; young men and women in jeans and boots and sneakers, some with raised placards, others with raised phones recording the protest even as they chanted along to the songs. We joined them. We threw stones at the police who stood in front of the café to protect the owner, who was cowering inside. We marched in circles up and down

the block, stopping traffic. By noon I was tired, and hungry, and beginning to feel bored. I could see Mark and Uta, she beautiful in her cutoff jeans and fiery red bandanna, side by side waving their placards like baits at the police. I decided to take a break. I crossed the road to a *Bäckerei* and ordered a sandwich and a coffee. I had two missed calls from Gina. When I left home at 6 a.m. she was still in her studio painting, and I hadn't told her where I was going. I called her back but there was no answer—she would be sleeping by now. Outside, the demonstration had almost doubled in size in the short time I had been in the *Bäckerei* and I could feel the tension rising all around. Time to go home. I edged into the crowd looking for Mark to let him know I was leaving, but soon I was carried by a tide of bodies making straight for the line of policemen standing behind their shields, their sticks raised. Stones and bottles and cans whizzed over our heads to crash against the policemen's shields. A shoulder knocked into me and I fell, knees hit my face as I tried to get up, shoes marched on my hands. Everyone was running, chased by the police. I kept trying to stagger up, but I kept falling back down under the ceaseless wave of knees and legs crashing into me. I stayed on the ground, mesmerized by a dully glowing square of brass embedded in the sidewalk—I had seen them before, *Stolpersteine*, they were called, meaning to stumble. There were names on them, entire histories, birthdays, transportation days, and the names of their final, terminal destinations. Four names, the Hartmanns: Elisabeth, Marcus, Lydia, and Eduard. All ended up at Sobibór, all died the same day, December 5, 1944. I was blinded by the rusted glow of the brass, shocked by the brutal indifference of history, teary with

tear gas, too winded to move. A hand was pulling me up, and for a moment I resisted, thinking it was the police, but it was Mark. He was smiling, an exhilarated look on his face. "Are you okay?" he asked. I stood up. My palms were grazed and burning, my pants torn at the knees.

"I am fine."

But he was already gone, hurling a stone toward the line of policemen. A tear gas canister landed next to me and I saw a wild-haired youth snatch it up and throw it back at the police, its arc of smoke hanging in the air like a dying thunderhead. To my right Lorelle was running straight at a row of policemen, using her ample bulk as battering ram against their shields. They knocked her down finally and hauled her away, screaming and kicking, to a police van. I stood there, disoriented by the tear gas, my eyes and nostrils streaming freely. I was alone on a tiny island, and all around me the sea was roiling and crashing with nameless rage.

"I have to go," I said to Mark.

"No. Not yet. This is it. This is our moment," Mark said. He was waving his arms as he talked, "This is our Sharpeville, our Agincourt."

I felt like laughing at his hyperbole. What moment, I wanted to ask, will this really change the minds of the so-called capitalists and racists and bring harmony and everlasting love to the world? And yet I couldn't help being impressed by it. I said, "You don't want to get arrested, not with your expired visa. Come now."

"Where are the others?" he asked.

"I don't know. I saw Lorelle being taken away. Come on."

We walked away, taking random turns, till the sirens and

chants were a distant susurration on the wind. We sat in a bar and ordered two beers. My phone rang, it was Gina. I was too tired and too rattled to answer. We finished our beer, but Mark wasn't ready to go yet. He called for another.

"That's the way," he said. He slammed his hand on the table. "Resist the system." We drank and ordered another round. I felt the edge coming off gradually. Outside, the smoky yellow streetlights were coming on as the sky darkened. The day had gone by already. A patrol car wailed past, its flashing blue lights mingling with the streetlight yellow.

"I should be going home."

"Come on," Mark said. "Another drink, on me." He looked drunk already. He called for a double shot of whisky.

"Not for me. Hurry up, I'll walk you home, then I am off."

On the way Mark stopped at a currywurst stand to buy a sausage. A boy, his face red with drink, his girlfriend tugging at his arm, flopped into the bench next to us. He bent forward, his face in his hands. "*Scheisse*," he kept muttering. The girl was dressed in a manga comic outfit, her face heavily made up, eyes slanted with kohl. Across the street a man in a hooded sweater stood in a dark doorway, whispering to passersby, "*Alles gut?*" never fully making eye contact.

"Let's go, Mark."

He couldn't walk straight, so I hefted his arm over my shoulder, bending awkwardly sideways since he was much shorter than me, and together we staggered toward the train station. At the abandoned church we found the door kicked off its hinges and lying on the floor just inside the threshold. The lights were on. The chairs were overturned, papers lay across tables and chairs.

"Fucking shit."

"What happened?"

"I don't know. Looks like we've been raided."

Mark went from room to room, picking up chairs and books from the floor. His room was at the end of a hall, next to the kitchen. His flimsy mattress was torn and almost cut in half. His backpack, which contained all his worldly possessions, lay open in the center of the room.

"Motherfucking pigs. It's the police, they've been targeting us for a while."

"Where are your friends?" I asked.

He looked at me and shrugged. "I have no idea."

"Well, what are you going to do, where are you going to sleep?"

He said, "I'll be fine." He didn't sound very convincing.

"Why don't you go over to your girlfriend's place?"

"Lorelle? Won't work. She has a flatmate. But hey, don't worry. I have places I can go to. I'll be fine."

I left him standing there with his empty backpack in hand, swaying on his feet, assuring me he was going to be okay, and then I remembered that he couldn't have gone to Lorelle's anyway even if she didn't have a flatmate; Lorelle had been taken away by the police. I was tired, I was sore, and all I wanted was to get home, take a shower, and crawl into bed.

I didn't hear about Mark's arrest till a week later, when I stopped by the church. There was something different about the place, the door was back on its hinges, and the yard looked like someone had run a rake through it. A pile of trash was neatly packed under a tree, waiting to be bagged. I knocked, but there was no answer. I pushed the door and went in. The ratty couches and lamps were gone. The lectern was still there, and I remembered Mark standing behind it to read from the Bible, mocking his preacher father. I felt a bit sad, and a bit hurt—they had left without telling me. They had my phone number, at least Mark did, he could have called. But then, they lived an improvised

and makeshift life, they had probably been chased out by the police and were even now holed up in another squat; they might get in touch after a week or so, after they had settled down. At least Mark might. I realized I missed them; I missed stopping by the church in the evenings when Gina was working and listening to them talk about everything, from global warming to despicable politicians to refugees, even when I secretly, arrogantly considered them naïve and hopelessly idealistic. Now I had to admit they were at least able to think of something, and others, apart from themselves, they were willing to throw stones at the police and even go to jail for their ideals—how many people could do that? Certainly not my self-centered, overambitious classmates back in graduate school, and definitely not Gina's oversensitive, even narcissistic fellow Zimmer artists we met regularly at dinners and openings and readings. Throughout the week I waited for Mark to call. Did he even have a phone? I couldn't remember. In the end it was Lorelle who called. She had been released from the police lockup a day after the demonstration. I said, "Where's everyone? I went to the church and there was nobody."

Mark's little group had disbanded, she told me. Stan had moved back to Mannheim, Eric to France, and Uta was back with her parents. The gap year from life has ended, the search for alternatives is over, I thought, the revolution lost. I felt a twinge of disappointment.

"And Mark?" I asked. Mark had been arrested, and that was why she was calling. She wanted to meet. She was waiting for me outside Neukölln U-Bahnhof, in a café across the street from the station. She called for a chai and I asked for a coffee.

She looked a bit different, more subdued, as if she hadn't been sleeping. Even the mandala on her cheek looked less fluorescent, the colors in her hair less celebratory.

"The last time I saw you," I told her, raising my voice over the street noise, "you were being hauled away by the police, kicking and screaming."

"Oh God, I was so high that day. They released me the next morning. It is routine. One of the thrills of the struggle, you might say."

"But what of Mark?"

A young man with hair falling to his shoulders and a long, mournful face loomed over our table and meekly whispered some words to Lorelle. He smelled of urine and feces and old sweat. He smelled acidic. His thick battered boots were crusted with layers of dirt and grime. She shook her head. *"Ich habe keine."* He turned to me. I looked away. He shuffled off to the next table.

It seemed after I left Mark that day at the church, he had gone out to get still more drunk, then he had returned to the church and started playing loud music, and that had attracted a cruising police car. They asked him why he was staying there, and if he had a place, and when he began to rail at them, they took him away. Things got more complicated when they discovered his visa was expired. Now it was a case for the immigration service.

"Well, where is he now?"

"In detention, at one of their centers. I was there yesterday and he told me to call you. He has no one. He needs help. They are going to send him back to Malawi—it is the worst thing that can happen to him. He cannot go back."

How definitive she sounded: He *cannot go back* to Malawi. What did she mean by that?

"Well . . . what can I do?" I asked.

"He needs a lawyer."

"What of those humanitarian NGOs—Amnesty International, can they help?"

"I have already talked to them, but this is not exactly their province. They gave me an address though, a lawyer. He belongs to another organization, they specialize in cases like this, and they work pro bono."

"Have you called him?"

"Yes, he is happy to help, but he needs to pay for access to documents and for making copies, et cetera."

"How much?"

"About two hundred euros. I don't have enough, I am afraid . . ."

"Of course, that is no problem." I was relieved it was only two hundred. I'd hate to have to ask Gina for the money. The lawyer's office was somewhere in Mitte, a twenty-minute train ride from where Mark was being held. It was a small office, with two desks, one for the lawyer, one for his assistant, a prim and sour-faced lady. Her black skirt was well below the knees; her sky-blue blouse was buttoned up to the collar, with lacy ruffs fanning round her neck and holding up her head like a neck brace; on her chest was a name tag, *Frau Grosse.* There was only one chair for visitors, so I stood. The lawyer's name was Julius Maier, but just call me Julius, he said, rising out of his chair to shake hands. He was slight of frame, almost insubstantial next to the grave and heavily present Frau Grosse. His father was from Burkina Faso, he added, as if to establish his

credentials, and his mother was German. Lorelle handed him the two hundred euros in an envelope. He counted it and gave it to Frau Grosse, who counted it again before returning it to the envelope and sliding the envelope into a drawer. I almost expected her to lock the drawer with a key attached to a chain hanging from her waist. She caught me looking at her and frowned; I turned away.

"First, your friend needs to prove he is not an illegal, and to do that, he needs to establish he is still a student."

"He came here as a student, it is on record. Why don't they believe him?" I said.

"It is on record, yes. But it is not that simple. He is now out of status, so he has broken his visa conditions."

"Is that very serious?"

"Very. He can be deported, or detained." He waited for me to comment, and when I didn't, he went on, "The best way to help is if he can show that he has applied for a visa extension. I have spoken to him, and he told me that he has not applied for an extension."

"Well, can he do that now?"

"To do that, he will need a letter from the school, saying he is still a student—but that will not be easy. He told me he hasn't been in school for the past year. He was in another school in Potsdam before coming here. His scholarship has been stopped. He has almost graduated, all he needs is to finish his final project."

It was a bureaucratic conundrum straight out of Kafka—to get a hearing he must prove he had applied for a visa extension (which he hadn't), but to apply for the visa extension he must prove he was still a student (which he was, technically,

even though his tuition had lapsed and he had not set foot on campus in a year, and because he had changed schools a few times his paperwork trail was as tangled as Bob Marley's hair). Still, the lawyer looked optimistic. Lorelle looked skeptical. I must have looked puzzled.

"But really," he said, "it is simpler if he asks for asylum."

"You mean like a refugee?"

"Yes."

"He won't," Lorelle said.

"Why not, if it will make it easier . . ."

"Well, he is not a refugee. He is a student."

We took a train to the detention center, a Brutalist edifice straight out of the Nazi architecture catalogue, where we were asked to fill out multiple forms. Julius filled them out and handed them to a lady, who looked like Frau Grosse's twin. She went over them line by line, running a thick finger over each line, before bringing out a rubber stamp and smashing it to the bottom of each page, making the table shake each time. She then looked at us and pointed—her hand rising with infinite slowness to hang in the air—to a row of chairs in a corner. We sat. I felt exhausted already. I felt like I was on trial for a crime and I would definitely be found guilty and hanged. I avoided the lady's glare and ran my eyes over the long, rectangular room. A row of square windows opened high up in one wall, with parallel iron bars blocking any hope of egress—if one were inclined to seek egress that way. A metal door to the side had a sign across it, *VERBOTEN*. A man came in and talked to Julius in German, and then turning to us he switched to English and asked us to follow him. We passed through many doors, each of which he opened with a key from a bundle of

keys in his hand, each door a different key, before finally asking us to sit in a sort of anteroom facing another door. A while later, the door opened and Mark joined us, accompanied by a guard who stood discreetly but visibly by the door. After the fortress-like entrance, and the multiple doors, and the bureaucracy, I expected to see Mark in chains. He was dressed in his usual red jacket and T-shirt. He looked subdued, and a bit lost and vulnerable without his hat.

"Thanks," Mark said to me.

"You'll be fine," I said to him.

Lorelle sat tense and straight in her chair, her eyes fixed on Mark, as if she wanted to cross over to him and hold him, but she remained seated, smiling whenever their eyes met. As it turned out, Julius's optimism was well founded. Mark was released two days later. I got a call from the lawyer and we met in his office. Mark was there, cap low over his head as usual, his red jacket over his layers of shirt and T-shirt, in the same Converse shoes and high-flying jeans. He was free, for the time being. The school had issued a letter acknowledging he was a student, the visa application had been submitted; Mark had been released into the supervision of the lawyer.

I shook Julius's hand, impressed.

"He has to be readily available if he is needed. He must not travel outside Berlin. They needed an address, just for formality, you know. We gave your address, is that okay?"

"Of course," I said. I did not ask him how he got my address. "But where is he going to stay?"

"At the Heim," Julius said, and when I looked blank he added, "The *Flüchtlingsheim*."

Refugee camp. Where asylum seekers were kept pending

the result of their asylum application. I turned to Mark to see what he thought. He was looking out of the window at a tree branch.

"But he is not an asylum seeker," I said.

Julius shrugged. "It is a temporary arrangement."

I said to Mark, "You know what, come to my place, you can crash there for a day or two before moving on."

Mark shrugged, wordless. Thank you would be nice, but then, he had been through a lot. Before we left, Julius took me aside. "How well do you know him?"

"About two months now. Why?"

He shrugged. "Well, I think you need to talk to him." He looked as if he wanted to say more but wasn't sure if he should. He looked over at Mark, then back to me. "Just talk to him. You know, to find out more . . . about himself."

"Okay," I said, puzzled. Was there something Mark was hiding from me? Surely he'd let me know if there was any danger to putting him up? We stopped at a bar and I bought Mark a beer to celebrate his freedom. "My first in days," he said. He was quiet most of the time. I wanted to bring up Julius's comment, but how did one broach such a subject? I decided I'd bring it up as tactfully as I could at an appropriate time. When we finished our drinks he looked up and said, "I hope your wife won't be upset with you bringing home a foundling."

"She'll be fine," I said. I knew that by taking him home I was crossing a line after which it would be hard to turn back. He was now my responsibility. Whatever he did, whatever happened to him, would have a direct bearing on me and Gina.

I heard the voices as I unlocked the front door, and I remembered we were hosting today. Gina had completed her *Travelers* paintings and was having her sitters and a few people from the Zimmer over for drinks and a viewing, and I was supposed to get the drinks on my way back. "Damn," I muttered, thinking of a reasonable explanation.

"All good?" Mark asked, eyebrows raised. I smiled and waved him in.

Gina was standing in the middle of the room, a glass in one hand, talking to a man in a Ralph Lauren shirt, half-unbuttoned to show his hairy chest. She opened her mouth to speak, then stopped when she saw Mark. Her eyebrows

arched, forming a question mark on her face. I went and
kissed her on the cheek. "Hi darling," I said. There were two
women out on the balcony, smoking, wineglass in hand. I
waved to them and shook the man's hand.

"You are Gina's husband," he said. "I am Dante." He
sounded French, or Italian, or Spanish. I wondered if he was
comfortable exposing his chest like that. I nodded and turned
to Mark, "This is Mark—a friend." I waited to see if Gina
would remember him, but she gave no sign she did.

"Mark, my wife, Gina."

Gina looked from Mark to me, the question mark still evident, then she gave him her hand. Mark, in his baseball cap
and jeans stopping at his ankles and backpack slung over one
shoulder and the stench of detention on him, looked so out
of place next to the elegantly bare-chested Dante that I felt
embarrassed for him.

"Come," I said to him. I took his backpack and led him to
the bathroom to wash his hands; I also needed a minute to
compose myself. But what I needed more than anything else
was a drink. In the kitchen there were two bottles of wine
on the counter, white and red, both open. As I looked in the
drawer for a glass, Gina entered. She closed the door and stood
with her back against the door, not coming in.

"I have been trying to reach you."

I filled my glass with wine and drank it all in one go. Gina
came and took the empty glass from my hand and placed it
carefully in the sink. I picked it up and refilled it. A week
after we got married two friends of hers had come to town
on their way to Baltimore, and Gina had wanted to introduce
me. She had cooked and I was supposed to grab the wine on

my way home from the library, teaching my ESL students, but I had totally forgotten. The annoying thing was that I wasn't doing anything, I had just sat in the library, browsing through a novel, and by the time I remembered I was three hours late. She was in bed when I came home and she wouldn't talk to me the next day.

"I forgot we were hosting tonight. I am sorry."

She looked radiant in her red dress, I told her.

"I kept calling. I left messages."

"I can still get more wine, if it is not too late . . ."

"Of course it is too late. Dante brought a few bottles. And who is the kid? He looks familiar."

"His name is Mark. He was here a while back."

"What is he doing here?"

"He needs a place to crash."

"To crash?"

"Yes. I'll explain later."

"You can explain now."

"Too complicated. Later."

"Don't drink too much, please," she said before she left. I finished a second glass, slowly this time. Facing the guests in the living room was the last thing I wanted to do; for that I needed some artificial cheer—and a change of shirt. As I walked down the corridor to the bedroom I saw the door to the studio was open. There were people in there, a man and a woman, talking in low voices. I stood at the door and cleared my voice. In the dim light I saw it was Manu, and the woman, the daughter was also there, standing in the shadows next to a canvas.

"Hi," I said. They all turned and stared at me, silent, as if

waiting for me to make an accusation. The woman moved a step closer to her daughter.

"I didn't know you were here," I said, keeping my eyes on Manu. They continued to stare at me in silence, and as the awkwardness mounted I went on, "I just came in. I was out to see a friend." Still they said nothing, and after a while the woman took her daughter's hand and, keeping as far from me as possible, squeezed past me through the door to the living room. I looked again at Manu, and after the woman. "I never got her name."

"Bernita."

"She doesn't talk much."

"She is shy," he said.

I stepped into the room and stood next to him, before one of the canvases. There were six in all, arranged in order of size, the biggest, a 60-by-50-inch, on the left, and the smallest, a 24-by-20-inch to the right. They were placed so that a single light from a lamp fell on them. Manu's portrait, the 60-by-50-inch stared back at us, thoughtful, a little tired, but filled with gravitas, like a defeated king amidst the ruins of his palace.

"A good likeness," I said.

On the next canvas was the woman and her child. I was seeing the finished paintings for the first time. Gina hated to show her work in progress, even to me. The woman was seated with the child asleep in her lap.

"Like the Pietà," Manu said. A woman holding her broken child, grieving as only a woman can. She was wearing the bulky winter jacket, her face staring down at the figure in her arms, the light falling on her covered head like a halo. Three

small canvases carried sketches of the child alone—I moved closer. No, they were not the child—not the woman's child. It was a white child, the boy from the motherless children's home, standing over the fence, shouting *Schocolade!* And yet, it wasn't him in the next canvas. It was a more generic child, an everychild. Anyone's child. And the next one was even more generic, genderless, neither white nor black; what was clear, though, was the almost accusatory pain in its liquid eyes. I pulled back and turned to Manu. I wondered what he thought of it. He was bending forward, his face close to the canvas.

"There is so much sadness here," he said. When I remained quiet, he went on, "But perhaps it is only my interpretation."

"Do you want a beer? I'll change my shirt and join you in a minute."

Manu had a daughter, he told me. They lived in a Heim.

"Why didn't you bring her?"

"She has her German lesson today."

I tried to guess his accent. "Senegal?"

"No. Libya. My father came from Nigeria, originally."

"Oh," I said.

Mark was on the couch, a glass of wine in hand, flanked by the two women who had been smoking on the balcony. One was Ilse, the PR person for the Zimmer, the other one I had never met before. Mark was describing his ordeal at the hands of the immigration officials to the women. Dante and Gina drew closer, and now there was a little group around Mark, who seemed to be enjoying the attention. He spoke with his trademark braggadocio, making it all sound funny. As I listened I felt like I was also hearing it for the first time, as if I hadn't been there with him, and I couldn't help but admire

his resiliency. The other lady, a brunette, in a blue dress that stopped mid-thigh, leaned toward Mark and asked, "Are you going to seek asylum then? It will be easier for you, no?"

"Mark is a student," I said, joining them.

"Oh, I see," she said, looking up at me. She looked to be in her forties. A journalist, from Frankfurt, I found out later. Her name was Anna. I wondered where Gina found her, most likely through Ilse. The fellowship was tireless in promoting its fellows.

"Why," Mark said, turning to me, a mischievous twinkle in his eye, "do white people always assume every black person traveling is a refugee?"

"They don't," Anna said. "I don't," she corrected herself. "I cannot speak for every white person in this world, can I?"

I left the group and went to the kitchen to pour myself a glass of wine, by the time I came back the woman and child had left. I saw Manu standing a little apart from the group, near the door, a glass in his hand. He was staring at the group, and when I followed his eyes I saw he was looking at Gina, who was talking to Dante. "Your wife is very talented," he said.

"Come and join us," I said, "don't stand here by yourself."

"I am afraid I have to go now. It is getting late."

I gave him his coat, and when I rejoined the group Anna was asking Mark if he had experienced any racism in Berlin, surely Berlin was the most liberal and welcoming of all European cities, no? Mark, unfazed, smiled and said, "I like it here. Even in Berlin I miss Berlin."

"Ha ha ha," Anna laughed, delighted. She had a rather unexpectedly loud laugh. "I like that. Can I quote you?"

Mark raised a hand, his face flush with wine. "Before you

quote me, let me add . . . I have also noticed this, the women always hug their bags when I am in the vicinity, without fail. Like this." He demonstrated. "With both hands. I didn't notice it at first, but then it became so obvious I couldn't ignore it."

Anna laughed, looking more guarded now. Gina threw me a look—Mark was my responsibility. He was making her guests uncomfortable. Dante, trying to salvage the situation, said, "But the race situation in Europe is good, no? Better than America? I go there often, for exhibitions. And they disrespect Obama, is true, is because he is black."

Gina said, "Well, it is not perfect, but it is not that bad either. We have come a long way since the 1960s and the civil rights struggles." She looked at me, but I had nothing to add.

"What is your experience, as an African in America?" Dante persisted, turning to me. I looked at his distressed jeans, his blue Polo shirt with his chest hairs springing out of the unbuttoned top, and I decided I didn't like him, but I smiled and told them about the first time I went to New York. I had approached a policeman at Penn Station to ask for directions, which is the logical thing to do anywhere in the world, and as I got closer to him I noticed his hand inching toward the gun at his waist. I had stopped and looked behind me, thinking surely it was someone else he was reaching his gun for, not me. Now he was gripping his gun tightly, but still I asked him for directions, my voice wavering, and he looked at me, unsmiling, and said, "Keep moving." When I told Gina that story a long time ago, she had been angered. She had called the police pigs and racists. She was fiery then, recently she had grown more tolerant, more oblivious of what was happening around her, her gaze focused only on her painting.

That night, after the guests had left, and Mark lay snoring on the couch in the living room, Gina said to me, "How long is he staying?"

"A day or two."

"How could you invite him without asking me first? If anything goes wrong . . ."

"What could go wrong?" I asked, and even as I said it I remembered the lawyer's worried expression as he asked me if I knew Mark well enough. I pushed the thought aside. "Is he going to set the house on fire, rob the neighbors? Come on. He may look a bit . . . disjointed, but he is okay. He just needs a place for a day or two to get his act together."

"What kind of trouble is he in?"

"You heard him earlier. He needs to sort out his papers. He is a student. A lawyer is working on it."

I lay awake most of that night, listening to Gina's soft breathing. I wanted to ask her about the baby in the painting, and what it meant, but she was already asleep. She slept with her face to the wall, far away from me. I lay sleepless all night long till the morning birds started chirping outside. I opened the window and poked my head outside and gulped in the morning air. I was never fully awake till I smelled the fresh morning air and heard the cry of birds in the trees, even in winter. The leaves were turning reddish on the trees. Already, summer was ending. When we came last October the leaves were already variegated and falling. Late in October I had stood at the window and watched a single leaf still clinging to a twig, thinking that must be the last leaf left on a tree in the whole street, in the whole city, in the whole world, and it was there, outside my window. Fall was my favorite season; an in-between moment, neither winter nor summer, and so brief. I loved to watch the leaves swirl and circle and rise and fall, driven by the wind and the passing cars to pile up against the fence by the sidewalk. I loved to watch the children from across the road play with them, picking up armfuls and raining them down over each other's heads. They'd hold hands and scream and jump up and down on the red and brown and dry leaves, soothed and excited by the crunching and breaking sound they made under their feet, their pellucid laughter rising through the street, up into the leafless trees to startle the birds, up into the upstairs balconies and windows still open as if in defiance of the coming winter.

Mark was already awake, seated on the couch, looking at the open door leading to the balcony and the top of the poplar trees lining the street. He was wrapped to the neck in a blanket, and seated like this, not in constant motion, he looked vulnerable, almost childlike. He had been out on the balcony for a smoke, and the smell had trickled into the room. I told him Gina had to go out for an event.

"Yes, I saw her," he said.

She hadn't said where she was going. Recently she seemed to be always coming in when I was going out the door, or going out when I was coming in; she was waking up when I was getting into bed. Yesterday in the morning we stood in

the bathroom side by side, but we couldn't speak because our mouths were full of toothpaste, we only stared at each other in the mirror over the sink, a brief eye contact before she bent down to spit into the swirl of scummy water spiraling into the drain. I often thought of Gina in her studio, alone all day, battling with colors and lines and fear and hope, coaxing the brushstrokes into shapes, a limb, a face, hair, eyes, and sometimes despairing, as Plato once said, of ever capturing that ideal form she saw in her mind. When we first came to Berlin everything seemed to be working out fine, but now I knew she sometimes stayed in the studio just to get out of my way, just as I went out to visit Mark and his friends to avoid her. Sometimes, when she came out of the studio and found me in the living room reading or watching TV, she looked taken aback that I was there, that I was me, and she was her, husband and wife, in a house, together, and I couldn't tell when this awkwardness had started. I wanted to hold her and just sit quietly, like we used to do a long time ago, but it required so much energy to do that, more energy than I possessed. Instead I would put on my jacket and walk the lonely Berlin back streets, and there is no loneliness like the loneliness of a stranger in a strange city.

Mark asked, "How did you two meet?"

"Let me get some tea first," I said. "Do you want some?"

"Coffee is better if you have it."

"No problem."

He was out of the blanket and already dressed when I returned with the beverages. I had met Gina at an Obama rally at the American University in Washington in March 2007. Obama had just declared for the presidency and Gina

was a campaign volunteer. I noticed her standing next to me, with her friends, all of them volunteers, wearing campaign buttons, and she was simply the most beautiful thing I had ever seen. Twice our eyes met, and I could see she was conscious of me too—I hardly heard a word the candidate was saying, I was busy plotting how to talk to her, but they left to be introduced to the candidate before I could summon the courage to approach her.

"What were you doing in America?"

"I went there on scholarship, in 2006—I was doing my PhD in history. As fate would have it, she was also a student, in the same department. A week later I met her in the library and this time I did not hesitate. When I mentioned I was from Nigeria she told me her father had been a Fulbright scholar in Nigeria. That is how it started. Your turn," I said.

"What do you want to know?"

"Tell me about Malawi. Do you have brothers and sisters?"

"Yes," Mark said. "Two of each, I am the middle child." His voice was serious, the frivolous and evasive Mark had momentarily disappeared.

"Tell me about them, your family."

"I . . . my father and I, we didn't see eye to eye. Did I mention he was a pastor?"

"Yes. What denomination?"

"It is a Pentecostal ministry, one of the few in Lilongwe. When I was a child he encouraged me to join the church drama group. I loved it. I had the flair, I guess, from very early. We'd dramatize stories from the Bible, mainly. I loved the performance, the power to make the congregation laugh with my goofiness, to bring them to tears sometimes, with

only words and gestures. I was always the lead. One day I'd
be the Prodigal Son, cast out, eating with the swine, and then
returning home to be welcomed home by my father, another
day I'd be Joseph, dumped in a well by my brothers. I can
understand why actors sometimes become schizophrenic. It is
easy to get carried away, and then coming back is a problem.
I really believed I was those characters. Even then I guess I
was trying to escape something, I don't know what. That was
my childhood, in the church, no outside interests. While my
friends were out there discovering sports and other interests,
I was in the church, always under my father's watchful eyes.
That's the sum of my childhood. When I finished secondary
school, I naturally wanted to study theater at the university,
but my father would have none of that."

"Why?" I asked.

He brought out a pack of cigarettes from his jacket pocket.
We stood side by side out on the balcony, smoking. "Well,
it was okay to be an actor in church, but not outside the
church. It was living a lie, he said. Making believe for a living. Ungodly, he called it. But with my mother's support,
I was able to get in. I invited the whole family to my first
performance. I had the lead role in *Sizwe Banzi Is Dead*, by
Athol Fugard. I was nineteen. I had worked hard to master my
role, you know, the lines, the movements. But still, even there
onstage, I could see the disappointment on my father's face."

"What exactly didn't he like?" I asked.

He dragged deeply on his cigarette, then he leaned over the
balcony and flicked away the stub. "He said it would bring
disgrace to the church. He said it was too worldly. You have
to understand, my father lived in the church, in the Bible,

for him there was nothing else. Well, I was so disappointed, I stopped going home. During the holidays I'd stay with my friends and we'd perform in small theaters and nightclubs and in the streets. We made enough money to live on. I had fun. My mother came to see me, and she begged me to come home. But I didn't go back. When I graduated I moved to South Africa to stay with my uncle Stanley. He is my father's youngest brother. He is a lecturer at a university, and he is the direct opposite of my father. I never went back home again. It was he who suggested I should look into going abroad to study further. He linked me up with his friend at the Goethe Institute in Johannesburg. I registered for German-language classes, and applied for a scholarship to come here to study. Just like that, everything came together."

"Have you ever thought of returning?" I asked. He shook his head and shrugged. "Sometimes. I miss my mother. And my uncle, and his wife and kids, and my brothers and sisters. But I don't see myself going back. Not soon anyway."

I wanted to bring up what the lawyer said, but Mark took me by surprise when he said he had to leave.

"Leave?"

"Listen, I am not sure your wife is happy with me being here. I could see it last night. And this morning she didn't reply when I said good morning."

I said, "I am sorry. But you really don't have to go. Gina's just preoccupied at the moment . . ."

"It's okay," he said. "Really. I appreciate all you have done for me."

I felt like Judas walking Mark to the bus stop, at the same time I felt a relief, which I tried to suppress. He said he had

friends who'd put him up, and if that didn't work out there was always the Heim. I reached out and gave him a hug, the Judas hug, and watched him run through a gap in the traffic, the wind lifting his ridiculous jacket behind him. He had lost some weight in the last few weeks. He caught the M400 bus and as it pulled away I saw him through a top deck window, waving. I waved back, my hand leaden.

My chest was heavy and my legs dragged as I walked back. Everything was changing. The leaves in the trees, the display clothes in the shop windows. There was an almost imperceptible chill in the air. I thought of home and the harmattan in November, and how it always made me sick, my mother said it was my body adjusting to the change in seasons. Our bodies always want to continue with what they know, pulled along by inertia. I hadn't spoken to my mother in a while. When I first got to America I used to call her every Sunday, talking through five-dollar call cards, the phone being passed from her to my father, to my sister and my two brothers. The plan was for me to return after my PhD, but then I met Gina, and the days turned into months, and the months into years, and then I just stopped calling home. The last time I called, over a year ago, my mother's voice had sounded so distant she could be talking about the weather to a stranger. I had handed the phone to Gina, but my mother always found it hard to understand Gina's American accent, and the call had lasted only a few minutes. I thought of Gina before the pregnancy. We used to sit by the window in the evenings, drinking white wine, watching the empty parking lot across the street, kids step-pushing their skateboards on the concrete, roaring down the pavement, jumping high in the air with skates glued to

their soles, falling, jumping up again, high-fiving after each success. I was so lost in thought I bumped into a woman looking into a display window, then immediately after into a man. I was on a strange street, I couldn't recognize the landmarks and the store names. The man was tall and fashionably dressed in a leather jacket. He held my arm by the elbow and shook it, jolting me out of my sleepwalk. "Hey. Watch it." I nodded and walked on.

9

As it turned out, my questions were answered one week after the day I walked Mark to the bus stop. It was the day of Gina's exhibition at the Zimmer Gallery, somewhere on Karl-Marx-Strasse. Gina hadn't commented that day when she came back and Mark was gone. Our life had reverted to its normal rhythm. We went out to dinners, and openings, and readings and performances by Gina's fellow artists. Today she looked happy as she guided visitors from painting to painting, answering questions about color, technique, concept. There was a solemn instrumental music playing in the background, her fellow artists from the Zimmer were all there. It was going to be an all-day

affair. I stood in a corner, trying to be helpful, chatting with Julia, the Zimmer director, a thin, tall, unassuming woman, with her partner, Klaus, a tall beefy man who kept downing glasses of Riesling like it was water. I had been there for three hours, and I was tired, and hungry, and I was thinking of where to go for a bite—I wanted something more substantial than the finger food on offer, I wanted to ask Gina if she'd come with me, and at that moment a man walked in. He looked familiar. He was with a group of three, and he saw me at the same time.

He left the group and came over. It took me a while to recognize him. It was the lawyer, Julius. He looked different in jeans and T-shirt. I told him it was my wife's exhibition. "Oh," he said, looking impressed. "I heard about the exhibition from my girlfriend." He pointed to one of the girls in jeans and bombardier jacket. "You know, I was going to call you tomorrow. I need to get in touch with Mark. Is he still staying at your place?"

"Actually no. Is everything okay?"

"Well, I need to get in touch with him. It is regarding the visa renewal application."

"He left my place a while back, but I can pass a message . . . I am sure I can locate him if necessary."

The lawyer hesitated, then making up his mind he said, "Well, it is urgent . . . I just found out today that his application for visa renewal was declined. I am sorry."

"Oh," I said, "I am sorry to hear that."

"Can you let him know, please?"

"Of course."

As he turned to go, he said, "This is none of my business,

but . . . you know, his real name is Mary. But I guess you knew this already? After all you are very close."

I looked blankly at him. Mary?

"He is a girl, or rather she is a girl. Mary Chinomba."

Mark, a girl? "Are you sure?" was all I could manage.

"Yes, of course I am sure. I saw the official documents. I see, you look surprised. You didn't know."

10

My phone calls to Mark went straight to a voice who told me, in clipped German, to leave a message, *bitte*, and after a while it stopped taking messages. I called Lorelle. She also hadn't seen him in a while, but she had heard he was putting up at a Heim close to the Görlitzer Bahnhof. We met at the station and walked together to the Heim. We passed empty and decaying buildings with graffiti in blue and green and black running down the walls, and shops with their pulldown doors permanently shut; we passed seedy corner shops with drunk men coming out of the narrow doorway with six-packs of beer under their arms and their beer guts spilling out of untucked shirtfronts, and mustachioed Turkish men

smoking from hookahs under beach umbrellas. We came out on a completely deserted street with a fence blocking the far end and long grass growing beneath the fence.

"Have you been here before?" I asked Lorelle. She shook her head.

We took a corner and entered another street, also deserted except for two men sitting on the pavement with their backs against the wall and their legs sticking out in front of them, still captive to whatever chemical was coursing in their bloodstream. They stared at us, their faces red and grimy, sucking greedily on their cans of beer, until we turned another corner. The Heim was an abandoned school building, most of its windows had no panes, and its yard was overgrown with grass and trash. The front gate opened into a driveway that led to the big gray building. On one side of the driveway was a smaller structure, which must have originally been the security post or an office building, now its windows were boarded with plywood turned black and peeling from rain and sun. Four men, three black, one Asian, stood at the doorway, talking in whispers. They stared long at Lorelle's hair and piercings, before turning to me. One of the men, with a red, yellow, green, and black Rasta man's beanie over his dreadlocks, nodded at me and I nodded back. At the main building's entrance, a huddle of men, dirty, unshaven, and visibly drunk, stood haggling over something. They looked up when they saw us, and one of them, the lone black man in the group, walked away. The smell hit us even before we entered the building: fetid and moist and revolting. Heim. Home. This was the most un-homely place I had ever seen.

"This is it?" I asked Lorelle. It was a four-story building

and from here I could hear voices and muted music coming from upstairs windows.

"This is it."

By the first landing was a bathroom, its entrance faced the staircase, half-blocked by a pile of trash falling out of and partially burying a trash can. A man came out of the bathroom, stepping carefully over the trash, a towel around his waist, his scrawny chest bare, his hair still wet.

"Hi," I said. "We are looking for a friend. Mark Chinomba."

His glance switched from Lorelle to me. He shook his head. "Where he come from?"

"Malawi," Lorelle said. "*Sprechen sie Deutsch?*" she switched to German, sensing the man's wavering English. He shrugged his scrawny shoulders. "Check upstairs."

Stuck to the walls by the stairs were handbills screaming slogans, *No to Borders! No to Illegal Detention! Asylum Is a Right!* They ran all the way along the staircase, some announcing events, in English and French, but mostly in German: drama group meetings, church group meetings, social worker schedules. We met no one on the second-floor landing, so we turned right into a double doorway that led into a long and dark corridor littered with old bicycles and broken tables and chairs and more trash. A row of doors faced us, most of them half-open, showing bunk beds with tattered mattresses on them in which men slept with their legs hanging over the sides.

I knocked on one of the doors and entered. A man stood in front of a small stove with a pot on it, in his hand was half a chicken, in the other hand a knife. The sight of Lorelle behind me seemed to startle him—obviously women didn't frequent this part of the Heim. He put down the chicken on the table

next to a pile of freshly cut peppers and onions and, wiping his hands on his pants, turned fully to us. No, he had never heard of Mark Chinomba. "From Malawi? No, he cannot be here. This room is Senegal."

Another man sat on his bed, watching a TV screen on a table next to the bed—it was an old TV, with the convex protrusion behind it. He didn't look up as we conversed with the man with the chicken; he continued to stare fixedly at the screen whose light illuminated his face, his expression swiftly changing with the images. There were shoes and more mattresses on the floor, cluttering the passage between the beds. A rancid smell hung over the room, rising from the cooking and the shoes and the unwashed bodies.

"Where are the Nigerians?" I asked, curious.

He pointed up, shaking his head. "You can't find Nigeria now. If you want Nigeria you come back in nighttime. Most of them sleep now."

I stopped at the foot of the stairs. I felt tired, depleted. I said to Lorelle, "I think I've seen enough."

She looked at me. "Don't you want to find Mark?"

On the next floor the door opened into a room much larger than the last one, a small hall, with all the mattresses on the floor. Most of the men appeared to be Asian, most likely Syrians, or Pakistanis or Bangladeshis, or Afghans, with a few black men, all with the same furtive, calculating look, all quick to shake their heads when we asked of Mark Chinomba. A few lay on their mattresses, fiddling with their cell phones, some sat around a table in the center of the room, playing a card game, their voices raised in dispute. As we passed in front of more open doorways and stepped over more

piles of trash—almost fainting from the stink—nodding at the men congregated in groups on the balcony or standing idly by the windows, I seemed to be passing through some region of Dante's *Inferno*. None of them had heard of Mark. The topmost floor was the women's floor, and from the stairs we could hear a voice trying to calm down a screaming child. Its shrill, piercing cries brought me to a stop.

"Do you think he'd be there, with the women?"

She shook her head. "No. Never."

We left.

The next day Lorelle called. "There's a film showing this evening, at the Neue Kino, it is a documentary about Mumia Abu-Jamal. A friend mentioned it. Mark is a big fan of Abu-Jamal," she said.

I had no idea who Mumia Abu-Jamal was, but I took down the directions she gave me. After the movie we sat in a little café next to the tiny cinema house. There were people seated at neighboring tables, still talking about the searing documentary we had just seen. Mark and Lorelle sat on a couch, holding hands, Lorelle gazing at Mark with a tenderness that looked alien on her hard, pierced face. She hadn't seen Mark in almost a month. Earlier, when we came in and saw him by the concession stand talking to the barman, they had thrown themselves at each other and locked lips, and the people nearby had cheered while I stood and watched them, absently thinking it must be painful for Lorelle to kiss with all the rings on her lips, but touched like everyone else by the performance.

"I had never heard of Abu-Jamal before."

"But how could you have?" Mark said, laughing. He looked

upbeat. "You live in a big house, with a beautiful wife. You live in America where everybody is a movie star and drives a big car."

"You make it sound like it is a sin or a disease to live in a big house."

"Well, I wouldn't go to see movies about men in big houses. I wouldn't make movies about them either."

"Quite a manifesto. What kind of movies would you make?" I said.

"Let me tell you the kind of movie I'd make. It is about a man in a tunnel. A long and endless tunnel, at the end there is his lover waiting for him, but he begins to realize that also, next to his lover, there is death waiting. But we never see him reach the lover, or death, just a single continuous shot of him in the tunnel, nothing more. The journey is the thing, the monsters that leap at him from the dark are all in his mind."

I nodded. "Nice allegory about the human condition. Beauty and death, side by side. We are all in a tunnel, pulled forward by love, but love is actually death in disguise. To desire is to die."

"Yes, and not to love is also to die," he said. He let go of Lorelle's hand and leaned toward me. "When I make my movie, it will be edgy. It will be Marechera. Dostoevsky. Caravaggio. Knut Hamsun. So edgy it will cut your heart to watch it. What is the point of art if it is not to resist?"

"To resist what?"

"Just to resist, period. On principle."

"That's the kind of films you want to make?"

"That's the life I want to live. Where art and life become one."

"Wait till you are older, and married with kids, with bills to pay."

He laughed and shrugged. "Maybe that will never happen."

Lorelle listened, her head on his shoulder, smoking a cigarette. She leaned forward and said, "Mark's made a short, it won an award."

Mark made a movie? My surprise must have shown on my face. Mark laughed and waved her away. "A short short. Thirty minutes long. Something I did for school project two years ago."

"But it won a directing award, here in Berlin."

"Nice," I said. "About a man in a tunnel?"

"You have to see it. I have a copy I can lend you," she said.

I wanted to talk to him about his options now that his visa application had been rejected, but he didn't appear to be interested in talking about it, and perhaps this wasn't the place.

"Try and call that lawyer. Today if possible. Julius. He has been trying to reach you." He nodded, and immediately changed the subject, "Hey, are you free next week? There's a vinyl record store you have to see. It is humongous, the biggest in Berlin, maybe in all of Europe."

"I am free."

"Good. We'll go, the three of us. We can have lunch afterward. Hang out."

"Great idea, but you must promise not to disappear again," I said.

Mark raised his beer and, laughing, quoted from Shakespeare, *"When shall we three meet again, in thunder, lightning, or in rain . . ."*

He looked happy, and that was how I'd always remem-

ber him, leaning forward to clink glasses, with Lorelle beside him, because as it turned out that was the last time the three of us were ever together again.

"*When the hurly-burly is done / When the battle's lost and won,*" I completed automatically.

A day after our meeting at the Kino, the refugee riots, as the papers later dubbed it, happened. The inmates at the Heim woke up to find the building surrounded by policemen, their vans and cars blocking all the exits to the streets. Next to the police vans were buses provided by the local council, long double-decker buses. A police spokesman, talking through a megaphone, told the inmates to pack their belongings and vacate the building—they had six hours. The neighbors, it appeared, had complained to the council, they felt threatened, their daughters and sons were not safe on the streets where refugees sold drugs, and got drunk and fought; the aliens had turned the entire street into a dumpster, trash

everywhere. Six hours to move out. The buses were there to take them to another Heim outside the city, meanwhile no one was allowed to go in or out. To hurry them along, the lights and water were cut off. But soon activists in the city heard of the blockade and descended upon the street, forming a human chain around the block, chanting in solidarity with the inmates, shouting at the police to leave.

"Mark texted me about it. Tension was high when I got there. Already the police were throwing tear gas at the activists, warning them to keep away. They wouldn't let us go beyond their perimeter," Lorelle said.

"Where exactly were they being taken?"

"Nowhere. It is a trick they like to play. They pile migrants into buses, promising to resettle them, and then dump them outside the city, in the middle of nowhere." She sipped her tea, as if to wash the bitter taste away. "It is a cruel thing to do to helpless people. You know what is written on the buses?"

"What?"

"Fahren macht Spass."

"Riding is fun?"

"That, accompanied by images of happy families holding hands—children and parents and even dogs. It is cruel."

"What happened to Mark?" I asked.

"I kept trying his number, but he never answered, and I began to hope that maybe he had managed to slip out."

She laughed and shook her head. "It was wishful thinking. Mark wouldn't do that. He loved such standoffs with authority. 'This is our moment', he would say, 'this is our Sharpeville, our Agincourt.' He was in there, barricaded with the rest. They had locked the doors from inside, blocking them

with iron beds and tables so the police couldn't break in. We could see them at the doors and windows, waving their shirts and holding hands. The police said they were ready to wait for as long as it took. It took three days."

"But, it wasn't even in the news . . ."

"The news covers what it wants to cover," she said, her voice flat. "I was there. Go online, look for alternative news sources, you'll read all about it. On the third day, when the police got tired of the standoff and threatened to break in and drag them out, the migrants soaked their mattresses, beddings, and floors in kerosene, they promised to set the building and themselves aflame. Some went to the roof and threatened to jump. Mark was there, on the roof. I recognized his jacket."

"What happened?"

"I saw his red jacket. I saw him fall, from the roof to the concrete pavement."

"He . . . he jumped?" I asked, waiting for a twist in the story. But there was no twist.

She said, "Afterward, I saw his body in the police car headlights before they took him away."

I said nothing. I continued to stare at her. We were seated outside a café we had often visited with Mark and Uta and Stan and Eric. Across the road was the church, looking more abandoned than ever. Mark was dead.

"They say he jumped."

"Well?"

"He wouldn't. He loved life too much. Others say he was pushed. I believe them." She lowered her head, her face was filled with the heaviest agony.

"Pushed? Why?"

"Because he was different, and even in that moment, that desperate moment, they couldn't forget that. Anyway, what does it matter now? He is dead."

Mary Chinomba. A preacher's daughter who loved to dress in drag, who loved to perform male roles onstage, who wasn't interested in the nice boys nudged in her direction by her parents. Who ran away from home to stay with her uncle, the only one who must have known and sympathized with what or who Mary was. The scholarship to Germany must have been the perfect solution for everyone involved, a godsend, literally.

"Once, you told me that Mark could not go back to Malawi. What did you mean?" I asked.

"A year after her arrival in Germany, Mary wrote her uncle a letter, pretending it was from her friend. The letter said Mary had died in an accident, and that the body had been cremated because nobody came to claim it. She signed the letter 'Mark.' That was the day Mary died."

"Did the uncle believe him . . . her?" I asked.

"The letter wasn't for the uncle, really, it was for the father, the family. She figured it was best for everyone concerned. Mark dropped out of her first university in Hamburg and became a nomad. He didn't want to be traced by accident. I asked him if he would go back home someday, and he always said, Maybe."

We sat down, watching our food go cold. None of us had the will to stand up and say goodbye.

"Tell me," I said, "how did you meet her?"

"Him," she said.

"Him. How did you meet him?"

Lorelle got married at twenty-two, against her parents'

will. The parents had been redeployed back to the US and wanted her to go with them, but she refused. After a few years, her husband, a DJ she had met at a party in a converted bunker, had turned abusive. "He beat me. I tried to leave him a few times but he threatened to harm me if I did. I eventually ran away to Berlin; I enrolled at the university. I met Mark, on the very first day. We became friends, much later we became lovers. A weird couple around campus, the cross-dresser from Africa and the freak from the US. Mark gave me the courage to ask Thomas, my husband, for a divorce. I grew up. Because of Mark."

I took her hand. "I am so sorry."

She nodded.

"So, you are going back to America?"

"I've been thinking about it for a while, now this . . . I feel as if things have lost their focus for me here. I want to see my parents, get to know them again. What about you?"

"I am not sure yet."

"Well, good luck. And when you come back to the States, give me a call."

•

I got off the bus at the stop next to the *Apotheke*. I walked past the retirement home, my head bowed in thought, and as I passed the school for the homeless children I saw him running to the fence, waving, chased by his eagerness, his face alight just as in Gina's painting. *"Schocolade!"* I averted my face and walked faster, but then I stopped and turned to him. I had to admire his persistence. I raised my hand and waved back. He stood with both hands on the top of the wall, just

like in the painting, his shock turning to delight as I called back, "Hello."

Slowly his hands dropped and he turned and walked back to his friends. I walked on beneath the poplar trees, my mind still churning.

The summer is ended, the harvest gathered, and still we are not saved. The line ran in my mind. I could see Mark standing behind the lectern, thumping his fist on the baize surface, his eyes flicking over his imaginary congregation, imitating his father.

"I am not going back," I said to Gina. I had not thought about it, but as soon as I said it I knew I had decided long before today. I would stay in Berlin, for a while. I could support myself for a few months teaching ESL while I decided what to do next. I could also do some work on my long-neglected dissertation. Gina was seated on the couch, a book in her hand. She didn't look surprised. I thought of our home in Arlington. The parking lot across the road, and us sitting on the balcony, watching the kids skating. That seemed like another life now; recently I couldn't find myself in that picture, next to Gina. She was sitting alone.

"We used to be so happy," she said. And I knew she meant before the miscarriage. "I thought if we came to Berlin, together, away from everything . . . I thought Berlin would heal us."

She sighed. The silenced lengthened, broken occasionally by birdcalls. Perhaps that was what we needed, silence. A little time apart. She looked directly into my eyes, and nodded. Somewhere, in the trees outside, a cuckoo's unmistakable call. I went to the window and looked up. A chittering, a flash of wings, gray and white and dappled. Then it was gone.

Book 2

CHECKPOINT CHARLIE

Manu walks up the driveway, then back, flexing his fingers and stamping his feet to keep the circulation going. It is almost midnight, two more hours to the end of his shift. His thick army surplus coat and the layer of woolen sweater under it feel useless against the cold claws of Berlin winter tearing into him. He is so hungry he feels weak. Stay awake, he whispers, stay alert, that's all you have to do for two more hours. He forces himself to imagine the clients staggering out, flush with drink and dancing. Part of his job is to hold the door for them as they come out trying to orient their senses to the cold, sometimes he helps them find their car if they can't find it by themselves. In the one month he has been working

here he's never had to lead a lady to her car, there is always an eager and muscular young man with the ladies as they come out, laughing and listing on their high-heeled boots. To be escorted home afterward by young men is why most of them come to the Sahara Nightclub, after all. Mostly white and older ladies, mostly black and younger men.

The Sahara sits like an island amidst the parked cars, its brash neon sign reflecting in red and green off the cars' shiny bodies. Both sides of the sidewalk are covered in snow, heaped up like sand at a construction site. He shivers again and takes another drag on his cigarette. He is not a smoker, he got this from his partner, the Turk, but neither is he a doorman, or a bouncer, or a Berliner, but here he is, holding the door, bouncing, smoking cigarettes, in Berlin. Two more hours. He curses the cold again but quickly catches himself; he is lucky to have a job at all given his status. His daughter needs new shoes now that she'll be starting school, new clothes, new underwear, including training bras—she gave him a list. She will be twelve in May. Bras. What does he know about bras, apart from how annoying they can be to take off when one is in a hurry! Ah, the cold, the blasted European winter. Perhaps, if he has some form of distraction, apart from smoking and listening to his talkative partner, the job, the bouncing, may be less tedious. Sometimes the clients come out to catch a quick cigarette, or spliff. He mostly ignores them. Keep it professional, the manager told him on his first day. Keep it professional or you are out. Gruff-looking, gruff-talking redhead, incessantly smoking. She wore jeans that were too tight at the thighs and calves, emphasizing her short, chunky legs, her hair was piled high

on her head, as if to give her extra inches. She looked up at him when he stood in her narrow office and told her he had heard of an opening. The office was dark and filled with cigarette smoke; on the walls were photographs of musicians and actors, some of them in the outlandish costumes of their art, some of them posing with the manager, there were bold, ostentatious signatures across the face of each picture. Next to the pictures was an old poster from the movie *Mandingo*. "Aren't you a bit too old for this job?" She blew smoke at him. He was only forty, he wanted to protest, and he might look a bit tired, but every muscle on him is real, earned in the strawberry and grape fields of Greece where he spent last season picking fruits, sleeping on hard floors, escaping the police and the neo-Nazis, and making sure Rachida was safe. The manager reluctantly nodded, acknowledging his lean, imposing presence, and said he could start tomorrow.

•

They come out, they smoke, they make small talk, and they go back inside to the loud dance music. Mostly young, mostly muscular, most likely West African. He wonders if they have wives back home, children, waiting to join them here in Europe, or waiting for them to come back rich and with all the right papers, the all-important papers that would open up life's cornucopia. He wonders what his wife would think if she saw him now, a bouncer at the Sahara. She'd understand, surely. Rachida needs a new jacket for the winter, new underwear. Just for the winter, in spring he'll find something somewhere, cleaning, construction, dishwashing. All temporary, till he gets his papers.

•

He recognizes the green jacket as the woman staggers out as if pushed by the loud dance music that follows her from inside the hall. He helped her with it earlier when she came. She arrived after 11 p.m., and she is leaving already. Maybe she doesn't like the music. Maybe she doesn't like the men. She staggers a little, pulling the jacket tight around her, looking around slowly. As he turns to her, mouthing *"Alles gut?"* and smiling, always smiling, trying to look as harmless as possible, she casts a contemplative stare at him, up and then down. The light falls directly on her and he notices her eyes are clear, probably not that drunk, just a bit disoriented, the brash lights and the cold do that to you coming out. His partner, Ahmad the Turk, pushes him aside and starts talking to her in his overfriendly, overeager way. She hugs herself beneath her jacket and, ignoring Ahmad, looks directly at Manu and says, "Can you help me find my car? It is somewhere out there." She points.

He takes the keys and goes out among the cars, pressing the beeper on the fob. The cold gets worse the further away he goes from the building. Ah, a Mercedes-Benz. Tucked away between a wall and a tree at the edge of the parking lot, as if she doesn't want it to be seen. New to the Sahara, most likely. He gets in and turns the key; loud music from the radio startles him, and he almost hits his head on the roof as he pulls back, then, relieved, he laughs at himself. He turns down the volume. The car smells of vanilla and sandalwood. Basma smells like that in the mornings, fresh, dressed for work. He leans back in the plush leather, he closes his eyes and lets the music wash over him like balm. It carries him away and he is

home, Rachida is two again and he is putting her to bed, she can't go to sleep without her favorite lullaby playing softly in the background. A loud knock on the passenger side window jolts him back to the present. Where is he? Green jacket. He wipes the moistness from his eyes before leaning over and opening the door for her. She gets in.

"Hallo," she said.

"Nice car. Scared I'd run off with it?"

She looks surprised by the question. Of course, she wouldn't expect small talk from the bouncer, only he isn't a bouncer, not really. "Well . . ." he mutters, and begins to step out, but her leather-gloved hand on his right arm stops him.

"Stay, please," she says. She removes her hand from his arm and begins to take off her gloves, a finger at a time. As she removes the jacket he notices for the first time the luxurious fur at the collar. She smells of perfume, rich, musky. The music comes to a stop, another tune starts.

She puts her hands over the air vent, turning them over slowly like meat on a grill.

"I have to get back to work. Will you be okay?"

She shakes her head and gives a small laugh. "I . . ." she begins, "I am no good when I've had more than two drinks. Can you drive me home, please? My place is not far."

"I can drive, but I am working."

"I asked your partner, he said it is okay. He says he will cover for you."

He looks at her, he looks outside at the pile of snow glowing in the dark. "Okay," he says.

•

They drive in silence. She sits with her head uptilted, her eyes closed. He enjoys the silence, the dreamlike ride in the deserted night streets. On a narrow back street a homeless man staggers into the road, looking like something out of Dickens with his overcoat blowing in the wind behind him, his long beard, his wild, baleful eyes caught briefly in the headlights, then he is gone. Manu follows her directions, conscious of her form, her smell, her swan neck illuminated by the streetlamps and the headlights of the cars they pass, and he knows she is conscious of him too for she sits half-facing him, expecting him to say something. She lives in Grunewald. He follows her finger down a quiet and dark street and eases the car into the narrow driveway, the tires loudly crunching the gravel on the cobblestones. He turns off the engine and they sit in the dark for a while, then she stirs, and he stirs. She points him in the direction of the U-Bahn and hands him a fifty-euro note. He hesitates, then he shakes his head. "No."

"Well, *gute Nacht.*"

•

They leave the Heim early as they do every Sunday. Sunday is a good day, he and Basma were married on a Sunday, and Rachida was born on a Sunday. If she is going to be there waiting for them with the boy, if a miracle is going to happen to them, it is most likely going to be on a Sunday. And so, every Sunday, for the past one year since they arrived in Berlin, he and the girl have taken the train from the station near the Heim to Kochstrasse U-Bahn, and from there they walk across Oranienstrasse to Checkpoint Charlie.

He is glad the trains are mostly empty today. He hates the

weekdays and the rush hours and having to stand face-to-face with other passengers, breathing in the smell of stale beer and sausage and cheese, listening to their loud, unrestrained chatter on their cell phones.

They sit side by side, away from the cold wind that blows in every time the doors open. At a station an official appears before him and demands to see his pass. He always maintains a month's pass for the two of them, no need to take chances. After the ticket check he feels Rachida tugging at his arm. "Father." He is muttering to himself again. He clasps her hand. She looks at his face, anxious. Recently it is happening more regularly. The sallow-faced young man next to them leans over to lock lips with his even sallower-faced girlfriend. His hair stands in a ridge on his head, held up by gel. The girl wears a biker jacket and knee-length boots. Manu looks out the window, willing Rachida to look away. As they get off the train they face a billboard with a completely naked man seated on a stool, leering into the camera, his crotch barely covered by his hands clasped over it. A few months ago Manu would have stepped in front of his daughter to block her view, but now he simply turns his gaze away. It is a new world, another culture. She'll get inured to it. Beside the naked man's picture is another of a starving, fly-specked black child, looking out plaintively at the passengers, asking to be saved from whatever hell the viewer imagines is lurking in the shadows behind her. What does Rachida think of it all? He looks down at her walking quietly next to him, her face set, trying to avoid the pedestrians, trying to keep up. She needs her mother.

As they come out of the U-Bahn and join a body of pedestrians waiting for the light to change, he feels a familiar mix

of hope and dread. Two weeks back, as they waited right here to cross, in this very spot, he thought he saw her in the distance, holding a toddler, the same height and hair shape as Omar. He pointed and they ran, ignoring the cars, pushing through the cluster of tourists on the sidewalk, past the mock MPs, one black, one white, standing in front of the guard hut on the median, hoisting the American flag, posing for pictures with tourists at two euros per picture. A child in a blue jacket momentarily separated from its parents stood in their path, alone on the sidewalk, looking about, trying not to panic. They turned left into Zimmerstrasse and hurried past the Stasi Museum, past the ancient Lada cars parked by the sidewalk, past the giant balloon waiting to take up its passengers for a lofty view of Berlin. Then they turned back, breathless, toward Stadtmitte U-Bahn.

"Where are they?" Rachida cried. There were tears in her eyes. The woman had disappeared, her black jacket swallowed by a sea of black jackets, then she reappeared crossing the road, hand in hand with the child. She was like a swimmer dipping and surfacing in a choppy sea.

"There," he shouted.

"Mother!" Rachida shouted.

They waited at the crossing, watching the pair receding further into the crowd. The light changed, they ran. He felt a clutch of pain in his chest, he needed to exercise. He realized he was pulling Rachida too hard, her hand almost slipping out of his moist grip. But they were catching up to the woman and the boy, who just entered a souvenir shop. Why was she not looking around, searching for them like they were searching?

Later, he sat on a bench by the roadside, his hands shaking,

trying to console Rachida as she covered her face with her hands, her shoulders shaking. The memory of the woman's surprised, then frightened face as he grabbed her hand shamed him. Her gaze went from him to Rachida, two demented faces in the middle of the souvenir store, he shouting "Basma, darling!" and the girl shouting "Mother!" Passersby looked casually at them and he wondered what they saw: a tired-looking man and a crying girl by the roadside, clearly foreigners, in their old and ill-fitting winter jackets—mostly, though, they didn't see you at all.

•

The lights change and they cross, he takes Rachida's hand at a crossing, pretending to guide her through the crush of bodies, but really just wanting something to hold onto. They loiter around the souvenir shops and then they turn back and head toward Stadtmitte U-Bahn. Their legs are used to these routes by now, rising and falling and turning automatically, only the eyes are on full alert, head swiveling, searching for the beloved faces. Hours later, when the girl's legs begin to drag, he stops and they enter a McDonald's. She orders a chicken sandwich. Again, he is reminded that only last year she was ordering the Happy Meal: six chicken nuggets, fries, and a drink. He tries to make small talk as she eats. He feels her eyes on him, full of questions, and he quickly smiles and touches her cornrows. "Your hair looks different. When did you do it?"

Her eyes light up as she runs her hand over the imbricated, dovetailing rows. "Hannah did it, last night while we were waiting for you to return."

Last night. While he sat in the car with the lady in the

green jacket, yearning to put his hand over hers, his lips against her neck.

"It's beautiful. We must thank Hannah when we get back. Maybe we'll pick up something for her."

They hang around till the crowd has thinned, and the doner kebab and imbiss stands by the roadside have closed and the tourists are replaced by another kind of crowd, younger, louder, walking hand in hand, and then they head back to the trains.

•

At the Heim, Hannah is waiting for them in what the inmates refer to as the garden. A barren and graveled space at the back of the huge and charmless building. It is littered with cans and plastic bags clinging to the base of the building, vestigial rosebush stalks, and iron benches presenting a windswept and dismal tableau. The inmates, especially those with children, come out on warmer days to sit on the benches and gaze at the slate-gray skies, enjoying a moment of quiet, pretending they are somewhere else, not at a Heim in a strange city thousands of miles from home.

Hannah turns her kindly, questioning eyes on him and he smiles briefly in response, saying nothing. Is that a flicker of relief on her face? He feels a spark of anger at her. He knows what she is thinking: for another week they will remain a make-believe family, till next Sunday when he and the girl go back on their search. They met in Greece and for one year they traveled together, almost a family, he and Hannah and Rachida, in the manner he has seen many people do on the road, childless women falling in with motherless children, wifeless husbands with husbandless wives, proxy partners for

as long as it lasts—then they parted when she came to Berlin ahead of them, and now they are together again. Sometimes he wonders what she wants from him. Love? Friendship? Protection? For almost two years she has never asked for anything that he wouldn't have offered without being asked. Protection, yes, friendship, certainly, but not love. She is a beautiful woman, and even in these circumstances she manages to look pretty, with long silken hair framing a face from which the joy and light are fading. She sometimes mentions a daughter and a husband back in Eritrea. She never offers more details, and he never asks for more. Details have a way of piling up, layer upon seductive layer, making you think you know the person, until one day you realize you don't. Stories are made up and traded as currency among homeless, rootless people, offered like a handshake, something to disarm you with. He has long stopped wanting to know—he knows better than to get too close. They are here for a new start, not to re-create or hold on to the past. The water they all crossed to come here has dissolved the past. But, he can't give up on Checkpoint Charlie. Because she is alive. He knows. If she isn't he'd know, and if she is alive she'd never rest until she finds them.

•

His partner, the sour-tongued, sour-tempered Ahmad, says, "What these young men want is power. When they fuck these women they think they own the world. By fucking them in the ass or the mouth or wherever, they feel they are fucking the whole of Germany. I swear, that's what they think. Haha. What do you think, Ghaddafi?"

"I don't know, Ahmad."

"You should know. You are educated. You must have an opinion."

"You are right, I guess."

"You are right I am right, Libya." He pauses, dragging on his cigarette. "Tell me, if you are Libyan, why are you so black?"

"My father is originally from Nigeria. He settled in Libya before I was born."

He never considered himself different from any Libyan till after the fall of the dictator when ordinary citizens, includ-ing his neighbors, some of them his patients, began attacking whomever they thought looked different, foreign. He doesn't tell the Turk this. He shrugs. "There are many like me."

The Turk is an ex-boxer. Ahmad the Turk, they called him in the ring. Once, he was a contender for the heavyweight title for the region of Bavaria, but he broke a wrist in the fifth round, he didn't even know his wrist was fractured till the next round. He just couldn't feel his hand anymore.

They stand side by side in the little alcove next to the entrance, sheltering from the cold, smoking furiously to keep away the cold. Ahmad is given to hyperbole, especially on nights like this when the cold is most bitter, and the women and young men that pass before them seem to be having all the fun in the world. He knew the Klitschko brothers, he claims. Once, he was a sparring partner for both brothers, three years back, when they came to Heidelberg and he got to stay with them in the Hotel Europäischer Hof Heidelberg, the most expensive hotel in town. Sometimes he gets overcome by nostalgia for his fighting days, usually when the weather dips too far below freezing, and the Sahara is deserted, then he'll smoke cigarette after cigarette while doing a little shadowboxing, his fighter's

muscles rippling under his jacket, and when he gets tired of that, he'll step into the bar to refill his hip flask with vodka.

"Muammar," he says, sipping his vodka, "these women come for company, a little fun, and our job is to help them get it. Right?"

"Right."

"One day, one of them asked me to walk her to her car, just like it happened to you that day. Hold my hand, she said, and we went. Beautiful. Young. Tits this big. I walk her to her car and she pulls me inside and begs me not to let her go home alone. I swear to Allah, Libya. Now we are holding each other in that car, and we go at it, giving no quarter, boom, I go at her, and she comes back, pow, she scratches my back until I bleed, I pound into her, she pushes up, I push down and now the car is rocking with our movement, and still we go at it."

He assumes a boxer's crouch, fists forward and raised. "Now we are locked together, like this, swaying together. She is a tigress. And all the while that woman Fairuz is playing on the car radio. Now we both fall back into the car seat, locked together, breathing heavily in each other's face. She holds me, like this, two hands around my neck, as if scared of falling off a cliff, harder, she says, harder, and then, I can't hold back anymore, my body shakes, I am down. I am out." He leans against the wall, panting in recollection. "Ah, Ghaddafi. Those were the crazy nights . . ."

Then he straightens up, looking past Manu into the night. "Hey, look who's here."

For two weeks the club had been shut down. A mysterious fire had started behind the bar, some say it was a jealous

husband who had followed his wife to the club. Not much damage was done.

In those two weeks, as he walked the streets of Berlin looking for casual employment, and even on Sundays at Checkpoint Charlie, he thought about her, attracted and guilty at the same time. He remembers her hand on his arm, a brief electricity, a frisson, and her mouth near his ear as she whispered, "*Gute Nacht.*"

Now he watches her approach. The cold has intensified over the last few days. As she approaches, swathed in her green jacket, he feels like turning and walking away in the other direction, into the cold night. She ducks into the tight alcove next to him and takes out a cigarette.

"How can you stand this cold?" she says. He hands her a light, saying nothing. She takes a drag and passes him the cigarette. They smoke, not talking.

"You should go in," he says. "It is warmer."

"I am okay here," she says. "I am not a very good dancer."

"Then why do you come here?"

"Maybe I need the company," she says. She turns and looks at him directly. The Turk slips into the bar and returns with a bottle of vodka. "I can't drink," she says. "I have to drive back."

"I can drive you," Manu says. The Turk winks at him and makes a shadowboxing motion with his fists.

"That will be nice," she says. She takes the open bottle and sips.

Later, in the car, he asks, "What is your name?"

"Angela."

"Like the chancellor," he says. At her house, they sit in the car for a while, listening to a piano concerto on the radio. The

night is quiet, all the windows are dark. A cat slinks across the balcony and into a garden.

"What do you do?" She turns, facing him. "I mean, before you came to Berlin."

He says, "I was a doctor. A surgeon."

She takes his hands and looks at them, as if by so doing to divine the truth of his claim.

"I knew there was something different about you when I first saw you that night. You looked out of place standing there, helping people to their cars. What happened? Where's your family?" When he says nothing, she rubs his hand in hers. "You have very good hands."

"Thanks."

"Your partner told me you are from Libya. Do you miss your country?"

"I have no country."

"Come inside."

He looks out the car window at the house, quiet, the darkness settled around it like a mist. "Perhaps not," he says gently.

"Come on, have a cup of tea before you go. I live alone."

He follows her into a big hall. He can tell it is a big house even though she doesn't bother to turn on the lights. A baby grand piano stands near a window in the living room, which connects to the kitchen in an open plan. A silver shaft of light comes in through the kitchen window, falling on the silver refrigerator and stove. She opens the fridge and takes out a bottle of gin, then she leads him through the living room, into a corridor, and then into a bedroom. She leaves him there, standing in the middle of the room, the bottle of gin and two glasses on the table next to him,

and disappears into the bathroom. Soon he hears the shower running. He looks around the dark room, feeling his way to a light switch. The overhead light comes on, transfixing him in its glare, he quickly turns it off and turns on the night lamp. He sits on an ottoman by the window, and takes off his thick boots. The boot is worn at the heels. He has been wearing it for two years now. When she comes out of the bathroom, wrapped in a flimsy robe, he continues to sit, motionless. She drops the robe.

"I have a wife," he says. His voice is hoarse, his eyes fixed to her voluptuous body.

She sits next to him on the ottoman, the heat from her body rising toward him. "And I have a husband. But we are separated." She takes his hand and places it on her breast, all the time looking into his face. Slowly she helps him take off his jacket, dropping it on the floor. He stands up, conscious of the bulge in his trousers. "I'll take a bath."

In the bathroom, still warm, the mirrors still covered in steam, he fills the tub with hot water. The heating at the Heim has broken down and bathing for the past month is simply turning on the freezing shower over his head and standing under it for as long as he can endure before dashing out of the bathroom. He dips his leg into the very hot water, and then the other leg, then slowly lowers his body; the hot water on his skin is a benediction and he almost cries out with pleasure. He sinks in to his chin and closes his eyes.

The sun coming in through the blinds wakes him up in the morning, and he sits up momentarily disoriented. Where is he? He is in a strange room, in a strange bed, and there is something important he has forgotten. When he sees the

naked woman next to him he gets out of bed and begins to dress. It is Sunday.

"Where are you going?" she asks, reaching out an arm toward him. He continues to dress, hurriedly, almost desperately. "My daughter will be waiting for me," he says finally.

"What is her name?" she asks.

"Rachida."

"Bring her, one of these days. I'd love to see her. I have horses, she could ride them."

•

Each time he goes back to Grunewald she asks him to bring Rachida, and each time he promises he will. He goes on weekdays when he isn't working, and on Saturdays before going to work at the Sahara. Occasionally he stays overnight, but never on Saturdays. He makes up excuses for that: he has to take Rachida to the park, he has German-language lessons—which he does, though not on Sundays. To Hannah and Rachida, he says he is out job hunting in Grunewald, and he tries to salve his conscience by getting them little presents, things he can afford, scarves for Hannah, sweets and trinkets for Rachida. Sometimes Angela hands him a grocery bag stuffed with packets of sugar, tea, fruits. "For your daughter." Hannah takes the bag each time, saying nothing, but her eyes are always filled with questions, which he avoids.

"Where are we going, Father?" Rachida asks. Her apprehension shows in the way she clutches his hand as they get off the train at Grunewald, she walks close to him, staring at the gated houses with vines running over the walls and fences. This is far from Kreuzberg and the Heim, far from

the touristy bustle and noise of Checkpoint Charlie, far from anything she has experienced since they came to Berlin.

"We are going to see a friend. She has horses and she might let you ride one."

She looks up at him, surprise and doubt on her face. How will she behave with Angela? he wonders. It will be fine. Angela is charming, easy to talk to, and surely she will be great with children. With her he can talk about the past. Lying in bed naked, post-coitus, the words come easily, gently coaxed by her attentive face, the right questions, and on each visit he tells her more. "Tell me about Libya," she always begins. He told her how the students at Rachida's school began to disappear, one by one. "What happened to all my friends?" Rachida had asked him, "they don't come to school anymore." The school population dwindled as the violence grew, the NTC rebels gradually took over town after town, those who could afford it left, till only the children of the poor remained. The worst part was when the teachers started to leave. By the end of 2010, almost all the schools in the area were closed.

"Every day I woke up, I took the kids to school, I went to work, I pretended that things would soon get back to normal. I was the only doctor left for miles around, when eventually even the sick stopped coming to the clinic for fear of the violence on the streets, I told my wife to take the children and leave. She refused, she wouldn't go without me. Then one day, I took the kids to school as usual and the gate was closed, not even the guard was there, that was when I knew it was time to go. When we came home, my wife was ready, unknown to me she had packed weeks before, and just waiting for me to

come to my senses. And still I was reluctant to go. 'But if we go, who will take care of the sick and the wounded?' I asked. 'Let the politicians take care of them,' she said.

"We decided to come to Berlin, that's where everybody was going. Also, I had an old school friend here, Abdul Gani. We had no plan, nothing. The most important plan was to get out of Tripoli alive. Also, I told her, 'If anything happens on the way and we are separated, continue on to Berlin. Look for me at Checkpoint Charlie. I'll wait there, every Sunday.'"

"Why Checkpoint Charlie?" Angela asked.

He shrugged. "I had read about it in books. It seemed as good a spot as any." Then he added, almost shyly, "In the movies lovers always meet at a prominent landmark, like the Empire State Building, or the Eiffel Tower."

"You must love your wife very much."

"Yes," he said.

"So, did you meet your friend, Abdul?"

"Unfortunately no. By the time we got here he had moved on. He now lives in America, in San Diego."

•

He wonders if Rachida can sense his nervousness, how his steps falter as they approach the front door, how his hand takes an infinitesimally long time to rise to the doorbell. The door opens and a man stands at the door, a man with a thin, unsmiling face, his hair graying. Manu can tell he isn't that old, mid-fifties. He looks at Manu, then the girl, then back to Manu.

"Who are you looking for?" His voice is challenging, his posture, one hand on his hip, is aggressive. Manu turns to

Rachida, unable to hide his confusion, he looks at the house number again, 47, then he says to the man, "I think we have the wrong house. Sorry to disturb you."

He pulls her hand and they turn to go. As they cross the road he hears Angela's voice calling, "Manu! Hey, Manu. Come back."

They take off their muddy shoes by the door. The man is seated behind the piano, running his fingers aimlessly over the keys. He doesn't look up when they enter.

"Joachim, this is Manu, a friend. And this is Rachida, his daughter," Angela says. She comes forward and frames Rachida's face in her hands, pulling it close, running a hand through her hair. "She is so beautiful, Manu."

"Hello, Joachim," Manu says.

Joachim remains bowed over the piano, his back curved over the keyboard until it seems he is going to tip forward, then he raises his hands and a tune rings out. It rises and falls, repetitive, rising and falling.

Angela leads the girl away. "My, you are so cold, come to the kitchen, I'll make you a cocoa. And you, Manu, I'll get you a coffee."

The man keeps playing, his head lowered, his eyes closed. Manu sits, feeling the awkwardness of the moment. Joachim is the husband. Angela has mentioned the name several times. He wonders what he is doing, why he is back. His eyes run over the familiar room, every surface is redolent of him and Angela caught in blind passion, panting and sightless and naked. The piano. She, bent over, her hair dripping into the keyboard, he behind her, his hands on her waist, together

banging out a sweet and strange tune. He begins to stand up, and just then Joachim turns and says, "Charles Mingus."

"What?" Manu asks, smiling. He takes a deep breath to regain his poise, always smiling to show he is harmless.

" 'Take the A Train,' by Charles Mingus. You know it?"

"No. I am not a musical person, unfortunately. I am a doctor." He adds the last with a squaring of his shoulders.

But the man interrupts him. "Did Angela tell you I am a musician, jazz?"

"I believe she must have."

He continues before Manu can answer, "Jazz is like life. You have to trust in chance, sometimes it will work, sometimes it will not work. It is like sex. When it does work, it is magic. Tell me, does it work like that for you?"

"I am not a jazz person myself," Manu says.

"I don't mean jazz. With my wife. The sex, is it magic, is it chemistry?" He has been playing as he talks, but now he stops. Manu turns to the kitchen, hoping Angela will appear. He can hear laughter from the yard outside, coming through the open back door. He hasn't heard Rachida laugh like this in a long time. He stands up. "Let me see how my daughter is doing . . ."

And just then Angela enters, a cup of coffee in her hand. She hands him the cup. She looks from him to Joachim, who has gone back to picking at the piano keys.

"What are you two talking about?"

Joachim continues to play, turning fully to face Angela. Manu stands up and heads for the kitchen and the back door leading to the courtyard. Rachida is in the barn, feeding a piebald mare an apple. She turns and sees him, her face alight

with wonder. She hands him the apple. "You can feed her, Father. Isn't she pretty?"

"Yes."

He can see into the living room from where he stands. They are shouting at each other. Joachim is trying to take her arm, but she shakes him off angrily and walks away to the kitchen. Joachim follows her, she leaves the kitchen and heads into the corridor to the bedroom.

"Come, we have to go now."

"The horse, Father, what of the horse?" she asks. She is wearing a pair of Angela's boots. He hugs her tightly, "I am so sorry, child. This was all a mistake. We have to go."

"But . . ."

"Hurry, Rachida, hurry."

As they pass through the living room, a door opens and Angela comes out. Manu whispers, "Sorry, we have to go now. Thanks for everything."

"You don't have to go." She goes to Rachida and takes her hand.

"I am sorry," he says, looking into her eyes. "This was a mistake."

Rachida looks with perplexity from her father to the woman.

"Come, Rachida," he says. Their feet landing on the hard snow makes hollow crunching noises as they leave.

•

"She says she can't go today. She is not feeling well."

Hannah stands by the door, a tense smile on her face. She is wearing a quilted housecoat that reaches below her knees.

"Well, it is Sunday. Please go in and remind her. It is Sunday."

"What happened yesterday? She came back distraught."

He searches her face, most of it covered by her hair falling forward like a veil. He wonders how much Rachida has told her. It is Sunday, he wants to repeat, but says instead, "Can I see her?"

He steps forward, trying to go around her into the women's section. The women and children occupy the top floor of the Heim, and although it is not forbidden, the men consider the women's section off-limits. If they want to see a woman, they stand at the entrance and send for her. Hannah remains static.

"Come," she says, "let's go to the garden."

In the deserted garden a plastic bag flies in the wind around the square space, and ends up stuck on the leg of the bench they are seated on, side by side. Hannah says, "I heard from my lawyer today. The review board has approved my asylum application."

He looks at her, speechless. Finally, he says, "Well, that is great news, Hannah. I am so happy for you."

She nods. "I have been allocated a place, a small place. One bedroom, and a living room. A bath, a kitchen."

"When do you leave?"

"No date yet, but soon."

"Rachida will miss you."

She nods again, silent. He adds softly. "We will miss you."

"You two can come with me."

"But we can't," he says.

"Why not?"

When he gives no answer she lays a hand over his. "You don't have to answer now. Think about it. Rachida is like my

daughter now. I want to know she is okay. I want to watch her grow into a woman."

•

A light snow is falling, turning the sidewalk white. He exits the train station and walks toward Checkpoint Charlie, alone. The mock MPs are at it again, posing with tourists. The wind in his face brings tears to his eyes. The diehards brave the bone-chilling cold, drifting like windblown paper from one display to the next, their faces barely visible pink splotches under scarves and hats. He continues on Friedrichstrasse till he sees the blue *U* sign in front of Stadtmitte U-Bahn. The lighted sign sucks him forward like a fly, and soon he is on the train, not caring where he is going. He changes trains a few times, from U-Bahn to S-Bahn and back again. Once, he starts and looks around, fearing he has forgotten something. "Rachida," he mutters. As he gets out of a station he notices the train tracks running in multiple directions: at times they look like fault lines separating sections of the city; other times they are stitches, holding the city together. Now he is walking by the Spree, alone, and where is everybody, the summer crowd sitting in the grass watching the tourists in boats gliding by. Lumps of dirty snow from the last snowfall litter the dry brown grass. He stands staring at the water.

He can hear Hannah's voice, rising from the water, "Why don't you take a break today?" And his voice, sounding horrified, "You know I can't. What if she comes today, the very day I decide not to go? I won't forgive myself . . ."

"Maybe it is time to let go, Manu."

"What are you saying?"

"Rachida . . . She knows her mother is never coming. She is doing this just to please you."

"What?"

"Listen . . . my husband . . . he is not coming either. He died, killed in front of my eyes."

"But you said he was coming, you are waiting for him." She was lying to him. Why was she doing that? But she went on, gentle yet still insistent, "We say things sometimes to keep our sanity. Your wife, she died, didn't she? And the boy, and you blame yourself."

"Shh. Stop. You know nothing about me."

He left her and ran out into the street, clutching at the hot molten pain in his chest, till he got to the train station. Now his face in the Spree stares back at him—tired lines on his forehead and around his eyes, deep like a freshly plowed field. His hair, when did it turn so white, so thin at the top? The wind blows over the water surface; ripples, waves rise, tall and towering like horses rearing up to attack, and everywhere he turns there are bodies floating, people screaming. He holds onto Rachida, he is a good swimmer, but Basma, where is she, she has the boy, he can't see them anywhere. Bobbing and sinking. Flotsam everywhere. But he won't give up. He will go to Checkpoint Charlie every Sunday. Rachida will come with him. They will walk past the souvenir shops and ice cream stalls, together. If they keep their memories alive, then nothing has to die.

Book 3

BASEL

A drive of twenty minutes outside the city toward Liestal and a confusion of intersections led to the tiny town where the woman lived. Katharina, that was her name. They'd left the autoroute and taken a narrower road that rose gently into the hills through little towns with cars bearing ski equipment clamped to their roofs parked in front of houses and hotels. Skiers getting ready to go off to the mountains, the taxi driver explained, he pointed ahead, French border. The border was even closer than Basel, which was still visible behind them, its tall buildings and communication masts rising into the cloudy sky. The house was tiny, separated from its neighbors by fir trees and grass hedges. Portia told the driver

to wait. She got down and stood before the door and peered into the glass panel before ringing the bell. A woman opened the door halfway, sticking only her head out in the crack between door and frame.

"Katharina?" Portia asked.

"Yes."

"I am Portia. David's sister. We spoke on the phone."

The woman nodded and opened the door wider. Portia paid the driver and followed the woman into the house.

"Welcome in Basel," Katharina smiled. She ran her hands through her hair, twisting it into a knot at the back. *To*, Portia found herself correcting mentally. It was the same in Berlin. *Welcome in Berlin*, they'd tell her. It was a direct translation from the German, she knew, but she corrected them anyway, mentally. Welcome *to* Basel.

"Sorry, it is a very small house," Katharina said. Her hair was raven black and tousled. A beauty, Portia noted grudgingly, if you like the petite type—she stood just over five feet tall. Part of the reason she was here was to see this woman whom her brother chose, to try to understand why he chose her. What was the attraction? She was an educated woman, a former lecturer at a university, a PhD. Was that part of the attraction, an intelligent person he could talk to, look up to, or was it the beauty? That would be a good place to start, an instant icebreaker. Why do you think my brother chose you? Unless of course if it was she who did the choosing. The house was a veritable dollhouse, the living room already felt crammed with only two of them standing in the middle. Two bedrooms at most. An open door led into a kitchen adjoining the living room. A square patch of tartan rug covered the

floor, on the edges of the rug were a couch, two armchairs, and a circular dining table by the window. A glass flower vase with a single red rose in it rested on the window ledge—it was a large window, almost taking up the whole wall, and it gave the small room an illusion of space. Next to the window was a bookshelf. Everything in its place, a tidy mind.

"It is a beautiful house," she said.

"Thank you," Katharina said, and, out of modesty or a stubborn determination not to concede the point about how unimpressive the house was, she pointed at the wood beams in the roof, thick and long and tubular. "It is an old house, my aunt built it. Long ago. Maybe twenty years now."

They sat down, the ice still unbroken. Katharina took out a picture of her aunt from the desk drawer and showed it to Portia. A large, stern-faced woman, hair tied at the back of her head, her back straight and her chest thrust out like a drill sergeant at a parade. She had died a few years back, at the age of eighty—an independent, strong-willed woman, who lived in a time when such attributes were considered unwomanly. She grew up poor, she never married, worked various jobs all her life: laundry maid, nanny, cook, bus driver, all the time saving her money, driven by one desire, to build her own place. And she did, saving every penny. She taught herself carpentry and some of the wooden furniture, like the bookshelves and dining table and chairs, she made herself. Katharina was her only niece, and they were close, and she left her the house when she died.

"Sometimes I feel sad. She didn't enjoy life, she saved and economized, and now she is dead. She should have enjoyed more, you know." As Katharina talked her eyes kept straying

to the passage leading to the door next to the kitchen, and a minute later the door opened and a man came out. Average height, about forty, leading a bull terrier on a leash. He was dressed in boots and a windbreaker, ready for the outdoors.

"This is Sven."

He shook hands with Portia.

The dog went over to Portia and she let it sniff her hands and her feet, circling her, before returning to Sven. He pulled at the leash, heading for the door, speaking softly to the dog in German. Katharina spoke to him in German and he nodded. *"Ja, ja."* His eyes behind his glasses blinked weakly as he smiled and said, "I am taking Rex for a walk. It is good to see you."

"Bye, Rex," Portia said.

Man and dog reappeared in the path outside the window, heading for the faraway tree line. Sven leaned down and scratched Rex behind the ears before taking off its leash. Rex bounded forward and the man followed till they disappeared into the trees. On the horizon a dense black cloud swarmed up over the fir and spruce forest, it changed into a storm of birds, a murmuration of starlings, shape-shifting, now a funnel, now a wave, now a sphere, now a sickle, rising and falling, breaking up and reconfiguring, fast and evasive and then it was gone.

Katharina said, "Sven and I grew up together. At one time we were engaged, we were going to be married."

"Oh," Portia said. "And?"

"It was a long time ago. Before I met your brother."

Portia waited, but Katharina didn't offer more, her eyes were fixed on the distant line of trees where man and dog had disappeared.

"What happened?" Portia pressed.

Katharina shrugged. "I talk about Sven if you like. But he is not too important for this, yes? Not concerned. My father and his father, they went to university together. Sven, he is a professor."

"So, it was expected then, that you two would marry?"

"Well, not really, not like arranged marriage. He was my first boyfriend and we like each other, and everyone thought we were going to get married. Yes. Is there anything more you want to know about him?"

Portia shook her head, surprised by the directness and abruptness of the question. So much for breaking the ice. She wasn't the one who brought up Sven—but she sensed the woman was merely circling, sniffing her up, two strange dogs meeting. Portia smiled brightly, this was going to be a chess game. "How old is he?"

"He is forty now. Five years older than me."

"So you were about thirty when you met my brother?"

"I was twenty-nine. Your brother was thirty." She stood up. "I'll get some tea. You want?"

"Yes. Any green tea will do."

Portia went to the bookshelf and looked at the titles: Bertolt Brecht, Goethe, Kierkegaard, Spinoza, all in German. Katharina had studied philosophy or something in that line. She wondered what they discussed, she and her brother, at night. She wondered why she was here, what purpose this visit would serve, after all, her brother was dead, gone. *Lycidas.* That poem had been running on her mind all day, driving her crazy—*For Lycidas is dead, dead ere his prime.* Three years dead. This inquisition, this raising up of the past, of what good was

it? But she was here, and Katharina was here, so she might as well get on with it. Outside, the fog was steaming off the grass, rising to cover the trees.

As soon as she came back with the tea, Katharina jumped into her story without further preamble. They had met at the Basler Fasnacht festival in Basel. "You know the Fasnacht? No? It is famous ceremony here. People dance and sing, mostly folk songs and political songs. People come from many countries to watch. That night, me and my friends, we were following the singers, they walk in the streets with their lanterns, dressed in traditional clothes. I was in final year for my PhD, and I was happy and carefree." She paused, her eyes wistful, perhaps reliving the moment of her past happiness.

"Was David there to watch as well?"

"He was there with his wife, this he told me later. They were having some argument, I think. She left and went home. And he was alone . . ."

"My brother had another wife, before you?" she asked, putting down her tea. Katharina smiled, her cup held in both hands. She nodded, amused at Portia's reaction.

"Yes, he had a wife. Her name is Brigitte. And his name it was not David. It was Moussa. When your brother first came in Switzerland he was staying in a refugee hostel outside town. It is old building near a farming village, nobody was staying in the building so they give it for refugees. It is remote, far from town, and the refugees were not allowed to go any-where, not church, or library, or public buildings. It was a new law. The government was trying to control immigration, too many new people coming in, and all over the country people are not sure how to treat them. There was suspicion.

The government even started paying refugees to return to their countries. About a thousand francs per person, I think.

"But Moussa didn't want to go back. He applied for asylum. They were allowed to work on farms, helping the farmers and also making some pocket money. When they first met, he was working on Brigitte's father's chicken farm and she had come to visit from the city. Her father and mother liked him very much because he is very nice, and sometimes he stayed for dinner after they work on the farm and they talk about things, what he planned to do. They even wanted to get lawyer for him to help him with his asylum application. But this day the daughter, Brigitte, she came with her two-year-old daughter. Brigitte was divorced. She was surprised to see him. Her parents have already told her about him, but she didn't know what to expect. He told me at first she was very hostile to him, she thought he was trying to take advantage of her parents. They were old, in their seventies. But later they became friends. Your brother, he was easy to talk to, yes? Very charming."

Portia caught the faint cynicism in Katharina's voice. It was understandable, for despite all that had happened, Brigitte had been the first wife and still a rival, even if only after the fact. She went on, "Very soon she was taking him to her place in Basel for weekends, and before a few months they were talking of marriage."

"And did you meet her, this Brigitte?" Portia prompted when Katharina paused for a long time, her eyes on the teacup, which she held before her chest in a meditative pose.

"I have met her. I don't want to sound mean, but she is a common person, not very educated, you know, she was an

assistant in a store. But she was lonely and just coming out of a divorce, and I think she loved him and her daughter liked him—he was very good with children. So why not, they try to get married quickly. And I think he told her that was the best way he can get his papers, and she wanted to help. So they went to the registry, but at registry they meet more problem. Instead of getting married he was detained for many days and finally he was deported back to Mali."

Moussa. Portia was hearing that name for the first time. She had a lot of catching up to do. David had left home fifteen years ago, she was nine then, and he was nineteen. All she remembered was a long-legged kid who played soccer with his friends in the backyard, who was protective of her, and whom she idolized. She remembered one morning, walking her to school, he had told her he was going away for a long time and she might never see him again, but he would write to her and he would always love her. He left the next day, to South Africa, she later found out, illegally. He had spent a year in prison there. He came back home, and when it appeared he had finally settled down and was ready to return to school, he left again one year later, this time on a boat to West Africa; from there he planned to cross the desert to Europe.

She imagined his deportation. In England, when she was doing her MA, a classmate from Kenya had told her about an uncle who had been deported but had somehow found his way back. He told her it always happened at night. She imagined her brother, alone or with other deportees, handcuffed, led by immigration officials through a deserted terminal, *at night*, to a waiting plane chartered specially for the purpose. It would be a long and interminable flight. Once, on a plane to

Frankfurt on her way to Zambia, an Arab family had boarded, man, woman, two children, escorted by immigration officials. "Why?" the man kept shouting, looking into the faces of the passengers as he passed through the aisle. "Is it because I am Muslim, because I am not white? You send me back to die? My blood on your head." In his seat, he banged his head repeatedly against the headrest and the armrest. "I kill myself before I go back." The children and the wife screamed with him, loud and sorrowful, delaying takeoff, till finally the pilot came out of his cockpit and spoke to the agents and the crying screaming family was led off the plane. She remembered the man, a portly, middle-aged man, in fishnet singlet and jeans—he must have been surprised by the agents as he watched TV or ate dinner with his family—and the quiet, tearful wife holding the two children, one on each arm. Did her brother also scream and beg to remain, and when they got to Mali, was he simply dumped at the airport with nothing but the clothes on his back, and who was at the airport to receive him? What do deportees feel: relief, shame, anger? Surely, they must feel relief to be away from all that European suspicion and alienation? And yet, some of them, no sooner do they arrive than they begin to plot their return. It is as if some homing device, focused toward Europe, is implanted in their brains and it never stops humming till their feet are on European soil.

"Why was he deported to Mali, why not to Zambia?" she asked.

Katharina looked at her and shrugged. "Because he told everyone he was from Mali. That his family is there. Even me. I didn't know his family is from Zambia till much later."

"What happened after the deportation? How did he return to Switzerland?" Portia asked.

"Brigitte, she promised she'd get him back. She got a lawyer who told her the only way he can come back is if they get married. So, she got on a plane and went to Mali and they got married."

Despite herself, Portia was impressed by Brigitte's tenacity. What was it about her brother that attracted these women? She took a sip of her tea—it was cold. What is it about black men that acts like a super-magnet to these white women: curiosity, the exotic factor, love, or is it pity? What is it about white women that black men can't keep away from?

"She must have really loved him," she said.

Katharina laughed. "Yes. Like a movie, yes? Very romantic. And also, very foolish."

"Foolish?"

"Well, it didn't last. They got married in a court in Mali, they came back, husband and wife. He got his papers, he started working at the rail station, everything was going well, then they were fighting. They live together less than two years only. He told me she wanted too much to be in charge, all the time, and his life became hell. He said his life was better when he was living in the refugee camp."

"And that was when he met you?"

"It was love at first sight. For both of us. After that night at the bar, it was only one month later he left her and he started to stay with me."

"Well, if you were so in love, why did you kill him? Why did you kill my brother? Can you make me understand that?" Portia asked. Katharina put down her cup, she went to the

table and pulled out a drawer and took out a cigarette packet. She opened the window and blew the smoke outside. "So, finally you ask your real question. This is the reason why you came. I wondered when you were going to ask."

Portia sighed. At last, the ice was truly broken.

•

In the taxi going back to her hotel, Portia watched the raindrops hitting the window and she imagined heaven and earth conjoined by pillars of rain. Rainy Basel. *He must not float upon his watery bier / Unwept, and welter to the parching wind.* It had been raining yesterday when they arrived in Basel. A wet welcome. It felt like it was raining in every town and village and hamlet all over Switzerland. It had been raining at the Hauptbahnhof in Berlin when they boarded the train, and it rained all the eight hours the train ride lasted. She closed her eyes, exhausted by the bad weather, by her session with Katharina. In her mind she played over and over again Katharina's words, her halting English, the hand gestures, the direct, combative stare, till toward the end when she ended the conversation abruptly. She was too tired, she said, the memories were too disturbing, she didn't know they would be so strong, could they continue tomorrow? She would call, she had Portia's hotel number.

•

He had insisted on taking a room with two separate beds. To give her some space, he said. Or, to give himself space. He was a married man, separated, but still married. He liked her, she could tell, otherwise he wouldn't have said yes to her

invitation. Come with me, to Basel. She had surprised herself. She hadn't known she was going to make the invitation
till she did it; in her defense, she had been drunk at the time.
Two days ago she hadn't even known who he was, and now
here they were, in Basel, together, even if in separate beds.
She loved having him here, she felt excited every time she
turned in her bed and saw him in the next bed, mere meters
away, a book in his hand, and he'd sense her looking at him
and he'd give her his easy smile and ask if she was okay. She
had wanted to go to Katharina's with him, but he had advised
against it. "We don't want to spook her." He was right. His
presence would have been a distraction.

He was not in when she entered the room, perhaps out for a
walk. She decided to take a bath before he got back. The room
was bare, almost utilitarian. A flat-screen TV was hooked to
the wall, the table was wooden, the chairs plastic, she liked
the spaciousness and the austereness. The beds were firm and
comfortable. She had found the hotel on the internet, attracted
by its proximity to the train station, and booked it hours before
they left Berlin. She loved the view of a wide, grassy fen
with willow trees and the fog hanging over it. Beyond it was
what looked like a river, or a lake. *Watery bier.* She imagined
drowned bodies floating in the water. She shivered. This was
part of the old city, nearby was the university and many excellent restaurants, according to the pamphlet given to them by
the receptionist when they checked in last night.

She had always wanted to see Berlin and had decided to stop over for a day or two before passing on to Basel. Luckily, she met a couple online who offered her a place to stay; they were out of town, somewhere in Denmark, and she had the use of their place for two days. She spent the first day indoors, sleeping. She had had to wake up at 4 a.m. to catch her Ryanair flight from Gatwick. She was reluctant to go out, even though she had a long list of attractions to visit—the wide, cold and wet Berlin streets were intimidating, and if only she spoke some German. All morning she watched American movies and sitcoms on television. Mostly old movies. Denzel Washington in *Training Day* sounding very fluent

in *Deutsch*. They reminded her of the Hong Kong kung fu films David had been so fond of, and how they'd laugh at the off-sync between the English voice-over and the actors' moving mouth. The Germans, however, were not so sloppy, the asymmetry between lip movement and voice-over lasted only a syllable, a half-syllable, and you had to be assiduously watching for it. She amused herself watching for it, giving herself one point whenever she caught one; an idle game to pass an idle rainy day. By midday she was tired of watching TV and beginning to feel like a prisoner, so she explored the flat.

There were pictures of Hans and Ina, her absent hosts, on the mantelpiece, hiking, biking, camping, in different countries, mostly tropical, maybe even Africa. She had spent the night on the couch in the living room; she felt like she was camping here. There were two bedrooms, the one next to the living room was the guest room, mostly bare, with a bed neatly made up and a table and chair by the window. She had gone there only to get the duvet and return to the couch and the TV. Everything was in place, ordered, organized, they must have cleaned before they left. In the morning she got an email from Hans, he gave her their hotel phone number and wanted to know if she was fine? He had forgotten to tell her there was food in the fridge, eggs and bread and cheese, she was free to use that.

The rain stopped by midday and the sun came out. Furniture was being moved in the next apartment, somebody was moving in, or out. She had to go out. She had no excuse, the sun was shining, she had a map, and she had only a day left in Berlin before she moved on to Basel. This, after all, was why she decided to stop in Berlin, to see the city and the historic

places she had read about in books: the museums, the famous streets, the WWII memorials.

She took a shower and changed into a pair of jeans and a T-shirt, as she stepped out into the corridor she noticed the door to the next apartment was open, in the doorway was a man on a ladder, a black man, and when he turned and looked at her, she knew he was African. What are the odds, she thought, as he returned her surprised gaze. She stood in the passage before the door, staring at him; she couldn't help herself. She had been starved of human contact for two days, black human contact, apart from the German-speaking Denzel Washington, and now right in front of her was a black man, an African, looking down at her from his ladder. But what if he wasn't African, what if he was one of those rare Afro-Germans she had heard about, who had lost all memory of Africa, who spoke nothing but *Deutsch*?

He was stepping down from the ladder now, a picture frame in his hand, his head tilted, mirroring the way her head was tilted to look up at him. She straightened her head. And then they spoke at the same time. "Excuse me . . ." she began.

"Can I help . . . ?" he asked. In English. Not German then. The accent was West African, probably Nigerian. Nigerians were everywhere. She had met many in Zambia.

"I am sorry," she said, blushing mentally.

"Can I help?" he said again. He was good-looking, not the sweet and lyrical Denzel Washington kind, but subtler, especially when he smiled just now. He had a stubble, he looked like he hadn't been sleeping well.

"I was wondering . . . I am looking for directions."

"Okay."

They stood side by side over her map.

She followed his directions to the Museumsinsel, and it wasn't as hard as she had feared. She wanted to see the Egyptian collection, but when she got there she couldn't get in because of the long line. It'd take hours. The line looped and curved in on itself. The Museum Island was like a fair, with determined-looking tourists coming and going—a group of red-faced young men came riding past her on a contraption that looked like a bicycle, with five or six riders facing each other in a circle, all of them pedaling on the multiple pedals, a huge barrel of beer on the flat board in their middle from which all were sucking through giant straws.

She loafed around for a while, browsing through the books and DVDs for sale, then she joined a sidewalk procession toward the Brandenburger Tor, bumping into bodies and muttering excuses, and when she finally got tired of loitering and taking pictures at the gate, she took a bus and returned home. A wasted day. She should have purchased the museum ticket online before coming, she should have bought it the day before, she remonstrated with herself as she sat on the bus. She was usually well-prepared, and to be caught this flat-footed annoyed her.

•

The neighbor's door was closed. Maybe he didn't live there, most likely a moving man hired to move things. But no, he didn't look like a moving man, something about the way he looked and spoke. She was surprised at how sharply disappointed she felt. She paused briefly before the door and listened, hoping to hear the sound of lifting, or music, or feet,

but all was quiet. It was almost 4 p.m. She opened her door and turned on the TV, she couldn't wait for tomorrow to come so she'd be on her way to Basel. Berlin had been a disappointment, her fault, not the city's.

But now the TV failed to occupy her and she wandered the apartment, from room to room, opened cabinets in the kitchen, read the labels on the wine bottles in the pantry. There was half a crate of red, and a full crate of white. She picked out a Bordeaux. She'd knock herself out and wake up tomorrow. She searched in drawers and cabinets for the corkscrew, but she couldn't find one. And, not until much later, after she had gone and knocked on the neighbor's door and, flashing her best smile, asked to borrow a corkscrew, please, and laughingly invited him to join her for a drink if he wanted and he said yes, why not, give me five minutes, and they were seated at her hosts' circular, three-seater dining table, raising glasses in cheers, not till then did she admit to herself that she could have drunk the Chablis with the screw cap but she had decided to drink the corked red as a pretext to go talk to and perhaps invite the neighbor for a drink. But, she had a good excuse; she had many good excuses: she was alone in a strange city and he was a fellow African and she was going stir-crazy.

"Portia," he said. "Very Shakespearean."

Her name was a cross she had borne all her life. But he wasn't making fun of her as the perplexed kids at school had done, he wasn't puzzled as the lecturers at university had been. In England, at postgraduate school, a classmate had asked her if it was a traditional African name.

"My father was a fan," she told him.

"So, how long have you lived here?" he asked.

"I don't live, here. I am couch-surfing."

"Couch-surfing?"

"Couchsurfing.com. Never heard of it?"

"Sounds like a porn site."

She laughed. Nice sense of humor. But what if he was dangerous, a rapist, an opportunistic ripper? Clearly he knew about porn sites. Well, too late now. Her mother would read all about it in the Zambian papers tomorrow. Hopefully, the circular glass table between them would offer her a minute-or-two head start before he reached her.

"It is a site that connects travelers with hosts, people willing to offer their couches to perfect strangers who might someday return the favor."

"I feel bad that you didn't get to see the museum, and you are leaving tomorrow. Do you want to go out? Grab something to eat?" he asked. A rapist wouldn't be asking her to go out, unless he was the brazen kind that gets his kick out of doing it out in public. A flasher-rapist.

"I want African food," she said. She hadn't eaten properly in over a day.

He thought for a minute. "The closest I can offer is Asian, but it is about twenty minutes away by train. It is good, promise."

She was still dressed from her outing, so she freshened up in the bathroom, picked up her handbag, and they left after a glass each of the wine. Restorative, the wine proved. She wasn't aware she had been tired from her first venture into the city. They took the train and sat side by side, but they couldn't speak for the din, so they smiled silently at each other whenever their eyes met. Two musicians, one a chubby child with

an accordion, the other a man-and-woman duo with a music box, vied with one another to see who'd break the noise barrier first. She watched the stoic Berliners absorbing the abuse, their faces impassively turned to the view outside the train window. A *Mots* vendor tried unsuccessfully to get her to purchase his newspaper but she had no change. He handed the vendor a euro coin and took a copy even though, he told her when they got off, he couldn't really read German. "You looked like you needed rescuing."

She thanked him. Was that the vibe she gave off, like she needed rescuing?

"This way," he said. They were on a busy side street, and almost every second or third store was a secondhand bookstore displaying English and German books in the window. Sandwiched between the bookstores and record stores were Asian restaurants: Thai, Vietnamese, Indian—people sat at tables on the sidewalk, reading menus, looking bored as Roma minstrels played popular tunes on their accordions and trumpets. Another bookstore. Inside a woman in a hat sat behind a desk, facing the street. She caught Portia's eyes and smiled, waving them in. Portia grabbed his hand. "Come, let's look at books." The interior of the store was a thicket of books, falling out of shelves, spilling out of cartons on the floor. It was hard to find a path around the room without stepping on books and magazines. Now Portia realized it was actually a man wearing a wig under the hat and a flowery red dress. Two men, actually, one in a blue shirt, youngish, sat further inside the store, half-hidden by a bookshelf. On the table before them were two glasses of red wine and a half-empty bottle.

"He is the real deal. He is Barack Obama before the celebrity," the man in the blue shirt was saying.

"Oh, you are a Cory Booker fan too," the man in the red dress said. "How good to know. I love that man. He is my mayor. I am from Newark, you know."

Americans, rolling their r's and flattening their a's. Portia pulled out books at random. They were used copies, "for rent or for sale," a sign glued to the shelf said. There was a whole section dedicated to Graham Greene. She ran her hand over the spines, reading the titles. Her father was a fan, he had sent her Greene's memoirs, *Ways of Escape* and *A Sort of Life* on her nineteenth birthday. She found the writing a bit too macho, a bit too Hemingwayesque.

The store appeared to be an apartment doubling as a bookstore. This was the living room, she could see the kitchen through a half-open door with dishes in the sink and a packet of what looked like cat food on a shelf. A closed door next to a shelf probably led into the bedroom, half-blocking the door were more boxes of books, some opened with books spilling out of them, some not yet opened. It was like a hoarder's haven here. She felt stymied by clutter, hamstrung. She waded back to the entrance where the man in the wig and hat and his friend were still talking about Cory Booker.

"They have Achebe here," he said to her. She joined him. A whole section dedicated to African authors of the earlier generation, Alan Patton, Mazisi Kunene, Naguib Mahfouz. He flipped through a copy of *Things Fall Apart*. It was an early edition, with a folkloric sketch of Okonkwo's face upside down on the cover, and Introduction by Aigboje Higo. Inside were more folkloric sketches at the start of each chapter.

"I'll take this," he said to the men at the table, "how much?"

But they were laughing so hard they didn't hear. Tears formed runnels down the face of the man in the red dress, cracking his makeup.

" . . . that is so preposterous," the other man kept saying. He banged his hand on the table and sipped his wine, all the time laughing. "Preposterous!"

Portia picked out a book and handed it to him. He looked at the title: *Prison Dialogues*, by James Kariku. "I remember this book. I had to study it for my secondary school finals."

"My father," she said.

"Your father is James Kariku?"

She nodded. She looked defensive, she had had this conversation many times before and was weary of it.

"No way," he said. He looked at her, then at the book, as if trying to determine if she was joking.

"I am Portia Kariku. If you want, I can show you my ID," she said, and turned away from him.

"Of course, I believe you, it's just . . . so unexpected. Okay. I'll take it and you'll sign for me."

"You buy it if you want, but I can't sign for you. I am not my father." Her voice had grown cold. He paid for the book and they left. What a clutter. Her skin crawled retroactively at the cat hair on the carpet and the spiderwebs on the roof and the dirty plates in the kitchen sink. How incongruous it all was, with the fancy storekeeper by the entrance, drinking red wine in his wig and la-di-da hat next to all that grime.

When they came out after eating, the very last sunrays of the day glistened on the wet cobblestones. It was an Indian summer day; the golden sunrays poured on the buildings and

trees and sidewalks like honey. They took a train back to Mitte. "Let's get off here," he said.

"This isn't our station."

"Yes. But it is a beautiful day. Let's walk," he said. She followed him along a line of stones marking where the Berlin Wall once stood, and soon they were in a throng of young people, all moving in the same direction. She looked at him, questioning.

"They are coming from the park over there, Mauerpark. Come." He took her hand and pulled her away from the crowd. She liked the feel of his hand in hers.

"I'll buy you a drink," he said.

They entered a tiny bar, its entrance almost invisible from the street. Inside was dark and empty save for the barman, who was standing behind the bar, his back turned to the empty room, staring at a TV screen over the shelf of bottles on the wall. One part of the wall was lined with cigarette and pinball machines. A door led into yet another section of the bar, perhaps the restaurant, from which they could hear loud voices and laughter. They sat down, and eventually the barman came over.

"Two shots of vodka for me," Portia said before he could speak.

He shrugged at the barman. "Same for me."

They downed the vodka in one gulp and then asked for a glass of wine each, red for him, white for her. "So," he said, "what do you do?"

"I teach," she said. "My mother has a school in Lusaka, I work for her."

"Do you like it?"

"I didn't at first, but it grows on you. The kids are adorable."

An old woman in a white faux fur jacket, its collar raised up around her neck, entered, in her hand a bunch of flowers. The front door light in her red hair was a brush fire at night. She shook the rain off her jacket as she looked around the empty room, then she limped over to them. She picked out a pink rose and held it out to Portia. The woman had a ring on every finger, including her thumbs. Portia shook her head.

"Take it," he said. He gave the woman a few coins. Portia held the red rose to her nose, then she placed it on the table next to her glass. "Thanks."

The old woman shuffled over to the bar and handed the barman the coins, she sat on a stool with her bunch of flowers on the counter in front of her.

"What are you doing in Berlin?"

"I came with my wife, over a year ago."

"Oh," she said. She pushed the flower further away. "Where's she now, your wife? Of course, you don't have to answer . . . forget the question."

Of course, she had seen the ring impression on his finger, but she hadn't given it any thought. They were two strangers in a strange city, soon they'd part and perhaps never see each other again.

"My wife left for America a few months ago. We used to live in a different part of town, in Charlottenburg. I moved here when my wife left."

"Who lives here?"

"A friend, who I met through another friend. Her name

is Lorelle. She and her roommate . . . they left for America. I am helping them take apart the furniture and get them into storage, in exchange I get to stay for a few months, rent-free."

"What do you do afterward?"

"Move on, I guess. I have to go back to the States and finish my PhD, eventually."

"Oh, what are you working on?"

"The Berlin Conference of 1884 . . . though I discovered that here in Berlin they call it the Congo Conference."

"That's an interesting topic. What's the title of your dissertation?"

"You really want to know?"

"Yes, really. I just finished my MA and I am thinking of going back for a PhD, eventually."

"You should. My title is, 'The Berlin Conference: Imaginary Borders and the Scramble for Africa.' What do you think?"

"I like it."

"Good. Now, your turn."

"Yes, my turn. Give me a minute."

She stood up and went to the barman, they talked and the barman led her to the cigarette machine and she came back with a packet of Marlboro. She opened it and handed him one.

"I don't smoke," he said.

"Me neither, but I feel like a cigarette right now."

They lit up and dragged in the smoke tentatively, coughing, their eyes watering.

"So, my turn. I am going to Basel. My brother used to live there. I am going to meet his wife."

"Basel. Switzerland. Where does he live now?"

"He died. I am going to meet his Swiss wife, Katharina. I have never met her before."

"Why do you want to see her now?"

"My mother wants to know how he died. The papers didn't say much. And Katharina was in prison for killing him, so we couldn't reach her."

"His wife killed him?"

"Yes."

A laying down of the ghosts. After her father died last year her mother had started talking about David more and more. Where did she go wrong, and why did he feel he had to go away? He had been so obsessed with emigrating. A month ago, when Portia was getting ready to go back to London to submit her MA thesis, her mother said to her, "I want you to go and see her when you finish with London. Talk to her. I want to know what happened, why he left us for her, what he was looking for." She handed Portia a photograph. The photograph, the one on the nightstand by her mother's bed. In the picture her brother was standing next to Katharina, looking at the camera with no expression. What was he thinking? The photo had come five years ago with a letter, the only letter he ever wrote since he left home. In it, he said he was fine, he was now in Switzerland, married to the lady in the picture, and they shouldn't worry about him. The next time they heard about him, he was dead.

Portia looked at her, shaking her head. "Mama, it will not bring him back. He had made his choices."

"But I want to know. I was a good mother, wasn't I, and a good wife?" And because all her life all she wanted to do was to please her mother, to make her happy, Portia said yes.

Her father had also left, long before David did, but her
father did come back. He came back irreparably damaged by
exile, and it could be said that the return was what ultimately
killed him. She didn't tell him all this, though she wanted to.
She felt she could tell him even the most intimate things and
he'd respond with respect and full attention. She wondered
what his story was. There was something lost and dreamy
about him, as if he was waiting for something, or someone.
What was he doing in Berlin, all by himself, his wife thousands of miles away in America?

She picked up the rose, sniffed it again, and said, "So, do
you give every woman you meet a rose? What would your
wife think?"

"That poor lady looked like she needed the money," he
said. The lady was bent over the bar now, a cigarette in one
hand, her drink in the other hand, the flowers on the counter
next to her. She was staring up at the TV screen, discussing
what was showing with the barman.

"That's a good reason. Well, thank you. I'll put it in a vase
when we get back."

After a while she said, suddenly, "My birthday is next week."

"Well, happy birthday in advance. How old?"

"You first. How old are you?"

"Old," he said. "Thirty-five."

"I am twenty-five."

"You are so young."

"You sound disappointed."

"I am not. I just feel . . . old at the moment. Superannu-
ated. What is your wish, for your birthday?"

She shrugged. "Joy, happiness, wisdom. What more can

one wish for? And, talking about happiness, I must mention you do look a bit solemn."

He shrugged. "I guess I have been indoors and alone too long. I have forgotten how to compose my features in company."

"Compose your features, that's an interesting way of putting it. Why are you unhappy?"

"Is happiness very important to you?"

"Well, isn't it, to everyone?"

"To some, yes. In Dostoevsky's *The Brothers Karamazov*, Father Zosima says the purpose of human existence is happiness. God Himself wants us to be happy. Creation is fulfilled when God sees us happy. We are only unhappy if our mind is not very clean, if we sin."

"Sounds like a rather convenient argument for the church."

"It does."

"Dostoevsky doesn't sound like he understood very well how life works. Happiness is important, but I wouldn't say it is the main purpose of human existence."

When they got back to the apartment they stood by her door. She wasn't ready for the night to end. She dreaded going into the empty apartment by herself, so she waited, playing with the key on the key chain. He said, "I'd invite you for a nightcap, but my place is a mess. The dust alone will give you an infection."

"In that case, come to mine. We still have some wine left." She hoped she didn't sound too forward, too shameless.

"Good. Let me get my phone. I left it when we went out. Ten minutes?"

Before he came back, she changed into a skirt and a fresh

T-shirt. He walked around the room, stopping to look at the record collection.

"Mahler, Beethoven, Bach. Snooty folk, huh?"

He turned to the pictures on the wall. "Turner. Kandinsky. Prints."

"You know painting?"

"Only by association. My wife paints."

He joined her on the couch. She handed him a glass of red wine.

"What if your friends walked in now? How would you explain my presence?"

"Is there anything to explain? We aren't breaking the furniture. At least not yet." She looked contemplatively at him.

He said, "You have nothing to fear from me."

She liked that he said that seriously, that he could tell she wanted to be reassured.

"Tell me something about yourself. Anything."

He told her about his friends, Stan, Mark, Uta, Eric, who used to live in an abandoned church. She listened. His voice grew sad as he described Mark's death. He stood up. "Let's play some music. I don't want to depress you." He slotted a CD into the Bose player.

"What song?"

"David Bowie. 'Heroes,'" he said.

She shook her head. "Nice, but . . ."

"But . . ."

"Too white for me. I am a lover of the blues. My father had a stack of them, records with brilliant album-cover artwork. Billie Holiday. Robert Johnson. Muddy Waters."

She went to the kitchen, her glass of wine in her hand. He

stood up and followed her. The kitchen was long and narrow, a window opened into a courtyard with a gnarled and twisted ash tree in its center. He stood by the window. "I have the same view from my kitchen."

"What of love?" she asked, coming forward to stand next to him. She could feel the drink, making her light-headed, but she didn't care. She leaned into him and pressed her lips on his briefly. "What does Dostoevsky have to say about love?"

He put one arm around her waist, saying nothing. She pulled away and began cutting a block of cheese into cubes onto a plate. She opened a tin and poured out cashew nuts and almonds beside the cheese. They faced each other, he still by the window, leaning against the sill; she resting her hips against the sink, her head tilted. She picked up the bowl and returned to the living room. He came and sat next to her, saying nothing. She wondered if they were about to cross a certain line, a certain border. She felt happy, expectant. She got up and sat on the floor before the TV, the remote in her hand, flipping through channels.

"You look beautiful, sitting there, like a TV fairy."

She turned and looked at him, still flipping through channels. She stopped at a channel showing a western, in German. "Do you speak German?"

"*Ein bisschen*," he said. "A little bit."

She fell asleep before the movie ended. When she opened her eyes he was still seated on the couch, the light from the screen playing on his face. She smiled up at him.

"I am putting you to bed, then I am off." He picked her up and carried her to the guest room, putting her down gently on the narrow twin bed.

"Don't go," she said.

"It is one a.m."

"If you go I can't sleep. I've been sleeping badly."

"These people, the owners, what will they think?"

"They won't be back for a few more days," she said, then added, sleepily, "Come with me, to Basel. I don't want to go by myself."

"**Y**ou've been humming that word for a while now. Lycidas."

They were in their beds, waiting for their room service meal, neither of them feeling like going out in the rain. He had her father's book of poems in his hand. He was seated, his back against the headboard, she was lying on her stomach, her face turned to him. Outside the gray cumulus clouds hung low in the sky, over the trees and roofs, and the deluge seemed to be rising from the marshy bog itself.

"It is a poem, by Milton. An elegy for a friend who died in a boating accident. All day it has been in my head and won't

go away. Perhaps it is the rain. It is making me sad." She went to the window and stared out into the night.

"Were you close to your brother?"

She shrugged, not turning. "He left when I was very young. I was around ten when I last saw him."

"Fifteen years ago."

She nodded. "Yes. My father was in Europe then, trying to be an exile."

"Trying?"

"He could have returned home anytime he wanted, but he refused."

"Why did he leave?"

She returned to the bed and sat down, facing him. The room was dim, only the light from the TV flickered weakly against the blue wall, the rays soaking into the walls, like water on sponge. "He got into trouble with the government because of his writings, not just his poems, but articles as well, in the newspapers. He was something of a rising star, I guess. Some people saw him as a possible future candidate for the presidency. He was young, smart and fearless, or foolish, depending on how you look at it. He belonged to that nationalist era in African politics that produced young idealistic men by the bucketful, and then promptly threw them behind bars or killed them—the lucky ones like my father escaped into exile to spend the rest of their lives in limbo."

"What did he write about?"

"Well, you have read his poems. His articles and essays accused the government of corruption, among many other things. He was part of a university-based group of intellectuals agitating for multiparty democracy, they wanted Kaunda

to resign. And they had a good following, and also supporters in America and Europe, which made them more threatening to the government, plus, they had a case, the economy was bad, people wanted a new beginning. I heard about it mostly from my mother, the rest I learned from history books.

"My mother met my father at university, just after independence in the sixties, they became lecturers at the same university, in the seventies. She was in the history department. He was in English. He was in prison for two years, then he was released and held under house arrest. While in prison he wrote his book of poetry, it brought him international attention when it was published by the Heinemann African Writers Series. He became an international celebrity—PEN awarded him the Freedom to Write Award, Wole Soyinka and Harold Pinter held a joint reading from his book in London. He was offered fellowships and visiting lecturer positions in England and America, but he didn't want to go. He wanted to stay in Zambia. Yet, despite numerous appeals and pleas, he never got his job back. My mother persuaded him to leave the country. She had just given birth to my brother and all she wanted was to be somewhere safe. They left in 1980, with the help of my father's foreign friends. They were in exile in England for ten years. My mother said it was the best years of their marriage, but she only saw that in hindsight. It wasn't a bad life, he had a job at the University of Leeds, teaching African literature, but while he was becoming more and more settled in exile, she was pining for home. Kaunda's dictatorship was over anyway. So, when she got pregnant with me she decided to come back to Zambia. My father told her to go on ahead, he'd join her in a few months. So, she took my brother and left. She returned

home and managed to make a life for herself. She started an elementary school. But my father didn't go back. By then he had developed a taste for exile."

Her voice was flat, bitter. She lay on her back, directing her words at the ceiling.

"How long did he stay back after your mother had left?"

"Seventeen, eighteen years. I never saw my father till I was eight, for me he was always a photograph on the wall, a wedding photograph with my mother, he in a suit, my mother in a wedding dress with yards of tulle flowing behind her. I saw him for the first time when we visited him in Copenhagen, Denmark, he was doing a fellowship there. We stayed with him for a year. I remember that year. It was cold, and my mother had no friends, she was always sitting by the fireplace, waiting for my father to return from some outing with his friends. Famous authors would stop by the house, all of them exiles, Soyinka, Mahmoud Darwish, Breyten Breytenbach— of course I didn't know who they were then, till later when my mother told me—and they'd talk poetry far into the night, about their countries, and exile, and they'd read poems they were working on or had just published.

"There was a little yard in the back, with a magnolia tree in the center, and when the weather was good I would ride my bike round the tree, round and round and round till it got dark and my mother would shout for me to come in. I think my mother hoped my father would come back to Zambia with us after the Danish fellowship, but he didn't. He had become something of a professional exile. He went from fellowship to fellowship, from asylum city to asylum city. All over Europe. And they loved him, even though he hadn't

written a book in over twenty years. He gave comments after
every coup in Africa, on every civil war that broke out, every
uprising, every plane crash. He was the Africa expert. He
wrote fiery opinion pieces in newspapers attacking the government in Zambia, even though by now the government and
most of the country had forgotten who he was. But in Europe
he was a hero, telling truth to power. They called him the
conscience of Africa. My father ate it up."

Her voice died down with a sigh. Their food came, they
ate in silence. She ate in bed, sitting up, her plate in her
lap, he moved to the chair by the window, flipping through
the book of poetry as he ate. She watched, and gradually
her expression darkened. Why was he keeping so far away
from her? Why did he come? And why were they in separate beds? In Berlin she had kissed him, and she thought
he would kiss her back, but he hadn't. Perhaps he was here
because he thought she needed protection, just as he thought
she needed rescue. Her sullen mood persisted and she didn't
answer when he asked her if she was okay. She went to the
bathroom and brushed her teeth, she got into bed and pulled
the sheets over her head. He came over and pulled back the
sheet. He lay down next to her.

"I can't sleep," she said. He held her, not saying anything.

"You mustn't be bitter against your father," he said. "Sometimes poets have to be imperfect so their poetry can be perfect. Reading him has taken me back to my school days."

It was the most profound thing anyone had ever said to her
about her father, and she felt grateful. Her mood lightened.
He kissed her head. Like a brother, she thought. She closed
her eyes. "Tell me a story."

"What kind of story?"

"Any kind."

He told her about a rich young man who was addicted to palm wine. One day his father dies, and many days after, his palm-wine tapster who draws his palm wine from the palm trees falls from a tall palm tree and dies. The rich young man misses his supply of palm wine, and his friends no longer come to visit. He grows despondent. So, he decides to go to the Dead's Town to find his tapster. It is a long and hazardous journey. It leads him from his town to various parts of the bush, places outside civilization, inhabited by all sorts of inhuman creatures. Thus begin his many adventures. He stays with a man who promises to give him directions to the Dead's Town, but he must first rescue his daughter, who has been attracted to a Handsome Gentleman and followed him into the bush. The Gentleman, it turns out, is not really a person but a wild creature of the bush. He had returned with his young bride to the bush, and as he entered, he gave back each bodily part that he had rented from a human being, until he was nothing but a skull; he then held the young woman captive. The rich young man searches for the host's daughter, finds her, and the two escape the bush . . .

She fell asleep listening to him, her head on his shoulder. When he stopped talking, she opened her eyes.

"I know that story. Amos Tutuola. My MA is in postcolonial literature, remember. But go on, did he get what he wanted? Did he get his tapster back?"

"He got more than that. He gained wisdom, he also got a magic egg with a never-ending supply of palm wine."

She drifted off, half-awake, half-dreaming, half-remembering;

she saw her father getting off the plane at Lusaka International Airport. He was home, finally. She could feel her mother's nervous excitement as they watched him at the customs counter, presenting his passport to be stamped. Her mother was wearing her best dress, her best jewelry. It was the happiest Portia had seen her in a long time. He, on the other hand, looked perplexed. He was in his black suit, with a white shirt and his best oxford shoes.

"Where are the secret police?" he whispered, he looked disappointed. He was expecting to be arrested, to be whisked away in a black car by security agents. In the car he kept asking about old friends, why weren't they there to receive him at the airport, surely they must have read in the papers he was coming back? He had written about it in the English papers. Her mother told him most of the old friends had retired, returned to the village. Many were dead.

As the days passed alarming signs began to show, he appeared disoriented, unsure where he was, or what day it was. He'd go to the window and peek outside at passing cars, expecting the house to be stormed by agents looking for him. He tried writing. He was working on a volume on exile, he intimated, but he couldn't make headway, the lines came out dull and uninspired. Soon he started talking about going back. He had been home just two months, but already he felt stifled. He couldn't work here, he complained. Once, they found him seated in the yard, under the cashew tree, in the pouring rain. Portia took him inside, even as he fought her all the way. Then one day, they came back from work at her mother's school, and he was gone. He had left a one-line note on the table: he was going back to England. When had he

planned this, when did he buy the plane ticket? They rushed to the airport, and when they got there they found him seated meekly on a bench in the departure lounge. He hadn't been allowed on the plane because he had no visa.

He thought he could just walk into the plane with no documents.

A month later he tried to leave again. An official, who happened to be her mother's cousin, called to tell them he was at the airport. He had attacked the immigration official who stopped him from boarding the plane. His passport had expired, and he still had no visa for the UK. This time her mother didn't go to the airport with her. When Portia got there, she saw him through the glass door, dressed in his best suit and white shirt, his carry-on bag in his hand, ranting as he paced up and down, waving his passport, and when she entered she heard him, in his careful professorial British English, asking them if they knew who he was. "James Kariku. You can look me up. Google my name. I am a poet. This country doesn't appreciate talent. In Europe they will roll out the red carpet for me. You think I am lying, go ahead, google my name!"

She stood at the door, too embarrassed to go in, though the three officials at whom he was ranting could see her standing there. Finally, she took a deep breath and went in. She whispered "sorry" to the officials and led her father to the car. In the car she broke down in tears and turned to him, asking, "Why don't you want to stay with us, Baba? Why do you want to leave?" He remained quiet, hunched against the car door, staring out at the line of jacaranda trees with their fire-red flowers looking ghostly against the night sky.

He kept to his room, and from behind the door they could hear the sound of his typewriter, banging furiously. When he died two months later, they found a pile of paper covered in gibberish, only one line was clear, repeated over and over again, "Down with the dictatorship." He was a resistance poet, it was all he knew, just like exile was all he knew. He had been home less than one year. Her mother said, "I made a mistake. I shouldn't have pressed him to return. Exile was his life. The return killed him."

•

"Think of him happy," he said. Her father had been happy in Denmark, drinking and arguing all night long with other poets. And she remembered the time she saw him in London. She had not seen him since that trip to Denmark, when she was eight. "I saw him in London, he had flown in from The Hague, where he had been living as a writer-in-residence. I was doing my MA at SOAS, it was my first year there, and it was a bad year. I was homesick. It was winter, wet and dark and cold, typical London winter. I couldn't read, I couldn't think, I'd spend days in my room, sleeping, only coming out to get supplies. I was diagnosed with depression due to the weather and the doctor told me to install bright fluorescent tubes in my room, to compensate for the gloom. Anyway, my father came to town. My mother called me from Zambia and gave me his hotel address and his number. I went to his hotel and they made me wait in the lobby. He was still sleeping, they said, but they would let him know I was there. I didn't tell them he was my father, I just gave my name.

"Then he came down. There were two people with him. I

hadn't seen him in a long time, but I recognized him, he still had his beard even though it was all salt-and-pepper now. I was sitting in a corner in the lobby—and he almost passed me. It seemed he had forgotten I was there. Then he saw me. 'Portia. You look exactly like your mother.'

"He gave me a hug. He introduced me to his friends, 'My daughter.' He looked happy to see me. But it was awkward. I didn't know how to be a daughter, and clearly, he had forgotten how to be a father. Plus, I didn't know what to call him, Dad, or Father, or Baba. I followed them to the reading, I even remember the title of the event: Poetry, Exile, and Resistance. But the truth is that he had long ceased to be a poet, and most of the resistance was imaginary. But the people there, they loved it. They didn't care. They didn't even know where Zambia was on the map of Africa. As far as they were concerned, all of Africa was one huge Gulag archipelago, and every African poet or writer living outside Africa has to be in exile from dictatorship. My father knew his audience and their expectation, he gave them what they wanted. He was dressed for the occasion, the beard, the austere dashiki. He read. He vituperated. He narrated his prison experience that had happened decades ago as if it were just happening now. The audience, they ate it up. They clapped. They cried. They bought books. I guess I also felt a bit proud. My father was a star, a minor one, but still a star.

"I followed them to dinner and spent almost two hours listening to him hold forth about African nationalism, pan-Africanism. What did it all mean? Ideas that at some time, long ago, meant something but are now empty as any political jargon, something to whip out and flash before the masses, or

in textbooks. I hate politics, what it makes people do, what it does to people. One of the ladies with him was his translator, she was nice. She was the only one who tried to make conversation with me. Her name was May and it turned out she was a lecturer at SOAS, she had translated my father into Greek, and I could tell there was something between them. She asked me about my studies, about my mother, but all I wanted was to talk to my father, alone, for just a few minutes, I wanted to ask him when he was coming home, if he missed my mother and my brother and me. I waited, but he wouldn't stop talking. So, I left. I told them I was going to the bathroom, I didn't return. I slipped out and returned to my room.

"The next day I left for Zambia, abandoning my studies. I knew if I stayed a day more I'd lose my mind. I did go back to finish my studies, eventually, but that year was my worst, ever. When I told my mother about the meeting she said, 'Something is wrong with us. Our men keep deserting us.' But I told her it was not us, it was them. There was something they wanted, something just beyond the horizon, something outside their grasp, they would keep searching for it till they died. He stayed on in London for about seven months, with his translator girlfriend, then he came home and that was the end of it."

"**W**as she upset yesterday?"

Katharina had phoned early in the morning to say she wasn't available to meet today as planned. Portia stood at the foot of the bed, her expression switching between perplexed to annoyed. She was already dressed up and ready to go out when the call came. He was also up, still in his striped pajamas, by the window with a laptop in his hand.

"Not really. She was a bit defensive, which is normal. I mean, she just came out of prison, I expected her to be a bit reticent, and even erratic, but I thought because I am his sister she'd want to talk to me about this."

She dropped her bag and sat down on the bed, her face

downcast. Her flight back to London was tomorrow. In London she'd catch a connecting flight to Lusaka. She imagined the disappointment on her mother's face.

He said, "Give her a call later, to see if she changes her mind."

They went out for a walk. The rain had stopped; the sun was out. They ate an early lunch in a roadside restaurant. When they came back to the hotel the receptionist handed Portia a note. "Miss, you got a call."

She took the note and read it. "The bitch. So whimsical. She is coming. She is having dinner with us. This evening."

•

Paintings of dinner scenes covered the restaurant walls, rising all the way to the ceiling. Corpulent gentlemen and thick-waisted women, reaching into plates piled high with all sorts of meat—huge-thighed chicken, enormous slabs of ham, gigantic shanks of lamb—their mouths bulging with food, glasses raised and dripping with blood-red wine. The rest of the wall was taken up by colorful frescoes of flowers and birds, giving a warm and cheerful ambience to the room. The painting looked like an epicurean Last Supper, a bacchanalia, with Jesus left out, perhaps hiding out of sight, horrified by the gluttony. Gormandize, Portia thought. Her secondary school principal, Mrs. Joyce Bisika, used the word often in her speech at Assembly, as in, "Girls gormandizing in the cafeteria, asking for extra portions. So unladylike," or, "Girls gormandizing on life with their shameless, unladylike behavior."

Katharina saw Portia looking at the paintings. "I hate them. They say it has been here even before the restaurant started. This used to be some kind of school cafeteria."

Katharina had arrived at exactly 4 p.m., alone. Portia had expected her to come with Sven, but there she was, by herself, waiting for them in the lobby, looking subdued and almost formal in a black knee-length dress. She said nothing when she saw Portia was not alone. She said she had made a reservation for them for 5 p.m. and the restaurant wasn't far from the hotel, so they walked. They walked through quaint, constricted streets, cobbled and sloping, and as they came down the hill they could see right into compounds below, most of them with open courtyards in which stood tall, leafy trees, and then they were in an open street.

"This is a shopping area, very touristy," Katharina said. Today she was friendly, even charming, at one point she took Portia by the hand as they walked, and Portia could see how a man would easily fall for her. The streets were crisscrossed with tram rails making the walk confusing, and not knowing where to look when crossing, they had to trust Katharina as they now dashed, now waited, now strolled through the wide, winding streets. They were not far from the university, and most of the people on the streets looked like students. They took a narrow alley and came out on another wide street. She pointed across the road at an imposing red stone building. "That is the *Rathaus*, the city council chamber." They crossed over.

"It is beautiful," Portia said. In the center of the courtyard, facing the street, was a sculpture of two gargantuan men, their arms and torsos impossibly twisted around one another in a silent, frozen combat, pulling at each other in strife and opposition, and yet balanced and equally matched. There was something elemental, almost mythic about them. Katharina took them to an imposing cathedral, from the cobbled court-

yard they could view the Rhine below, and across the water in the distance the city itself. They looked down into the sluggish, frigid water, and Katharina, now enjoying the role of tour guide, told them how in the summer young men and women would dive into the water and drift downstream, their clothes tied in a waterproof bag which they also used for flotation.

She looked at her watch, "Time for dinner," she said. The restaurant was next to the Jean Tinguely Fountain, a little basin populated by curiously shaped sculptures and wheels and scoops, all playful, all lighthearted, but now all frozen and trapped by winter's breath.

"So, you go back tomorrow," Katharina said. They had finished their meal and were finishing off a bottle of wine. Katharina had looked amused when Portia said she didn't eat meat and ordered a fillet of sea bass. "But your brother loved meat. In fact, all the Africans we met really liked meat. You are the first African I am meeting who doesn't like meat."

Portia opened her mouth, then closed it again. To Katharina's credit she shook her head and immediately apologized for her comment. "I am sorry. That sounded so silly."

"Tell me more about him," Portia said. But Katharina shook her head firmly. "We make deal. Today, I am your host. I show you Basel. We eat, nothing serious. You come to my house tomorrow and we talk about your brother. I feel happy today. Nothing sad."

•

They checked out of the hotel early in the morning. Her flight was in the evening, from Basel to London, from there

to Lusaka through South Africa. He would take the train back to Berlin.

"Why?" she asked Katharina as they sat down at the circular table by the window. They were alone, the men had gone out with the dog.

Katharina nodded and smiled. "Maybe I ask you the same: Why do you want to meet someone who killed your brother? And if you had followed the trial you know I didn't plead guilty. I said I didn't kill him."

"But you were found guilty, and sent away for three years. Very lenient. In most countries you'd hang."

Again, Katharina nodded and smiled. "Okay. You are his sister. You deserve to know. I tell you everything."

"Not everything. You can skip the sentimental stuff, the romantic meeting and 'love at first sight.'"

"But what if it is true, the sentiments as you call it, the romance, even the love?"

"Well, convince me. That it was all true, that you loved him, that he wasn't a victim."

"Victim how? Of what?"

"Of your anger and jealousy. Of the whole system, of Europe."

"No. Moussa was never a victim. He knew what he wanted, and how to get it. That night, after the dance, my friends wanted me to go, but no, I said. I stayed talking with him till the bar closed at midnight. I was in love."

That was the day they met, at the twilight of his first marriage. After that night, after that dance, she told Sven their engagement was not going to work. "I didn't love him. He was a good, decent guy, but I wanted more at that time." She

shrugged. "I was not so young anymore. Time was passing for me. I wanted more . . . excitement."

She looked out the window at the distant figures in the mist, dog, men, and Portia wondered what she was thinking.

"Exactly two weeks after that meeting, he left his wife and moved in with me. I was staying in a little place near the campus, one bedroom and a kitchen. Twice Brigitte came to shout at him and beg him to go back, but he said no, he wanted divorce. She didn't give him the divorce till after one year."

"And your family?"

"Well, that is another story. My father is a theologian, you know. I am the only child. He is a good man, he didn't object to my relationship, but he didn't say yes. Every year we used to go on a retreat, we go with my family and the people in my father's church, and I wanted to bring Moussa, but my father said no. I either come alone, or I should not come at all. It was the most painful thing. I realized also how serious all this was. I talked to my mother, I begged them to talk to Moussa, to try to understand him. We had a big fight. I told them I was sorry to be source of embarrassment for them. Everything they had taught me was a lie then. They said we should love strangers, we should never judge people by how they look. It was the most disappointing time of my life. I was very close to my father, you know. I looked up to him. I asked him, What if he turned up in your church, would you turn him away?

"We got married. Just the two of us. I did not invite my family. My mother wanted to come but I told her no, I had no family. After the wedding we went to Mali. I took some time off from my studies, and he got time off from the railway where he worked. He had told me a lot about his father

in Mali, and his brothers and sisters, and I wanted to see them. He never mentioned that they are not his real family. I only knew what he told me, that he was from Mali."

Portia bowed her head and shrugged. "I guess he was ashamed of his real family." She wanted to know what this other family was like, the one he chose over his real family, over his mother and his sister and his father.

"In Mali we stayed in a hotel in Bamako. It was my first time in Africa and it was different than what I expected. It was big, and noisy, and everybody was busy. I thought it would be a bit like India, I was in India once, in Goa. But it was different. The house was on the outside of the city. Our first night he left me at the hotel and went to greet the family alone. I was surprised, but he told me that was the tradition. The next morning, we went together to greet his father and his mothers, there were four wives of the father. He is an Islamic teacher and there were many children learning with him. He received us in a little room, just outside the main house, and he was seated on a mat and we sat next to him, I had to cover my head because women were not allowed into the room with open head. Moussa had warned me about that before, so it was not a problem.

"The father was old, with a white beard, but very active. Also, he spoke good French, and I also know French, so we were able to communicate. He welcomed me, and he said Moussa was a good and dutiful son and he hoped we would have a happy life. Then he begin to tell me how Moussa came to him from the sea. He said it was God who told him to go to the sea that day, and he found Moussa and two other young men at the waterfront, they had just arrived and they

didn't know where to go next. He brought them home. He said from that day Moussa became his son. I listened. I was confused. This is the first time I am hearing that the man is not Moussa's real father. But I didn't say anything there. I keep quiet and I pretend as if I know. After telling me the story of how Moussa became his adopted son, the old man prayed for us. Next, we went into the house to meet the women. It was a big compound behind a mud wall, with different sections for the wives and their children. There were many children and they all came to touch my hand, my hair, my nose. They were very excited by the visit. They ran out to invite their friends to come and touch me. We sat in the senior wife's living room, this is Moussa's mother, his adoptive mother now I know, and all the other wives joined us. They giggle when I speak. They find everything I do funny because it was the first time they were seeing someone like me in their house. We gave them a little money and the presents we brought, mostly clothes for the children, and for the wives. Finally, we went back to the hotel. For me, the holiday was already spoiled because of what I learned. I ask him, Why didn't you tell me about your real family? What kind of marriage is this when I don't even know where you really come from, your real family? He said he was planning to tell me. But when? I asked him. I say to myself, What other things is he keeping from me? I think like that in my mind. I make him promise to write to his mother, his real mother, and to tell her about me, about our marriage, with a picture of us, me and him. We didn't stay long in Mali. We had planned to stay one week in the hotel but we had to leave after three days."

"Why?"

"Why? Because now I am angry with him. I feel I don't know him anymore. Also, people kept coming to see us, his friends, more family, they'd knock on the door as early as six a.m. They will bring food, and they'll sit for hours and they won't go. It was impossible. Every day. I mean, this was supposed to be our honeymoon. So, we left to spend the remaining three days in Senegal. Things were better there. We met a German couple, tourists, Ingrid and Hermann, they said they came to Senegal for bird-watching. They wanted to see the African gray owl. Moussa went with them once, but I was not interested. By that time, I was tired, I wanted to come back."

"A very short visit then," Portia said.

"Well, that was our honeymoon. We came back with many plans. Moussa wanted to go to university, because he didn't finish his education, you know that. He also wanted us to make peace with my parents. He talked about parents and how important they are. When he talked like that, I find it confusing, because he himself was not at peace with his real parents, and he never told me why. Now maybe you can tell me."

"I . . . wish I could tell you. He wanted another father, I guess, another family," Portia said, turning away to the window.

"Why, what is wrong with his real father, your father?"

"My father . . . he left us. He was a poet, a political poet. He lived in exile all his life. He died recently."

"I didn't know that. I am sorry for your loss."

They sat without speaking for a moment, then Katharina took a deep breath and continued, "Anyway, my plan when we came back from Mali was to finish my PhD, and maybe one day, to have children. Well, it was not easy. Moussa didn't

have many friends, and some of my friends now started to avoid us. It was interesting. I would call, and they'd be busy, or they wouldn't answer the call. At my graduation only my husband and his one friend from the railway came, everybody else have their family there, and friends, we only three of us.

"After my graduation we decided to move to Geneva. It was becoming too lonely here in Basel. We had only two friends, a Nigerian woman, Obi, and her Swiss husband, Alfred. Geneva was more international. There were more mixed families, and we became part of that community. There were also many international cultural events . . . at one point our social life revolved only around international events, at embassies, at cultural festivals, at weddings, well, this is Switzerland, after all. Very international.

"I knew what I was going into when I married an African. But, still . . . The most painful was my parents. It was over one year before we finally made peace with them. It was Moussa who said to me, Let us go and meet them. He said he felt guilty, that it was because of him that my family left me. Well, we went. We knocked on the door and my father opened the door. He looked surprised when he saw us there. He wasn't expecting us. I felt sad when we all sat there, in the living room, with my parents, as if we are strangers, and my mother asking us if she can make tea for us. I wanted to say to her, Mother, I am your daughter, I have not changed. Why do you talk to me like this? And my father . . . ah, it was so painful because I used to be so close to my father, you know. But funny enough, they started talking, my father and Moussa. My father said he had a funeral service to attend the next day. And Moussa said his father oversees so many funer-

als in Mali. My father was interested when he learned that
his father was an imam. And so they started talking about
religion. My mother and I moved to the kitchen to talk.
She wanted to know if I needed anything, if he was treating
me well. I said I needed nothing, that I was fine. That I just
missed her and my father. So, for a while things were back to
normal with my parents.

"I started work in Geneva. Teaching at a research institute
affiliated to the university, as a junior faculty member. I was
making some money, but we needed more. He still worked
for the railway, the plan was for him to go back to school,
but he always made excuses. The truth is, he couldn't afford
to go back because he was sending all his money back home
to Mali, I discovered that later. I had to pay for everything.
Sometimes he was supposed to pay the bills, but he wouldn't,
he will forget, instead he will send the money to Mali. I discovered also that he had taken credits from the bank, just to
send to his father. I saw the letter from the bank, reminding
him to make payment. I was disturbed. He said he sent the
money because his father was dying, and I said why didn't
he tell me. He had told me about his father being sick, but
I didn't know it was so serious, that he was dying. He said
I didn't listen to him anymore anyway. Ah, it was so frus-
trating to talk with him. I never talked about this to anyone
before, not even my mother, but you are his sister, so I am
telling you everything.

"He started accusing me of not wanting to have children,
and I said I couldn't take care of two children, him and our
baby. And he lost his temper, he said I was calling him a
child. He said I was disrespectful, and that I was racist like

all my friends. He had changed. We had those fights, but we always make up. But one day, it got so bad. He was praying, on a mat . . ."

"He was very religious then?"

"He didn't use to be, but suddenly he became religious and will pray five times a day on a mat. He will fast during the fasting time. And he even said that I must change my religion, that a wife must have her husband's religion. I said religion was not very important to me, and we started to argue. But anyway, that day it got so bad. I had just come back from work and right there in the mail was another bill I thought we had paid. He was going to pay, it was water, or electricity, I can't remember. I had a bad day at the office, the students, you know, they make you angry sometimes and I was beginning to think maybe teaching was not the best thing for me. It seems every decision I have made so far have been bad decisions, and then there was this bill. I couldn't take it anymore.

"He was in the living room, praying on a mat. I couldn't wait for him to finish. I started waving the letters at him, I threw them in front of him, but he ignored me. I went to the kitchen and made tea. In the kitchen drawer I saw more bills, and I saw a Western Union receipt, he had sent almost a thousand francs to his family and here we were, our light bill unpaid, and also we were already behind on rent. When he finished praying we started arguing, and I pushed him in the chest and I said I had had enough of the marriage, I said I was leaving. That was when he took a knife, a kitchen knife, and pointed it at me. He said he would kill me and then he'd kill himself. I had never seen him like that before. He was shouting and banging on the table, and he put the knife on my

chest, right here. It was late at night and the neighbors called the police. But by the time they came he had calmed down. But I didn't sleep there that night, I ran to a friend's house. And that was it, that was the end of our marriage. Two years of marriage, three years since we first met in that bar on Basler Fasnacht, and it was over.

"I was exhausted. I called Sven and he came with me to the house to get my things. Moussa couldn't believe I was really leaving. After all, we had fought and made up before, but this time I was afraid, for my life. Maybe I was overreacting, maybe it was all in my mind, but I kept seeing him with that knife, and he had changed. I was afraid. He begged me, but Sven said he'd call the police if he interfered, so he just sat there with tears in his eyes as I took my things. I was crying too. I think I still loved him. A little bit, but I couldn't trust him anymore. I left my job and moved back to Basel.

"I had a little breakdown at that time. Everything for me had ended. At this time my former friends came back. And I am shocked at all the nasty things they say. They think they are trying to make me happy. They will say, You are lucky you didn't have any children with him. Or they ask, What did you guys talk about all the time? Did he even know how to use fork and knife? I told them that's it. Leave me alone, don't ever come back. What right did they have to judge him? What have they ever stood up for in their whole life? I told them I was ashamed to be their friend. I am sorry. He is your brother, but I have to tell you the truth. Some people here are very racist. I don't want to upset you."

"Do I look upset?" Portia asked. A woman had once screamed in her face in the Tube in London, dementedly

shouting, "Fucking foreigner!" Foreigner, for some reason, was the worst form of insult the woman could think of. She had read in the papers about people being thrown out of moving trains by skinheads for being black.

"Don't worry about upsetting me," she said. "Just go on with your story."

But still, she was touched. She had misjudged Katharina. Despite everything that happened, she had been truly courageous, going against her family and friends, standing up for love.

"Did you see him again, I mean, before the last time?"

"Yes. I'll tell you, but first, I go out for a cigarette."

They went out together and stood by the door, smoking.

"I saw him. He also moved back to Basel. I couldn't stop him, he had the right to do that. But we didn't meet. We made contact only through my lawyers. I needed a lawyer because I didn't feel safe. Of course I sometimes see him at the station where he worked, at the Hauptbahnhof. And he will wave to me and I will pretend I didn't see him. And then, I don't know what happened, I came back one day and I found him waiting for me here. I don't know how he found my address, maybe through one of our old friends, maybe he followed me, I don't know. But he was waiting for me outside the door, and he waited for me until I had opened the door, then he came and said we should go in and talk. He said he was going back to Mali. I didn't believe him and I said he should leave. He left. Just like that. He just looked at me sadly and he shake his head and he left. I was surprised.

"Then the next day, I got off the train, and there he was. It was late in the evening, on a Sunday. The platform was

almost empty. I think he came on the same train with me. I am not sure, but I think he followed me. I turn and he was there, coming toward me. I stood there, I was terrified. He looked so serious. You understand, I was not thinking clearly at this time. My aunt had just died, and then all the pressure from him. I stood there, paralyzed. I wanted to scream for help, but I just stood there, watching him still approaching, and the place was deserted, just me and him. He said nothing, he came and hugged me. I remember a train was coming in then. It honked, very loud, and that added to my panic, and at that moment the train lights flashed into my eyes and it was as if I was released from chains. I . . . pushed him with all my might. I thought he was going to kill me. I am sorry. You know what happen next. There was the trial. At first, I didn't want to defend myself, I wanted to die, to be punished. I caused his death. I kept seeing his body, cut into pieces. But my father said, What is the use? Best to tell the truth and fight for my freedom. We got a lawyer and, you know the rest. They gave me three years, not for murder, but for what we call *Totschlag*, manslaughter."

·

The community cemetery was located on a hillside populated by pine trees. It looked like a park, peaceful, the sort of place one would want to be buried in. They were the only people there, Sven was in the car, waiting for them.

"I have never been here before," Katharina said, "I was in detention when they buried him."

It was one of the few community burial grounds in Basel that had a section for Muslims. They found his grave next

to a tree, tucked away at the back of the neat rows of head-
stones, all ritually positioned to face the east. It was raining
again. They clustered solemnly under one umbrella over the
headstone, speaking in whispers as if scared they'd disturb the
dead. Portia felt the tears fill her eyes. It was hard to believe
that under this stone lay her brother's remains. What drove
him, what did he seek, so far away from where he was born,
why so restless, and was he finally at rest, here, in this foreign
place? No wonder philosophers and poets always describe life
as a fever, a burning raging fever from which we all seek
relief. Her father had sought his in his activism and exilic
delusions. Her brother had left home and taken a boat to Mali,
and he had ended up in the home of the preacher who became
his father, but the fever had still raged, driving him to Europe,
and she wondered if it was all worth it. He had died at thirty-
three, so young. Would his soul fly back to Africa, back to
where he was born? She had started thinking more and more
about death, since her father died. And she, what did she seek,
what was her fever and how did she seek relief from it? She
wanted to make her mother happy. She wanted to find out
more about her brother—but she could hardly call that a fever.
And what was the use blaming it all on their father—he was
a shitty father, of course, but ultimately we all make our way,
driven by our own appetites and predilection.

On the way to the airport they passed people standing at
bus stops waiting for the next bus, it was wet and watery and
windy, somehow that was how she always imagined Europe
to be. Katharina sat silently in front, next to Sven, looking
at the passing landscape. Earlier, in the cemetery Portia had
asked her what her plans were. "I am not sure," Katharina

said with a shrug. "For me I cannot stay in Basel again, not in Switzerland. I have lost my friends. Maybe I go to another country, maybe Germany. I have my education. Of course I come back to Basel once in a while since I have my house, but I have to find a new life somewhere."

When they got out of the car Katharina stood in front of Portia, her eyes wet. "I have nothing more to say, but I want you to know I am sorry and I really loved your brother. But there was so much problem between us and it was never going to work. It is life." She rejoined Sven in the car, walking away without looking back, her shoulders heaving violently.

Now there were just the two of them, sitting on a bench, not talking much. Her mind was here, and also in Lusaka. She was walking down a tree-bordered path toward a modest brick house in front of which her mother was standing, waiting for her. She still wasn't sure what she'd tell her mother, she wasn't sure if the journey had been a success or a failure, but she was glad she came. She mentioned this to him. "I didn't want to come, you know. I told my mother, What is the point? Plus, he is already dead. But this has been worth it. I met you."

"I am also glad I came."

She wrote down her number and her email. "Call me, or write. I am also on Facebook. Will you?" He held her tight for a long time, then they parted. Walking toward her gate, she imagined him watching her until she disappeared. She refused to turn back, if she did she'd break down and run back to him and say, "Come to Lusaka with me." He had said yes to her once, why not a second time? But, she had no claim on him. When she asked him drunkenly that night to come to Basel

with her, she had been surprised when he said yes. Perhaps
he also needed to get away, deferring a final decision by aim-
less motion. Now he had a train to catch, he had to return to
Berlin, back to the house in Mitte, cluttered with boxes that
he had to put in storage. His mind was in between places.
Eventually, she was sure, he would make the right decision.
Maybe he would go back to his wife. She hoped he wouldn't,
she hoped he would write, she hoped they would meet again.
She came up on the escalator and there, through the glass, she
saw a plane on a runway speeding for takeoff. She watched,
impressed by the certainty, the power, every bolt, every screw,
every drop of liquid focused on that takeoff. Nothing tentative or hesitant. It was amazing, and beautiful.

THE INTERPRETERS

It was fortuitous that I bought a ticket for the French TGV train instead of the Deutsche Bahn, which, it turned out, was on strike today. It meant I had to go through Zurich to transfer to a Berlin train. I passed through a line of disappointed Deutsche Bahn customers waiting for answers regarding their travel. As the train pulled away from the glum faces on the platform, I tried to suppress a smug feeling of false prescience we all get when things work out for us and don't work out for others in the same situation. It was three hours to Zurich, so I closed my eyes as soon as we got under way. I jerked awake as the train came to a stop at the Zurich station. I stood up and ran to my next train, I felt sluggish,

slowed down by sleep, but I made it before the doors closed. I put my head down and slept off again. The next time I woke up a border policewoman was standing over me. We were at the German border, the train had come to a stop and the police were going around the train, checking documents. There were two officers in the carriage, the other, a man, was talking to another passenger a few seats away from me. I couldn't help but notice that the other passenger was also African, with the tall thin frame and curly hair common to some East Africans. A Somali, most likely; with him was a boy of about twelve.

I handed the officer my passport.

"Nigerian," she said. She looked at the picture in the passport and then at me in that way immigration officers always do, then she asked me if I had bought any watches or jewelry in Switzerland. I wasn't worried about my documents, my German visa still had two more months on it, and I'd be long out of Europe before it expired. The other passenger seemed to be involved in a long discussion with the officer who had now taken his document, a piece of A4 paper, and was consulting with the female officer. They went back to the Somalian and asked him a few more questions before returning the document to him. Our eyes locked and he nodded at me, I nodded back. I closed my eyes, but I couldn't return to sleep. When the train stopped at the next station and I opened my eyes, I saw he was sitting opposite me. "This seat is free, yes? You don't mind if we sit with you?" he asked. We were the only black people in the carriage, and it was natural for him to assume some solidarity, a closing of ranks, the same way some black people would carefully avoid talking to another

black person in a room full of white people. Obviously he was starving for company. I nodded. "Please."

He looked to be in his middle to late fifties, but when he smiled he had a twinkle in his eyes and it took away five years from his face. "I see you from there, you look sad. That's why I join you."

"I look sad?"

"Is about a girl, maybe?" he said, leaning forward, eyes twinkling. I thought of Portia on the plane. I smiled, saying nothing. He pressed on, "This girl, she is your wife maybe?"

"No, not my wife."

"I see. I understand. But you love her."

"Why do you say that?" I asked, not sure if I should be offended by his persistence or not.

"I see in your eyes. I travel a lot and I see many things. I know love when I see love. You tell this girl you love her?"

I laughed at his intensity.

"Are you traveling in Europe?" he asked. I caught the odd phrasing. Of course I was traveling in Europe, but I understood he meant something else; he wanted to know the nature of my relationship to Europe, if I was passing through or if I had a more permanent and legal claim to Europe. A black person's relationship with Europe would always need qualification—he or she couldn't simply be native European, there had to be an origin explanation. I told him I had been to Basel with a friend, and I was now going back to Berlin via Frankfurt.

He said, "I live in Munich. Two years now in Munich. I take this train to Munich." He had the hoarse voice of the cigarette addict, with the accompanying phlegmy cough and

nicotine-stained teeth. I turned to the boy, who was staring at the passing landscape where the day was slowly evanescing into night. He had a vacant look on his face.

"What's your name?" I asked. He looked from me to his father, then he turned back to staring out at the landscape.

"His name is Mahmoud. He don't like to talk. He is shy of strangers," the man answered. The boy looked at him, the annoyance briefly flashing in his eyes the way all kids at that age are always annoyed at their parents. He said something to the boy, and I asked him, "Is that Somali you are speaking?"

"No, that is Turkish."

"Ah, you are from Turkey!"

"No, Somalia. But we lived in Turkey long time. He speaks Bulgarian as well, and Arabic, and some German, and English."

"Wow. A walking Rosetta stone," I said.

"Stone?" He looked puzzled.

"How did he learn to speak so many languages? He is so young."

"My son, he have very small school education. He learn everything from travel."

"I see."

"We have been to many countries, but now we live in Germany. This boy, he has been traveling since he is four years, now he is fifteen."

"So, you are going back to Munich?" I asked. Clearly, he wanted to talk. I wasn't particularly in the mood for talking but I was intrigued by the boy, who sat silent, looking out at the passing landscape—rather quiet for someone who spoke so many languages. I wanted to hear him speak, I wanted to test him.

"Tell me something in Bulgarian," I said. He didn't even turn from the window.

"We go to Munich first, then maybe we go to Bulgaria," the father said.

"You are going to Bulgaria today?"

"Yes, maybe, but first we go to Munich. Listen, is a long journey, many hours before we come to Frankfurt. If you want, I tell you my story. To kill time. It is long story, but interesting, and is all true. I swear, by Allah, it is all true."

The offer was made matter-of-factly, it sounded reasonable, we had a long trip ahead of us, what better way to shorten the trip? I leaned back in my seat. "Go ahead." I could always feign sleepiness if it got boring.

•

His name was Karim Al-Bashir and he was born in Somalia, long before the tribal wars and internecine killings started. His father was not ethnic Somali, he came from North Sudan as a young man and settled in Mogadishu, the Somali capital. The father, Al-Bashir, married into a good and moderately well-to-do family of traders, he was hardworking, and lucky, he prospered. His father-in-law gave him a loan and he started his own business, selling provisions in a corner store. His first son, Karim, was born one year after the marriage. Al-Bashir died in a car accident when Karim was only twelve years old, and suddenly the young Karim had to assume the responsibilities of an adult. With support from his uncles he was able to continue his father's business, buying and selling. He got married at twenty and had his first daughter before he turned twenty-two. And then gradually things began to

change. In 1990 President Siad Barre died and overnight Somalia descended into political chaos. Time passed. Factions organized around family ties and tribal loyalty divided the country into fiefs overseen by tribal warlords. And thus began Karim's personal nightmare.

In his phlegmy voice he said, "One day a young man come to my shop and says he wants to marry my daughter, Aisha. She is only ten. She is too young, and I want her to finish school. But I am afraid of telling him no. This is a powerful man, the son of the local warlord, even though he is young, everyone knows him. His name is Abdel-Latif. He go around with a group of bad boys, all with guns, and they can shoot you, just like that. So, I go and tell my in-laws. My mother-in-law she knows about this man Latif and she tell me, Be careful. She say I must not give any answer now, we wait and see, maybe he lose interest and go. But every day this man he come to the shop. He will sit and his friends will take a few things and not pay, cigarette and biscuit and Coca-Cola, small things, and I will smile and smile, and he will remind me that he wants to marry my daughter. He begin to call me his father-in-law, just like that. One day he say, 'Why you don't want me to marry your daughter, you think I am not good enough? Are people from where you come better than us Somalis?'

"And now I know. It is not only about my daughter, Aisha. He wants to destroy me because my father is not originally from Somalia. That day, we have a family meeting, my wife's two brothers, Mustafa and Abu-Bakr, and my wife and her mother and father. I can see in their eyes that they have no hope for me. My father-in-law, he say, 'We will go to Abdel-

Latif's father, I know him very well, he is my namesake, Muhammad. We grew up together, if his son will listen to anyone, he will listen to his father.' It is our only hope. The only other choice is to run away to another town far away, but even that is not hundred percent safe, because these people they can have friends and family in different towns and they can get you. That night we go to see his father, Muhammad, who is namesake of my father-in-law. He is an important man, he live in a big house and there are many people all waiting to see him. Many cars are parked outside the house. It is in the evening, after the Maghrib prayer. We sit on a mat in the outside room, four of us, me and my father-in-law and Mustafa and Abu-Bakr, my wife brothers. Soon he come in and people greeted him. Though others are there before us, the moment he see my father-in-law he invite him forward. 'Muhammad,' he say, 'what a surprise, what a pleasure to see you here in my home.' They go aside and they talked. When they come back, I can see there isn't much hope on my in-law's face. But we don't leave immediately, food is brought in by two young girls, their head covered in hijab. Plenty food, because he is an important man. Rice and chicken. We eat together, from the same bowl using our fingers. Then we left.

" 'He'll talk to his son,' my father-in-law say. 'He'll reason with him.'

"That night, I go to sleep full of hope. Since the whole thing start, I cannot sleep very well, both me and my wife. The country has changed. People shooting guns every day on the streets. People go about in fear. Women are punished for very small reasons, like not covering their heads, or not marrying the person the mullahs say they must marry. Well, we

wait to see what will happen after the promise from Muhammad. Our answer come two days later. Latif and his friends
came to my shop. My shop is not big, just a small room in
front of the house, facing the road in a quiet part of town.
Suddenly we hear gunfire, ta-ta-ta, they fire gun on the door
of my shop. I thought I was dead. Bullet everywhere. My
eldest boy, Fadel, he is just seven years, he always stay with me
in the shop, he run into the house, me I lay on the floor waiting for them to come in and kill me. They come in, three of
them, Latif is leading. They stand over me where I am lying
on the ground. 'Stand up,' he say to me. I stand up, and as I
look into his eyes I know it is going to be my last day. It is not
the eyes of a normal man. His senses have been turned by the
terrible plant they eat, kwat. You know kwat? It is like drug.
They eat it from morning to night and is very bad. It make
you go crazy. He is chewing like this, in handfuls.

"He look at me and he say, 'So you think my father can save
you from me?' My hand and my leg start shaking, and all I can
do is to pray in my mind that they kill me quickly and that
they don't touch my wife and children. He tell me to go into
the house and to bring my daughter and her mother. He say
he want to hear from their mouth that they have no objection
to this marriage propose."

"Proposal," I said.

"Yes, proposal. So, I go in, but the house is empty. My wife
when she hear the gun, and she see Fadel running inside, she
take the children and they run to her father house. I come back
and tell him that they have heard the gun and they are afraid,
they run and I don't know where they are. I am sorry. 'Okay,'
he say. 'Just prepare your daughter for the wedding. It take

place next Friday, five days from today.' This talk is happening on a Sunday, I remember everything as if is today. I tell him I have no problem with that. I only have one request. More time, please. One month maybe, so I can buy my daughter new clothes and pots and other things for the marriage, I am poor man and I need time to get the money together. 'Two weeks,' he say, and they left. I sit there, too afraid to go out. I can't believe I am still alive. When I see the gun I think my last day has come. As soon as my legs become strong to walk, I go to my in-laws' house and tell them what happened. We have another meeting.

"My father-in-law, he say, 'You have two choice here. You can stay and let him marry your daughter, or you can leave town. You decide.' 'No,' my wife said. All these time she have been quiet and left all the decision to me, but now she speak, very strong. 'That man will never marry my daughter. What son-in-law is this? He is crazy man and one day he will kill my daughter. My daughter will never sleep in the same room with that man. Never.'

"And that is how we leave our country Somalia. First my wife and children leave for Hargeisa to stay with her aunt, my mother-in-law's sister. I stay behind and continue to open the shop, to pretend everything is okay and normal. Latif and his boys sometimes stop in front of the shop to ask me if I am getting ready for the wedding, and I always say, Yes, insha Allah, when they ask me where is Aisha I make excuse, I tell them she have gone to school, or she have gone to the market with her mother. They will take a few cigarette and small small things from the shop and they will go. I wait, and one day before the wedding, I leave town. I follow my wife to

Hargeisa. I leave everything we own, everything, including the goods in my shop. I tell my in-laws to sell everything they can sell and send us the money after. This is the beginning of our life on the road."

"What year was this?" I asked.

"2002, is twelve years now. I feel sad to leave Mogadishu. I feel in my heart as if I will never see Mogadishu again. I feel sad for my family also. I have three children at the time, Aisha, who is only ten, and Fadel who is seven, and this one, Mahmoud, who is only four when we leave, and his mother was pregnant that time. Now Mahmoud is fifteen, almost sixteen. I leave Mogadishu with three children, now I have five children. Two were born on the road."

The boy, Mahmoud, who had been quiet all this while, his face glued to the window, gazing at the small towns and countryside and farms outside, now turned and whispered to his father, the father nodded. The boy stood up and headed for the toilet at the end of the carriage. He had a limp, perhaps even worse than it appeared because he walked self-consciously, trying to minimize the limp with a stylish roll of his body. Karim saw me staring after the boy and he said, "He is a good boy. He speaks four languages, and all he learn on his own. His brother speak five language. I speak three."

"What happened to his leg, was he born like that?"

"No, no, he wasn't born like this. He get accident. It happen in Yemen. I tell you my story, I tell you everything. It is a sad story, but still, we thank God we are alive together and we are healthy. I have seen people who suffer more than me. I have seen people die in the forest, trying to cross the border. Once, me and my boys, when we are leaving Turkey through

forest, we saw a woman and her daughter in the bush. They are looking around, and I ask her can I help you, are you in trouble? She say she was looking for her husband grave. He died when they tried to cross into Bulgaria with human smugglers. He just fall down and died. The smugglers help her quickly bury him in the sand. That was many days ago, but she came back because she kept thinking of him. 'You come back to do what?' I ask her. She say she come to say *du'a* for him, to pray for his dead body, she and her son, the son is maybe five, maybe six years old, she say only if she pray for her dead husband can she be able to go forward. Now they look for the grave and she can't find it, it was over a week since they buried him and everything look different. She go from one little place that look like grave, then she begin to pray, then she go to another pile of sand, about four times I see her go from one sand to another. Sometimes while praying she forget what she is doing and she begin to fall asleep because she is so tired and she didn't sleep for many days, then she will start again, then she will forget the words and she will start to cry. We leave her there, she and her son. I tell you, I have seen so many suffering. My story also is sad, but I have seen more sad stories in my traveling. My boy, he broke his leg in Yemen. And you know all his dream is he wants to be a football player. He wants to grow up and play for the Turkish club, Galatasaray."

"How did it happen?" I asked.

Now we were in Cologne. The noise made by passengers coming in and going out, the sound of their laughter and their German words formed the background to our talk. The boy was back from the toilet. He looked glum, too serious for a

kid. His father turned to him and said something in Turkish and the boy looked at me, then he turned back to the window. After a while he stood up and took some money from his father to go to the canteen. At the table to our left a German family was staring pointedly at us, their faces impassive, making no attempt to disguise their curiosity.

"Life in Yemen was not easy at first. But good thing is that we are safe and we are together as a family, this is the most important blessing. We register with the United Nation refugee service, and they give us small money every month, not much, about fifty dollars each. That is not enough for food and house, but things cheap in Yemen. And soon my in-law was able to send us small money from what they sell of my property back in Somalia. We rent a small place, just two rooms and a little kitchen. The children in one room, me and my wife in another room. Sana'a, the capital of Yemen, is a small city. The buildings is not much different from Mogadishu. Large families live in large compounds, with many children and the women wearing their veil and people walking on the narrow streets, just like Mogadishu. There isn't much work to do, but soon I meet some Somalis and one of them, Othman, he invite me to work with them. We buy cigarette and small small things we can buy cheap in Yemen and we take it to Somalia and make some profit, not much, but enough to survive."

"Was it dangerous?"

Karim laughed and shrugged. "Well, what we are doing is smuggling, you know. I don't ask too much question. My partner is young Othman. There are many Somalis like him in Yemen, they live in the refugee camps, with no wives or

children. I don't even think they are real refugees, just busi-
nesspeople. He sometimes talk that his brothers are Somali
pirates and they kidnap big ships on the sea and make big
money, but something happen and his brother die and they
stop doing pirate work. He doesn't say more than that. Now
they smuggle people from Somalia to Yemen and other countries. And then they take back cigarette and other small things
to sell in Somalia. Me, I did not join in smuggling people,
but I join in buying and selling cigarette. Still, my wife, she
was not happy. She said I can't do this kind of business. But
I tell her, What can I do? We can't live on fifty dollars every
month. We will die.

"Well, everything is good for a time. Everything go fine.
We are happy. My children start going to school and we can eat
good. My wife give birth and we move to a bigger house, not
too bigger than the last one, but with three rooms. This is our
first year in Yemen. The Somali community is very small then,
but soon things start to change. More people start to come,
then Othman start doing more people smuggling, and he want
me to join him. I will not lie to you, I did join him for a time,
and the money was good. Then my wife become unhappy,
she say, 'Why you do this? Are we not managing okay, what
if you get arrested, what if you die, then what will happen to
us? Now we are in this strange land, you can't break any law.' I
say I will think about it. And that day, as I go to meet Othman
to tell him I can't do people smuggling anymore, they tell me
Othman is dead. He died in a boat on the sea. His people were
sitting in the room and they are crying and I quietly left them.
That same day my son fell from the veranda. Because we are
on the fifth floor, in our new house, it is cheaper to rent the

fifth floor, the ground floor is more expensive because no elevator or anything and everybody want ground floor, and there is a little garden in the yard. Well, my son was playing with his brother, Fadel, and he is leaning on the rail and it broke, he fell and thank God he survived without any major broken bone, but he broke something in his kneecap and from that day he was limping like this. At first we didn't know that his kneecap broke. But after a while we see that as he grow, his left leg is not growing like the right leg."

"Did you take him to the hospital?"

"Yes, but in Yemen, there is nothing they can do. Yemen is small country, and poor. They tell me the only place you can get help is in Europe, Germany, or France. I look at my son who all his life wants to play football and I promise myself that I will bring him to Germany or France as long as I am alive."

They were three years in Yemen, from there they moved to Syria. The family continued to grow. There were five children now, three girls and two boys. They got to Syria in 2005. In Damascus their life improved almost immediately. There they'd spend the best seven years of their lives since they left home. The economy was good, Karim was able to get a job with no difficulty, as a kitchen assistant in a hotel he described as the best hotel in all of Syria. His face lit up as he remembered. "Food is not a problem. I get plenty food from the hotel. Food they want to throw away, good food, the best food in the world because this is a very big hotel. I tell them no, I will take it. That way I didn't have to spend my money on food. No more fighting with the wife, and the kids all go back to school. My oldest son, Fadel, he is now ten, and my

daughter Aisha is almost fourteen; she was only ten when we left Mogadishu. My wife have not seen her mother or her father for over three years.

"In Damascus we decide we will not get in touch with the Somali community. The last experience with Othman was not good. But we are able to keep in touch with our family back home. They tell us things in Somalia are getting worse every day. Every day Shabaab is growing bigger, now there are bombs on the street. Some of my wife people and my uncles have now moved to refugee camps in Kenya. We hear that Abdel-Latif, the evil young man who caused us to leave home, is now one of the most powerful men in all the country. Seven years in Syria, and we would have stayed even longer but for two reasons, one is my son's leg, we have to get to Europe, and second reason, every day Syria is becoming like Somalia. War has started everywhere and even the Syrians are running away from the cities to the countryside, some are leaving the country. And so my wife said, 'We have to go, we are not safe here with our children.' We left Syria in 2012, we follow a group that is leaving for Istanbul in Turkey."

Karim fell quiet, and before he turned to the window I saw his eyes fill up with tears. The boy was asleep, his head resting against his father's shoulder. Outside, night had leaped onto the landscape, and we could be anywhere, Turkey, Syria, Yemen, Germany, it didn't matter. What mattered was to hear what happened next. I wanted to know what happened in Turkey, why was it only him and the boy on the train, where was the rest of the family, Fadel, the girls, the mother . . . ?

"In Turkey things very difficult. My wife almost left me. We have only one room and a parlor for me, my wife, and the children. We are always fighting and the children couldn't even go to school. When we live in Syria my wife and daughter are able to get work, sometimes cleaning, sometimes cooking, and in the hotel there was always food, leftovers, chicken, rice, fish, and we were never hungry, we eat rich-people food. But in Turkey, all the foreigners are treated bad. I only get the worst job, in a furniture company, we carry furniture to people houses, sometimes we repair furniture, and as you finish one job, another one is coming. You have to work many hours, for very little money, they just force you to work overtime with no pay, whether you like or not. If you complain, they say okay, go, other people want your job. You work like slave. My wife say, We can't continue like this. If we continue like this, we will die. We have to decide. We have to go to Europe now.

"Every day I worry: how we get money to travel, where do we stay in Europe? I was afraid, I was tired, I miss my home and I miss Mogadishu and my shop and my simple life selling little things with my family. I know if I enter Europe, I may never come back to my country forever. So, me and my wife, we agree, I say, I will take the three older children with me, she will stay with the two young ones. I go first, if everything work out fine, she will come after me. But my wife, she say, No, take the two boys, I stay with the girls, Aisha who is nineteen and Fatima who is eight and the youngest, Khadija, who is only three. She say girls must stay with their mother because they are women and they need their mother. I agree.

"The next big problem is, how to go to Europe? My son, this one, he say, 'Baba, can we not take our hundred euro that we get from the refugee service people and fly to Europe?' We laugh. It is not so easy. Our two choice to travel is to go through Greece, and directly to Western Europe, but if we go through Greece we have to fly and we have to have papers and do registration and fingerprint and so many things, the other one is to go from Istanbul, which is near the border, then we walk across the border into Bulgaria, which is East Europe, but it is still Europe because Bulgaria just join the EU. Finally, we decide we will go by foot to Bulgaria.

"So, we say goodbye to my wife and my daughters. That night we did not sleep. All of us, we cry all night. I didn't know if I will see my little girls again, and my wife. But we have to go, there is no choice. In Istanbul we meet the people who will help us across the border to Bulgaria. Ten hours we walk with my two boys, in night, from nine p.m. to seven a.m., always hiding. Ten hours and we have to hurry all the time because of danger and we have to stay with the other people in the group and the smugglers who are guiding us. My boy, this one, with his leg, he get tired and he cannot walk anymore, and he start to cry. I tell him we are doing this so we can get medicine for his leg. He said no, he doesn't want it anymore, he say he only want to go back home. He is tired. Me and his older brother we carry him, under the arm, like this. That is when we saw the woman and her son who are looking for the grave of her husband to say the *du'a* for his soul. It is long time ago, but I feel sad and scared every time when I think about it. That woman alone in the forest with her son, not knowing whether to go forward to Europe or to

go back, because her husband died. What can she do, where can she go?

"As we got to the Bulgarian border the border police come out and arrest us. We are happy to be arrest, I tell you. As they put us in line, one lady come, she is not Bulgarian, she come from France or Belgium, I think, she say to me, 'Are you together with these boys?' I say, 'Yes, they are my children.' She say, 'In that case you are lucky, because we treat family different. We will keep you together and you will get a better room and food and everything will be fine. Just always remember to join the family line.' We very happy, me and my children. We think, this is the end of our journey, our suffering is over. But we don't know this was just the beginning of our bad luck."

I said, "What do you mean? You had made it to Europe at last, with your kids, and the nice lady had promised to assist."

Karim shook his head. "Ah, she is nice, but the Bulgarians are different. They are not like real Europeans, I tell you, they are more like Asians, and they just join the EU, they are not very friendly."

"What do you mean?"

"I'll tell you. They bring truck to take us to town, and because of what the lady said, I take my boys and join the family line, but a man come and say to me, 'Hey, you can't join this line, this is only for women and girls, are you a woman?' I say, 'No, but I am with my children. The lady say I am to stay with family because I am together with my young children.' The man say, 'Where is your wife?' I say, 'My wife is not here, only me and the boys.' The man say, 'Okay, join the men.'

"I want to argue more, but I can see they are getting angry. They say to me, 'Hey, we don't care who you are.' This is after I show them my refugee protection paper from UNHCR in Yemen, they say as far as we are concerned, you have no right here. You enter this country illegal and you are a criminal. So just shut up. Now I see my boys are beginning to cry and people are staring at us. Everybody is tired and I don't want trouble, so I join the men in the line and we enter big truck, like military truck. We drive far and we can't see outside because we are sitting on the floor inside this truck and there are many men, many from Morocco, Algeria, Eritrea, Nigeria, Ghana, Mali, Afghanistan, Syria . . . everyone speaking different language. When we get to the home, which is actually a prison . . ."

"What do you mean prison?" I interrupted.

"This place used to be an actual prison, but now is empty so they use it for refugee but it is really prison. Very big stone building with iron bars and many floors, with women and family on one side and the rest for men, all packed into small tiny rooms. As we are coming down from the truck to be registered, we see the woman again and I quickly run to her. 'You,' she say. 'Where did you go? Why are you not with the families?' I told her what happened. She turned and talk angrily to the man who say I cannot join the family. They argue, then she say to me, 'Don't worry, from now on, I talk directly to his boss. You will be fine. Just finish registering and I will see you inside.' She was angry. We register and we go inside and all the time I keep looking for her, but I didn't see her again. They begin to take us to the rooms, and I tell you this is a bad bad prison. As we go to our rooms the refugees

who are there already, they stand by the door and shout at us and spit at us. My children they are crying now. 'Where are we, Baba?' they ask me. They have never seen anything like this before. I tell the official, 'But you can't do this, you can't put my small children in the same place with all these men. It is not right. Look at my youngest boy, he only seven, how he stay in the same room with all these men?' I touch his hand when I talk and now he is angry. He push me away and call me illegal alien. He say, 'If you don't like our accommodation, you can go back to your country.' Still I try. I say, 'But I am a United Nation protected refugee, see my paper here. You can't do this to us.' He say he does not care about any rights and protection, and I can wait when I go Western Europe. Here is Eastern Europe, they don't care about this. Still, we are a bit lucky, they put us not in the long big room with dozens of men, but in a smaller room with four other people, with my children we are seven in the room. There are bunk beds, and my boys are able to get the top bunk bed, one on top of my bed, the other on the next bed. We stay in that place for one year. It is a bad place, a prison. There are guards everywhere, these guards they work with prisoners before, so they still treat us like prisoners. The food also was bad. We all have to eat in the cafeteria, and even if you are not hungry you cannot take your food to your room, not even bread. It was hard for the young boy because we eat at five p.m. and by eight to nine before we sleep he is hungry again and he will be crying."

He was quiet for a while, looking out of the window. The boy was still sleeping. The father gently ran his hand on the boy's head, his eyes faraway. The memories of that grim place, the prison as he so bitterly called it, had darkened his face,

and yet, when he looked at the boy, his eyes softened and he sighed and turned back to me.

"It was not all bad, you know. We are lucky to be in that little room away from others. It is only seven of us in our room, in the other rooms there are twenty, thirty people. And most rooms are doing segregation, the people stay together in one corner according to their country or color or religion. The Algerians and Pakistanis and Syrians, they stay together. Our room is black people, African. But I tell you, after a few days, the Algerians and Moroccans, these people who didn't want to stay with us, they run away from their room and come to our room because they say, Hey we African too. They say the other rooms are too much fanatics. Too much argument and fighting over religion and Arab Spring and little little things. Our room is called TV room because everybody like to come and watch TV in our room, even though they also have TV in their room. Any chance they get, they come to our room. The TV room is more fun. If you see any refugee who was in Bulgaria, ask them about TV room and they tell you. It was popular place. People everywhere, some playing cards, some eating, some listen to music, some fighting!"

Was that nostalgia in his voice? Did he perhaps in some little corner of that recollected room etch his name in the wall: "Karim Was Here"? Why do people do that only in places of bitterness and suffering and sweat: prisons, locker rooms, grimy toilets; but never in fancy hotels or restaurants or churches? Is it to affirm their existence in those places that try to diminish the human in them, a cry against extinction? Karim sighed and went on, "And sometimes they call my children to interpret for them. Sometimes when there is

argument and two people can't talk to one another, because one speak English and the other is only speak Arabic and maybe the other Turkish and even Bulgarian, it is my children who help them talk. This is a good thing for us, because everybody in the prison now know Fadel and Mahmoud. One day, the big overall prison guard, his name is Bogdan, but everybody call him Boss Bogdan, he come to the TV room. He stand by the door like this and say, 'Who is Fadel?' At first I fear, I think, what has my son done now? Is he in trouble? But my boy he stand up and he say, 'I am Fadel.' The officer enter the room and he speak to Fadel in Bulgarian, but Fadel his Bulgarian is not very good yet. Boss Bogdan speak in English, now they talk, and they laugh. Then Bogdan switch to Turkish. The younger one, Mahmoud, he jump in, because his Turkish is a bit better, and the officer turn to me and he say, 'Interesting family.' Boss Bogdan he say, 'Okay, come quick quick, we go to my office.' A lawyer is having meeting with one refugee in his office, and the lawyer speak only Bulgarian and English, the refugee he speak only Arabic. Many of the refugee they only speak Arabic and nothing else. Fadel he go and he translate for them. Boss Bogdan is very impress. And suddenly he become friends with my boys. Sometimes he ask them to come to his office and read a letter for him, or just to talk and to watch TV, like his own children. When he go on inspection around the prison, they go with him. They walk with him from floor to floor, talking to the prisoners, my boys they translating for him what the prisoners are saying. He give them extra food and little little present. From that day, many refugees who want to talk to their lawyer, they come to look for Fadel and Mahmoud. Many of them want to

leave Bulgaria immediately and they need lawyer so my children have to interpret for them all the time. If Fadel is busy,
then Mahmoud will translate. For that they respect us and they
always tell me, These children are very smart, you must take
them to school. And even though they say it as a praise for me,
I still feel sad because of the life we are living. I always think,
what if we are back in Somalia, and everything is okay, and
we are living in our small house with our shop. My daughter, Aisha, who is almost nineteen now, she would have been
married, and maybe I will be a grandfather. Fadel would have
started taking over my little business by now, and maybe we
will have another shop by now. But here we are in this place
and we don't know what will happen to us today or tomorrow.

"One day, Boss Bogdan he call me and say, 'These boys,
they are very intelligent, they should be in school, not in a
prison like this. We will see what we can do for you.' I tell my
boys and they dance and jump. I look at them and I begin to
cry. Fadel who was big and strong in Syria, he is now so thin
his eyes are big in his head. And Mahmoud, he doesn't like
the prison food and he has been having stomach problem since
we came here, his back is all covered with rashes and we have
no doctor, no health workers. People die in their rooms from
sickness and there is nothing anyone can do for them. Every
day they take out dead bodies. Mahmoud, as he is growing
taller the limp in his leg is becoming bigger. Whenever we
talk to the mother she ask, 'Are you really in Europe, how
soon can we come and join you? The girls are getting bigger
every day, and they miss their brothers. The youngest one is
always asking for you, because you used to play and carry her,
now she cries and ask for Baba.'

"One day a woman, her name is Sonia, she come and say Boss Bogdan send her and she is going to help us. She belong to a charity that work with refugees. She say she have find us a place to stay, but it is outside town, not too far, but it is cheap. It is a little house in a big bloc of houses, they all look the same, with one room and one living room and a kitchen, but for us it is like a palace. We can cook and take shower and have a little privacy. Sonia, she pay the first rent, and she say after this I have to find work and continue to pay my own rent.

"So finally we leave that prison. We leave TV room and everybody is sad. But it is not easy to get work. Me I have no training, I am a shopkeeper, and also, Bulgaria is not a rich country. Even the people of Bulgaria they can't find work, they want to leave Bulgaria and move to France and Germany, just like me. But I keep trying, every day I take the bus and I go to town to look for work, I go from hotel to hotel from shop to shop, anything I can find, and sometimes I don't come back home till night. Sonia keep coming every day. She try to help. But nothing. Soon however a bigger problem begin. Every day the Jehovah people come to our house to preach to us."

"You mean the Jehovah's Witness?" I asked. He pronounced it *Yehova*.

A family of five in the seats behind ours, mother, father, girls and boy, were talking at the top of their voices, one of the girls kept trying to sing in a shrill voice. Karim had to raise his voice to be heard. "Yes, these people are not good people. They are like the Al-Qaeda." There was so much anger in his voice.

"Why do you say that?"

"I tell you why. When they come first time, I tell them, me I am not Christian, I am not even a very good Muslim, all I want is to take care of my children and for my family to be safe, just leave us alone. Please, please, don't come again. Leave us alone. Then one day, I come home from looking for work, and Fadel is not around. I ask his brother, 'Where is Fadel?' He say to me, 'Fadel he go out with the Jehovah people.' I say, 'When did this thing start?' He say, 'For many days now. One day the Jehovah people come when you are not around and they become friends with Fadel. They come every day and talk to him and he begin to follow them.'

"When Fadel come back I just look at him and I can't speak. I ask him, 'Why you do this, Fadel? What you want with these people?' He stand there, he say nothing, just looking at me. I look at him, and I see that my boy has grown up. He is already a man. He has a little mustache already. Some beard is already on his chin. I tell him, 'Look I don't care what religion you follow, you can be Catholic or Protestant Christian, but not this people. They will break our family. They are like cult.' He say nothing, and I know it is too late already. I search his room and I find a Bible and a cross that the Jehovah people give him. The next day I did not go to look for work. I stay at home to watch him. They did not come that day, but in the night, Fadel he ran away from home to stay with these people. They have plan it long time. Now, I don't know what to do. I go look for Sonia to ask her to help me, but when I see her, she tell me, the social service people they want to speak with me. Fadel has told them that his father, me, Karim Al-Bashir, is a religious fanatic, and I am forcing him not to be Christian. I go with her in her small car to the office. Fadel is waiting

for me with the Jehovah people, three of them. Two men and one woman. That day, I cry. I stand there in the office and I look at my boy, sitting with these people, the Jehovah people, and me sitting there, and I don't know what to say. I wanted to go away and let him do what he want. But then I think of his mother, I think of him when he was a little boy, when he was playing with Mahmoud and he fell from the balcony and how he was crying and saying sorry, it is his fault, and how he didn't eat food for two days because of his sadness for his brother. I say no, I will not give up my first son so easy. I will fight these people.

"Sonia say the only thing I can do is talk to the Muslim Council of Bulgaria. I didn't even know there is a Muslim Council. She tell me, Yes, there is Muslim Council in Bulgaria, they are mostly from Turkey, but they have been in Bulgaria many years and they are very strong, they even have like thirty percent in parliament. Maybe they can help and talk to the government and government can help me get my boy back. So, I go to these people. I meet one of them in mosque, during evening prayer, and after he take me to his house. I tell him everything that happen with my son. Well, he is angry when he hear everything, he say it is not right to break family because of religion, and he say he will help me. We try to meet Fadel, but he will not meet with us. We only meet the Jehovah people and they say Fadel doesn't want to see us. Every time we try to set up meeting, he will not come. His brother say they sometimes see him walking with the Jehovah people, dressed like them in black jacket, and they go from house to house to preach. The Muslim Council, they get a lawyer and the lawyer say I must say that the boy is young,

and he has to stay with me. So, we have another meeting at the social office, and they say he say I am religious fanatic and he is afraid to stay with me. But I say he is my son and he too young . . . and he is . . ."

"Underage."

"Yes, he is underage, so they can't take him from me. But the social people say okay, they will keep him and when he is eighteen he can decide what he want. In a few months, he will be eighteen. Now, I don't know what to do. Finally, I begin to give up. What can I do? I am a poor man, this is not even my country. I say to the Muslim people, I give up. I have to leave here, I can't stay here anymore, we have to go to Germany. Because I think of all we have come through, from Somalia to Yemen to Syria and Turkey and Bulgaria, and I say, Well, we are lucky we are still alive. I think of that woman and her son in the forest trying to pray on her husband grave. And I say to myself, I don't want to lose my other son. They say no, you must stay, we will put Mahmoud in Islamic school and he can become good Muslim and we will keep fighting for the other one. But I don't want to be trap in religion and fighting over religion. I am tired, and I still have no job, and life in Bulgaria is too hard. If Fadel want to see me one day, he know we are going to be in Germany. So, we put together all our money and we get some help from the Muslim Council and we come to Munich."

"How has it been in Munich?" I asked.

His face looked drawn in the poor light of the train carriage. The family of five had finally quieted down and we didn't have to shout. He shrugged. "Sonia, she connect us with another charity in Munich, a church. They give us place

to stay, me and Mahmoud. I have a lawyer, he help me apply
for asylum and I have document to stay in Germany for five
years. He say we will fight my case and we will win. We will
get paper for my wife and my daughters to join us. He say
the German government care very much about family and
education, and they will not send us back to Somalia because
no school there for the children, and maybe my son will soon
have his operation. I am happy for that."

"What of your wife, have you been in touch?" I asked.

He lowered his head. "I talk to my wife. I say soon maybe
now she can join us, because the lawyer say it is now possible
to get them to come. I have not seen my daughters in almost
three years and I don't know how they look now. You know
women grow fast and their face change. My wife say Aisha
now has a boyfriend, and he want to marry her, but Aisha say
no. She say she will not leave her mother alone." He looked at
me, his expression an alloy of sadness and pride and despair.
He said, "Why God give me such good daughter and such bad
son? Why? When I tell my wife about Fadel she get angry.
She start to cry, all the time on the phone. She say I lost her
son. She say is my fault. She say she will never join me in
Germany if I don't find Fadel. So, every day I call Bulgaria, I
ask Sonia if she hear about Fadel and she say she hear he has
move to Switzerland, to another Jehovah people. Switzerland,
how possible? Well, I go to Basel in Switzerland, two days
ago. We stay with friends Sonia introduce to us, and we ask
everywhere, all the Jehovah people, but no Fadel. We can't
find him. I don't know what to do. Maybe I go back to Bulgaria. Maybe I wait. Maybe my wife will change her mind."

His eyes searched mine in the gloomy carriage, and I saw

the hunger on his face. He was hungry for hope, hungry for a break. He shouldn't feel down, I told him. He had come a long way from Somalia. His boy would be fine. I patted the sleeping boy gently on the head before leaving them. We were in Frankfurt and I had to change for my connection to Berlin. I waved goodbye to them, my mind already moving on to the next thing. I had an hour to kill, and it wasn't till I sat down in the empty food court with a cup of coffee before me that I realized I had left my bag on the train. The bag in my hand was Karim's—it was similar to mine, a black leather valise, but a bit older, more tattered. I jumped up and ran down to the platform, foolishly hoping the train would still be there, but the platform was empty, and was this the right platform to begin with, it was a big station, and the platforms all looked the same, with the German signs incomprehensible to my fatigued eyes. I stopped the first uniformed person I saw. He shrugged. He couldn't help. He looked at my ticket and spoke into his phone, he pointed up, I had to go to the information office upstairs, maybe they could help. But, as I dragged my feet toward the escalator, an ominous feeling descended over me, I felt I had dreamt this scenario before and I knew how it was going to unfold. Everything was in that bag, including my passport and my green card.

At the office I stood in line, lost in thought.

"*Nächste*," the lady behind the counter barked at me. When I didn't move she snapped louder, "*Nächste, bitte!*" her German sense of order ruffled. The man behind me gave me an impatient nudge, muttering angrily in German, and still I hesitated. What would I tell the woman, even now my bag was flying away in the night, would Karim get down

at the next station and report the bag? He didn't have my address or number, and would he even notice he had the wrong bag before he got to his destination? I could follow him to Munich and try to locate him, but he said he might soon be leaving for Bulgaria. I needed to keep calm, I was tired, sleep-deprived, I decided to go on to Berlin, to think things through on the train. I had my ticket at least. I left and went back to the platform.

I saw the same officer, standing on the platform. He looked at me suspiciously when I asked him for the train to Berlin. "You find your bag?" he asked. Just then a train pulled into the station, and I saw a face at the window, it was Karim—he was back, looking for me. I ran toward the train. The officer called after me, trying to tell me something, but I was already entering the train. Through a window I saw the officer waving urgently at me, but I made my way down the aisle, toward that face at the window, and why was the train so dark, it felt like a continuation of the darkness that had settled over me since I discovered my bag was missing. The train jerked forward, almost throwing me into the lap of the person sleeping in the aisle seat next to me. I groped my way to an empty seat at the back, one row next to Karim, who even as I sat down I realized was not Karim, and flopped down by the window, looking at the receding platform dotted with sleepy passengers holding their tickets in one hand and their bags in the other.

I sat, tense and alert—I'd get off at the next station and catch any train to Berlin. But the next station came and passed, and the next one, and still the train didn't slow down. I fought to keep my eyes open, I couldn't work up the strength to turn to not-Karim, to ask what train this was. The sense of doom

settled more firmly over me like a blanket. Soon the lights and buildings gave way to monotonous open country. I jumped to my feet and rushed up the aisle looking for an official to ask when the next stop was. I passed through the carriages, eyes glowed at me from the seats, faint reflection of the light outside rose from dark faces; there were no officials to see. I dropped into a seat, exhausted, and immediately fell into a deep stupor. A baby was crying in my sleep and when I woke up it was still crying. Perhaps it was the crying that woke me up. We were pulling into a station, and I got up, trying to see the name of the station, definitely not Berlin Hauptbahnhof, my destination.

More people were coming on, there was a commotion by the door, curses and shouts, a man fell and then stood up again. There were guards, holding guns, forcing more people onto the train. Now I noticed the people being forced on were mostly women and children. Mostly Asian and African.

"What train is this? Where are we?" I asked the man next to me.

He shrugged. "We are at the border."

"What border?"

"Italy. That guard was speaking Italian. I speak the language." He said the last with pride.

The train started to move again.

"Italy?" I asked, flummoxed. Perhaps I hadn't heard right. "I am going to Berlin."

"You are on the wrong train, my friend," he said, and started to laugh. Another man joined in the laughter. I looked around the dark train. "What train is this?"

"We are being deported, don't you know?" the man asked.

His words were gentle, chiding almost, as if he were talking to a slow child. The exhaustion redoubled heavily on my
shoulders. The train grew darker, the way the light fades as
day ends abruptly in winter. I stood up. If only the baby would
stop crying. I wanted to go and talk to the mother, to tell her
to feed him, to do anything to shut him up, but suddenly my
willpower left me and I sat down again, my brain simply shut-
ting down, and I couldn't keep my eyes open. When I woke
up we were being led off the train to buses waiting by the
curb outside the station. It was a small station, with a single
track passing through it and a single exit on either side of the
track. I hurried over to the soldier.

"There's a terrible mistake. I got on the wrong train."

I showed him my ticket to Berlin. He called to another soldier and they conversed for a while, the other soldier shrugged
and turned away. I felt my heart sink.

"I cannot help you here. You make complaint when you
get to camp," the soldier said, gently turning the barrel of his
gun toward me. The weak morning sun splashed itself over
the trees and concrete buildings as we came out of the station
and into the buses. I couldn't read the signs, they were in Italian, probably. We followed the direction of the sun, meandering and climbing through sleepy villages and hamlets and
endless olive farms.

The bus was worse than the train. At least in the train there
was more space and more air. In the bus the press of bodies
and the cries of babies and the cursing of men intensified. The
crying baby was in the same bus, and the mother's cooing
continued, trying to calm it down, until suddenly it stopped.
I could understand how it must have lost its will to cry any-

more, the same way the energy had drained out of me earlier. I waited for the cry to resume, but it didn't. We were in some countryside, and suddenly we could smell it, the sea. The smell was unmistakable, salty, minerally, and then we could hear the distant rush of water against the coastline. Somehow I wanted the baby to cry again, to articulate the feeling inside me, a deep, confused cry.

Book 5

THE SEA

As he drove down the sloping road to the camp he caught a glimpse of the sea below. The southern Italian sun was gleaming on the waves and for a moment it all came back, the woman lying half-covered in the foaming waves on the beach, and he running toward her. At first he thought she was dead. The camp sat on the slope of a hill by the sea. Today the sea was restless, roiling and snapping at the foot of the hill, spouting foam like an enraged leviathan. This hilly landscape, which in his childhood had looked postcard-idyllic with its view of the endless blue Mediterranean below, was now ruined by the slapdash red brick structures and white tents covering it, and the smell, the unbearable smell.

His late uncle, who had been in a prisoner-of-war camp in WWII, said the smell was unmistakable, it was more than human effluence and trash, it was the smell of misery and despair. The tents were more recent; the brick structures had been there since the 1920s as offices and temporary staff accommodations when the hill was mined for copper, when the copper veins ran out in the 1940s the mine was turned into a military camp, and when the war ended the site was abandoned to wild goats and rodents, and for decades its brick structures and iron roofs rusted away in the humid, acidic sea air. When, a decade ago, the refugees started coming and the small island started running out of space to keep them, the town council voted to salvage the rotting structures and turn the place into a refugee center. The migrants were brought here as soon as they arrived in their boats, to be examined by the doctors, to be deloused, to be registered, and officially welcomed to Europe. As Matteo drove past the sign that said *Welcome Centre*, he couldn't help grinning at the lack of irony by whoever had proposed the name. A bored-looking guard nodded at him and he parked his motorbike under a tree and climbed the four concrete steps to the camp director's office. He wondered why the man had sent for him. They had been together last week—a body had washed up on the beach in front of his house, and he had called the director to come pick it up. It was not the first time. Twice, a leaky boat with shivering, terrified, and surprised-to-be-alive families had beached on his property and he had driven them in his truck to the refugee center. All except the woman and the child.

North, they all want to go north, the director shouted into

the phone as Matteo entered the tiny office. The man caught his eye and nodded.

Yes, Germany, France, England. This is not a prison, you understand, they are free to go if they want. He put down the phone and stood up and shook Matteo's hand. American reporter. He wants to know if this is some sort of detention center. Whatever gave him that idea.

Perhaps he wants to borrow my truck, Matteo thought. The refugee center was badly underfunded, and the director was often asking for help, which Matteo was always willing to offer. Most of the town's inhabitants, men women children, had at one time or another volunteered at the camp.

Come, the director said, I have something to show you.

They descended the steps and followed the path leading to yet another gate which opened into the camp proper. The ground underneath was hard and pebbly; this stark, ugly landscape was somehow offset by the sea, white foam turning to soft aquamarine. Between the hill and the sea was the camp. A central structure dominated the entire camp—rectangular and unremittingly utilitarian, its aluminum roof arched over the concrete building, square windows cut into the concrete at precise, regular intervals. This was the medical center where all newcomers were examined by doctors, nurses, and other volunteers. Matteo had volunteered here before, more than once. On busy days it looked like a marketplace, men and women and children dehydrated from their long ordeal on the sea were stretched out on cots and hooked to drips for rehydration—it was never a pretty sight: some had feet rotting in their wet shoes, some had shit and vomit caked to their skin and hair, some were delirious with fright from being trapped

between dead bodies for days in the boat—pregnant women had to be checked to see if the baby was still alive, or not, in which case emergency cesarean sections were performed right there on the floor, more serious emergencies were flown out by helicopter to bigger and better-equipped facilities in Palermo and nearby cities.

Matteo hadn't been to the center in over a month, but nothing had changed, it was overcrowded as usual, it was meant to hold five hundred people, but it always had over two thousand migrants, some just arriving and waiting to be processed, some leaving. Toilets had been converted into sleeping spaces, it was either that or leave women and children exposed to the weather. As they descended further into the camp he saw them coming from all directions, men and women and children, in their hands were bowls they presented at a table where two men stood behind three huge aluminum basins from which they ladled out food, which the inmates began to wolf down immediately without waiting to sit.

The director, still not explaining where they were going, said, There are more in those tents. Some are too sick to come out.

They came to a tall fence facing the sea. Matteo was about to ask what exactly they were looking for when he noticed the line of bodies standing or sitting, men and women and children, all facing the sea, their faces pressed against the fence. They were not talking, just facing the sea, away from the kitchen and the diners. Nearby a woman sat on the hard pebbly ground, moaning softly, all the time knocking her head against the fence. They did not turn when Matteo and the director approached.

What are they doing here? he asked.

The director pointed at the woman and whispered, They say she sits here every day to listen to the voices of her children who drowned.

Matteo imagined the voices rising from the impassive depths, woven into the wind and waves, faint and then dying, snuffed by the wet air, but since they say sound never really dies, the voices must continue, diminished, inaudible to ordinary ears, but still detectable with the right listening device, like a mother's ears. The director came to a stop abruptly. His voice still at a confidential pitch, he said, A week ago a man hanged himself in one of the bathrooms. Another woman went crazy and started screaming for no reason around the camp, she was subdued, but that night she stabbed herself to death. Another man managed to scale this fence and threw himself into the waves, he drowned immediately.

In the distance a fishing boat, or a ferry, rose and dipped, leaving a contrail of churning sea behind it. Coast guards, most likely, on patrol. In the sky a Frontex helicopter circled in long and widening loops as it searched the inscrutable waters.

I don't understand . . . Matteo tried to hide his impatience. The director raised a hand, urging him toward a man standing alone by the fence, also staring into the water, quiet and motionless. The day was dying and soon the mild Mediterranean sun would dip into the sea, its last rays slanting over the water and the coastline, turning the skyline and the white sands and the rooftops russet, and the aquamarine water black.

Who is he? Matteo found himself whispering, not sure why. He has been here for a month now. He has been passed

from camp to camp. He is very sick and I fear he cannot last much longer.

Now Matteo noticed how frail the man looked, with the wind flapping his baggy shirt and pants, threatening to sweep him over the fence and into the sea. He was of average height, his clothes hung on his gaunt frame and a beard covered his chin. The director was staring at the man with a regretful look on his face. Matteo wondered why the man was important, why his case differed from the other hundreds around him.

The director turned to him. He was brought here with a bunch of others, deported from the north. This has been happening more and more often, migrants rounded up and dumped into trains and sent back to their first European country of entry, usually Italy or Greece. They want to send them back to their countries, or at least to Libya or Egypt, but the government often forgets about them. After a while most of them simply walk out and return to the north. This one, he came to my office two weeks ago. He was not a refugee, he said. His documents went missing and he ended up on the train by accident. I didn't believe him of course. You get such stories every day. Once, a woman from Togo told me she was a queen in her hometown, she had been chased out by rivals and should therefore be given automatic Italian citizenship, not even asylum, citizenship. She demanded to be taken to the king of Italy.

What did you tell her?

I told her we had no king. I get all kinds of stories here. But this guy, he persisted, and I agreed to take him to the US consulate in Palermo. We went and he placed his complaint,

but they said there was nothing they could do about his green card. They said they'd flag it if it ever appears anywhere and let him know. He can apply for a replacement only in America or in his home country, Nigeria, meanwhile, he can apply for a visitor's visa, but he needs his Nigerian passport to do even that. They gave him some forms to fill out.

If he is not a refugee, then he shouldn't be here, Matteo said.

Yes, I told him the same thing. But it appears he has nowhere to go, or nowhere he wants to go. I also suspect he doesn't have the means to go anywhere . . . but most important, he doesn't appear to want to go anywhere.

Doesn't he have family, a wife?

He mentioned a wife, but I got the feeling he doesn't want to call her. The director sighed and with a last look at the man turned and started uphill back to his office.

You believe him? Matteo called after him. The man hadn't once looked at them.

I retire next week. This is my last week here. I can't sleep at night. I see dead babies and drowning mothers. The director's face was gaunt as he stared at Matteo, his eyes hollow with sleeplessness. I don't want to leave any loose ends, you understand.

How does that involve me? Matteo asked, even though he was beginning to suspect just how. Giuseppe, the director, was a childhood friend. They had grown up in cottages next to each other, their fathers, fishermen, and sons to fishermen, and grandchildren to fishermen, co-owned a fishing boat, till Giuseppe's father died five years ago, drowned on a fishing expedition off the Tunisian coast. Unlike Matteo, who had

never left the island, Giuseppe had studied at the university in Palermo before returning to the island. He had been the camp director for three years now.

This man will die if I don't get him help.

Suicide?

No, he doesn't look suicidal. But he seems to have lost all will to live. I have seen it happen before. When I told him that he was free to go, that this was not a prison, you know what he told me? He said he was thinking about it. About his next move. Go back to Germany, I told him, get in touch with your friends. But he said no, not Germany.

Maybe he wants to go to his country, Nigeria, Matteo suggested.

Maybe, but he has been here over one month now. He is ill. You see how he looks. I have seen people like that. They grow apathetic, they withdraw, they neglect their health, and they die.

And why do you believe I can help him if even he doesn't want to help himself? That's why you called me, isn't it?

Well, he came from Berlin. He has lived there for over a year. I thought that might interest you.

•

I stand by the fence till the sun sets. This is the best spot to watch the water change color with the dying sun. I don't want to go back inside. Last night the man, boy really, on the bed next to mine was screaming in his sleep, and this morning he refused to get up, he lay there, staring at the ceiling. He is not more than twenty, and usually he is very chatty, always talking about his journey across the desert and his prospects

in Europe. England is his ultimate destination, he and every-one else. If not, he would settle for Germany. And should we travel together, do I have any money, and how long have I been in this camp. Then the lapse yesterday. I have seen many like him, the high spirits alternating with depressed silences. This is my third camp. The first was Lampedusa, then Greece, then this island. Every camp is different, and yet the same.

I spend my time staring at the water. If you stare at it long enough you notice the gradations of color, the minute shift-ing spectrum between green and blue and indigo. Once, the director came and stood next to me, this was a day after we had gone to the American consulate in Palermo, he asked me what I looked for in the water. Nothing, I told him. I have always been fascinated by water. I was born in a landlocked town, with no rivers or lakes, the streams were seasonal, formed by flash floods of the rainy season. As kids, after it rained, we stood on the banks to watch the moving mix of water and mud and tree limbs and dead birds and the occasional goat or dog and marvel at the power of water. Rainfalls were the most spectacular events, magical, and anything seemed possi-ble, giants could fall from the sky, trees could be uprooted and tossed about like twigs, humans could wash up by the roadside, sometimes chunks of ice fell, making holes in the roof and shattering car windshields and windowpanes. Hail. After the rains, vultures sat for hours on baobab trees, their cinereous wings soaked and useless, waiting for the sun to come out. It was the most pathetic sight, these huge ungainly creatures, yet still birds, still built for flight, and yet, for this moment, before they dry out, stuck on tree branches, wingless.

Try to get out of here, the director urged, if you stay here,

you will die. I have seen too many die here. Healthy, normal people. The next day they fall ill and the next day they are dead. I listened. I nodded. I thought, Who is to say if I am not dead already, the people around me could be shadows, wraiths, like me. If I am alive, then I am barely alive. Barely walking, mostly standing and staring at the water.

I feel his gaze, he and the other man, a new face, a reporter, perhaps, but he has no notebook, no bag for his recorder, and he doesn't have that hungry, vulpine look reporters have. Just another islander, a church member perhaps, another attempt to save me, to get me out of this camp. He was quitting, he told me. He seems desperate to save me. No man can save his brother, or pay his brother's debt—or something to that effect. Some poet said that. I pretend not to see them, and finally they turn and they leave. I am thinking, I wanted to tell him. I have all the time in the world. I have nothing to do but stare at the water and think. I am trying to decide if I want to go out there, to live, or to wait here and embrace whatever comes. No, I am not a fatalist, I am not reckless, but I feel if I wait here long enough, presently something would be revealed to me, someone would step up to me, a familiar face, or a total stranger, a child, a man, a woman, and they would say, Listen. And they would tell me a story, a fable, a secret, something so pithy, so profound, that it is worth the wait. Listen, they would say, listen carefully.

•

The next day the man comes back alone and offers to take me into town, if I have time. Time. He is mocking me, perhaps. Time is all I have. He introduces himself, Matteo. A friend to

the director, and perhaps like the director he also suffers from a savior complex. But I indulge him. All I have is time, after all. I have been here one month, and I have never been into the village. We go in his small car, up the hill, past a line of trees, and we are in the town center. It is a small town, its narrow stone-cobbled streets meandering between white-painted houses and a central church facing a square with a water fountain with the statue of a lion rampant in its middle.

We park by the fountain and walk around the quiet town. Sleepy old men and women sit in front of cafés under umbrellas and awnings, drinking coffee in the hot afternoon sun. We come upon a busy street leading away from the fountain, a street market is in session; we pass a butcher's stand displaying haunches and sides of sheep hanging on hooks.

I grew up here, Matteo says, waving at a familiar face. I know literally everyone in this town.

After the market is a line of stores selling clothes and ladies' bags and shoes. The clothes on display make me self-conscious about my own tattered clothes; I have been wearing the same thing for weeks now and I must look like a scarecrow. More and more I notice in front of hotels and pensions African and Asian men sitting in little groups on steps and on benches, talking in whispers. Their faces have a speculative, haunted look, as if weighing how long they could stay in this small town before wearing out their welcome.

Come, let's have coffee, Matteo says.

We sit outside one of the cafés and order coffee. From here the sea is visible in the distance. There are a few men and women sitting at nearby tables, most of them stare curiously at me as we sit down. A group of young men at the next café

stare pointedly at me and whisper among themselves. The waitress refuses to look at me and addresses herself all the time to Matteo. I order tea. When she comes back she slaps the teacup in front of me and stands there waiting for payment. Matteo says something sharply to her and hands her some money. She gives him change and walks away.

I am sorry, he says. There is anger in this town. Half of the population has left.

Why? I ask.

The economy is bad. People blame that on the refugees. In the last five years the refugee population has almost surpassed the population of the locals, and so more and more locals leave. As he speaks an African woman drifts into view, she is wearing a colorful print dress and leading a child by the arm. She walks slowly, meditatively, and she could be in her hometown, going on a visit to the neighbors'. More brown faces pass as we sit, Indians, Arabs, Africans. I drink my tea. The bell at the church tolls the hour. From where we sit the church steeple is visible, pointing forlornly into the glaucous air. Matteo says in the Middle Ages anyone who broke the law would be hoisted up in a cage in front of the church and left exposed to the elements till they died. It was useful as a crime deterrent.

The director told me you used to live in Berlin.

Yes, I reply. I want to thank you for the coffee, and for this. I wave my hand.

We can do this again tomorrow if you like, he says.

He has something to tell me, or to ask me, I can tell, but he is waiting, sizing me up. We go back to the camp as the sun is going down. He comes again the next day, at the same time,

and we go back to the same café. The same waitress brings me my tea, with croissants, avoiding my eyes as she places down the tray. I watch the Africans pass, and in the distance the blustery sea is bluer today.

I'll tell you a story, Matteo says. He sips his espresso and lights a cigarette. He has an angular face, his skin is sunburnt. He is a housepainter, he tells me, he used to be a fisherman, like most men in the town. His hands are covered with streaks of green paint. It is about a woman, he says. Think of it as a fairy tale.

·

Once upon a time a man came upon a woman lying on the seashore, half-covered by the foaming waves. A mermaid, he thought. Her lower body was in the water, her wet hair falling over her face, her clothes wave-torn. He stood over her, the waves crashed and receded and crashed back again, she appeared dead. Then he saw the child some distance away from her, struggling to rise, tied to a life buoy with a piece of red cloth. He ran over and scooped up the child. It was a boy, about one year old, with seaweed tangled in his hair and water pouring out of his mouth and nostrils. The woman was moving, raising a hand toward him, trying to speak, her voice weak. He ran back to her and brought his ear close to her. Help, she croaked, pointing at the boy. Please. He tried not to panic, he looked around, seeking help, but the beach was empty. Only the waves washed against the sand and rocks of the narrow bay. He pulled the woman away from the waves. He took off his shirt and covered her naked chest.

Can you stand?

She tried to stand but her legs kept giving out under her. He put an arm under her shoulder and, the child in one hand, he led her to

his house not too far away from the beach. He lived with his old father, Pietro, in a house that had once been full of the voices of his brothers, but his brothers had all left for the city, and three years ago his mother had died. Only he and his seventy-year-old father lived in the big house, which was now crumbling as houses tend to do in this weather.

For two days mother and child slept, side by side, on the queen bed in one of the bedrooms. The man sat on a chair and watched them, scared they might be slowly dying from some secret injury, an internal hemorrhage or infection contracted in the water. He watched the woman turn and kick and roil in her sleep, re-creating the motions of the sea that had recently disgorged her. The child whimpered and held on tightly to the arm of the woman. All night long he watched, sleepless and anxious, sometimes raising his hands as if to still the restless motions of the sleeping pair, then retracting them. Fancying the couple were too still, he placed a hand on the woman's chest to feel the heaving, up down, up down, of her breathing, then he placed a moist finger under the child's nostrils to feel the draft of its breath.

Come, his father, Pietro, said, go and rest. There is nothing you can do. I'll watch over them and I'll call you as soon as she wakes up.

The woman woke up that night. She stared at the old man dozing in a chair by the window and she looked neither surprised nor alarmed. Her first action was to reach over and cradle the sleeping boy in her arms. The old man brought her a bowl of soup and watched her as she drank.

•

They say I collapsed while standing by the fence, watching the water as I always do. I have no recollection. I wake up and a

doctor in white is crouching over me, shining a flashlight into my eyes. I am in the medical center.

Can you hear me? the doctor asks.

I close my eyes and turn away from the light.

How do you feel, any headaches? he asks.

No, I reply, well, a little bit.

I try to sit up but the doctor pushes me back to the cot. I have seen the doctor before, there are two of them, him and a woman, they take turns, each dropping in about twice a week. He is not up to forty, about my age, with a receding hairline and a permanent frown of worry on his face. He sits on a chair by the cot, the frown deepening.

You are dehydrated and malnourished. We are going to keep you here for a few days and give you saline solution.

In the morning the director comes, and he sits down on the same chair the doctor sat in and shakes my hand, as if congratulating me on something I have achieved. You are leaving, he says. It is all settled. The man, your friend, Matteo, he is taking you with him. You can stay with him till you get better.

I want to protest that Matteo is not really my friend. I hardly know him, or when and how this was all settled, but I don't want to sound ungrateful. Matteo looks harmless, polite, ready to listen, I am sure I will get along with him. Still, I don't want to be in someone's house, I don't want to be obligated to anyone. But I am too tired to argue. Back in my corner, I get my things together. I don't have much. A toothbrush given to us by the camp, a comb, a change of underwear, a sock, my slippers—I put them all in a polythene bag and I sit to wait for Matteo.

The room is empty. The bunk next to mine has a new

occupant. The young man has left a few days back. He wanted me to go with him, he said we'd make a good team. He was from a small town in Nigeria, he told me, not mentioning the town or the state. He was poor and felt he stood no chance in his hometown of ever achieving the good life, so his mother sold their land and gave him the money to pay his way across the Mediterranean. I imagine him on a train, or in the back of a truck, or walking on a bush trail, going north. I admire his optimism, which, inevitably, will get shattered, it is impossible that it won't, but still I admire it. In a corner of the tent I hear a radio, BBC, the announcer's voice interrupted by static. I used to listen to BBC a lot as a child. Another voice is on the phone, always on the phone, the ubiquitous cell phone, the only link to the world left behind.

I am in Italy. Everything is good. Everything is working fine. Soon I go to Germany. Yes, insha Allah.

I think of Karim and his son Mahmoud, and how he chose the wilderness of exile over home. I remember the pain in his voice when he said he knew he might never see Somalia again. Once upon a time, to be away from the known world was exile, and exile was death. Through the tent entrance I see a group of young men, about four of them, they always gather there, by the hillock, talking earnestly, they keep to themselves, sometimes it appears they are arguing. They make phone calls. They are planning their route, their forward path. They talk bravely, boldly turning their back on all they know, embracing change and chaos, and yet, sometimes I catch the nervous note in a laugh, I imagine them back in their tents, on their cots, pining for home. I hear their voices heading toward the gate, going into town, to

try to earn some money, or to make connections, to hustle. Endlessly hustle.

•

The first day she was able to stand up, she followed a door, which led into a larger room, and then into another room. Some of the windows were broken; the walls had cracks in them. An air of decay and forget-fulness pervaded the entire house, and even in her semi-somnambulistic state she could tell there was no woman's touch anywhere, and that, for some reason, made her sad. She stood in a room between a kitchen and another room, a dining room perhaps, and looked around, lost. It was some sort of storeroom; there were boxes under wooden shelves, and cans of paint piled on top of each other, there were brushes on a table, the paint dry on the bristles, some of the paint had ran down on the table, making lines, now dry and multicolored. Then the old man entered.

My son is not here, he has gone to work. Do you want something? I want to go outside. Please.

He looked closely at her for a while, then he nodded. He led her by the hand through a side door, then down a flight of half a dozen lichened stone steps, down a vine-hedged path, and they were in a garden. This used to be a beautiful park and people would come from the village just to sit here and look at the roses, he said. As they approached a fountain, the smell of dead leaves in the water rose in the air. Nearby a nymph held a cracked vase, in her abdomen and shoulders were what looked like bullet holes. He led her to a bench facing the sea.

This is where my son found you, Pietro said, pointing. And sud-denly she was agitated again. He reached out and took her hand, she looked at him without recognition. The children, she cried. She wrung

her hands. Where are the children? He took her back inside, and they passed through the many doorways until they came to the bedroom. The boy was there, sleeping. The worry and panic left her face, she sat on the bed and folded the boy in her arms, burying her face in his chest, all the time whispering to him.

She looked up and the old man had gone, in his place the younger man was standing there. How much time had passed, she had lost track.

What is his name? he asked.

Omar.

What is your name?

She shook her head. At night she dreamt of fire and loud explosions in the sky. There was a man, and a girl. And there was water, so much water, and she was swimming in it, kept afloat by the orange life buoy around her middle, she and the child. She dreamt the same dream in a loop, over and over, and the dream always ended with the man standing over her, telling her it was all right, she was safe.

He whispered again, What is your name?

She shook her head, desperately now.

Come.

He led her to the bathroom and stood her before the mirror. Toothbrushes with flat, chewed bristles stood in a cup over the sink. The mirror was stained by soap suds and dirt, there were cracks in it, a long diagonal crack ran from bottom to top, cutting her face in two. Her hand flew up to her face, as if in reaction to the cut in the mirror. She ran her fingers through her hair; she touched her cheeks and her lips and her eyelids, as if touching the face of another.

I am sorry. I don't know.

Behind her in the mirror he smiled in encouragement. He said, It will all come back to you. Take a bath, then rest. He left. Alone in the bathroom the woman looked at her face in the mirror, she saw the

grime, the sand and sea salt in her hair, and try hard as she might, she couldn't remember who she was or where she came from. All she could remember was the sea. She undressed and ran her hand slowly over the cesarean scar on her abdomen.

•

This is my house. It is not much, but here you are safe, the man said gently.

She looked up at him, the word "safe" registering in her sea-muddled mind. Her eyes at first questioned him, then they trusted him, and could that be the moment that he fell for her, for her eyes, so huge, so beautiful. He fell and it was a long and bottomless fall.

She was scared of the dark, she told him. She slept with the lights on, and sometimes he heard her screaming in her sleep. At those times he'd sit on the chair till she slept, sometimes he knew she only pretended to be sleeping, like a child, her eyes closed, listening to him breathe and move in the chair, but he knew she found his presence reassuring. Once she woke up when the lights were off. She raised a hand and pointed to the window. Light, she said. Please. She remembered the dark boat; all she wanted as they rode the waves up and down was a ray of light to touch her skin. Please, she repeated.

Once she had overcome her fear of waking up in this strange place, she loved to take walks in the mornings, while the boy still slept, to walk in the park and sit on the bench and stare at the water in the distance. The man watched her from the house, through the kitchen window. A week ago she wasn't here, a week ago he didn't know her, now here she was and all he could think about was her. She was a mother, a wife, perhaps greatly loved by a husband who was now probably dead in the water, his corpse beached and half-buried on some European shore. Of course he might not be dead, he might

be somewhere, ahead, or behind, sitting with his cell phone in hand, waiting for a word from her. The man was surprised by the quick jealousy he felt at the thought of a husband waiting for her.

She could stay here, he said to his father.

Why not. She had no memory of a past, or a destination; sending her to the camp would be cruel. With a child. This would be a new beginning for her, for them. He could give her that. He would give her that. But he had to take it slow. He didn't want to scare her.

•

We used to be fishermen, Matteo told him, but not anymore.

Why did you stop fishing? the man asked.

Fishing became too painful, Matteo said, and he did not elaborate. He went on, I taught myself how to paint. The painter left the island, so I am in some demand at the moment.

He had been a week in the house now, and already the memory of the camp was fading from his mind. He remembered the woman who sat by the fence and said she could hear her children's voices from the depths of the sea. And the camp director, Giuseppe, who must have retired by now. Every morning he took a walk on the beach, for about thirty minutes. The doctor ordered it.

It is up to you if you want to recover or not. You are young, nothing is really wrong with you. Your malaise is really in your mind. Of course your body is weak, due to poor diet and other minor infections. But it is in your power to get better. Eat well, exercise. It is the best medicine I can prescribe for you, the doctor told him.

The doctor was an old man, a childhood friend to Pietro. He had sat on the chair next to the bed, the very bed the mer-

maid must have lain in, and he wondered if the doctor had also attended to her when she lay here, lost and sick with fear. He was wearing a white doctor's coat, as if he were in a hospital making his rounds, his doctor's bag by his side.

Tell me, the doctor asked, are you married?

Yes, he nodded.

Don't you miss your wife, don't you want to be with her?

Did he miss Gina? He thought of home before he met Gina. He had two sisters whom he hadn't seen in over ten years. They were much older, married with grown-up children, and when he was a child they never really had time for him, and apart from the occasional phone call, they hardly met. His father was a retired government contractor and he had been born when his father was in his fifties, too old and too tired to take much interest in him after the initial joy of having the much-desired male child. Once, during his early months in America, he missed his mother so much he felt embarrassed by how much he missed her, but after a while he got over that. Gina had replaced his family, and he was not lonely anymore. He missed Gina, he missed her so much it felt like there was a hole in his chest, but he knew with time her memory would get blurry and it would be like a dream, recollected vaguely at unexpected moments. He felt scared when he thought of that. He didn't want to forget her. He wanted to call her a thousand times every day, but for what purpose? He had avoided calling her so far, he felt ashamed at the way they parted. Time would fill up the void in their hearts left by the other, fill it up like an empty well gradually filled up with household junk till people have forgotten that it was once a well. Those who dug it would die, those who knew it was a

well and even drank from it would move on, and its time as a well would be forgotten.

Twice the doctor came back to see him, and he always stayed for dinner. Meat, and vegetables, and pasta, but never fish. They sat, the three of them, eating and watching the sea through the window, in the distance a boat circled the water. Pietro's dog lay in the corner, its eyes closed. Coast guards, Matteo said; no, that is the *carabinieri*, the police, the doctor argued; wrong, Pietro said, squinting his old eyes, it is a private boat, one of the rescue volunteers.

Matteo told him the doctor's story: he had left the village to go to Rome to study medicine, he had married there, making a good living, but he missed home, he missed the sea, and when in 2013 he saw in the news, with the rest of the world, the bodies of over three hundred migrants fished out of the Mediterranean in the nearby island of Lampedusa, he had gone there to volunteer, and he had never returned to Rome since then. He moved back to the island and opened his own practice. He volunteered at the refugee camp, and old as he was, he went out with the rescue boats daily to search for capsized migrant boats.

Before leaving, the doctor ordered him to rest, he still wasn't as strong as he thought he was, it would take time for his body to recover. He tried to read after his walks. There were books in the house, on bookshelves in the living room, all in Italian, except for one in English, translated from the Italian, *The Leopard*, by di Lampedusa. Matteo asked him if he wanted to go out on the boat with them, they were going round the island, he and Pietro—the island was so small you could go round it a dozen times in a day—and at first he said

no, but once they were on the water he liked it, until he grew
seasick and started to vomit and had to be helped out of the
boat to his room when they got back.

•

He said, You have been here six months now. Tell me, what do you
remember?

She said to the man: Omar is my son, I know that, instinctively, but
I don't remember his birth date, or his favorite color. I know I am a good
mother. I will do anything for him, I will give my life for him, willingly.

But there was more she was not saying, recently she had started
to dream of other faces, a man, a girl, and when she woke up her
head ached from trying to follow those images. All day the headaches
persisted, a dull blunt pain at her temples. Other images came up
unbidden, street names, faces, she remembered a car number. 1980.
She saw herself walking down a street and into a white house with a
date palm tree in front of it, with two children holding onto her hands.
A boy and a girl. It was a happy place, but she couldn't get past the
doorway, she always stood by the door, and when she opened the door
everything was blank.

She said, There's a man. There is a house, white. We live there, I
am sure. It is burning. There are gunshots and buildings are crumbling
about us. That is all I can see, the man, the house.

He said gently, sadly, Don't think about the past. You are safe
here. I'll take care of you both.

•

We are in the kitchen. I stand in the corner watching Matteo
cook. He throws a slab of red, bloody meat on a skillet. Next
to it long stems of asparagus are steaming in an open pot. He

cooks well, self-sufficiently, waving me away with a napkin whenever I offer to help. I stand by the open window, feeling inadequate. From somewhere in the house a radio is playing, a woman's voice singing a sad opera tune. I pass him the salt, I clear the table of onion skin, and when I run out of things to do, I engage him in small talk: why does he live alone with his father in this big house, where's the rest of his family? It is hard to tell if he is young or old, his face is indeterminate, sometimes when he sits facing me in the room, bent forward in his chair, he looks old and wise and tired. He must have witnessed a lot of things thrown up by the waves in front of his door. I have seen some myself since I have been here, pieces of clothing, children's toys, a shoe, a cell phone case, when walking on the beach.

We have settled into a routine, I wake up, I walk on the beach, when I get back I wash the dishes if there are any to be washed, then the rest of the day I sit in the park facing the water. Sometimes staring at the beach, I see the old man appear out of the distance, with his dog, and then I'll join him and we'll walk together quietly, the waves lapping at our feet, the distant roar rising and falling, soothing, and at such moments I almost forget how malevolent and predatory the sea can be. I feel indolent, and for the first time in a long while I have started thinking about what to do, where to go. But, when I bring this up with Matteo at dinner, he shakes his head. You are not fit. You think you are, but you are not. The doctor said you need at least a month before you can even think of traveling.

And to take my mind off my restless thoughts he takes me for a walk into the town. We go past the water fountain, past the

church, past the café. He points, There is the telecommunication store. It does more business than all the other stores in town.

There is a line of dark-skinned men in front of the store, they are buying SIM cards and call credit, they will call home and let their family know they are alive, they have made it to Europe. As we pass them some of them turn and stare at us curiously, I look back trying to see if I can recognize a face from the camp. I wonder, are they disappointed yet, is this what they expected, these empty, cold and wet cobbled streets, the deserted hotels, the crumbling aged houses? Behind the square is the museum—Matteo says it used to be a fortress, long ago, in the time of Garibaldi, and in front of it is a statue of a soldier on a horse, wielding a sword. The fortress juts out of the rocky ground and over the water, defiantly facing the African shore in the distance. It is surrounded by a wall bearing gun towers at intervals, each tower has a rusty cannon facing outward, ready for the enemy to emerge, spectral, from the sea mist.

We go from room to room in the museum, starting from the ground floor—the entire museum is dedicated to military history. The artifacts are curated to start from the earliest and most rudimentary weapons, spears, lances, bayonets, with drawings of ancient knights dressed in chain-link body armor, on foot and on horses, charging into the fray, and then progressing to rooms showing more sophisticated and contemporary weapons, guns, pistols, muskets, rifles, cannons, and machine guns. There are pouches of gunpowder, grenades, rockets. Here is a history of a militarized Europe, of war and conquest and devastation.

Back in my room, I stare out into the park, the dying light

has thrown dappled shadows of the tree leaves onto the flowers. Somewhere behind the house Matteo has shown me a tilled patch of ground where the mermaid in his story had tried to make a small garden last spring before she left. It isn't big, just a practical, workable portion, which she tried to bring alive, pulling out the weeds, crushing the hard lumpy clay with a shovel and soaking it with buckets of water, transferring some of the living roses from the flower beds in the park and planting them in a row. It was tough making plants grow in the acidic, saturated sea air, yet she persisted, daily, doggedly, and at a point he realized she was not really convinced she could make anything grow, really, she was just killing time. She was sowing her fears, her doubts into the ground—who was she, where was this place, who were these people she was staying with?—and hoping some answers would sprout, magically, out of the soil. Matteo would watch from the window, and he saw how she sometimes forgot where she was, squatting and staring at the soil absently for minutes, muttering to herself. Then she caught herself, she looked around guiltily, she sat on one of the iron benches, her head bowed, and he knew the tears were running down her face as she stared out to sea. He came out, casually, as if he were just passing by, taking a walk on the beach, he sat next to her, pretending he didn't notice her covertly wiping her eyes, and he talked disconnectedly, trying to take her mind off her troubles. When she appeared exhausted, when he saw her attention wavering, her eyes turning to the water, he stopped talking and led her back to the house. He'd sit and watch her sing to the child a nursery song in a strange language.

•

She was conscious of him staring at her from the house. Soon he would come out and ask her, anxiously, if she remembered anything at all. They would sit for hours, hardly talking. Once, he pointed at the tall stone building near the water and said it used to be a fortress before it was converted to a museum. A fortress with moats and drawbridge—the moat was now dry, the drawbridge broken. Then he turned to her and whispered suddenly, Sophia.

Sophia? she asked.

You don't remember?

She repeated the name over and over in her mind, trying to see if it resonated, if it struck a chord. Should I know the name? she asked, her face beginning to look confused.

It is your name, he said.

The words came of their own will. He hadn't planned it, but as he spoke it all made sense. At first he thought with time she'd forget who or what she was looking for, where she was going, and settle down. This would be home. She'd get used to the sea, and the house, and him, show him some love. But she had been here for months now and he couldn't wait any longer. And now that he had started talking he couldn't stop. And as he spoke he also believed what he was saying. Every word rang true. Because he wished them to be true.

We were lovers, many years ago. I visited your country. We met. We fell in love.

She turned to him. She ran a nervous hand through her hair. Then what happened, did we break up?

No. We couldn't get married because your parents . . . well, they had another man they wanted you to marry. And I left. I had to come back home. I was heartbroken.

Then what happened?

You promised you would never forget me. You promised you would come find me someday, no matter how long it took.

And you, you waited for me?

Yes, I promised I would never leave my island, I'd wait for you. Time passed, I had almost given up. Then there you were, in the water. You came like you promised.

She wanted to believe him, she wanted her days to have meaning, she wanted the headaches to stop. She believed him. She said, I am sorry. You must have suffered, waiting for me. She took his hand. He leaned forward and kissed her on the lips.

You came, that is all that matters.

That night she tried to make up for the pain she had cost him as she lay under him, her arms and legs locked around him. In the other room the child slept alone for the first time.

•

Carefully they dressed up in the new clothes he had bought for them. She wore white, and over that a red spring jacket. The child wore a blue jacket and khaki pants. The man wore a black suit, a white shirt, and a blue tie. They drove in the tiny car to the town center, the boy sat with his face pressed to the window, following the backward swirl of the lampposts and the narrow streets that receded and convoluted and rose and fell. They got down at the square. The boy watched a family, a man a woman and their daughter, throw bread crumbs to dun-colored pigeons that fluttered and settled and fluttered again as people passed. They sat on a bench before the fountain, the man and the woman. They watched the boy join a group of children dipping their hands in the fountain. The town hall was a few meters from the fountain, and the registrar was waiting for them. The registrar asked if

the woman wanted to freshen up in the restroom before the ceremony, she said no.

Good, he said. Please, come this way.

Afterward, the family of three had lunch in a Greek restaurant, then they entered the car and drove back home.

•

In the evenings he took her on a drive around the town. It became their routine. Far from the town center, on the road that followed the coastline, with a clear view of the water, half-circling the town. He drove fast, trying to outrun something behind, some memory, some history that doggedly followed in their wake. They drove, his eyes on the strip of empty road ahead, her eyes on the ineffable view of the sea and sand. They came upon a ghostly housing development of villas and apartments, grand and untenanted. They passed courtyards and gardens that had started to run to seed, over roads eaten away by neglect and weather. The waves' whoosh was a lover's lament of loneliness. They drove round and round, through some developer's failed dream of sand and sea that came up against harsh economic reality, and not a single human being was in sight. The streets between the villas and apartments were named after famous cities, Naples, Paris, Milan, Barcelona, Berlin, Frankfurt, Athens, Florence, Vienna, each one deserted.

•

And then one day she woke up suddenly, it was midnight, but the moon was shining into the room, and she could see everything, clear as day. He sensed her movement and asked, Is everything all right?

She turned to him, and he saw that something had changed in her eyes. She said, My name is not Sophia.

What did you say? He sat up and moved to the opposite side of the bed. She was looking out into the garden, the light on her face, her back to him.

My name is not Sophia. She turned to the man. Calm.

Well, what is your name?

She shook her head, overwhelmed by the memories racing into her head, a flash flood carrying so many things in its stream. He waited, his breath coming out with difficulty. He had seen this before. Soon would come the panic, the tears. He waited.

I have a husband.

I am your husband.

She raised a hand, and in the movement there was a sadness he had never seen before. Please, don't say that. I remember everything.

She looked at him, her eyes bitter.

Well, what is your name?

Basma, she said, and repeated the name slowly, savoring it, like the name of a newborn, uttered for the first time, Basma. I have two children, Omar and his sister, Rachida.

The man stood up. He was naked. He quickly put on his clothes and sat with his head in his hands, saying nothing, not looking at her. That day she moved out of his bedroom and into the guest room with her son. She didn't come out all day, and all day the man stayed in his room, and she could hear him through the wall, pacing up and down, she could hear his father knocking on his door, but he didn't open it. At night she lay awake, and her mind was like a churning sea, throwing out to shore bits and pieces of floating memory.

As he paced his room he asked himself why he was surprised, surely he knew this day would come, his father had cautioned him about it. He loved her, he loved her like he had never loved anything before. He felt like dying.

Be brave, his father said through the door, maybe she loves you too. But she has a child, and a husband. Let her decide what she wants to do.

When she finally came out, she was dressed to leave. She had a little plastic bag with a single change of clothing in it, the boy was dressed in his blue suit. Father and son were seated at the dining table, she went to them and sat, and they could have been a family at dinner, except there was no food in front of them. Finally, he said, Please don't go.

How she had changed. Already he could see the resolute, confident woman she must have been. Where was Sophia, the woman who had flailed about, plucking at plants in the garden, singing soft lullabies to the boy?

She said, her eyes staring neither at him nor at the old man, We were the last to get out. We made our way to the coast and paid five thousand American dollars each to get on a boat. I was scared, I didn't want all four of us on the same boat. What if something went wrong? I told him, go on ahead, find a place and come back for us later. But he wouldn't hear of it. Without you and the children, I die, he said. So we left, all of us. They shot at our boat as we left the coast. I don't know what happened, or why. There was confusion, the screams began and never stopped. Have you ever been on a refugee boat? Pray you never do. Pray your country never breaks up into civil strife and war, that you are never chased out of your home. The boat was really nothing but a death trap, an old, rickety fishing trawler that should have been retired a long time ago. Because we paid five thousand each we got to sit on the upper deck where we could get a bit of fresh air. Some, who were down below in the hold, stacked on top of each other, died within hours of our departure—the children and the pregnant women died first. We saw them bring up the bodies and throw them

in the water. Our engine was on fire, the captain wanted to turn back, but we begged him to go on. We would rather die in the water than go back. There was nothing to go back to. My husband tried to save us as the boat sank. He is a great swimmer. He held me and the boy and I held the girl and for an hour we floated, clinging to a raft. A helicopter appeared overhead, and we thought finally we were safe, but after circling for a few minutes it left. I told my husband to let me go, to save the children, but he wouldn't. We decided that he would take the girl, and I would take the boy because he was smaller. He gave us the life jacket. We drifted. I tied the boy to my back. Something, a log, rose out of the water and hit me in the head, and I must have fainted. When I woke up you were standing over me, and I couldn't remember a thing. I guess my mind didn't want to remember. After a while I stopped trying to remember, it was easier to listen to your stories. Sophia. How badly I must have wanted to believe I was Sophia, and that this place is my home and I have not lost a husband, or a child.

He stood up and went over to her. *Is there no way I can convince you to stay? You are making a mistake.*

Was there really a Sophia?

He went back and sat next to his father, he stared out the window. The sky was low and darkening; it was setting to rain. Seagulls flew over the water in cycles, making weak and shallow dives. He lowered his head, his elbows rested on the table.

Yes, there was a Sophia, but that was a long time ago. Someone I knew as a kid.

She stood up and took the boy's hand. He stood up and followed them to the door. *You don't have to go today.*

She turned and looked at him. *I have to go. I thank you for saving my life. But I am angry at you for lying to me. I have a husband and another child, I belong to them.*

You don't know if they are alive. You don't know where to find them. Stay. I can help you find out where he is.

I know where he will be. In Berlin. We agreed, if we ever got separated, to wait there. In Berlin. He has a friend there. Every Sunday we promised to go to a spot and wait, Checkpoint Charlie.

The man followed her out of the house, down the lichened stone steps. She stopped briefly in the garden and looked at the roses that had started to sprout, now wilting in the autumn chill. He took them in the small car to the ferry depot to catch a ferry to the mainland, the first stop in their uncertain journey. As she got out of the car he handed her an envelope.

Take this, he said. Our marriage certificate, you will need it. You can't travel without some form of documentation. You'll also need money. Here. Please take it.

She began to shake her head, opening her mouth to utter no, but he pressed the papers into her hand. You can destroy it as soon as you get to your destination. He stood by the car and watched her and the boy join the line of passengers waiting to get onto the ferry.

•

Finally, the story has come to an end. We are in the park, sitting on the bench on which he and the woman must have sat so many times before, nearby is the patch of ground where she attempted to start a garden.

Basma, I say. Is that why you helped me, why you brought me to your house, in the hope that I might have some knowledge, some information about her?

He shrugs. His eyes are dark, hooded, and for the first time I see how withered and tired he looks.

He says, I am like a man drowning, and I must grasp at

every straw. Have you ever been in love? Surely your wife, or another?

I think of Gina, and I wonder where she might be now. In America, probably, right now she'd be in a studio, in her overalls, painting, trying to capture on canvas something elusive, something even she can't put a name to. Our story is over, the ink has dried, each of us must move on now and it will be as if we had never met, never loved, and never dreamt together.

Maybe not your wife, Matteo says shrewdly, reading my face. Maybe another.

I think of Portia, and I feel light and breathless with longing. I would like to see her again. You are right, I say to Matteo, there is someone else, but I doubt I will ever see her again.

Why did you let her go?

I didn't let her go. Circumstances got in the way.

Far away we can see old Pietro staring at the water, next to him the dog chases seagulls as they skip and flutter over the waves. He looks like he belongs here, megalithic, one with the rocks and sand and waves that throw themselves at his feet like supplicants. The dog yelps, then retreats and returns in a playful dance with the waves and the gulls.

Did you go after her, Basma? Did you try to find her, to convince her to come back?

He says, I went to Berlin, twice, but I just sat in my hotel room and watched the streets through the window all day, then I came back. Twice. I didn't have the will to go into the streets looking for her. I thought, what if I saw her with her husband, her children, and what if they were happy together? I couldn't bear it. So I took the train and I came back. I promised myself to forget her, but then, when the director told me

you were from Germany, from Berlin, and since you have been among the refugees, I thought, perhaps you might know something, anything.

I say, What of her husband, what of her children?

He says, What of me? What of love? His voice is at once pleading and also defiant. I can't sleep. I think of her all the time. I want to know if she is okay, and the boy.

So I tell him of Manu, the doctor turned bouncer, who sat for Gina, who went every Sunday to Checkpoint Charlie hoping to see his wife and son there. As I tell him I see his countenance fall and his eyes grow more hooded. He is a good man, even if a little unusual, and I owe my life to him. We continue to sit as the sun goes down, turning the water and the sand purple and pink. The iodine smell of the sea is in the air. In the distance the old man appears, heading for the house, the dog by his side, in the sea a rescue boat rises and dips on the water, searching for distressed migrant boats.

That evening we leave in the boat as if we were going fishing, then we head south and keep going. I watch the coast recede and shrink—somewhere out there is the refugee welcome camp on its hilly perch, and I imagine the inmates seated against the fence watching the water and the distant African coast hidden in the mist. I imagine the Syrian woman, knocking her head against the fence and moaning the name of her vanished children, and of her destroyed hometown over and over, Aleppo.

We will be a few hours, Matteo says, you should go down and get some rest.

Earlier, before we set out, he asked me if this was what I wanted, if I wasn't better off staying on in Europe, going

back to Berlin, or even staying on the island with him and the old man. I lie on the bunk downstairs, using the tiny backpack Matteo gave me for a pillow. All my worldly possessions are in there, a pair of pants, some underwear, the book *The Leopard* by Tomasi di Lampedusa. I close my eyes but I can't sleep, under the engine sound I hear the susurration of the wind on the water, and soon I am on the deck, standing by the rail watching the water. It is dark, the fog lies thickly over the water and there is nothing to be seen but the inky black. I feel as if there is no deck under me—I am standing over the water, and when I bend down I see my reflection glowing up at me, my forehead glistens with sweat. I am . . . I look terrified. A restless, writhing motion fills the water. Fish. A school of them in a feeding frenzy, but when I bend closer, my face almost touching the water, I see they are not fish, they are human. Bodies floating face-up, limbs thrashing, tiny hands reaching up to me. Hundreds of tiny hands, thousands of faces, until the surface of the water is filled with silent ghostly eyes like lamps shining at me, and arms reaching up to be grasped; they float amidst a debris of personal belongings, toys, shoes, shirts, and family pictures all slowly sinking into a bottomless Mediterranean. I drift past, and they drift past, and God drifts past, paring His nails. I pull back, tears on my face. *I had not thought death had undone so many.* I repeat the line over and over, rolling it over my tongue like a prayer, till my whisper turns to a scream. A hand on my shoulder is shaking me.

Wake up, Matteo says, we are here.

I sit up and grab my bag, discombobulated from my vivid dream, and follow him up to the deck. At first I don't see any-

thing, then gradually over the bow a finger of light appears. Then more lights. Faint, wavering needlepoints of light.

Tunisia, he says, we can't get any closer than this, I am afraid.

We drop the tiny, inflatable dinghy into the water and using a small rope ladder I lower myself into it. I look up at the face looking down at me anxiously. The dinghy wobbles and rises and falls with the waves, then I begin to paddle. I feel like a man treading water, then I begin to pull away, carried by the flood tide, and soon the coastline is rushing at me. With a mighty heave the water spews me onto land and I am on all fours, my eyes and ears and mouth filled with briny seawater, but underneath me is the firm African soil. I grasp a handful and feel the emotions overwhelm me. I stagger to my feet and look back to sea, but there is nothing to see, only mist and black rushing water.

Book 6

HUNGER

When I got her email saying she'd be in London in July, and if I happened to be in the neighborhood she'd love to see me, I packed my bag and got ready to travel. The invitation came at a good time—I had completed my dissertation defense back in Virginia and I was contemplating whether to return to Nigeria or to stay on in the US. Her father's English mistress, who was also his translator, had died and her son had discovered a box full of her father's things, including unpublished manuscripts, and she was going to London to pick it up. The flat was in a high-rise on Boswell Street, a narrow back road tucked away in the warren of roads behind Russell Square. There were similar buildings

on both sides of the road housing boutique hotels and one
or two art galleries, others were council flats with balconies
littered with satellite dishes and children's toys—plastic cars
and bikes too big to store indoors and too new to throw
away, blocking the space between the doors and the stairs, a
veritable fire hazard. Not too far away was a park, a rectangle
of green enclosed in a chain-link fence, where workers from
nearby offices sat during their lunch break to catch half an
hour of air and sunshine. The offices were mostly hospitals
and labs that seemed to be concentrated in the neighborhood, over three hospitals within a radius of a few blocks,
there were also pubs and cafés. The park soon became our
favorite spot, and in the first week we spent hours there every
day, mostly in the late afternoon when the workers had left,
watching the pedestrians pass, sometimes staying till the lazy
summer sun finally dimmed at around 8 p.m.

I had never been to London so she sent me a careful description: *Take the Heathrow Express and you don't get off till you get
to Russell Square station, I will be in a red shirt holding a "Welcome
to London" sign.* As promised, she was standing at the station
entrance, unaffected by the stream of passengers coming in
and going out through the turnstile, the wind pulling at her
long skirt and red button-down shirt, and as promised she had
a *Welcome to London* sign which she held stiffly in front of her
with both hands. She actually had a sign.

I waited for her with my bag next to a phone booth as she
dashed into the Tesco opposite the station to grab a packet of
tea and sugar and a bottle of wine. Later, she confessed she
hadn't recognized me at the station till I stood in front of her
and whispered, —Hi Portia.

In the bathroom I stared at my reflection in the mirror:
my hair had thinned and turned white at the sides. Friends in
Nigeria and in the US had looked at me once, twice, sometimes thrice before uttering my name, with a question mark,
unsure if it was really me. My bones showed at the collar, my
cheeks were sunken, but I liked to think the fire still blazed
in my eyes.

—What happened? she asked.

—I am fine, I said.

The flat was small, large enough for two, an end unit on
the third floor with a single bedroom, a living room, and a
kitchenette. From the stairwells and behind doorways came
voices of children and mothers trying to be heard over the
drone of the TV. May, the late owner of the flat, was a lecturer at SOAS, she had lived here with Portia's father before
he finally moved back to Zambia. She retired four years ago,
the year he moved to Zambia, and she died a year ago, three
years after him. She was a pretty woman, even in old age:
her picture next to the TV showed a steady kindly gaze, with
deep laugh lines around the mouth and eyes. She had married
once, early in life, and had a son from that marriage, he now
lived in Australia, an accountant with a tidy bookkeeper's
mind, and it was he who wrote to Portia's mother about the
box belonging to her late husband; he said Portia could stay
in the empty apartment while she was in London, the flat was
paid for till autumn when he'd come and clear away whatever
was left before turning over the flat to the landlord. Here the
two aged lovers, the exiled writer and the retired lecturer, had
spent their days and nights, alone save for occasional outings
to readings and theaters and perhaps dinner with old friends:

retired teachers, editors, writers—some of them exiles living anonymous exilic lives in the big, gray city.

We did not sleep early that first night—it had been two years since we last met, and then for less than a week. I had thought I would never see Portia again, and to have heard from her, and now to actually be with her, left me speechless. I tried to tell her how I felt, but lacking words I simply held her and kissed her slowly on her lips and all over her face before leading her to the bed. Afterward we opened the bottle of wine and sat staring at each other, smiling wordlessly. What were we to one another, lovers, friends, strangers? We sat by the window and talked till the weak, watery sun inched its way over the trees and the morning birds began to chirp. I hadn't talked to anyone like this in a long time. It felt good. I told her about my time at the refugee camp, and about Matteo and his father. When I finished the tears ran down her face.

—I am so sorry, she said.

—Why, sorry for what? I tried to sound cheerful, lighthearted.

Later, when we crawled back into bed, she showed me a picture on her phone. Me and her, standing in the courtyard of the cathedral in Basel, overlooking the Rhine.

—Do you remember? she asked.

It seemed a lifetime ago. I looked different then. I said, —I feel like the guy in the John Donne poem.

—Which poem?

—I don't remember the title, but it is about a lover who left on a long trip. Before leaving he hands his girlfriend his picture so she would remember how he looked in case he returns all worn out and changed by time.

—I know the poem, she said. You really haven't changed that much.

She put her head on my shoulder, running her hand over my chest. —You are the same inside. And that's what matters.

•

When I woke up Portia was hunched over a rugged, much-traveled red Echolac suitcase with combination locks, taking out binders and notebooks, one item at a time. She took out a moleskin diary and flipped through the pages. I went to the kitchen and filled the kettle with water to make tea. My mornings never came into focus till I had a cup of tea in my hand. I made two cups and placed one on the table beside her.

—Thanks, she said.

—What's that? I asked.

—My father's notebooks. There are at least five of these. I am not sure what to do with them.

—What's in them? I asked, taking it from her.

—All sorts of things. Poems, diaries, essays, articles.

She held her tea mug in both hands. She looked around the room. She had been here four days before my arrival.

—Do you think they were happy here? she asked, staring at May's picture, almost glaring at it. There was an unuttered subtext to her question. Was he happier with this woman than he had been with my mother? she was asking.

—Who can tell? Remember, he left her and went back to Malawi to be with your mother. That says lot.

Portia too had changed. Physically she was the same, a bit softer around the eyes, a little fuller around the hips, but the quick clever girl had turned into a quieter, more patient

woman. I liked her this way. She was now a mother, she said, almost casually. She showed me a picture on her phone. A curly-haired, twinkle-eyed boy, with a smile like his mother's. She had married the German in whose apartment I first met her in Berlin, couch-surfing. He had turned up in Lusaka three years ago, and he needed a couch to sleep on. That was how it started. He had broken up with his girlfriend, Ina. He was on an assignment, a film company was making a documentary on the 1884–1915 German genocides on the Herero in neighboring Namibia, and he was writing the script. He didn't need to be in Zambia, actually, but he remembered she lived there and he wanted to see her. He stayed for two weeks, and every night he took her and her mother out, to dinner, to dance, to cinema, and on the final day before he left he told her he loved her, he wanted to marry her. Her mother liked him, she thought he was a gentleman.

—By then, Portia said, I had given up hope of ever seeing you again. When we parted in Basel, you were supposed to get in touch. I gave you my email, I didn't have yours. When you didn't write I guessed it was because you didn't want to.

She didn't give Hans an answer right away, she held out for six months, till one day her mother said to her, —What do you want, my child? Does this person—this Nigerian—even know you are waiting for him?

And so she called Hans in Germany and said yes. He flew back and they got married in a small church in Lusaka and they moved back to Berlin, back to that same apartment where we first met, and every time she passed my door, where she first saw me standing on a ladder, she'd linger, hoping the door would open and I would step out and say, —Hi, can

I help? Finally, she couldn't bear it anymore, she told Hans she couldn't live in that house, she told him it was because of the pregnancy, she didn't like climbing the stairs daily, she wanted to live near a park. They moved, out of the city toward Wannsee, but even then she felt Berlin closing in on her, daily, slowly. She fell ill constantly, she was sick for home, sick for something she didn't know. She stayed indoors and cried all day. Hans thought it was the pregnancy, the hormones, and he said yes when she decided to move back to Zambia, ostensibly to give birth at home, to be with her mother.

—I felt myself descending into depression, I was losing track of time, of my mind, and I feared I'd harm myself, she said. Hans didn't come to Zambia with her, he sensed that something had ended. The marriage had lasted less than a year.

—What's the baby's name? I asked.

—David, she said, we named him after my brother. My mother did.

Hans came to visit after the baby was born, twice, he tried to convince her to return to Berlin, but she said no. Her stay in Berlin was over, and going back wouldn't be fair to him. She didn't know how to tell him it had been a mistake. She told him she wanted to raise her child in Africa, surrounded by family. Some days she woke up in the night to scour Facebook, trying to find me. Several times, she called my Berlin number and listened to the German voice telling her the subscriber didn't exist. That was when she decided to write to Gina to ask for my email.

—It was the only way I knew how to contact you. I remember you mentioned she was a Zimmer fellow, so I wrote to them asking for her contact, I told them it was

about a painting. They were helpful. I wrote to her and she wrote back.

—Yes, Gina forwarded the email to me.

•

Of the three of us, Gina had perhaps changed the most. Since Berlin she had become something of a world traveler, when I arrived in Virginia a year ago to complete my PhD she was just returning from a six-month stint in Paris, and was on her way to Venice for the Bienniale. She had visited Germany again, many times, had been back to Berlin, and once she spent a month in Dresden. We met in a restaurant in Chantilly not too far away from Dulles Airport, she had an hour to spare before her flight to Rome. I was staying in a drab hotel off Highway 66 in Manassas, and each morning I'd pick up the phone to call her, then put it back again, and when I finally called she told me it was fortunate I called that day, she was on her way to the airport. She sounded happy to hear from me. She looked different, she had a red scarf around her neck, its color reflected against her skin, making her cheeks and her eyes glow.

—You look great, I said when I sat down.

—You don't look well. What happened? Why didn't you call? How long have you been in the States? Why are you staying in a hotel?

—Which question do you want me to answer first? I asked, raising my hand.

—All of them.

So I told her of Italy, of the refugee camps, of the two months I spent in Tunisia trying to convince the Nigerian

embassy I was Nigerian. Finally, they put me on a plane with over a hundred deportees and dumped us at the airport in Lagos.

—Where is your American wife? my mother asked me when I got home. I explained to her that we were separated, but each time people came to see me, she would tell them, "He came back alone, but his American wife is coming soon to join him." I could hear the shame in her voice, her son who had gone to America had returned poorer and thinner than he had left. I left as soon as I recovered my health. My father cleared his bank account and gave it all to me; he wanted me gone to spare my mother the pain of having me there, of having to explain to people why my American wife still hadn't arrived.

Our tiny apartment was still there if I needed it, Gina said. She wasn't staying there. It felt too big for her alone so she had moved in with her parents and used it only occasionally to paint. The light there was always good in the afternoon.

—It belongs to you as much as it does to me. How long are you here for?

—I don't know. I am meeting my supervisor tomorrow. I'll leave as soon as I defend my dissertation, maybe six months, maybe a year.

—I'll be away for over a year, she said.

The waiter was standing over us, a smile on his face, his pencil poised. Gina ordered a salad, I ordered the sea bass with asparagus.

—You look weird with your hair all white, she said. She

reached over and touched my hair, as if to confirm the white was real.

—Tell me about your travels, I said.

She told me about Dresden. She had spent a winter month there, painting, and sightseeing. Their guide told them Dresden was the most bombarded city in the Second World War, if not in all of history, 3,900 tons of bombs dropped by Allied bombers, destroying up to 90 percent of the town, and then, after the war, when the town had a chance to rebuild, they decided to re-create most of the buildings exactly as they had been before the bombardment. Their guide took them to the Altstadt to see the rebuilt cathedral, the Frauenkirche, which took almost ten years to reconstruct, with architects using 3-D computer technology to analyze old photographs and every piece of rubble that had been kept.

—They had the choice to do something new, make a clean break from the past, but they decided to rebuild the city like it was.

—Nostalgia, I said, they were homesick for their past.

She looked disapproving. —Not all of us have that luxury, of a past. My history doesn't offer me much in that respect. Once I go past Martin Luther King and Rosa Parks, there is nothing else but the plantation and after that the insurmountable Atlantic. So, I have learned to look forward, to embrace the new and to shape my future. I find it weird, this clinging to the past.

Gina, I realized, was saying goodbye to me. I felt sad, and proud all at once: I liked what she had become. I was a part of her past, therefore I had contributed to her present. I reached across the table and took her hand. And we sat like that, hold-

ing hands, not talking, till at last she looked at her watch and said, —Time to go.

—Have a safe flight. And . . . take care of yourself.

•

—Did you see her when you went to the US? Portia asked.

—Yes, I said.

She was sitting with her head bowed, doing her nails. Her voice sounded remote, almost cold.

—Did you stay with her?

Portia had these dark moments. This morning I woke up and found her crying into her pillow, when I asked her what was wrong she told me about a girl she saw when we were in Basel.

—I didn't tell you at the time, but I saw this girl, a schoolgirl, a black girl, about six or seven years old. Her hair was nicely braided. The whole class was going somewhere, walking in a neat file, their teachers walking beside them. The black girl was alone at the back of the line. All the other kids were chatting and laughing, except the black girl. I saw her nice braids, and her little red barrette, and I thought of her poor mother, she'd be anxious all day thinking of her little daughter, the only black girl in the class in that strange, cold country.

•

I told her about my stay in the US—I stayed for exactly one year, and I never saw Gina again after that goodbye in the restaurant. It was strange being by myself in our small apartment overlooking the empty parking lot, in the evenings I almost

expected the door to open and for Gina to walk in, back from work. In the closet she had neatly stacked my clothes and books and binders in a corner.

Our photos still hung on the walls and on the stand next to the TV. In the wedding picture I looked so young and happy, in a black suit, Gina was smiling into my face in her white wedding gown, a bouquet of flowers in one arm, and around us were the faces of her family and our friends. Some of the faces I now couldn't put names to.

The year passed by quickly. I worked on my thesis at night, in the day I walked around the city, I rode the train to the end of the line, I went to the National Mall and walked with the polyglot crowd at the Cherry Blossom Festival. I stood under the Washington Monument and watched parents and children pulling and running after kites, I passed the Tidal Basin to the new Martin Luther King monument and read the wise quotations on the wall. Once, I went to the public library near the apartment and walked between the aisles, running my hand on the book spines. I sat and read the papers, hoping someone would recognize me—this was where I used to teach ESL classes and had formed a nodding acquaintance with most of the staff—but no one did. I passed in front of the information desk, the lady manning the desk was called Jill, and I had often stood there and exchanged small talk with her, but now she smiled vacantly at me and asked if I needed help finding a book.

Gina called me on Thanksgiving Eve from Venice, Italy, and asked if I had any plans for Thanksgiving. I didn't. She said she hoped I was not planning to sit in the apartment alone. She had told her parents I was around and they were

expecting me for dinner. The next day I dressed carefully and bought a bottle of wine and got into a taxi to go to her parents' in Takoma Park. Her whole family would be there, cousins, nephews and nieces, uncles and aunts—I was particularly fond of Uncle Keith. On my first Thanksgiving with them before we got married, before dinner the whole family had gone to a nearby park to play football. It was something of a family tradition, Gina told me. I knew nothing about football, but I was conscious they were all sizing me up, trying to see what kind of in-law I'd make. I gamely chased the ball with them, I endured being knocked down multiple times by Gina's six-foot-four, two-hundred-pound knucklehead cousin, Ruben, who was playing football at college. Finally, when I could do so without loss of face, I left the players and joined the old folk cheering from the sidelines. I stood next to Gina's father, who nodded at me encouragingly, and Uncle Keith, who looked at me and said, —That was an awful performance. Clearly you know nothing about football.

I nodded, trying not to appear miffed. My knees were scraped, my ribs were sore from collisions. I thought I had handled myself well under the circumstance.

—Yes. I am more of a soccer person, I admitted.

Uncle Keith, it turned out, was a former football player, now a coach. He walked with a limp, which he got when he broke his leg playing. —Listen, all sports are essentially the same. Decisive victory is the aim of every game, just as it is in war, because all competitive games are descended from warfare. Remember that.

Now my taxi was in Takoma Park and almost at the house. Suddenly I knew I couldn't face them. I couldn't imagine

myself seated there, trying to appear cheerful, trying not to have to explain to the whole assembly why my marriage to their daughter, niece, sister, cousin, was no more. I couldn't. I told the driver to stop. I paid him and told him to keep the wine. I got down and went into a restaurant and ate by myself, then I returned to the apartment and sat in front of the TV till I fell asleep.

On my last day in the apartment, before leaving for the airport, I signed the divorce papers which Gina's lawyer had sent over by courier. I sat in front of the computer and tried to compose a short, sincere email to her: *Thanks for the past we shared, and good luck with the future,* but it felt inadequate. I deleted it, turned off the computer, and left.

—No. I didn't stay with her. She was out of the country. It is over between me and her. I signed the divorce papers.

—Well, what next? You have your PhD. Are you going back to the US, to become an American, or back to Nigeria?

—I haven't decided.

She went back to her nails. After a long while she said, — Come with me?

—Where? Basel? Again?

She laughed and shook her head. The dark cloud had lifted. —No, not Basel. To Lusaka. If you want. And, I can offer you a job. My mother is retiring, so I will be running the school. You can work with me.

—I have never been to Zambia. I don't know what to expect.

—Oh, you will love it. She put down the nail polish. Her

face lit up, her voice became eager, joyful. The kids are great, you will love them. And, it is quiet, peaceful. You will have time to think while you decide what to do next. You can expect to stay with me and my mom. Plus . . .

She held my gaze, a wicked smile on her lips.

—Plus what?

—All of these. She stood up and gestured at her body, shaking her full, braless breasts and her curvy hips. —Think about it.

•

Portia and I sometimes walked from Boswell Street all the way to the British Library. She used to live not far from the library when she was at SOAS, she said. She pointed out a Pret a Manger. She said she and her roommate used to have lunch there every day for a whole term, the roommate's boyfriend worked there.

—This roommate of yours, was her name Portia? I teased.

—You are jealous. Some emotion, at last.

—What do you mean? I can be emotional. I am emotional.

Sometimes we took the opposite route, toward Holborn station and on to the British Museum, or to Covent Garden to mingle with the tourists watching the painted jugglers and magicians. Once we stumbled on a pop-up street market selling food from every corner of the globe. We joined a line at a Thai stand, then we sat and ate in the open air, tears running down our eyes from the spice. It was getting dark when we came back. A crowd was standing in front of our building, some of them holding placards.

—A protest, Portia said.

There were actually two protests, the one in front of our building entrance, and another one across the road, on both sides men and women held up signs, the two groups appeared to be in opposition to one another. Two police cars were parked by the curb at a distance, their lights flashing.

—What is happening? Portia asked a lady next to her. The lady was wearing a tracksuit, as if out for a jog, except she was pushing a child in a stroller—the child looked contented, swaddled in blankets and sucking its thumb. It appeared a man was hiding in our building, the lady told us breathlessly, an asylum seeker, being sheltered by a humanitarian organization. She pointed vaguely to a window, —Up there.

At that moment a bus cruised by, and as it passed the crowd before our entrance gave a loud cheer. I looked at the bus puzzled, till I saw what they were cheering. On the side of the bus, in huge black letters were the words: *Foreigners Out!* The other group shouted jeers and threw water bottles at the bus. The bus disappeared at the end of the street, and as we stood there it came back again from the direction where it first appeared, eliciting the same response from the two groups as before. I wondered how long it had been circling the block, round and round, slowly, like a shark circling a drowning swimmer.

—He is Nigerian. His name is Juma. We were back in the room and Portia was on her laptop. I went over and sat next to her. An organization, calling itself "The Guardians," appeared to have been hiding the escaped asylum seeker for weeks now, moving him from one safe house to another, evading the police and immigration officials. His asylum application had failed and he was about to be deported when he escaped with

the help of the group, who claimed the deportation order was illegal since they had an appeal pending. Nativists had finally traced him to our building, and what we saw downstairs was a standoff between them and the anti-nativists.

—It says here he has been on hunger strike for months, and he swears he'd rather die than be deported.

Juma appeared to be quite popular, there were dozens of articles and opinion pieces about him in the papers, some supporting him, others calling for his arrest and deportation. The home secretary had vowed to deport him. There was a photo of him under one of the articles, a gaunt, pensive, yet defiant face, staring unblinking at the camera.

The next morning, I woke up and went to the window almost expecting to see the demonstrators still there, and the bus with its ominous sign circling the block. Had there really been a large red bus circling the block, or was it all a dream? And the police car by the curb, and the woman with her child in a pram, breathlessly describing to Portia what was going on. The wind blew dead leaves and pieces of paper down the deserted street. Only plastic water bottles trapped by the curb and a few discarded placards in the grass bore testament to last night's protest. It was only 6 a.m. on a Sunday, the streets were empty, the city was still asleep, recovering from the weekend's endless parties and drinking, getting ready for Monday.

As I sat on the windowsill, looking out, enjoying the quiet, waiting for Portia to wake up, I became aware of voices coming from the hallway outside. The voices had been there for a while, quietly buzzing, and now they seemed to be coming from right outside the door, arguing in lowered tones, as if afraid of being heard, or of disturbing the still-sleeping

neighbors. I opened the door and poked out my head. A door down the hall near the stairs stood half-open, the voices were coming from there. I put on my shoes and went over to the door and knocked, the voices stopped, when no one came to the door I stepped in, not sure what I was doing, or what I was going to say. A young man, dressed casually in tracksuit top and jeans, was standing in the middle of the room, alone, and didn't appear surprised to see me. Where was the other voice?

—I'll be with you in a moment, he said, and he went back to his phone, furiously typing a message with his thumbs. Behind him was a table loaded with cartons stuffed with folders from which pieces of paper were falling out. The room was sparsely furnished, a table by the wall, a couch in a corner. I wandered over to a window which opened to the street and looked out at the same view as the one from my room. Now I could hear movement from another room, the sound of things being dismantled, books taken off shelves and put into boxes—that must be the other voice. A windowpane behind the table was broken where a brick had sailed through it last night. I had no doubt this was where Juma was being kept. But where was he? I waited for the young man to look up from his phone, but he kept fiddling with it, sending out texts and staring at the screen, waiting for the ding of the answer. Just then the owner of the second voice came out from the inner room, carrying a carton filled with books.

—You look like you are moving out, I said.

He stopped, carton in hand, and looked from me to the phone-obsessed young man, not sure what to make of me. He ran his hand in his hair and looked around the empty room. He must have been in his twenties.

—The landlord wants us out by the end of the week. You saw the damn fascists throwing rocks at us yesterday. Who are you?

I said, —I live down the hall. I heard the commotion yesterday, and I wonder if everything is okay?

The other young man finally looked away from his phone and said, —You are not from the *Metro*? I thought you were from the *Metro*.

—The *Metro*? I said blankly.

—They were sending a reporter for an interview . . . forget it. What do you want? Now he looked suspicious, turning to the open door as if expecting more people to come in. He went and closed the door.

—I am your neighbor. I heard all the noise last night. And, I am Nigerian, like Juma. If I can be of help . . .

He ran his fingers through his hair, a thoughtful look on his face, weighing me. The other young man dropped the box on the table and stretched out his hand to me. —I am Josh, this is Liam.

We shook hands. Liam appeared to relax.

—Well, Josh said, I have to head out. Nice to have met you.

He left and now it was just me and Liam in the half-empty room.

—Listen, I began, I hope I am not disturbing you or . . .

—Come, Liam interrupted, let me show you something.

I followed him to another room that looked like a study, with bookshelves against one wall. He stood in the middle, staring at me. This was where they must have kept Juma. It looked like a monk's cell, with a narrow cot in a corner, a bare redwood table with a single book on it, a chair; a naked

lightbulb hanging from the ceiling threw a dull yellow spray of light on everything. I picked up the book. It was *Hunger*, by Knut Hamsun.

—He read that over and over, as if he was preparing for some exam, Liam said. His voice was low, almost reverential. I opened the pages idly. I could understand why a starving man would read a book about food, but not why he'd read a book about a starving writer. It seemed masochistic.

—Is it true, I asked, that he has fasted for seventy days?

He started to answer but we heard a knock on the door and he hurried out. The reporter, most likely. I put down the book and followed him. A man in a shabby rain jacket and a backpack slung over one shoulder was talking to Liam. I nodded to the newcomer and headed for the door.

—Well, good talking to you . . .

Liam stepped toward me, almost blocking my path, and said, —Listen . . . I was wondering . . . you are Nigerian, right?

—Yes. I am Nigerian.

He lowered his voice. —Can he call you? It'd be lovely for him to have someone to talk to, someone from home.

—Where is he?

He glanced at the reporter, who had gone over to the table and was taking out a notebook from his backpack. —Well, we don't know.

—You don't know?

—Last night, when those fascists started gathering outside, we smuggled him out, through the back entrance. Molly took him to a café near the square to wait out the protest. He gave her the slip. He went to the bathroom and he never came back.

—Who is Molly?

—My colleague, one of the volunteers.

I said, —I am in flat number 20 down the hall. If there is anything I can do . . .

On impulse, which I would soon after regret, I gave him my number. Perhaps I felt the unfairness of it, the crowd with their placards, like a lynch mob, and the bus like a shark circling the block, while the gaunt, terrified Juma lurked in his room, unsure what his fate was going to be. I couldn't help but be in solidarity with him; I had known so many like him along the way, I had been one of them.

Portia noticed me checking my phone.

—You are not listening to me, she said. She was telling me about a cousin in South London. Her mother had called and wanted her to go see him.

—I am sorry, I said, and told her of my meeting with Liam, of the tiny, empty room a few doors down the hallway.

—And they don't know where he is? The Guardians don't sound very professional to me. Who are they?

—Well, I met only two of them, both are young. And there is a third, a lady, but she wasn't with them.

When the phone rang it was almost 10 p.m. The voice was low and apologetic, they were outside and could they come in for a few minutes? We were already in bed. Portia, tired of poring over her father's notebooks, was watching another episode of *Doctor Who* on her laptop, she watched the show addictively, sometimes I watched with her—a Dalek had the doctor trapped, and this time it looked like there would be no intergalactic escape through the trusty phone booth.

—They want to come here? Right now? Portia asked, tearing her eyes away from the screen. It is late.

—They are at the door.

—Bloody hell, she muttered. I changed and went to the living room. Portia cleared the empty teacups from the table while I removed the wine bottle and opener from the windowsill. The doorbell rang. I went and opened the door. There were two of them: Liam, still wearing the track-top and the jeans, followed by a tall, sturdy young lady. She was strikingly tall with a ponytail severely twisted at the back of her head—she looked capable, ready to take charge. Like a nurse, I thought.

—I am Molly, she said. Her grip was firm, and she was a nurse, as it turned out.

I pointed to the couch. —Sit, please.

Liam began to apologize for the unexpected visit, and for the late hour, but I told him it was fine.

—We couldn't come earlier because they are out there again.

We had seen them through the window, arrayed in the same formation as yesterday, including the big red bus.

—Have you found him yet?

—No, Liam said. The worry lines were pronounced on his face. Molly, on the other hand looked calm, unflappable.

—He is fine, I am sure, she said.

—How can you be so sure? Liam snapped.

—If he had been found, if something had happened to him, it would be on the news by now.

Liam and Molly had met Juma at the hospital where Molly worked. He had been brought there from the detention center after he had started his hunger strike and his health

was failing. The officials wanted to force-feed him, pushing tubes down his throat. Molly was the nurse assigned to him, and she was horrified by what she saw. When she was alone with him she asked him about himself and gradually he opened up to her. Liam, her boyfriend, had also been following Juma's story in the news, and together they decided to intervene. One day, Juma tried to escape. Molly met him in the hallway, he was barefooted, his bedsheet wrapped over his hospital gown, he looked confused, searching for the exit. She led him, protesting, back to his room and told him she could help. —You can't make it this way, she told him. I have a plan.

The next day she brought a pair of sturdy boots, a jacket with a hood, sunglasses, and a pair of jeans. She hid them in the men's toilet and as soon as the guard was out of the way she led Juma to the toilet where he changed, and then to her car in the underground garage. It was easy, easier than she had hoped. She took him to her one-bedroom apartment, which she shared with Liam. That was how it began.

—Why? I asked. You could lose your job, or go to jail.

—I have lost my job already, she said calmly, and I don't care if I go to jail. I just couldn't sit and watch them try to force-feed him with those tubes, it is horrible, inhumane. It is illegal.

—So, who else is in your organization? I asked.

—Well, we are a small organization, Liam said, looking at Molly.

—How small? You must need a lot of logistics to keep ahead of the immigration officials.

—Well, there are only three of us. Me and Molly and Josh.

—Just three of you? Portia asked, giving voice to my surprise.

—Well, we have done well so far, Liam said defensively.

Liam was a postgraduate student at the University of East Anglia, Josh was a schoolteacher, both were passionate advocates for migrants' rights. Molly was passionate about health care and justice in general. They had made up the name, The Guardians, to make themselves look professional, but there were only three of them. How did they manage it? It hadn't been easy, and as they spoke I could hear the stress reflected in their voices. The organization was born when Juma stayed in their little flat, sleeping on the floor in the living room, then, when they got a tip-off that officials were coming, they moved out. In the past few months they had moved Juma to five different locations, mostly the houses of friends, some of whom didn't even know who Juma was or what exactly was going on. Others knew and were willing to help on principle. All the time they had kept the media involved, sending detailed information about Juma's hunger strike, about the government's effort to arrest him even though his case was under appeal. They were excited when Josh told them they could bring Juma to this place—the flat belonged to his uncle, a banker who had been posted to Spain and left the flat in Josh's care. I tried to hide my disappointment. The whole plan sounded shockingly rickety, and it was just a matter of time before everything came crashing around their heads. I was not so sure I wanted to be involved in it, that would be foolhardy.

—Well . . . I began, turning to Portia.

—You will need help, she said to Molly, leaning forward. How can we assist?

—Yes, how can we help? I echoed, reluctantly.

But, as it turned out, their request was pretty modest. They wanted me to inquire discreetly among the Nigerian community if anyone knew Juma's whereabouts, if some Nigerian family or organization was hiding him. They felt bad that they had lost him. I didn't know any Nigerian groups in London and I doubted if he'd go to any of them for help, but to cheer them up I promised to ask around.

·

Last night, unable to sleep after our visitors had left, Portia had gone back to her father's diaries and had discovered a forgotten picture tucked in the pages of one of the notebooks. It was her, at age one, the picture was turning yellow at the edges, but the likeness was unmistakably her. She was standing outside in a park or in a yard, it was a spring day, behind her a field of green followed by a row of fir trees overlooking a lake. She was facing the camera, striking a pose, her hand on her hip, laughing.

—I have no recollection of this, she said. She sounded perplexed.

In the back of the picture was a date, and a place. *April 1992, Leeds.*

—My mother never mentioned a visit to Leeds when I was one.

—It is definitely you, I said. The same nose, the same mouth, the eyes confident and beautiful even at that age. On

the back of the picture there was a poem, handwritten, dedicated to her. She read it out, slowly.

SPRING
(for Portia)

It is spring, child
Feel the juices, only last month frozen—
Like the lake outside this window—
Let the juices flow

Stand, totter, fall, then stand again
See, the rabbits are out again
And the leaves on the larch

The colours are here again—
Blue daffodils, yellow dandelions,
And green, evergreen for you.

Rejoice with the vine and the poplar,
Shout viva! for the winter was long,
And the sun is here again!

—It is a beautiful poem, I said.
—He wrote it for me. In Leeds. There was wonder in her voice. She called her mother, who confirmed that yes, they had been to Leeds when she was just one, it was a brief visit, they stayed only one month, March to April. It was her father's last year at Leeds, the next year he moved to Norway

and they never saw him again till Portia was ten. She read the poem to her mom through the phone.

—I am not sure what to do with the diaries, she said later. So far she had located over twenty poems in the five diaries she had found, not all the poems were complete, some were only fragments, about the weather, the sea. Several were dedicated to May, his mistress. One, titled "Home Songs," was more complete than the others. In it he talked about his childhood and the first day he left home to go to boarding school. There was in all, about twenty years' worth of writing, all unpublished. The diary entries were sporadic, going entire years without any entries, but toward the end of his life, from 2009 to 2011, he kept a constant flow of notes with several pages for every single day.

—You should get in touch with his publisher.

—They are all retired by now, or dead.

•

We took the National Rail at Charing Cross. It was after the morning rush hour, and the crush of bodies began to thin out as we went further southward, till there were only about six of us in the carriage. A man seated across the aisle was cackling loudly to himself, his long narrow beard shook and wriggled as he laughed. He looked tired, his eyes were red and he kept sipping at his coffee in between laughs, long noisy sips. Portia glared at him, then turned away to look at the passing scenery outside. Balconies with laundry hanging from the rails, brick walls with unreadable graffiti on them. Next to the laughing man was a young woman trying her best to ignore him. She couldn't be older than fifteen, one hand held onto a stroller

with a child in it, the other hand held a phone to her ear. She was dressed in pink sweatpants and a flimsy T-shirt against which her tiny breasts strained.

I watched her hand, the long nails painted red, tapping on the phone with its diamante-crusted case, its red colors matching the colors on her nails. The words flew faster now, her fingers tapping a beat on the phone as she emphasized each word in a mash of accents, Caribbean, West African, and South London. It was a slow train, stopping at every station on the way. The laughing man stopped at Gillingham. At Crayford the young woman stood up to exit. Then came Abbey Wood. We got down.

That morning, Portia's mother had called to remind her to go see her cousin, who hadn't been back to Zambia since he left to study in England. She had handed the phone to me and said, —My mother, and when I looked at her blankly she had nodded encouragingly. —She wants to say hi, she mouthed.

—Hi, I mumbled. I had never spoken to her mother before, I didn't know how her voice sounded. She asked about the London weather, and whether we had been to Piccadilly Circus. I answered "yes" and "no" to the strong, clear voice on the other side. Finally, she asked me to make sure Portia went to visit her cousin, Jonah, because his mother was sick and was worried about him.

—I am sorry, Portia said afterward, I took you unawares.

—It's okay, I replied. I was surprised, and impressed, that the mother was fine with the idea that her daughter was here with me, alone, in London. But then, Portia had always made it clear how close she and her mother were. I wondered what she had told her mother about me. Did the mother worry if I

was a responsible person, if I was taking care of her daughter? Of course, she must, what mother wouldn't.

I thought of my mother. When I came back from Italy she had pretended I was not home when friends came to see me, or she'd say I was asleep. One day my father said to me, —Your mother had built so much hope on you. She used to tell her friends one day she'd go visit you in America, to meet your wife and play with your children.

My father looked tired, he sat there, not looking directly at me. —Listen, I don't know what happened to you. I just hope you did nothing illegal. I hope you can go back someday and set your affairs in order.

We exited the station and followed the line of litter by the sidewalk, papers, beer cans, cigarette packets, marking the path like signposts. We passed a Waitrose, a curry shop, a laundromat, Portia taking seemingly random turns as guided by her cousin's voice on the phone, and finally we were facing a cluster of council houses behind tall birch and elm trees somewhere off Abbey Road. The houses looked identical: semi-detached, each with a picket-fenced garden at the back and green plastic trash containers at the front. A line of square flagstones led to the front door. Portia rang the doorbell and the door opened. A man in his thirties stood there, still holding the phone to his ear, dressed in Arsenal FC jersey, shorts, and soccer boots, looking like he was about to step out to the training field. He hugged Portia and shook my hand.

—Come in. You guys are just in time. The match has just started. Ten minutes in.

We followed him into a narrow hallway, stepping over a pile of mail covering the doormat, and into a dark and poky living room illuminated by the light from the big TV screen dominating one wall.

—Sit down, Jonah said, his eyes on the screen.

Now I noticed two kids, a boy and a girl, seated on the floor directly facing the TV, they were also wearing Arsenal jerseys. One said Thierry Henry on the back, the other said Pires, the father was Patrick Vieira.

—Hey, Tom, Sheila, say hi to your auntie Portia. The last time she was here was when? He turned to Portia.

—Four years ago? I was at SOAS then, so about four, five years now.

—Wow, Jonah said. Tom was only four then, and Sheila was two. Look at them now.

Tom and Sheila turned briefly and shouted, —Hi Auntie Portia, in unison, their faces dull and expressionless, then they turned back to the screen. Arsenal was playing Tottenham Hotspurs. Jonah sat on the edge of his seat, wrapped up in the game, following every strike, every save, groaning or cheering. Often he'd lean forward and clap his son on the back. The kids were as animated as their father.

—Did you see that, did you see that, Dad? the boy shouted. He ran to the kitchen and we could hear him telling his mom what had just happened. The mother had only briefly stepped into the living room to welcome us and then returned to the kitchen, a small woman with a pinched, fierce face. At half-time Jonah stood up and stretched. He looked hopeful—the game was tied at 1–1. He went to the kitchen and came back with three cans of beer, he handed one to me, one to Portia,

and opened one for himself. —To Arsenal, he said, raising his can. I have a good feeling about this one.

His wife came in and sat on the arm of his seat, draping one arm over his shoulder, and it looked to me as if she was restraining him. Jonah waved his beer at her in a salute. She had a half-smile on her face, she refused to meet my eye, or Portia's, she kept her eyes fixed to the TV, but it was obvious she wasn't watching the game. The halftime break was over, the players were coming out of the tunnel, making the sign of the cross as their legs touched the field, some bending down to touch the grass, finding their way to their positions. Things took a downward turn for Arsenal in the first ten minutes, and by the end of the match they were down 3–1.

Jonah crushed his empty beer can and flung it against the wall. He jumped up and rushed to the kitchen, his wife threw an apologetic look at us before she followed him, and soon we heard the sound of a scuffle. I stood up, but Portia shook her head. I sat down. The children were still seated, staring at the screen where the pundits were analyzing the just-concluded match. They looked as if they were waiting for the players to come back from the locker room, and the game to restart, and their team to reassert its invincibility.

Jonah came back, a bottle of Smirnoff vodka in his hand. He flopped into his seat with a loud sigh and slapped the bottle on the table, he didn't glance at us, not even once. We watched as he filled a glass to the brim and drained it in one go, and repeated the same twice. Half the bottle was gone in a few minutes. I heard the steps of the wife slowly climbing the stairs, each step squeezing out a loud creak, and then the sound of a door closing and it was like a light switch turned

off. The children continued to watch the screen. Portia was looking at her cousin, a sad look on her face. He sat slumped in his seat, his face buried in his hands, shaking his head violently, and soon a muffled cry came out between his fingers.

—Goddamn you, Gunners! he sobbed, why, Arsenal, why?

After a while the wife came down, she stood at the door, looking at him.

—We will be going now, Portia said, standing up.

She walked us to the door, her back straight, her head high.

—He lost his job, you know, she said, looking directly at Portia, the half-smile on her lips. He had a good job at the factory, then the drinking started. He can't keep a job. Security, deliveryman, waiter, taxi driver, he has tried everything. Now he has stopped trying. He watches football and he drinks.

•

The protesters were gathered again, about a dozen persons on both sides of the road, as usual the nativists were closer to the entrance, bunched together, holding up their placards and shaking them in the air. They jostled us as we passed through them, calling out: "Go back!" and "Where is he?" and "Fucking illegals!" Portia calmly opened the front door while I stood behind her, positioning my back against hurled missiles or words. I pushed the door shut behind me and held her before the stairs where she stood, shaking and unable to climb. I felt the shivers traversing her body and I held her tighter till they ceased. For the first time I began to contemplate the possibility of our moving out to a hotel, we might not be safe here. The hallway leading to our door was dark, and so at first I didn't see the two figures standing in front of a

door next to ours, huddled in the dark, dressed in long coats, the taller figure was checking in her bag as if for a key, but as we got closer she looked up and I recognized the face: Molly. At the same time she said, —It is me, Molly.

—Hi Molly, I said.

The other lady remained a step behind Molly, her face in the shadows. Now I saw she was black, and her head was covered in a head scarf that fell to her shoulders like a veil. They followed us inside and sat on the couch and now, in the brighter light of the living room, the second lady's face looked vaguely familiar. I had seen those eyes somewhere. Portia went into the kitchen to make tea, I followed her.

—I wonder what they want, I whispered, and the other lady looks familiar, doesn't she?

—It is not a lady, Portia said, it is a guy, it is *him*. Didn't you see his shoes, and the hands?

Of course. She was right. I returned to the living room, and yes, it was him, the head scarf was off, now lying in a pile next to his feet, next to the muddy, broken, laced-up dress shoes. He sat hunched forward, hands clasped between his knees, his eyes looking out at me, waiting, unsure of his welcome. It was a face used to being turned away, kicked out, a pariah dog. I sat, facing them, waiting for Molly to speak.

—We found him, she said.

Juma had wandered back by himself, disguised in a head scarf. Molly looked sheepish, like she was about to make a request she knew was outrageous, one she shouldn't be making. I steeled myself for it.

—Where is Liam? I asked.

She looked at her phone. —I am expecting his call. He has

gone to meet a pastor at St. Luke's. He is one of our supporters, he has promised to put Juma up for a while. It is not safe
for him here anymore.

I turned to Juma and smiled. —Hello.

He shook my hand, then lay his palm over his heart. The
gesture took me by surprise, it was a common part of greeting
back home, to put the right palm over the heart after a handshake, but I hadn't seen it done in a long time, and I certainly
wasn't expecting to see it here.

—Hello, he said. His voice was hoarse, whistling out of his
mouth, the long hunger strike had drained him. He accepted
the cup of tea from Portia.

—Thank you. I can drink tea and water only, he said. He
seemed careful to explain how scrupulously he was observing
the rules of his hunger strike.

Molly said, —I am sorry to surprise you like this. But Liam
said you are from the same place as Juma, that you are willing to help.

When I said nothing, she looked at Juma, then at Portia.
She lowered her head. —We have nowhere else to go.

Another brick had been thrown into the window last night,
and the landlord was threatening to call the police, he wanted
them out immediately. Tomorrow, if things worked out with
the pastor, they'd move to the church, but tonight they needed
a place for Juma to stay. They feared either the police or the
nativists outside would come banging on the door at any minute. They couldn't even slip Juma out through the back, the
protesters had discovered the back entrance and some of them
were stationed there. Molly and Juma had been hiding in the
stairwell and in the hallways, waiting for us, since 2 p.m. We

had not headed home directly after leaving Portia's cousin's house, we had wandered aimlessly for a while, then we went to the British Museum to view the Egyptian collection, we stopped at a Caribbean restaurant for dinner, and from there, instead of taking the train back, we walked about for almost an hour, then we sat in the park for a while, and all that time they were waiting for us, skulking by the doorway, going up and down the stairs, careful not to be recognized by residents who passed them in the hallway or on the stairs.

—Listen, I began, we don't own this place, like you we are sort of caretakers . . .

—It is okay, Portia said from the kitchen. I smiled and shrugged at Molly. —He can stay. For a night.

After Molly had left, I asked Juma if there was anything he needed. He needed the bathroom. He said he hadn't showered in two days. I showed him the bathroom, and the extra towels in the closet. He took off his broken shoes and walked to the bathroom in the flip-flops I gave him. Portia stood looking at the shoes, the heels were so eaten away I wondered how he was able to walk in them, the socks, stuck into the shoes, were patched and grimy. —These socks need to be aired, she said, they stink.

We debated what to do with them: throw them in the trash and get him new ones tomorrow, or take them to the laundry, which might not be worth the trouble, they were practically coming apart in threads. We decided to take the shoes with the socks out and place them by the door—he would find that least offensive, it was customary back home to leave shoes

out by the doormat. And then there was the matter of food: what if we wanted to cook, Portia liked to make omelets in the morning, would that interfere with his hunger strike? It would be extremely cruel to cook while he struggled with hunger. Fine, we would skip breakfast tomorrow, and if he was still here at lunchtime, we would eat out—it wouldn't kill us to alter our routine for one day. Hopefully Liam would be here to get him before the end of day. Portia hung his boxy jacket in the closet, the scarf she also hung carefully next to the jacket.

He sat in front of the TV, his eyes glued to the news. I wondered if he was waiting for news about himself. I asked him, —Where did you go to yesterday? They were searching for you.

—I took the bus, he said.

—The bus?

He nodded. —Yes. It is really safe on the bus.

He explained that when he first came to England he used to take the bus at night, in winter it was the warmest and safest place he could be. He'd take the bus plying the longest routes, his favorite was the one going to the airport, and he'd stay on for hours, sometimes as long as three hours on one bus, back and forth, only getting down to look for something to eat.

—I was new in the country, I had only my bag, a very small one, containing just my toothbrush and one change of clothes and a book or two. I was afraid to go anywhere or do anything. The bus seemed the safest place to me.

—And the drivers, didn't they complain?

—No. Sometimes I'd hang around at the airport. I didn't stick out, so many faces coming and going. And there is good food there, in the bins outside. I did that for months before they caught me.

—Who?

—The immigration. A driver must have reported me. He stopped talking abruptly, his eyes glued to the TV. Portia nudged me and whispered, —He needs rest.

She gave him a blanket and asked if he needed anything before we turned in. No, he didn't.

In the bedroom I said, —What if Molly and Liam don't turn up tomorrow?

She seemed less worried than I was. —They will come.

After we turned off the light I stood briefly by the window. The protesters were still out there, standing with their signs, some sitting by the curb smoking, in the corner the police car waited idly.

He was still sleeping when we woke up. We decided to let him sleep and we went out for a walk. We ate in a little place just opening, the owner looked sleepy as she went from table to table, arranging chairs and laying down the cutlery. When we finished we stopped by a fruit stand and Portia bought a crate of apples. He was awake when we returned, watching TV. Portia first put the apples in a bowl by the window, then, with a guilty look at Juma, she moved the bowl to the kitchen. He noticed and said to her, —You really mustn't worry about me. And, as if to further put her at ease, he broke into a story about fruits. He seemed to have a story for every

occasion—it was his way of communicating, with stories of all he had been through. Or perhaps it was his way of trying to forget his hunger, and he did it with unexpected stamina, his hoarse voice droning with no inflection. His English was adequate; the English of a non-native speaker, learned mostly from books, making up his own pronunciations of words he had never heard spoken.

—Once, he said, in Greece, two years after I had left home, a friend and I were attacked by skinheads. They trapped us in a building for two days, with no food.

—How did that happen? I asked.

He looked at me and then at Portia, straight in the eyes as he spoke, pinning us down, making sure we paid attention.

—Well, my friend and I had been picking strawberries for over a month for a farmer who then refused to pay us, and when we complained, he had sent these youths after us. We were passing through Greece, trying to make our way to France and then to London. We never planned to stay long in Greece, we arrived at the harvest season, and my friend, Hassan, I met him in a camp in Italy, he is an Afghan, he said it would make sense to arrive in France with some money to pay the people smugglers, or guides as they preferred to be called, who'd get us to England, and so we worked. Five euros a day, plus food. We worked, and at first the farmer was paying us regularly, he'd send his manager in the evening each day with his little bag of money and we'd line up and he'd hand out our money. And then the pay stopped coming. The first day we thought it was a mistake, we went to work the next day, and the next day, now he was owing us for a few days, and when a whole week passed with no word from him, we went

to his office in a group to protest. But he had been expecting us. The police were there, he must have had them on standby, like he had done this before. They told us to leave the farm, and we did, peacefully. We went back to our tents. We were camped in a park outside of town. Early the next morning the skinheads came in their black shirts. They started breaking our tents and beating us with baseball bats. There were many of us, a few hundred, including women and children, but we were no match for this dozen or so young men. They were full of fury, and now, looking back, I wonder why they were so angry, they were clubbing children and women, kicking them, screaming. Well, we ran away in different directions, my friend and I entered an abandoned building and we were trapped in this building for two days. The skinheads knew we were in there, but they didn't come in to get us, they waited outside, it was a game for them, they wanted to starve us into submission. Two days, with no food, only a little water in a bottle, and no heating. They waited in a bar across the road, taking turns to watch us, and when the bar closed they waited in the street, they knew we wouldn't be able to slip out, there was only the front exit. We could see them, occasionally coming out to look up at the building, in their black shirts and boots. My friend Hassan almost gave up. I told him to hold on, he was crying and begging me to allow him to surrender, then miraculously we found a can of preserved apples in a closet in the kitchen. We opened it and drank the juice, then we ate. We were able to last a day longer on that can, and that day the skinheads gave up, they just left, and we were able to get out. When we opened that can and I took out a piece of apple, the smell of it brought tears to my eyes. I remembered

all the fruits I ever ate growing up, the mangoes, the bananas, the melons, the pineapples. I wanted to go home. The longing for home was so strong I could feel it in my stomach. It was a moment of weakness I never allow myself to indulge in anymore. Hunger is a tool. It is power. By refusing to eat, you are telling your enemy, There is nothing you can do to me anymore. If I am willing to starve myself to death to prove a point, what else is there to fear?

—Why did you leave Nigeria? I asked him.

The stories kept coming, discursively, randomly. He sat on the couch, the blanket draped over his lap covering his knobby knees and shrunken calves. The sentences tumbled out and it was nothing short of fascinating that so many words could be coming out of this small frame. In the refugee camp in Calais, he had met a woman who used to be rich back in her country, she had a restaurant and a big house, cars and servants, and then she had to leave to save her life. In the camp, bereft of everything she once possessed, she would put on airs, she would refuse to eat, wouldn't take a bath, she would lie in her tent, on a mattress, calling out the names of her maids, now back in her country, to come and clean up the place, to draw her a bath, she would get angry when she got no response and she would storm out of her tent and stalk the little space before the tent, throwing out curses, waving her hands at the children gathered to watch her tantrums. It was sad to see. He didn't know what happened to her afterward. He was there for just two days, but it was the bleakest place he had ever been, the Jungle, they called it, worse than Niger, or Greece, or Germany. In Germany, he had witnessed a demonstration in Berlin, at the Oranienplatz. A man had stayed

up in a tree for three days, defying the police who had come
to break up the refugee tents. Juma's voice was full of admiration. The police were flummoxed, they didn't know how to
handle the man. He stayed there, in the cold European winter,
hugging a tree branch, in the falling rain, shitting and pissing
on himself, with no food, and only rainwater to drink, but
not coming down.

They came and took him away in the afternoon. The landlord, it appeared, had relented after a call from Josh's uncle,
he had given them two more days, and then they had to
move out.

—Will he be okay? I asked Liam.

I realized Juma might not be all there, mentally. His travails
had taken a toll on his mind and often he appeared to be lost,
drifting and sometimes hardly aware of where he was or what
he was doing. Liam shrugged. —We have no idea. Our greatest fear now is the authorities. Our contacts told us to expect
a raid at any moment. We are trying to mobilize the media,
to build up some public pressure to stop them.

The demonstrations began early that afternoon. From our
room we could hear the chants, swelling and ebbing, they
sounded like soccer fans in a stadium, without the density,
without the mass, but there was no mistaking the passion. I kept
my ears cocked, expecting to hear the sound of boots marching to door number 12, for a call for them to open up, or for a
battering ram breaking down the door. But nothing happened.
There was a brief mention of Juma on the news, on Channel 4. The shadow immigration minister was condemning the

Home Office's cruel and inhumane immigration policy, and the promise to create a hostile environment for immigrants. Migrants' rights groups were urging their members to go on hunger strike in solidarity with Juma. Inmates in detention centers all over the country were refusing to eat.

—Something is going on down there.

Portia was by the window, looking out at the demonstrators. I joined her. Today the anti-nativist group was larger, some had Juma's name boldly printed on their placards.

—Well, it seems our friend is winning hearts and minds, I said. I feared that this newfound support might work against him. The government wouldn't like to lose face, and might feel compelled to act quickly. My fears were justified, as it turned out.

The next day the police came. Early in the morning, when the street was still asleep, and the sidewalk was still littered with picket signs and water bottles and cigarette butts from last night's protests, we heard loud banging on a door down the hall and I jumped up and rushed to our door. There were five of them, dressed in riot gear and helmets. The door opened and they walked in. Now Portia had joined me at the door. She slipped her hand into mine and held tight.

—What is happening? she asked. But she knew what was happening. After a while they walked out again, two hefty men holding him by his thin, twig-like arms, his skinny, shoeless legs barely touching the ground. Behind them came Molly, also being led by the arm, and then Liam and Josh, and all the way down the stairs Molly's combative voice rang out clearly, —You can't do this. It is not right. You have no right.

Then the footsteps ceased, and the front door closed. We

rushed to the window and caught a sight of the top of the police van pulling away.

—What should we do? Portia asked. She was close to tears.
—Is there nothing we can do?

I watched her face crumble, like a child's sand castle on the beach dissolving before the waves.

—I am sorry, I said, holding her.

—It is not fair, she said, echoing Molly, it is not right.

When I was in secondary school I had witnessed a public execution, when such things were still happening in Nigeria. Three robbers had been brought to the soccer field on the outskirts of town and we had come to watch, children, men, women, some with infants tied to their backs. The robbers, their hands tied behind them, were led out of the military pickup and lashed to sand-filled oil drums. I was surprised at how young they looked, like teenagers, their faces sleepy, dazed. We watched the soldiers line up in front of them, and after a barked order from a captain the soldiers opened fire. It was quick, and brutal, and in a minute the men, who a while ago had been alive and young and maybe even hopeful, were now dead, their heads lolling on their necks, and their lifeless bodies being untied and dumped into the pickup. Later, my friends told me that I kept screaming as the shots rang out, over and over: It is not fair! It is not fair!

—I know, I said, hugging Portia tightly, my cheek against hers, feeling the tears streaming down, and I wasn't sure if they were all her tears or mine, I am so sorry.

It was the last time we ever saw Juma, in the flesh. But his images kept popping up everywhere. The news was a brush-fire roaring the name of Juma. There were debates and hurried

justifications for what happened. On every TV channel the red-faced home secretary faced a battery of microphones and tried to give plausible explanations why the government found it necessary to spend all that money to deport the Nigerian, and bungle the whole thing in the process.

That morning, they had taken him straight to Luton Airport and bundled him into a specially chartered plane to fly him straight to Nigeria. I imagined the scared Juma huddled in his seat in the plane, empty but for the two security officials sitting on either side of him, too weak and confused to protest or resist, the night outside the window taxiing past, and then the uplift into the clouds. In Abuja the Nigerian government refused to grant the plane permission to land and it had to turn back to London, with its perplexed passenger, after a brief stop in Malta to refuel.

·

It felt strange to come out of our building and not be met by the protesters, with their placards upraised, faces snarling, and shouting obscenities. Molly and Liam were waiting for us by the entrance, and I remembered how they had waited on the stairs that day, two weeks ago, Molly and Juma, like two undercover characters in a B movie. When Liam called and said he had a letter for us from Juma, we had invited them over, but they said they'd rather meet elsewhere, in a pub nearby, and I didn't blame them, the building must hold unpleasant memories for them.

It had rained overnight and there was still a chill in the air, rooks in a nearby rookery called valiantly to each other, lending some cheer to the dull, damp day. We sat in a crowded

café behind a bus stop, there was a match on TV and the excited crowd vociferously cheered and jeered the progress of the match. We sat in the back, away from the screen, and ordered a beer each.

—Where is he kept? Portia asked.

In reply Liam handed me the letter.

—His lawyer gave me this. For you both.

Portia and I opened the letter as soon as Molly and Liam left. As Portia read it out aloud, Juma's voice jumped off the page, and it felt like he was there with us, his impossibly sonorous voice coming out of his scrawny, diminished frame, continuing his narrative thread where he had stopped two weeks ago:

You must have heard on the news by now, or from Liam, how my deportation didn't work, and how I am now back in the UK. Let me just say I never thought I was coming off that plane alive. But I don't want to talk about that ordeal, it is too painful. Instead, I want to tell you why I left home. Remember, you asked me, and I never got a chance to tell you. Well, to answer your question, I have to tell you my whole story. But then, some of it I have already told you, and some you have experienced yourself in the course of your travels. This will be a long letter, but I have time here at the detention center. I spend the days reading books sent to me by kind charities. Today I am reading The Lonely Londoners. *It is about immigrants from the West Indies. Their English is sometimes hard to understand, but I empathize with their situation. "Are the streets of London paved with gold?" a reporter asks one of them. Very funny. I guess most of them didn't come for gold, they came for a better life, for a better chance. I imagine their lives in the Bayswater,*

how they negotiate the streets filled with signs and graffiti telling them, "Keep the Water White!" Nothing has changed. As I write, I remember that bus with its warning sign driving round and round the block. But to go back to my story, I'll take you to the night I left home. It will take me a few days to finish writing, so you will have to forgive me if in places it feels disjointed or if I become repetitive.

The school where I taught had been attacked by religious extremists. One of their aims is to stamp out Western education. We had been hearing of them for weeks before they came, how they go from town to town, attacking police stations and taking away guns, and attacking local banks and taking away money, every day we see a steady stream of people fleeing from the killers, they pass through our town in increasing numbers. Some have been walking for two or even three days, mostly women and children. I remember one woman, she must have been over seven months pregnant, and when we advised her to stop in our village and rest, she refused. She wanted to put as much distance as she could between her and the killers. We didn't ask her where her husband and the rest of her family was.

That night our village was attacked. The school where I taught was attacked first. It was located a little outside of town, and from our house we saw the flames rising in the night sky. They went to the principal's house and killed him and his wife and three children. They drove through the town in their pickups, firing into the air and shouting religious slogans. I tell you, I have never known fear like that. Each shot was so loud, imagine someone knocking on your door with a rock in the middle of the night, the sound cutting through your dreams. My old father came to my room and told me to run. He handed me a little package, in it was all his life savings. He is over seventy, he and my mother, and they said they were not run-

ning, they'd stay there and face whatever fate had in store for them. "The worst they can do to an old man like me," my father said, "is to put me against the wall and shoot me. As for your mother, they don't kill women. But you, if you stay they will take you and turn you into a killer."

My father was trying to make me feel better about going away, and I knew he was right, but it was hard to turn away from them and leave, knowing I might never see them again in this life. Well, that is how I left home, with only the clothes on my back.

Why did I leave my country? Well, I didn't even know I was leaving my country. We ran all night long, we crossed a stream, and in the morning they told us we were in another country, Cameroon. We camped in an open field at a school, sleeping on the grass, men and women and children, still too dazed to know what was happening. But our ordeal was not over yet, in fact, it was just beginning. Two days later the terrorists crossed the stream and attacked that schoolyard, killing over half of the people as they slept in the open, the rest of us, the lucky ones, we had to run again. We ran for a whole day and when we finally stopped, they told us we were in another country, the Federal Republic of Niger. I was a refugee. I had no family, no home, no friends, the people running with me were my new family.

I was in Niger for over six months. We were kept in an open field, over ten thousand of us. There was no town or village around us for miles, in the distance there were nothing but baobab trees and scrublands and a few nomadic settlements. I don't want to bore you with the details, I don't want to say how much I suffered, or what kind of suffering I witnessed, but imagine this: over ten thousand people living in a place the size of a secondary school, how much food would be enough to feed them, how many emergency toilets

would be enough to serve them, and just imagine the darkness at night because there was no electricity, and the mosquitoes were everywhere because it was the rainy season and sometimes the tents we were in would be swept away by the storm and we had to sit like that, huddled under the falling rain till morning came. And every day people died like flies. You would see a child today, playing in the dirt, tomorrow they'll tell you he died in the night. Often I'd look around me and ask myself, Where am I? Who am I? How did I get here? I saw how others had already become used to this lifestyle. Strange how life goes on. There were people actually giving birth, and getting married and children going to school, all in our ever-burgeoning camp. But my eyes were always turned toward home, I dreamt every day of my father and my mother, and I wondered what had happened to them that day I left.

Every once in a while, officials from the Nigerian government would visit to assure us things were getting better at home, the war was being won, and that soon we would go back home. Six months. The same story. But instead of shrinking, the camp grew daily with new arrivals. And one day I said to myself, You are never going back home. At night we listened to the radio, mostly BBC and the German Africa radio, and from there we learned that the war was only growing, the killers were taking more towns and villages, and they had already established what they called a caliphate, and soon they would be attacking villages here in Niger. Twice our camp was moved, away from the border region. And that was when I finally accepted that I might not be going back home, not so soon anyway. To stay in the camp would be to die, no doubt about that. I decided to leave. Others had left already, mostly the young and strong and healthy. Every day men came from Libya and Algeria and Morocco to tempt us to leave with them. I gave them the money my father

*gave me, we left, there were ten of us, three men and four women
and three children, two boys and a girl. I will not bore you with how
we sat huddled in the truck, hot and baking in the merciless heat, or
how the truck broke down somewhere in the middle of the Sahara
Desert, near the town of Agades, and how we joined other groups of
travelers to walk the rest of the way, with no food, and little water,
and how we refused to look back when those walking alongside us
suddenly slumped and fell into the burning sand, never to stand up
again. I made it to Libya, only to be arrested by border police. I was
in prison for many days, weeks, or even months, who knows? We
were kept in a dark room and forgotten, in that room I heard different stories from those who had been there for days and weeks and
months: they said we were being kept there to be sold to people who
would harvest our kidneys and hearts and other organs. Others said
no, we would be sold to rich households to work forever as slaves. I
will not tell you how, to survive, we had to drink our own urine, or
that only about six out of the twenty men locked up in that room
eventually made it out. I had sworn to myself I was going to make
it. I had already started training for hunger. One day we heard the
sound of gunfire, and then our door was thrown open by men carrying guns and they told us we were free to go, just like that.*

I was in that hell in Libya for a year.

*I worked, when I was able to, I won't tell you what manner of
work I did, but I was able to save up a thousand dollars after a year.
Why did I leave? How do I know? I knew that to stay alive I had to
keep moving. I found myself in a group getting ready to cross the Mediterranean for Europe. They gathered us at gunpoint in a little harbor
in the middle of the night, hundreds of us, men and women and children, families mostly. It was a sad sight to stand there with that group,
knowing that each one of them had a similar or even a more sad story*

*than mine. I saw a man and his wife and two children, dressed in
expensive coats and shoes, the wife was carrying a very fine handbag,
as if she was in an airport waiting to fly for a holiday.*

*Later I discovered why our guides had us at gunpoint. You were
not allowed to protest where you were assigned in the boat, regardless
of how much money you paid for the crossing. It was tight. It was
noisy. Next to me a group of women was singing, Hallelujah! They
kept singing. It was like a church revival. I was positioned down
below deck, next to the portable toilet that served the over three hundred people in that rickety vessel, and which soon overran with urine
and feces. I will spare you the details.*

*The boat sank of course, less than an hour after we set out. I
don't know what happened, I was down there, next to the toilet.
Some said we were shot at by a militia boat, some said it was the
same traffickers who wanted to take us back and make us pay all
over again, I don't know, and right now it is not that important how
or why it happened. All that matters as our boat sank into the water
was that I couldn't swim, and that people were clawing their way up
to the deck, kicking and screaming and holding onto their children's
hands. Most of them, like me, didn't have life jackets and couldn't
swim. I was saved by that stinking toilet. One moment I was down
there below deck, next moment I was underwater, and then I came
up, and in front of me was the blue plastic portable toilet. Some
pocket of gas, or maybe all that decomposing shit, was making it
float. I held on. I wouldn't float for long, I knew. All around were
people struggling, floating, screaming. Children floated past, and
their mothers, belly-up before sinking, plastic slippers, bowls, books
briefly floated, and soon there wasn't anything at all. There was
nothing, no heaven, no earth, no boat, only water and the sound of
wind over water. It didn't take too long for the toilet to sink, luckily*

for me at that moment a dinghy came by, and they pulled me in. In the dinghy were two rescuers and a father and his daughter.

The father was the most heartbroken, wretched man I have ever seen. His wife and his son were out there in the water, and he was here in the flimsy craft with his daughter. He pulled at his hair, he strained his eyes looking into the horizon, hoping to catch a glimpse of them. He was a good swimmer and he jumped into the water and swam around, searching, and then his daughter, about ten years old, began to cry and call after him and he quickly came back. He sat, torn and helpless, and me and the other men held him, scared he was going to do harm to himself. I said, remembering what my father said to me the night I left home, "If it is God's will, you will see them again." But he kept looking around, standing up, screaming into the wind till night fell, till his voice grew hoarse, and then he sat down and held his daughter in his arm and together they cried and none of us could console them. Often I wonder what happened to them, father and daughter, if they ever reunited with their family. Later, I learned, that of the over three hundred of us who left Libya that morning, only me, the man, and the girl and five other people survived.

Why did I survive? I often wonder. I am not a very religious man, but you can't go through the things I went through without realizing there is a God, somewhere, in the affairs of men. But sometimes, also you wonder if there is a God, why does He allow such things to happen. Why are some people born to suffering and heartbreak, while others from the day they were born till they die know nothing but happiness and pleasure? Is God biased, what did I do to face so much suffering? What did that man and that little girl do to be separated from their family? I mentioned this once to a clergyman I met in Germany. I had spent the night in an empty church, cold

and hungry, in the morning the clergyman woke me up, and with-out saying a word, offered me food and shelter for that night. We got talking and I asked him that same question. Is God partial? He said sometimes our suffering only prepares us for a great destiny. I laughed in his face. How were the men and women who perished in that boat being prepared for a great destiny? They are dead. Dead. Is God having a laugh somewhere in His living room, playing chess, or watching TV, oh, I see, we are the TV, a reality show about sur-vival. I get to thinking like that, sometimes, but then I tell myself, Hey, at least I survived, I made it.

I did mention this was going to be a long letter. But now I am almost at the end. I have already told you some of the story, how we were trapped in a building in Greece for two days without food, I and a friend of mine, Hassan the Afghan. He it was who told me of Eng-land, and said we must make that our target. But first, we needed to raise some money, which is why we were working in that farm picking strawberries. I remember those two days in that abandoned building, and I remember the sounds of the skinheads' voices at night, their footfalls as they walked around, waiting for us to come out, I remember the smell of fear and sweat on our bodies. Sometimes we would crawl to the window and look into the square at the restaurant where people sat dining, smell the aroma of food wafting up when the wind blew in our direction, driving us mad with hunger.

We eventually made it to Calais in France, through Germany.

Hassan had some contacts in Calais, and he said from there to England was a very short distance. He made it sound so easy, and so I wasn't prepared for what I met there. They called the place "the Jungle," and it was a jungle. The day we got there, at the edge of the camp, we witnessed a fight. A man was stabbed with a knife. Just like that. An argument had started when one man accused

another of stealing his bicycle, an Indian man, who said no, he just used it to go to the city to buy some grocery and he was returning it. But they started fighting and the other man, an Eritrean, stabbed the other one in the neck. That was our welcome to Calais Jungle. I remember the smell, and the trash, it was everywhere.

Hassan took us to his friends and they started talking in their language, I noticed one of them looking at me suspiciously. They offered him a cup of tea but they did not offer me anything. It is strange, I thought. I said I was going to go out, to ease myself. Now the younger of the men actually talked to me, in English, he said be careful, it is a jungle. He looked as if he was trying to scare me, but I felt grateful for his warning, after all, he was the first person to even notice me. I thanked him, and I walked out. I wanted to see if I could spot a known face, anything. I saw a man, a black man, and I went up to him and asked him where he was from. Why do you want to know? he asked, he looked angry. He looked mad, his eyes were wild and his mouth was so smelly when he came close to me and put his face next to mine. I turned and left. Hey, he shouted after me, hey. I kept on walking. I felt scared looking at him, and I asked myself, was I also like that? Did I smell like that, did I look crazy and I didn't even know it? It had been a while since I took a bath, or ate properly, or changed my clothes.

We were there for only two nights, but the memory of that place will never leave me. I already told you the story of the woman who was once a rich person in her country, Eritrea. She refused to talk to anyone. She would sit in the tent and call out orders, she would call out the names of her maids: Esther, come here right now. Bring me my meal, it is past mealtime, Esther. Or she would tell them to run her bathwater. There she sat, in the doorway of her tent with everyone looking at her curiously, like an empress, surrounded by all the trash

and her clothes torn and smelly and the flies all over her. Those who
knew her said she had lost everything to the government of her country
when she escaped. Houses, cars, and her husband was arrested.

Anyway, we left after two nights, and I was feeling lucky, and
thankful, that we had made it. We were led to the trucks where
they were camped for the night, far away from the Jungle. What if
we were caught, I asked, but the smugglers assured us it had been
arranged with the truckers, all we had to do was secure ourselves
under the truck and hold tight, and to get off as soon as the trucks
entered the UK. But my friend did not make it. He must have
fallen asleep, or something must have gone wrong with his harness,
all I heard was the scream as the tire ran over him, and then a wet,
squelching noise.

The night before we had stood on the beach in Calais, looking across the water at the lights on the other side. My friend said,
That is Dover Beach. He knew a lot about England. His father
had studied there, and he had gone to an English school in Afghanistan, it was as if all his life he had been preparing for this moment.
"England," he said, and there was awe in his voice. He asked me if
I knew the famous poem on Dover Beach, and when I said no, he
quoted a line, from memory. He said the writer's name is Matthew
Arnold. The writer had stood on the opposite shore from where we
stood, looking at the French shore. I don't remember all the lines,
but there is something about the "eternal note of sadness." I know
what that means.

Well, that is my story, my friend. That is how I came to England.
That is why I left my country. You know the rest. Now I am here,
in this remote detention center, waiting to find out about my fate.
Liam and Molly still come to visit me. I still continue with my hun-

*ger strike; I have gone a hundred days now without eating. I have
no illusions about how this is going to end. The government thinks
I am going to relent and give up, I can't. I am tired, actually, and I
know in the end this will not change anything, they will continue to
detain people, long after I am gone and forgotten. A doctor came to
see me. He warned me that my fasting will cause irreparable damage to my body if I continue. He looked worried. He took my blood
pressure and looked into my eyes and my mouth and my ears. He
was trying to scare me, to make me give up my hunger strike, to
break my will. I told him I am fasting not because I want to anymore, all that has lost any meaning to me. The truth is I have lost
all desire for food. I even try to put something in my mouth, but I
always throw up after eating. I can't eat. My teeth are falling out. I
can't find any food to my liking. They gave me everything to tempt
me, meat, fruit, vegetable, trying to entice me to eat, but I can't keep
anything down. I want the perfect food. I tell them I want manna,
or ambrosia, the food of the gods themselves, and they thought I
was joking, but I am serious. I want the perfect food, but where can
I find it here on earth? I want my mother's food, the one I grew
up eating. I want the first food I ever ate in this world. I want my
mother's milk, but by now I am sure my mother is dead.*

The café had quieted down. The game was over; our stay
in London was also over, we had only two days left. Tomorrow Portia was meeting with her father's editor, whom she
had been able to track online, to hand over the notebooks
to her; I had offered to go with her but she said no, this was
something she wanted to do alone.

Now she wanted to know if I was coming to Lusaka with
her. She stood up and said, —I am going to freshen up, and

when I come back I want you to say yes. She leaned over and placed her lips over mine before heading for the restroom. I watched the men's eyes follow her as she made her way across the room. She looked stunning in a knee-length black dress that hugged her hips and emphasized the slenderness of her waist. I felt proud that she was with me, and often I wondered why she chose me when she could have any man she wanted, and why did I hesitate, why couldn't I say yes?

Soon she was back, she sat facing me, she took my hand.
—Have you decided?

I imagined her home in Lusaka, and it was as if I had been there, she had talked about it so much that I could see the school, the jacaranda trees, the children in their neat school uniform. And she would be there with me, every day. But how would I fit in, and would it matter, as long as we were together? Things would fall into place. I stared at her and I marveled at how much she had changed from the young impulsive girl I first met in Berlin. How beautiful and restrained she had become. She had suffered too, that was why.

—What if I am not who you think I am, what if something has shifted and broken in me since you last saw me?

—We will start from somewhere. Plus, you must admit, you don't seem to do well by yourself. Last time I left you, you ended up in a refugee camp.

•

I thought of Juma, he'd be in his tiny cell at Harmondsworth Removal Centre, perhaps reading, drifting in and out of sleep, too weak to stay awake for long. Liam and Molly will keep visiting him, daily, dutifully, not knowing anymore what

drives them. They talk about the weather, how summer is almost over. Juma's voice has grown hoarser and flimsier, and the visitors have to draw nearer to hear him. Liam asks him if he needs some water and he says, Yes. He takes a tiny sip, wetting his chapped, shaking lips. Then the lucidity leaves his eyes and they leave him. The next time they come the officials deny them entry, they say he has been moved to another facility, no one knows exactly where, Liam and Molly will protest, they will talk to the lawyer, but eventually they stop coming, worn out, they stop making inquiries, for even the kindest and most empathetic of us can get emotionally fatigued. Liam returns to Norwich to focus on his studies, Molly goes with him to take up a new job at the N&N hospital. The din in the media quietens. Juma sits in his cell, thirsting for mother's milk, unable to eat anything else, he shrinks, he regresses, back to childhood, curled up in a corner fetus-like, his flesh withers, his bones become as frail as twigs. One day the guards open the door and he is not there, only a pile of twigs on the floor. The cleaner comes and sweeps up the twigs and bags them and throws them into the dumpster.

I stood up and helped Portia with her jacket, then I put on mine. I said, —Yes. Let's go.

END

NRTH